Practical Generative AI on AWS

*Building generative AI applications with Amazon
Bedrock, Amazon SageMaker JumpStart, and Amazon Q*

Munish Dabra

Jay Rao

KP Babu

bpb

www.bpbonline.com

First Edition 2026

Copyright © BPB Publications, India

ISBN: 978-93-65894-653

To View Complete
BPB Publications Catalogue
Scan the QR Code:

Dedicated to

To my parents, my wife Preethi, and my daughters Ishita and Mahika, your support, inspiration, and values make this possible.

- Munish Dabra

To my parents, my wife Rikita, and my son Avyaan, your support, sacrifices, and joy give purpose and meaning always.

- Jay Rao

To my parents, my wife Deepali, and my children Sri Advay and Samhitha, your love, support, and joy inspire my journey.

- KP Babu

About the Authors

- **Munish Dabra** is a principal solutions architect at **Amazon Web Services** (**AWS**). He helps enterprises build **generative AI** (**GenAI**) and agentic systems that work reliably in production. Through his work with customers across diverse industries, Munish has gained extensive experience with the challenges of building GenAI applications at scale. He regularly shares these insights through technical blogs and speaking engagements at multiple AWS events. Known for his practical approach, Munish focuses on bridging the gap between GenAI potential and real-world implementation.

- **Jay Rao** is a principal solutions architect at AWS, specializing in AI/ML technologies. He has guided numerous customers through their GenAI journey, from foundational implementations to advanced AI systems, spanning prompt engineering, RAG pipelines, and multi-agent architectures, transforming proof-of-concepts into production-ready deployments. As the author of *Computer Vision on AWS* and a recognized thought leader in the AI space, Jay brings technical expertise with a unique ability to make complex concepts accessible. His practical experience and implementation strategies are reflected throughout this book. A frequent speaker at AWS events, Jay is known for demystifying advanced AI concepts and providing actionable guidance for successful AI adoption.

- **KP Babu** serves as a senior GenAI/ML specialist solution architect at AWS, specializing in enterprise GenAI implementation that balances cutting-edge innovation with responsible deployment practices. With extensive experience across diverse customer engagements, he has developed deep expertise in architecting GenAI systems that meet stringent security and compliance requirements. Babu is particularly focused on designing autonomous AI agents and orchestration frameworks that allow organizations to automate complex workflows while maintaining appropriate oversight. Through his technical publications and speaking engagements, he translates complex implementation challenges into practical guidance, consistently emphasizing that successful AI agents must reliably address genuine business problems by effectively reasoning, planning, and taking action within well-defined enterprise contexts.

About the Reviewers

❖ **Harsha Sanku** is a solutions architect at AWS and a passionate AI enthusiast. His work focuses on hybrid edge architectures, including AWS Outposts, Local Zones, networking, and other AWS core compute technologies. Harsha is dedicated to designing scalable, resilient cloud infrastructure systems and driving the migration and modernization of on-premises workloads to accelerate cloud adoption. An AI enthusiast, Harsha is often catching up with Amazon SageMaker and Bedrock to explore how GenAI can enhance enterprise applications and deliver smarter customer experiences.

❖ **Kamal Manchanda** is a seasoned senior solutions architect at AWS in India, bringing 16 years of comprehensive experience in the technology industry. With a wealth of experience in cutting-edge technologies, Kamal has established himself as a thought leader in the realm of cloud computing and advanced analytics.

His expertise spans a diverse array of fields, including big data analytics, search solutions, and lakehouse architectures. Kamal has been at the forefront of implementing innovative solutions that harness the power of these technologies to drive business transformation and operational efficiency for AWS clients.

In recent years, Kamal has developed a particular focus on AI, specializing in both GenAI and agentic AI. His work in these emerging fields has contributed to groundbreaking advancements in machine learning and autonomous systems.

Beyond his technical prowess, Kamal is known for his ability to translate complex technological concepts into actionable strategies for businesses across various industries. As a respected voice in the tech community, Kamal frequently shares his knowledge through speaking engagements, workshops, and technical publications.

Acknowledgements

Writing this book has been an incredible journey, made possible by the extraordinary community of people who supported, challenged, and inspired us along the way.

We thank our families and friends who supported us throughout this endeavor. The late nights, weekend writing sessions, and countless conversations about the book required patience and understanding that you provided without question.

To our AWS colleagues and leadership team who encouraged us to think deeper about GenAI and gave us the opportunity to engage with customers, your trust and support has been invaluable. The countless discussions, brainstorming sessions, and shared learnings have shaped this book in fundamental ways.

We are grateful to the customers we have worked with over the years. Your real-world challenges and creative use cases shaped every chapter of this book. Your feedback on what matters in production, all of it is woven into these pages.

Thank you to the open-source community, especially the maintainers of frameworks like LangChain, LlamaIndex, and other tools that make building with GenAI accessible. Your work has been instrumental in our learning journey.

To our technical reviewers who caught our mistakes, challenged our assumptions, and pushed us to explain things more clearly. Your contributions made this a much better book.

Finally, to everyone at BPB Publications who shared our vision for a comprehensive, practitioner-focused guide to GenAI on AWS. Thank you for your partnership and guidance throughout this process.

Preface

GenAI is not just another technology trend, it is a fundamental shift in how we build software and solve business problems. Every organization we work with is asking the same question How do we navigate AWS's GenAI ecosystem to successfully implement solutions for our specific use cases while ensuring our systems are secure, scalable, and enterprise-ready?

That is why we wrote this book. We wanted to showcase the full spectrum of AWS's GenAI capabilities, from Amazon Bedrock's managed foundation models to Amazon Q's Business-focused AI assistant, from Amazon SageMaker Jumpstart's flexibility to the power of open-source frameworks. Each service addresses different needs, and understanding when to use which tool is crucial for success.

The gap between exciting demos and production-ready systems is vast. We have seen too many organizations struggle with hallucinations, unpredictable costs, security vulnerabilities, and AI systems that work brilliantly in testing but fail when faced with real-world complexity. Building enterprise GenAI applications requires more than just API calls to foundation models, it demands a comprehensive approach to architecture, security, observability, and governance.

One of the most exciting recent developments in GenAI is the rise of autonomous agents, AI systems that can reason, plan, and take actions to accomplish complex goals. We dedicate two chapters to this topic because we believe agents represent the future of how businesses will leverage AI. Imagine customer service agents that truly understand context and can resolve issues end-to-end, or analytical agents that can explore your data and generate trends and insights without constant human guidance. This is not science fiction; we are building these systems today.

Throughout our work with enterprises across industries, we have identified the patterns that separate successful GenAI implementations from costly failures.

This book emphasizes that security is fundamental, integrating measures like guardrails and controlled data access to protect sensitive information while maintaining utility. It highlights the importance of observability from the start, advocating for monitoring that captures system performance, model behavior, costs, and business outcomes. We explore strategies for scaling and ensuring reliability, sharing architectural patterns that allow applications to grow seamlessly with demand. Additionally, we guide you in selecting the right tools, whether managed services, customizable platforms, or open-source frameworks, and introduce the agent paradigm, where AI systems go beyond static responses to act autonomously and responsibly.

This book takes you on a complete journey:

Chapter 1: Introduction to Generative AI and Foundation Models - The chapter establishes the foundational concepts essential for understanding GenAI. We explore what distinguishes foundation models from traditional ML models, examine the principles of effective prompt engineering, and guide you through properly configuring your AWS environment with appropriate IAM policies and service limits.

Chapter 2: Getting Started with Amazon Bedrock - This chapter provides a comprehensive introduction to Amazon Bedrock, AWS's fully managed platform for building GenAI applications. You will explore Bedrock's capabilities including agents, knowledge bases, and guardrails, navigate the console and interactive playgrounds, and understand the platform architecture and development ecosystem.

Chapter 3: Experimenting Foundation Models in Amazon Bedrock - This chapter offers hands-on experience with the diverse models available in Amazon Bedrock. Through systematic experimentation, you will develop an understanding of each model's strengths, limitations, and optimal use cases, enabling informed model selection for your applications.

Chapter 4: Building Generative AI Applications with Bedrock APIs - This chapter transitions from console-based interaction to programmatic implementation. You will learn to integrate Bedrock APIs into applications, implement robust error handling, manage rate limits, and build production-grade code following AWS best practices.

Chapter 5: Using Amazon Bedrock Knowledge Bases - This chapter introduces retrieval augmented generation patterns for enhancing model responses with proprietary data. This chapter covers vector databases, embedding strategies, and techniques for building context-aware applications that leverage organizational knowledge.

Chapter 6: Using Bedrock's Managed Agents - This chapter represents a paradigm shift in how we think about AI applications. You will build agents that can reason, decompose complex tasks, interact with multiple systems, and achieve business objectives autonomously. Through a hands-on customer support agent example, you will learn agent architecture, knowledge base integration, action groups for backend systems, and production deployment with debugging and optimization techniques. From customer support automation to intelligent data analysis, this chapter provides the blueprint for creating AI agents that deliver real business value.

Chapter 7: Using Open-source Frameworks with Amazon Bedrock - This chapter explores the rich ecosystem of frameworks that accelerate GenAI development. We begin with comprehensive coverage of LLM frameworks, including LangChain and LlamaIndex for building RAG applications and managing prompts. The chapter then transitions to purpose-built agentic frameworks like Strands Agents SDK, LangGraph, and CrewAI with an extensive deep dive into Strands for production-ready agent systems. You will learn to leverage these frameworks' unique capabilities for building sophisticated AI applications that integrate seamlessly with Amazon Bedrock.

Chapter 8: Building Custom Models with Amazon Bedrock - The chapter addresses model customization through fine-tuning techniques. We examine when customization is necessary, guide you through the fine-tuning process with Amazon Bedrock, and discuss performance optimization strategies.

Chapter 9: Monitoring and Observability - This chapter ensures your GenAI applications remain performant and cost-effective in production. You will learn comprehensive monitoring using Amazon CloudWatch and CloudTrail, analyze model invocation patterns and audit API calls, and explore open-source observability tools for GenAI applications. The chapter covers best practices for monitoring Amazon Bedrock, setting up automated alerts, and optimizing resource utilization.

Chapter 10: Security and Responsible AI - This chapter addresses critical governance requirements for AI deployments. We cover implementing guardrails including content moderation and watermark detection, ensuring data privacy, managing compliance requirements, and establishing frameworks for responsible AI use within enterprise environments.

Chapter 11: RAG and Model Evaluation - This chapter provides methodologies for systematically evaluating GenAI performance. You will implement both automatic and human-based evaluation techniques, conduct A/B testing, measure retrieval quality using frameworks like Ragas for RAG systems, design custom evaluation metrics, and establish continuous improvement processes for your applications.

Chapter 12: Building Generative AI Assistant using Amazon Q - This chapter explores Amazon Q, AWS fully managed AI-powered assistant designed to enhance business productivity and streamline workflows. You will learn to create custom assistants that understand organizational data, automate routine tasks, implement secure access controls, and integrate with existing business systems to improve decision-making and operational efficiency.

Chapter 13: Getting Started with Generative AI on Amazon SageMaker Jumpstart - This chapter explores SageMaker AI's comprehensive ML hub for rapid AI development. You will learn various ways to access foundation models through JumpStart, explore pre-trained LLMs, deploy text generation models through hands-on examples, and fine-tune models on custom datasets with best practices for optimization.

Chapter 14: Best Practices for Developing Generative AI Applications - This chapter consolidates practical wisdom gained from production deployments. Topics include model selection criteria, performance optimization techniques, cost management strategies, and architectural patterns for scalable AI applications.

Chapter 15: Real-world GenAI - This chapter explores enterprise use cases and architectural patterns across industries, including customer service, financial analysis, and healthcare documentation. Each example includes architecture diagrams, implementation considerations, and lessons learned from production environments, along with common challenges and solutions for enterprise GenAI implementations.

Code Bundle and Coloured Images

Please follow the link to download the
Code Bundle and the *Coloured Images* of the book:

https://rebrand.ly/dcdc35

The code bundle for the book is also hosted on GitHub at
https://github.com/bpbpublications/Practical-Generative-AI-on-AWS.
In case there's an update to the code, it will be updated on the existing GitHub repository.

We have code bundles from our rich catalogue of books and videos available at
https://github.com/bpbpublications. Check them out!

Errata

We take immense pride in our work at BPB Publications and follow best practices to ensure the accuracy of our content to provide with an indulging reading experience to our subscribers. Our readers are our mirrors, and we use their inputs to reflect and improve upon human errors, if any, that may have occurred during the publishing processes involved. To let us maintain the quality and help us reach out to any readers who might be having difficulties due to any unforeseen errors, please write to us at: errata@bpbonline.com

Your support, suggestions and feedbacks are highly appreciated by the BPB Publications' Family.

At www.bpbonline.com, you can also read a collection of free technical articles, sign up for a range of free newsletters, and receive exclusive discounts and offers on BPB books and eBooks. You can check our social media handles below:

Instagram

Facebook

Linkedin

YouTube

Get in touch with us at: business@bpbonline.com for more details.

Piracy

If you come across any illegal copies of our works in any form on the internet, we would be grateful if you would provide us with the location address or website name. Please contact us at business@bpbonline.com with a link to the material.

If you are interested in becoming an author

If there is a topic that you have expertise in, and you are interested in either writing or contributing to a book, please visit www.bpbonline.com. We have worked with thousands of developers and tech professionals, just like you, to help them share their insights with the global tech community. You can make a general application, apply for a specific hot topic that we are recruiting an author for, or submit your own idea.

Reviews

Please leave a review. Once you have read and used this book, why not leave a review on the site that you purchased it from? Potential readers can then see and use your unbiased opinion to make purchase decisions. We at BPB can understand what you think about our products, and our authors can see your feedback on their book. Thank you!

For more information about BPB, please visit www.bpbonline.com.

Join our Discord space

Join our Discord workspace for latest updates, offers, tech happenings around the world, new releases, and sessions with the authors:

https://discord.bpbonline.com

Table of Contents

CHAPTER 1
Introduction to Generative AI and Foundation Models

Introduction

This chapter provides an overview of generative **artificial intelligence (AI)** and **foundation models (FMs)**, exploring their significance, and far-reaching impact. We will examine the importance of FMs as game-changing technologies driving innovation across industries. You will discover **generative AI (GenAI)** use cases and **Amazon Web Services (AWS)** ecosystem integration, learn prompt engineering techniques, and setup your AWS account to begin your GenAI journey.

Structure

The chapter covers the following topics:

- Overview and significance of generative AI
- Importance and impact of foundational models
- Generative AI use cases
- AWS ecosystem for generative AI
- Prompt engineering
- Setting up AWS environment

Objectives

By the end of this chapter, you will have a firm grasp of GenAI. You will understand the importance of FMs as foundational technologies driving innovation and the key use cases of GenAI. Additionally, you will be equipped with the knowledge to leverage the AWS ecosystem which is specifically designed for GenAI, enabling you to harness its capabilities effectively. Furthermore, you will learn the art of prompt engineering, mastering different techniques to optimize your interactions with these advanced models. Lastly, you will have an AWS account setup, ensuring you have the necessary infrastructure to embark on your GenAI journey.

Overview and significance of generative AI

AI has undergone remarkable advancements in the last two decades, fueled by significant technological breakthroughs. The convergence of high-performance computing, vast amounts of data, and advanced algorithms have propelled AI to new heights. The development of deep learning techniques, particularly convolutional neural networks and transformer models, has revolutionized fields like computer vision, **natural language processing** (**NLP**), and speech recognition. The introduction of powerful hardware accelerators, such as **graphics processing units** (**GPUs**), AWS Trainium, and Inferentia, has enabled the training of large neural networks at unprecedented speeds. Additionally, the availability of massive datasets and the rise of cloud computing have facilitated the development and deployment of AI models on a global scale. These technological advances have paved the way for AI systems to tackle increasingly complex tasks, from self-driving cars to language translation, and have laid the foundation for the emergence of transformative technologies like GenAI and FMs.

You may wonder where GenAI fits in relation to AI, **machine learning** (**ML**), and deep learning. The following figure will help you visualize this:

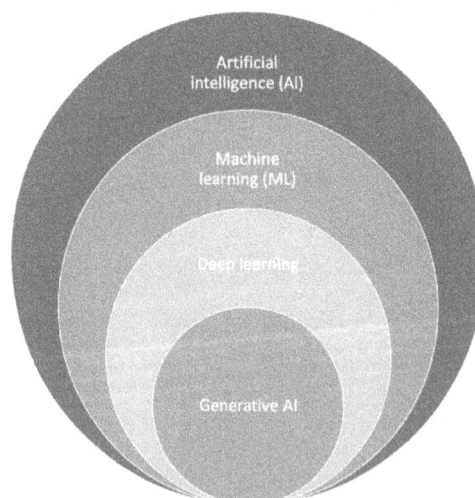

Figure 1.1: Where GenAI fits

AI is any technique that allows computers to mimic human-like intelligence and perform tasks that typically require human intelligence, such as learning, reasoning, problem-solving, decision-making, and perception. ML is a subset of AI that uses computers to search for patterns in data, rather than relying solely on pre-defined rules or instructions. Deep learning is an advanced subset of ML, composed of deeply multi-layered neural networks (inspired by the structure and function of the human brain) to learn and make intelligent decisions such as speech and image recognition. GenAI is a subset of deep learning that focuses on training neural networks to create new data, such as text, images, audio, or video, from scratch or based on existing data. It leverages the ability of deep learning models to capture complex patterns and generate novel, realistic outputs, opening up new possibilities for creativity and content generation. There are several studies published on how GenAI has the potential to drive a significant increase in global economic output and can provide a substantial lift to productivity growth.

GenAI models offer powerful capabilities to drive research, innovation, customer experiences, business process optimization, and employee productivity across organizations and industries. These AI systems can explore complex data, uncover new patterns, summarize content, outline solutions, and engage in natural conversations, accelerating research like drug discovery in pharmaceuticals while enabling personalized customer service through chatbots and virtual assistants. GenAI can optimize processes by extracting, summarizing, and evaluating data, generating synthetic data for ML, and supporting creative tasks, software development, report generation, and content creation to boost employee productivity. Moreover, it has the potential to democratize creativity and innovation by automating and augmenting tasks that previously required human ingenuity, such as generating stories, artwork, and computer programs or automate business processes which go beyond deterministic workflows. With applications spanning marketing, healthcare, and beyond, GenAI is reshaping problem-solving and creative endeavors, pushing boundaries of what was once thought possible as these transformative technologies continue advancing. While GenAI is still an emerging field with ongoing **research and development (R&D)**, its potential impact on our society and economy is immense.

Importance and impact of foundational models

GenAI is powered by a class of models called FMs. FMs are large-scale ML models capable of producing output based on one or more input prompts, typically in the form of natural language instructions. Their underlying architecture draws from intricate neural networks harnessing advanced techniques such as **generative adversarial networks (GANs)**, transformer models, diffusion models, and variational autoencoders. These models possess the ability to generate content by learning patterns and relationships from data, allowing them to create new outputs that align with the provided prompts or instructions. A good example is image generation with FMs. The model analyzes an existing image and uses what it has learned to create an enhanced, sharper, and more clearly defined version of that image. It does this by predicting how to improve each pixel based on the patterns it has learned from many other images.

With text, FMs work similarly. By understanding the context of the previous words in a piece of text, the model can make an educated prediction about the most likely next word that should follow. It calculates the probability of the possible next word and selects the one with the highest likelihood of being correct based on learned patterns and relationships. Diffusion models, for example, create new data by iteratively making controlled random changes to an initial data sample. In essence, these advanced models can study data, learn the underlying patterns, and then use that understanding to generate new data points that fit those patterns.

One of the most prominent examples of FMs is **large language models** (**LLMs**) like *generative pre-trained transformer-4 (GPT-4)*, *BigScience Large Open-science Open-access Multilingual (BLOOM)*, *Meta Llama*, *Amazon Nova*, and *Anthropic Claude*. These models are trained on massive datasets, allowing them to develop a deep understanding of natural language. By leveraging their knowledge acquired during pre-training, LLMs are specifically focused on language-based tasks such as summarization, text generation, classification, open-ended conversation, and information extraction.

The true hallmark of LLMs is their remarkable versatility across an array of tasks. This stems from their massive parameter counts, which imbue them with the capacity to learn and represent highly sophisticated concepts. Take LLM like *Meta Llama 4 Maverick 17B* model for example, it has over 400 billion parameters, granting it the ability to generate fluent content from minimal prompts. It is a natively multimodal model excelling in image and text understanding, making it suitable for versatile assistant and chat applications. The model supports a 1 million token context window, giving you the flexibility to process lengthy documents and complex inputs. Through pre-training on a staggering corpus of internet data spanning diverse domains and formats, these models gain an incredibly rich understanding of language. They develop an innate sense for the intricate patterns and nuances that enable coherent communication.

What sets LLMs apart is their talent for taking this broad knowledge and applying it adeptly to virtually any context or use case presented to them. From creative writing to analysis, coding to **question answering** (**QA**), LLMs adapt their deeply learned representations to produce contextually appropriate and substantive outputs. Their versatility equips them to serve as a universal tool across domains traditionally siloed by specialized models.

FMs are becoming increasingly larger and more powerful. These models represent the culmination of years of work focused on scaling up their size and complexity. For instance, *Bidirectional Encoder Representations from Transformers (BERT)*, one of the pioneering FMs released in 2018, had 340 million parameters. Fast forward just five years to 2023, and *DeepSeek* trained R1 with a staggering 671 billion parameters. This rapid scaling underscores the immense potential of these models as research continues pushing the boundaries of their capabilities.

Generative AI use cases

GenAI use cases, at a high level, would fall into three categories, customer experience, employee productivity, and process optimization. Let us take a look at use cases in each category in detail, starting with customer experience.

GenAI technologies can significantly enhance and optimize the customer experience in several ways, as follows:

- Hyper-personalization allows businesses to deliver highly personalized experiences, curated offerings, and communications tailored to individual customers, increasing engagement and satisfaction.

- Conversational analytics empowers companies to analyze unstructured customer feedback from surveys, comments, and call transcripts to identify key topics, detect sentiment, and surface emerging trends. This insight enables more responsive and tailored service.

- Chatbots and virtual assistants streamline customer self-service by automating responses to queries through AI-powered conversational agents, reducing operational costs while providing convenient 24/7 support.

- Intelligent advisory systems translate complex questions from customers into semantic meaning, analyze context, and generate highly accurate conversational responses, facilitating effective communication and issue resolution.

- Personalized recommendations leverage customer data to create customized promotions and product suggestions, delivering a more relevant and valuable experience.

By harnessing GenAI across these areas, businesses can optimize customer interactions, deliver hyper-relevant experiences, and drive engagement, loyalty, and operational efficiency. The above use cases illustrate how these AI capabilities can transform and elevate customer service and personalization.

Let us explore use cases related to increasing productivity. GenAI can significantly improve employee productivity across various domains:

- GenAI can accelerate product development by generating multiple design prototypes based on specified constraints, streamlining the ideation phase.

- In sales and marketing, it can generate personalized emails, scripts, and engaging content automatically, saving time and resources.

- Code generation tools powered by GenAI can provide code suggestions based on developer requirements, accelerating application development.

- It can automate repetitive tasks like report generation, accurately summarizing financial data and projections, and reducing errors.

- GenAI assistants can quickly retrieve relevant information, summarize content, and provide accurate answers, aiding employees in their daily work.

- In healthcare, it can interpret medical images, generate reports, enhance clinical trials through data synthesis, and create transcripts from patient interactions, improving diagnosis and treatment.

- GenAI can optimize product designs in manufacturing by rapidly evaluating numerous options, ensuring cost-effectiveness.

- Conversational AI agents trained in product manuals can provide swift technical support, reducing downtimes.

- AI can generate structured data from unstructured sources like product catalogs, enhancing business value.

Overall, GenAI's capabilities span diverse industries, automating tedious tasks, augmenting human efforts, and driving productivity gains, allowing employees to focus on higher value, strategic work.

Finally, GenAI can play a pivotal role in process optimization across various industries by automating and enhancing crucial tasks:

- Dynamically update planograms based on inventory levels, sales trends, competitor data, etc. to optimize stocking and merchandising strategies.

- Evaluate different supply chain scenarios to improve logistics operations and reduce costs.

- Quickly generate financial documentation like investment reports, loan policies, regulatory communications, etc.

- Automate **intelligent document processing (IDP)** to extract valuable insights from large volumes of unstructured documents, enabling mortgage providers to streamline loan application processing by automatically extracting and validating key information from financial documents, tax returns, and employment records, while allowing insurance companies to enhance underwriting efficiency by using AI to analyze claims history, medical records, and risk assessment documents to make faster, data-driven decisions.

- Accelerate drug discovery by aiding protein folding, sequence design, molecular docking, etc. while reducing R&D costs.

- Optimize clinical trial enrolments by matching eligible patients based on inclusion or exclusion criteria and co-morbidities.

- Simulate production to identify improvements, uncover hidden insights from data, and boost predictive accuracy without disrupting operations.

- Drive product innovation and automate business processes by developing new AI-powered tools for end-users, e.g., stock screening by using natural language search, wealth management for brokerage clients, and institutional investment analysis.

- Maximize media content value for search, discovery, content localization, compliance, brand safety, and monetization by integrating ML into media workflows.

Overall, by automating repetitive tasks, generating tailored content, and uncovering valuable insights from data, GenAI emerges as a powerful process optimization tool applicable across domains from manufacturing and supply chains to finance, healthcare, and beyond.

AWS ecosystem for generative AI

We started this book with what GenAI is, then we explored FMs and their importance, and then we uncovered various promising use cases that can take maximum advantage of GenAI capabilities. Now, let us discuss AWS portfolio of GenAI services.

AWS GenAI services are grouped into three categories or a three-layer stack, as shown in the following figure:

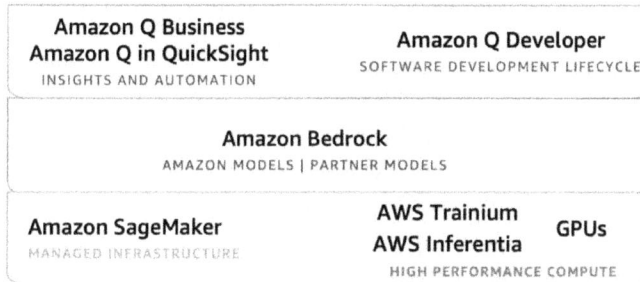

```
┌─────────────────────────────────────────────────────────────┐
│  Amazon Q Business                                            │
│  Amazon Q in QuickSight        Amazon Q Developer             │
│  INSIGHTS AND AUTOMATION     SOFTWARE DEVELOPMENT LIFECYCLE   │
├─────────────────────────────────────────────────────────────┤
│                   Amazon Bedrock                              │
│              AMAZON MODELS | PARTNER MODELS                   │
├─────────────────────────────────────────────────────────────┤
│                              AWS Trainium                     │
│  Amazon SageMaker                            GPUs             │
│                              AWS Inferentia                   │
│  MANAGED INFRASTRUCTURE     HIGH PERFORMANCE COMPUTE          │
└─────────────────────────────────────────────────────────────┘
```

Figure 1.2: *AWS three-layer GenAI stack*

The bottom layer refers to the infrastructure to train and deploy GenAI workloads, ranging from price performance accelerated computing (third-party GPUs and hardware accelerators powered by AWS custom silicon chips) to high-performance and low-latency storage to cutting-edge networking. The ability of AWS to provide such capabilities has allowed LLM providers such as *Anthropic, Cohere*, and *Luma AI* to train and deploy their models on AWS. Exploring deeper into the bottom layer infrastructure is beyond the scope of this book, however, if you are planning to train your models, you should explore different computing, storage, and networking options available to you on AWS.

Next, at the middle layer, AWS offers a serverless service and platform called Amazon Bedrock. It is a fully managed service that offers customers a choice of high-performing FMs along with a comprehensive set of capabilities for building GenAI applications. At its core, Amazon Bedrock provides access to cutting-edge FMs from leading AI providers like *Anthropic, AI21 Labs, Stability AI, Mistral AI, Cohere, Meta,* and *Amazon* own Nova models. The list of providers and models available through Amazon Bedrock is expected to continue expanding as the field of GenAI advances and more organizations contribute to their FMs. This breadth of options allows you to experiment with various FMs, and you can select the ones best suited for your use cases. Amazon Bedrock offers key advantages for enterprises leveraging GenAI, easy customization of FMs by using proprietary data through fine-tuning, and distillation, fully managed agents for executing complex tasks by dynamically invoking **application programming interfaces (APIs)**, and native support for RAG to securely connect FMs with proprietary data sources for generating accurate, and context-specific responses.

Amazon Bedrock offers a wide range of use cases, from creating original content like short stories and social media posts to answering questions by synthesizing information from large data corpuses, generating realistic images from language prompts, providing contextual product recommendations, and summarizing textual content. With its serverless experience, you can get started by experimenting with FMs in the playground, creating agents, and integrating the service into your applications by using familiar AWS tools. Overall, Amazon Bedrock simplifies the development of GenAI applications by providing a choice of high-performing FMs, comprehensive customization capabilities, data security, and compliance features, and seamless integration with AWS services, all while abstracting away the complexities of infrastructure management. We will explore Amazon Bedrock in great detail in future chapters of this book.

AWS also offers a GenAI playground called PartyRock. It is powered by Amazon Bedrock, and it is an engaging and user-friendly app-building playground. Within seconds, you can craft your unique apps, share them, and delve into the world of GenAI, all without writing a single line of code. It is very informative but it is built for educational purposes, so we will not be exploring that in this book. Amazon recently expanded access to Amazon Nova models through a new website allowing you to explore Nova models including three models (Nova Micro, Lite, and Pro) that generate text from different modalities, and two additional models for generating high-quality images (Nova Canvas) and videos (Nova Reel) from text and image input.

At the bottom layer, AWS offers Amazon SageMaker AI, which is again a fully managed ML service that enables developers and data scientists to build, train, and deploy ML models quickly. Among several capabilities, SageMaker AI offers JumpStart, a ML hub with a wide variety of public FMs to accelerate your GenAI journey. With SageMaker JumpStart, you can evaluate, compare, and select FMs quickly based on pre-defined quality and responsibility metrics to perform tasks like article summarization and image generation. We will explore how you can leverage Amazon SageMaker Jumpstart for your GenAI workloads in chapters eight and nine.

At the top-layer of the three-layer GenAI stack, AWS offers GenAI-powered applications and services that are easiest and quickest to adopt. AWS offers Amazon Q which is a GenAI assistant, powered by Amazon Bedrock, to help users in several areas. Amazon Q encompasses two products: Amazon Q Business, and Amazon Q Developer. Amazon Q Business is a powerful AI assistant that harnesses the collective knowledge and data within your organization to provide fast, relevant insights and solutions. By seamlessly integrating with your company's information repositories, codebase, and enterprise systems, Amazon Q Business can rapidly answer pressing questions, troubleshoot problems, generate content, and automate actions. When you engage in a conversation with Amazon Q Business, it will deliver immediate and contextualized information, advice, and recommendations tailored to your needs. These streamlines workflows accelerate decision-making processes and fosters creativity and innovation across your workforce. With Amazon Q Business, you can unlock the full potential of your organization's expertise and data assets, empowering employees to be more productive, agile, and innovative. Another top-layer service is Amazon Q Developer, an AI assistant that helps with building, operating, and transforming software for developers and IT professionals, encompassing far more than just coding support. It provides end-to-end guidance across the entire development lifecycle, including code testing, deployment, troubleshooting, security vulnerability scanning and remediation, application modernization, AWS resource optimization, and data pipeline engineering. Additionally, it empowers data scientists with streamlined capabilities to develop analytics solutions and build both traditional AI/ML and cutting-edge GenAI applications with greater efficiency and ease. It is trained on billions of lines of code and leverages advanced language models and ML techniques to understand the context and intent of the code being written. It supports over a dozen programming languages, including Python, Java, JavaScript, and Go, and integrates seamlessly into popular IDEs and code editors. Amazon Q is also integrated into various AWS services such as Amazon QuickSight (create and customize **business intelligence** (**BI**) visuals by using natural language instructions) and Amazon Connect (enabling customer service agents to provide a better customer experience). We will explore Amazon Q in *Chapter 12, Building Generative AI Assistant using Amazon Q*.

Lastly, AWS offers a specialized GenAI-powered service, AWS HealthScribe. It is a *Health Insurance Portability and Accountability Act* (*HIPAA*) eligible service designed to empower healthcare software vendors in building clinical applications that can automatically generate accurate and comprehensive clinical notes. By combining advanced speech recognition technology with cutting-edge GenAI, HealthScribe analyzes patient-clinician conversations in real-time and transcribes them into structured clinical notes. By leveraging the power of GenAI and ML, HealthScribe not only enhances efficiency but also ensures accurate and detailed documentation, ultimately improving clinical workflows and supporting better healthcare outcomes. AWS HealthScribe is out of scope for this book, check-out AWS Documentation for more information.

Prompt engineering

Prompt engineering refers to the process of carefully crafting the input prompts or instructions given to LLMs or GenAI systems to guide and control their outputs. It is a crucial aspect of working with these models, as the quality and specificity of the prompts can significantly influence the generated content.

Prompt engineering has become increasingly important as GenAI systems have become more widely used. Prompt engineers play a crucial role in helping users get the most out of these powerful AI models. Their job involves developing a variety of prompts, scripts, and templates that users can customize to get the best results from the AI. By experimenting with different types of inputs, prompt engineers build a library of prompts that application developers can then reuse in various contexts. This is important because it makes AI applications more efficient and effective. When users provide open-ended input, the application can use a carefully crafted prompt to give the AI model the necessary information and guidance it needs to generate a relevant and accurate response. For example, in a chatbot, a prompt might provide the AI with details about the user's location and the specific product they are looking for, allowing the chatbot to give them a more helpful and tailored answer.

Prompt engineering also offers several key benefits. It gives developers more control over how users interact with the AI, preventing misuse and ensuring that it responds appropriately. It also improves the user experience by helping them get the right results the first time, and it can even help mitigate biases that may be present in the AI's training data. Finally, prompt engineering can increase the flexibility of AI systems. By creating broadly applicable prompts, prompt engineers can enable organizations to reuse the same prompts across different applications and business units, allowing them to scale their AI investments more efficiently. Overall, prompt engineering is crucial for unlocking the full potential of GenAI and delivering better outcomes for both developers and end-users.

By now, we understand what prompt engineering is and why it is important. Let us define what a prompt is. A prompt is the way you communicate with a GenAI system. It is a piece of text that you write to tell the AI what you want it to do, like create a story, generate an image, or answer a question. *Figure 1.3* depicts the relationship between prompts and FMs, explaining the pivotal role prompts play in guiding the generation process.

Refer to the following figure for a better understanding:

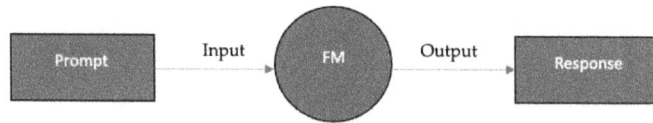

Figure 1.3: *Interaction with FMs*

Let us see it as an example:

User prompt:
```
Who invented penicillin? Where were they from and where did they do the
invention? Please be brief in your response.
```

Output:
```
Alexander Fleming, a Scottish scientist, invented penicillin in 1928 at St.
Mary's Hospital in London, England.
```

Model used: *Anthropic Claude 3 Sonnet*

The prompts you provide are important because they give the AI the context and details it needs to create something useful and relevant. If your prompt is too short or vague, the AI might struggle to know exactly what you want. But if you provide specific information, the AI can use that to generate something that is tailored to your needs. Prompt engineering is the process of refining and improving your prompts until you get the results you are looking for from the AI. It is about experimenting and trying different approaches to see what works best. With some practice, you can learn to craft prompts that bring out the best in the GenAI system and help it in order to create content according to your preference.

The prompt can have several elements, but typically it is made up of instructions, context, tone, style, output format, length, detail, and constraints.

Instruction (also called **task description**) is the core part of the prompt, where you specify the task or action you want the AI to perform. For example: `write a 500-word product review for the new XYZ wireless noise-cancelling headphones`.

Context is any relevant information about the task, setting, or domain to help the AI understand the specific requirements. For example: `you are a tech blogger writing a review for your audience of tech-savvy consumers who are interested in high-quality audio equipment`.

The prompt may specify the desired tone (e.g., formal, casual, empathetic) and style (e.g., persuasive, informative, creative) that the AI should adopt in its response. For example: `use an engaging, conversational tone and a balanced, objective style to evaluate the headphones' features and performance`.

The prompt may specify the desired format for the AI's response, such as a short paragraph, a bulleted list, or a more structured document. For example: `organize the review into the following sections: Introduction, Product Overview, Sound Quality, Noise Cancellation, Comfort and Design, and Conclusion`.

The prompt may indicate the expected length and level of detail required in the AI's response, such as whether a concise summary or a more comprehensive analysis is needed. For example: `the review should be approximately 500 words long and provide a thorough evaluation of the headphones' audio performance, noise-canceling capabilities, design, and overall user experience`.

The prompt may include any limitations or constraints that the AI should consider, such as word count, period, or specific guidelines. For example: `your review should not contain any profanity or overly subjective language, and it must be based on factual information about the product's specifications and performance`.

By including these elements, the prompt provides the AI system with a clear understanding of the task, the context, the desired tone and style, the expected output format, the required length and level of detail, any constraints, and any additional information that can be used to generate a high-quality product review for the XYZ wireless noise-cancelling headphones.

Prompt engineering techniques

Prompt engineering plays a pivotal role in unlocking the true potential of FMs by enabling efficient adaptation to diverse tasks through techniques like zero-shot, few-shot, and **chain-of-thought** (**CoT**) prompting. These methods demonstrate how carefully crafted prompts can enhance the effectiveness of FMs on complex tasks without the need for extensive model retraining.

Zero-shot prompting is a technique that allows FMs to generate responses for a task without providing any explicit examples of the desired behavior during the prompting process. Instead, the prompt relies solely on the FM's pre-training and its ability to understand and generalize from the instructions provided. This approach is particularly useful when you want to quickly evaluate an FM's capabilities on a new task or when you do not have any specific examples to include in the prompt. It leverages the FM's broad knowledge and language understanding capabilities, enabling it to generate relevant outputs based on the task description alone.

The following is an example of a zero-shot prompt for a task that involves generating a short story based on a given title:

```
```
Title: The Forgotten Lighthouse

You are a creative writer. Your task is to generate a short story based on
the given title: "The Forgotten Lighthouse". The story should be engaging,
descriptive, and have a clear narrative structure with a beginning, middle,
and end. Do not provide any examples, but rely solely on your understanding of
the task and your pre-training to generate the story.
```
```

In this example, the prompt provides the title of the story and instructions for the task, but it does not include any specific examples of what the story should look like. FM must rely on its pre-training and language understanding capabilities to generate a coherent and engaging short story based on the given title and instructions.

Zero-shot prompting is a powerful technique that showcases the remarkable capabilities of FMs to understand and generate relevant outputs based on natural language instructions alone. While this approach is straightforward and provides a starting point for evaluating FMs, it may not always yield accurate or desired results for more intricate tasks. It is worth noting that for more complex tasks or when higher accuracy is required, providing a few examples (few-shot prompting) or breaking down the task into intermediate steps (CoT prompting) can often yield better results.

Few-shot prompting is a technique that allows FMs to learn from a small number of examples provided in the prompt, enabling them to perform a task more accurately. Unlike zero-shot prompting, where the FM relies solely on its pre-training, few-shot prompting provides a few input-output pairs or demonstrations of the desired behavior, allowing the FM to learn in-context and adapt to the specific task. This approach is particularly useful when zero-shot prompting does not yield satisfactory results or when the task requires more specific guidance. By providing a few examples, the FM can learn the patterns and expectations associated with the task, increasing the likelihood of generating accurate and relevant outputs.

The following is an example of a few-shot prompt for a task that involves sentiment analysis:

```
```
Your task is to identify the sentiment (positive, negative, or neutral)
expressed in the given text. Here are a few examples:

Text: "The service at this restaurant was excellent, and the food was
delicious."
```
```

```
Sentiment: Positive

Text: "I'm incredibly frustrated with the constant delays and poor
communication from the airline."
Sentiment: Negative

Text: "The weather today is mild and partly cloudy."
Sentiment: Neutral

Text: "The new software update has some exciting features, but I've
encountered a few bugs as well."
Sentiment: ?
```

In this example, the prompt provides three input-output pairs that demonstrate how to identify the sentiment expressed in a given text. The FM can learn from these examples and then generate the sentiment for the new input text provided at the end of the prompt. Few-shot prompting is an effective way to tackle more complex tasks by providing a few examples that guide the FM toward the desired behavior. The number of examples provided can vary depending on the task complexity, with one example (one-shot), three examples (three-shot), or five examples (five-shot) being common choices.

By leveraging the in-context learning capabilities of FMs, few-shot prompting allows for rapid adaptation to new tasks without the need for large training datasets, making it a powerful and efficient technique for a wide range of applications. Furthermore, CoT prompting enhances FMs' capabilities in tackling complex reasoning tasks by breaking down the problem into intermediate steps. By combining few-shot prompting with CoT prompting, FMs can effectively solve intricate tasks that require step-by-step reasoning.

CoT prompting is a technique that enhances the reasoning capabilities of FMs by breaking down complex tasks into intermediate steps. This approach encourages the FM to generate a step-by-step thought process, or CoT, leading to the final solution, rather than directly outputting the answer. CoT prompting is particularly useful for tasks that involve complex reasoning, such as arithmetic problems, logical puzzles, multi-step word problems, or building autonomous AI agents. By explicitly prompting the FM to think through the problem step-by-step, it can better leverage its language understanding and reasoning capabilities to solve intricate tasks that may be challenging to solve directly.

The following is an example of a CoT prompt for a multi-step arithmetic word problem:
```
Question: There are 15 bookshelves in the library. If each bookshelf can hold
30 books, and there are already 270 books on the shelves, how many more books
can the library hold before the shelves are full?

To solve this problem, let's break it down step-by-step:

Step 1) Calculate the total capacity of the bookshelves:
```

```
Number of bookshelves × Books per shelf = Total capacity
15 × 30 = 450 books

Step 2) Calculate the remaining capacity by subtracting the current number of
books from the total capacity:
Total capacity - Current number of books = Remaining capacity
450 - 270 = 180 books

Therefore, the library can hold 180 more books before the shelves are full.
```

In this example, the prompt first provides the word problem and then instructs the FM to break down the solution into step-by-step reasoning. The FM generates a CoT, explicitly stating the intermediate steps required to solve the problem, such as calculating the total and remaining capacity. By following this step-by-step approach, the FM can effectively tackle complex multi-step problems that might be challenging to solve directly. CoT prompting can be combined with few-shot prompting by providing a few examples of step-by-step reasoning before presenting the actual problem to be solved. This combination can further enhance the FM's ability to reason through complex tasks effectively.

CoT prompting is a powerful technique that leverages the language understanding and reasoning capabilities of FMs, enabling them to tackle intricate problems that require breaking down the solution into intermediate steps.

The **reasoning and acting** (ReAct) takes the standard prompting approach a step further by enabling dynamic reasoning through interactions with external knowledge sources and environments. This comprehensive report explores the ReAct framework, its implementation, benefits, applications, and how it addresses critical challenges in GenAI, such as hallucination and limited reasoning capabilities. Traditional prompting methods primarily rely on a language model's internal knowledge, which can lead to limitations in reasoning and factual accuracy.

ReAct addresses these limitations by combining two essential capabilities, as follows:

- **Reasoning traces**: Verbal step-by-step thinking processes that help models track progress, handle exceptions, and adjust plans according to situations.

- **Task-specific actions**: Interactions with external environments or knowledge bases (using tools) to gather additional information necessary for problem-solving. This interleaved approach creates a synergistic relationship between ReAct, mimicking human cognitive processes where we often alternate between thinking and gathering information.

There are many evolving techniques such as the **tree-of-thought** (ToT) prompt the model to generate multiple possible next steps and elaborate on each path using a tree search method, enabling a comprehensive exploration of the problem space. Maieutic prompting iteratively delves into explanations, pruning inconsistencies and enhancing reasoning capabilities. Complexity-based prompting conducts multiple CoT rollouts, selects the longest chains, and identifies the most commonly reached conclusion, harnessing the model's ability to handle complex tasks. Generated knowledge prompting conditions the model on relevant information before completing the main task, improving output quality. Least-to-most prompting guides the model to list subproblems and solve them sequentially, leveraging previously solved components. Self-refine prompting employs an iterative approach where the model solves, critiques, and refines its output, fostering a self-correcting and self-improving process. Directional-stimulus prompting incorporates hints or cues, such as desired keywords, to steer the model's output toward the intended direction. Prompt chaining breaks tasks into subtasks, chaining prompts to perform transformations or additional processes on generated responses, improving reliability, controllability, and transparency.

Prompt engineering is a dynamic and evolving discipline that demands a synergy of linguistic prowess and creative expression. Crafting effective prompts necessitates a delicate balance of language mastery and imaginative thinking to elicit the desired responses from GenAI tools. This iterative process requires a deep understanding of language nuances coupled with a creative mindset to continuously refine and optimize prompts, unlocking the full potential of these advanced AI models.

Setting up AWS environment

In the following chapters, you will need access to an AWS account to run the code examples.

Note: **If you already have an AWS account, skip this section and move on to the next chapter. AWS provides Free Tier, which allows you to try services free of charge based on certain service usage limits or time limits. See https://aws.amazon.com/free for more details. Amazon Bedrock is not covered under free trial.**

Follow the instructions at **https://docs.aws.amazon.com/accounts/latest/reference/ manage-acct-creating.html** to sign up for an AWS account, then proceed, as follows:

1. Once the AWS account is created, sign in using your email address and password and access the AWS Management Console at **https://console.aws.amazon.com/**.

2. Type **IAM** in the services search bar at the top of the console and select **IAM** to navigate to the IAM console. Select **Users** from the left panel in the IAM console and select **Create user**.

3. Enter a **User name** value, then check **Provide user access to the AWS Management Console - optional** box. For the question, **Are you providing console access to a person?**, select **I want to create an IAM user**.

4. Keep the **Console password** setting as **Custom password** and enter a password. Uncheck **Users must create a new password at the next sign-in - Recommended** box.

The following figure shows how you can setup an IAM user in an AWS account:

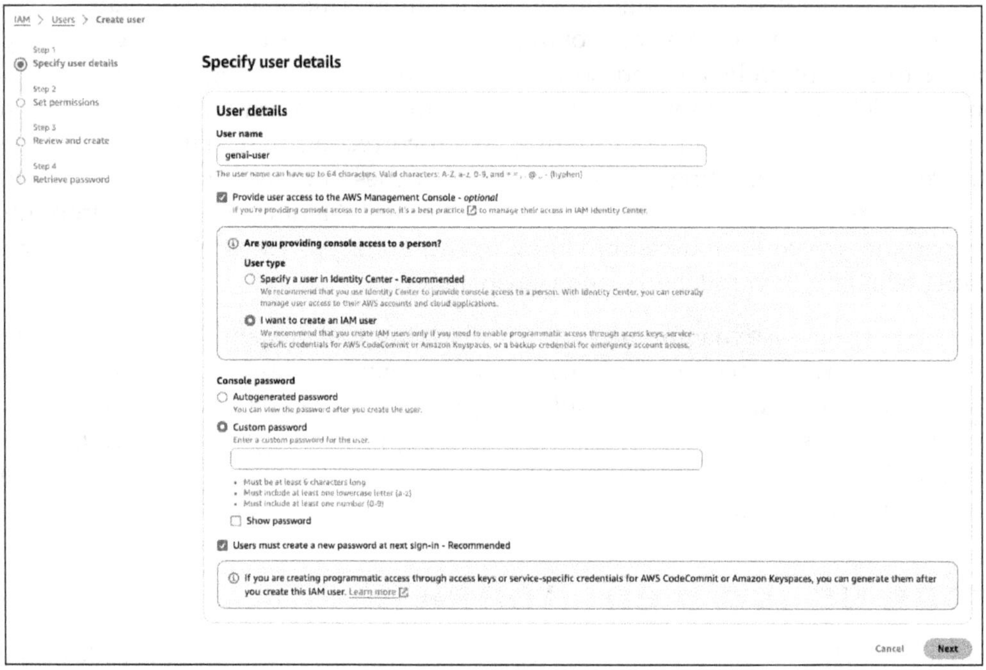

Figure 1.4: Setting up your IAM user

5. Select **Next**, on the **Set permissions** page, select **Attach policies directly** and select the checkbox to the left of **AdministratorAccess**.

The following figure depicts how you can add permissions to the IAM user you created in earlier steps:

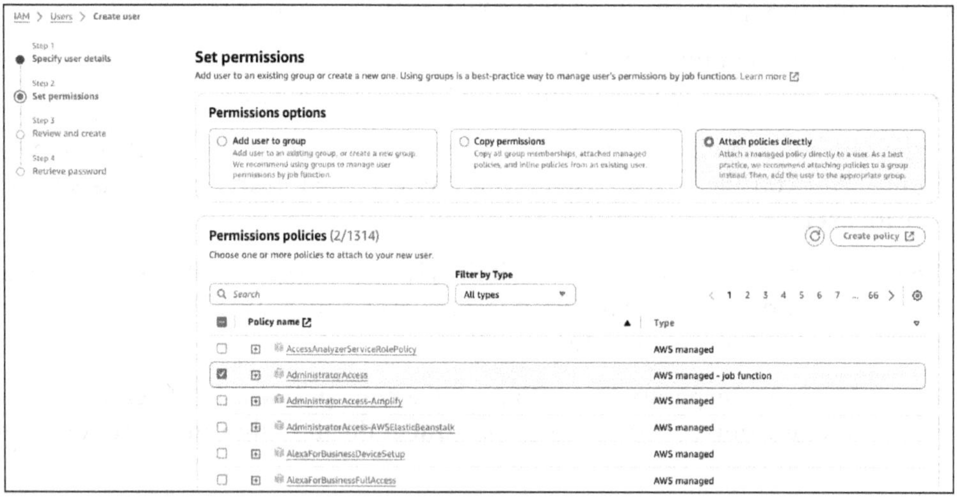

Figure 1.5: Adding permissions for IAM user

6. Select **Next** to go to the **Review and create** page then, select **Create user**.

7. Go back to the AWS Management Console **https://console.aws.amazon.com** and select **Sign in**. Provide the **IAM username** you created in the previous step along with a temporary password, and enter a new password to log in to the console.

Creating Amazon SageMaker AI studio domain

We will be using Jupyter Notebooks to run our code in the following chapters. Execute the following steps to create a classic studio domain in Amazon SageMaker AI:

1. In the AWS Management Console, type `SageMaker AI` in the services search bar at the top of the page, and select it to access the Amazon SageMaker AI console.

2. On the left panel, select **Studio**, and then the **Create a SageMaker domain**.

3. At the top right of the **Notebook** instances page, select **Create Notebook instance**.

4. Select **Set up for single user (Quick setup)** and select **Set up**. It will take a few minutes for the studio domain to get created.

    The following figure shows the presented choice while creating a SageMaker domain:

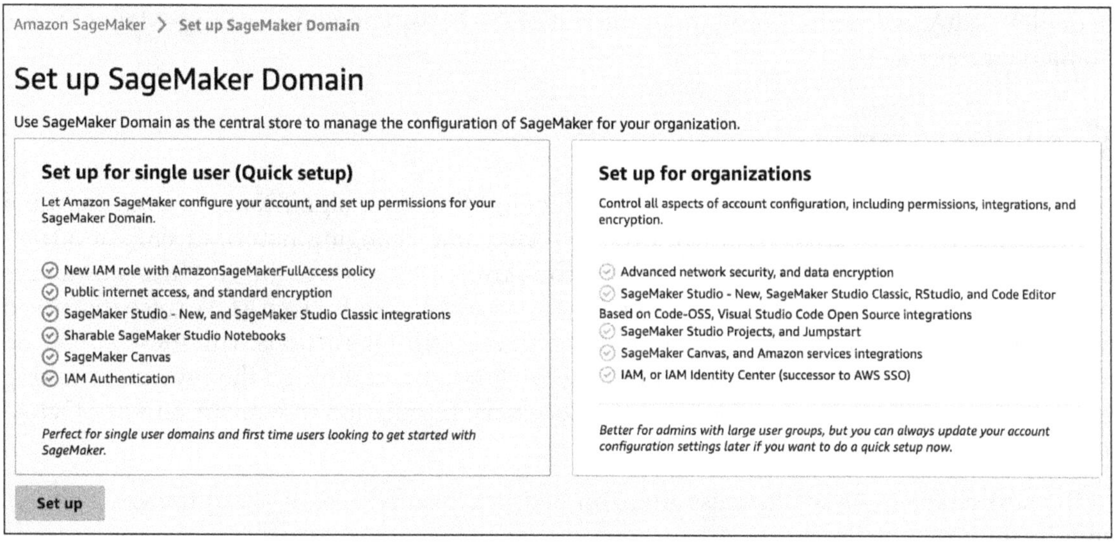

Amazon SageMaker ❯ Set up SageMaker Domain

Set up SageMaker Domain

Use SageMaker Domain as the central store to manage the configuration of SageMaker for your organization.

Set up for single user (Quick setup)

Let Amazon SageMaker configure your account, and set up permissions for your SageMaker Domain.

- ⊘ New IAM role with AmazonSageMakerFullAccess policy
- ⊘ Public internet access, and standard encryption
- ⊘ SageMaker Studio - New, and SageMaker Studio Classic integrations
- ⊘ Sharable SageMaker Studio Notebooks
- ⊘ SageMaker Canvas
- ⊘ IAM Authentication

Perfect for single user domains and first time users looking to get started with SageMaker.

Set up for organizations

Control all aspects of account configuration, including permissions, integrations, and encryption.

- ⊘ Advanced network security, and data encryption
- ⊘ SageMaker Studio - New, SageMaker Studio Classic, RStudio, and Code Editor Based on Code-OSS, Visual Studio Code Open Source integrations
- ⊘ SageMaker Studio Projects, and Jumpstart
- ⊘ SageMaker Canvas, and Amazon services integrations
- ⊘ IAM, or IAM Identity Center (successor to AWS SSO)

Better for admins with large user groups, but you can always update your account configuration settings later if you want to do a quick setup now.

Set up

Figure 1.6: Creating SageMaker domain

5. Once the status is **InService**, you are ready to proceed. Under **User profiles**, you will see a default user created. Select **Launch** and then click on **Studio** from the dropdown. All future chapters will provide instructions for executing the code examples.

The following figure shows how you can access SageMaker Studio in the domain you just created:

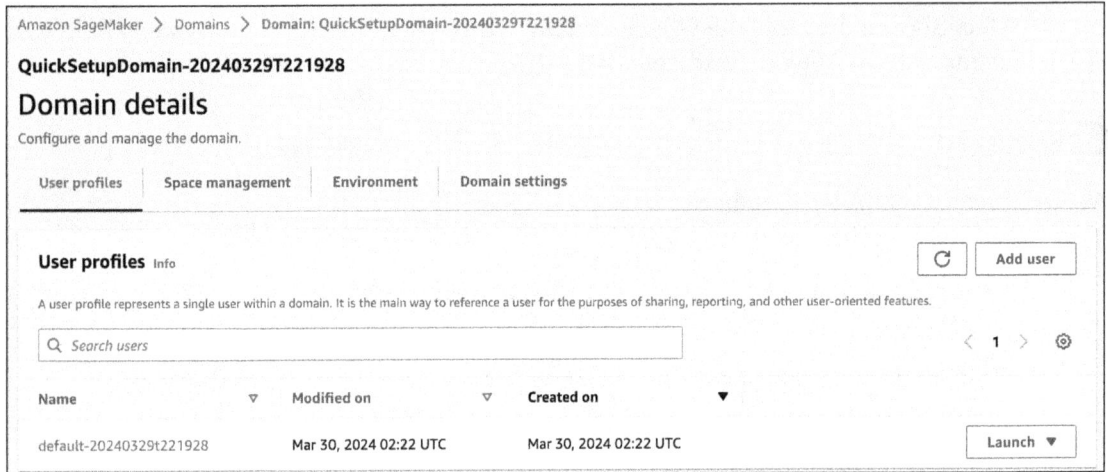

Figure 1.7: SageMaker Studio access

Now, you are ready to deploy the code examples that will show you how to use AWS services to deploy GenAI solutions. Throughout the rest of the book, you will use a SageMaker Studio domain for these steps.

Conclusion

In this chapter, we covered GenAI and FMs, highlighting their significance and far-reaching impact across various industries. We explored the game-changing nature of FMs and their potential to drive innovation through numerous use cases, showcasing the transformative power of GenAI. Furthermore, we explored the AWS ecosystem for GenAI. We also discussed prompt engineering, unveiling techniques to optimize your interactions with these advanced models and unlock their full potential. Finally, we guided you through the process of setting up an AWS account, ensuring you have the necessary foundation to embark on your GenAI journey.

In the next chapter, we will discuss Amazon Bedrock. You will learn about the key features and capabilities of Bedrock.

Points to remember

- GenAI is a subset of deep learning focused on training neural networks to create new data like text, images, audio, or video.

- FMs are large-scale ML models that power GenAI, capable of producing output based on prompts or instructions.

- LLMs like GPT-3, BLOOM, Mistral, Llama, DeepSeek, and Claude are prominent examples of FMs, trained on massive dataset to develop natural language understanding and in some models multimodal (image, audio, video) understanding.

- GenAI has numerous use cases across customer experience, employee productivity, and process optimization in various industries.

- AWS offers a three-layer stack for GenAI infrastructure to build and train AI models (computing, storage, networking, and Amazon SageMaker AI), platform providing models and tools to build AI applications (Amazon Bedrock), and applications to boost productivity (Amazon Q Business, Amazon Q Developer).

- Prompt engineering is the process of crafting input prompts to guide and control the outputs of GenAI models, using techniques like zero-shot, few-shot, and CoT prompting.

Exercise

1. Now that you have learned about the fundamentals of GenAI and AWS's capabilities, it is time to get hands-on. Visit **https://nova.amazon.com**, a new website to easily explore Amazon Nova FMs, where you can experiment with different prompting techniques and see the results in real-time. This playground allows you to attach images, videos, and documents, craft your own prompts, and engage in interactive chat sessions. Try it out and see how different approaches affect the AI's outputs.

Join our Discord space

Join our Discord workspace for latest updates, offers, tech happenings around the world, new releases, and sessions with the authors:

https://discord.bpbonline.com

CHAPTER 2
Getting Started with Amazon Bedrock

Introduction

In the previous chapter, we discussed the fascinating world of **generative AI (GenAI)** and how **large language models (LLMs)** are revolutionizing multiple domains. These models now power diverse applications that enterprises use daily, from helping financial analysts generate visual insights with automated charts and reports, to enabling software companies to build intelligent platforms that can process customer inquiries through voice and text, to assisting healthcare providers with medical image analysis and patient care summaries. However, accessing, customizing, and deploying these LLMs requires significant resources, expertise, and computational infrastructure.

This is where Amazon Bedrock comes in. Amazon Bedrock is a fully managed service that offers the easiest way to build GenAI applications using high-performance **foundation models (FMs)** from leading AI companies like *Anthropic, Cohere, Meta, Mistral AI,* and others, as well as models developed by *Amazon* itself. With Bedrock, you can easily experiment with and evaluate different FMs to find the best fit for your use case without the need for costly infrastructure or specialized AI teams.

Bedrock offers more than just a collection of FMs. It provides a comprehensive set of tools and capabilities to build GenAI applications with a focus on security, observability, privacy, and responsible AI practices. This includes techniques like **retrieval augmented generation (RAG)**, fine-tuning, and continued pre-training, which allow you to customize the models with your data. Additionally, you can build autonomous agents that integrate with your enterprise systems and data sources to execute complex workflows.

Whether you are a developer, data scientist, or business leader, Amazon Bedrock provides a comprehensive platform to harness the potential of GenAI. Let us explore how Bedrock can simplify and accelerate your AI journey.

Structure

The chapter covers the following topics:

- Overview of Amazon Bedrock
- Key features and capabilities
- Navigating Amazon Bedrock interface
- Ecosystem of framework and tools
- Amazon Bedrock platform enhancements

Objectives

By the end of this chapter, readers will gain a comprehensive understanding of Amazon Bedrock's core capabilities and how it streamlines the process of building GenAI applications using FMs. You will learn to navigate the Bedrock console, including accessing models and utilizing interactive playgrounds for hands-on experimentation. Additionally, you will receive an overview of Bedrock's essential features, such as knowledge bases, agents, and model customization options. The chapter will also cover the security and monitoring capabilities available in Bedrock to ensure you can build production-ready GenAI applications. Finally, you will discover the ecosystem of development tools and frameworks that support building with Bedrock, providing you with a well-rounded perspective on leveraging this powerful platform.

Overview of Amazon Bedrock

Amazon Bedrock is a fully managed service that provides access to high-performing FMs from leading AI companies like *AI21 Labs, Anthropic, Cohere, DeepSeek, Luma, Meta, Mistral AI, Stability AI, WRITER,* and *Amazon* itself. With a unified API, you can choose from a wide range of FMs to find the one that best suits your specific use case. Bedrock empowers you to build sophisticated and production-ready GenAI applications by offering comprehensive capabilities, including model customization, model evaluation, and agent creation, while prioritizing security, privacy, and responsible AI practices. Amazon Bedrock is available across multiple **Amazon Web Services** (**AWS**) Regions, allowing you to deploy your GenAI applications closer to your users and data sources.

By using Bedrock, you can easily experiment with and evaluate top FMs, tailoring them to your unique requirements. Techniques like RAG, fine-tuning, and continued pre-training allow you to customize these models with your data, enhancing their performance, accuracy, and relevance. Additionally, you can develop intelligent AI agents that execute complex tasks by integrating with your existing enterprise systems and data sources.

As a serverless service, Amazon Bedrock eliminates the need for infrastructure management, enabling you to focus on building innovative GenAI solutions. Using familiar AWS services, streamlining deployment, and accelerating time-to-market, you can securely and seamlessly integrate these capabilities into your applications.

Key features and capabilities

The following are some of the key features of Bedrock to help you build secure and production-ready GenAI applications on AWS:

- **Interactive playgrounds**: Builders often experiment with different FMs to identify the correct model and price performace for their specific use case, as each model offers unique capabilities. The Amazon Bedrock provides Chat/text, and image playgrounds for you to experiment, compare, and evaluate different FMs, explore sample examples, and try out different prompts or inputs, inference parameters, or configurations to generate desired responses from these models.

- **Data-augmented responses**: FMs, while powerful, are trained on broad datasets and may lack specific knowledge about an organization's business domain. As a result, these models can sometimes hallucinate or generate responses that are inaccurate or inconsistent with the organization's domain knowledge. To mitigate this issue and improve response accuracy, it is crucial to augment the FMs with additional information or context relevant to the organization's domain.

  Amazon Bedrock addresses this need through its Amazon Bedrock Knowledge Bases feature. This capability allows users to integrate their enterprise knowledge and data sources, enabling the FMs to augment their responses with relevant information from these data sources. Users can easily upload and manage their data sources within Bedrock, which will be queried during the response generation process. By leveraging the organization's proprietary knowledge, the FM's outputs can be enhanced, reducing the risk of hallucination and improving accuracy for the specific use cases.

- **Intelligent task automation**: To extend the capabilities of FMs and build sophisticated GenAI applications, Amazon Bedrock offers Amazon Bedrock Agents. This feature enables end-users to automate complex tasks by orchestrating interactions between FMs, data sources, applications, and user conversations. Agents can seamlessly integrate with various components to execute multi-step workflows tailored to an organization's needs. For instance, an agent could assist with travel planning by generating personalized itineraries, booking reservations, and emailing confirmations to users.

- **Tailored model training**: Base FMs excel at answering questions across a variety of topics. However, for specialized domains like legal, finance, cybersecurity, and healthcare, tailoring the model's knowledge to the specific domain can significantly enhance its performance. Amazon Bedrock allows users to customize FMs through techniques like fine-tuning and continued pre-training, using domain-specific or task-specific data. This tailored approach optimizes the models for generating accurate and contextual responses within the target domain or use case.

- **Optimized performance**: Delivering consistent performance and meeting **service level agreements (SLAs)** is crucial for any organization, including for their GenAI applications. Amazon Bedrock addresses this requirement through its Provisioned Throughput feature, which enables users to reserve dedicated capacity for their workloads. This feature ensures predictable model inference performance and helps organizations maintain consistent response times for their production applications, making it ideal for business-critical workloads that require reliable throughput.

- **Model evaluation**: To ensure the selection of the most suitable FM for a specific application, Amazon Bedrock provides model evaluation capabilities. Users can leverage built-in or custom prompt datasets to evaluate and compare the outputs of different FMs. This feature enables users to identify the model that best aligns with their application's requirements, optimizing performance, and ensuring the most appropriate model is chosen for their use case.

- **Content moderation**: Ensuring responsible, and ethical content generation is a critical consideration in GenAI applications. Amazon Bedrock addresses this need through its Amazon Bedrock Guardrails feature, which enables users to implement safeguards and content moderation capabilities. With Amazon Bedrock Guardrails, users can prevent the generation of inappropriate, offensive, or unwanted content, ensuring that their applications align with their organization's values and guidelines for acceptable content.

Navigating Amazon Bedrock interface

Let us explore the Amazon Bedrock interface and its key features, which are critical for creating GenAI applications on AWS. To begin working with Bedrock, you will need to setup the appropriate permissions and request access to specific FMs. Amazon Bedrock offers models from various providers, and each model requires explicit access approval and proper **Identity and Access Management (IAM)** configurations before you can start experiment or use them in your applications.

Model access

As discussed earlier, Amazon Bedrock provides access to multiple FMs from different providers. To access these models, you first need to request access through the Bedrock console. Navigate to the **Model access** section by going to Bedrock configurations model access, as shown in the following figure:

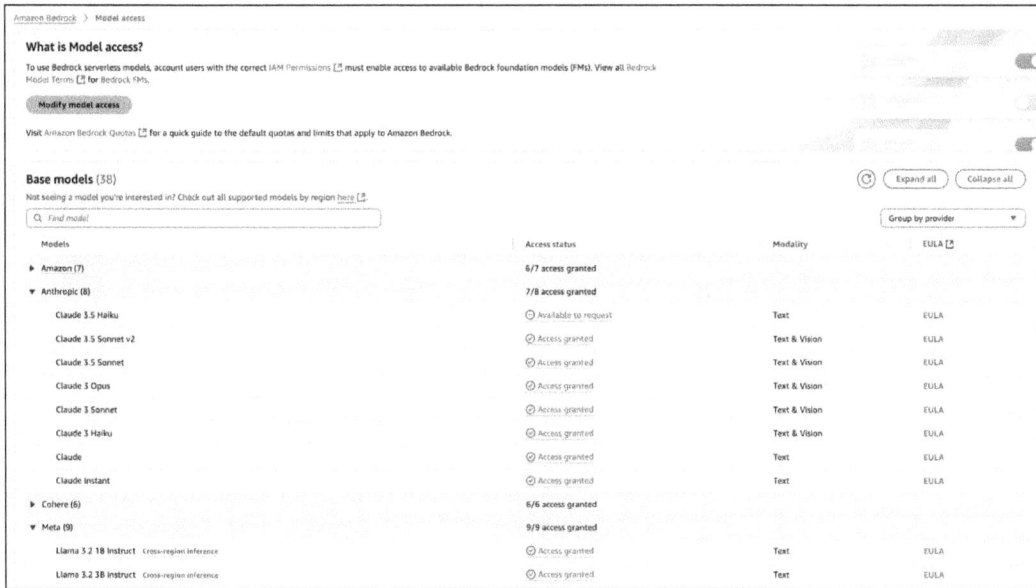

Figure 2.1: *Model access in Amazon Bedrock*

If your AWS account is managed by your organization, you might not have the required IAM permissions to request or access all or some of the Bedrock models. In this case, you may need to request additional permissions from your AWS platform team. Certain third-party Bedrock models, such as *Anthropic's Claude* models, might also require AWS Marketplace specific access. After gaining access to the desired models, they will be available for use within your Bedrock environment, allowing you to experiment, evaluate, and integrate them into your GenAI applications.

Playgrounds

The Amazon Bedrock provides interactive playgrounds that allow you to experiment and compare different FMs, explore sample examples, and try out various prompts, inputs, inference parameters, or configurations to generate desired responses from these models. Prompts are input text that you submit to the FMs to receive a response. They can contain questions, instructions, or sample examples for the model to learn from. Inference parameters or configurations are settings that you can adjust to influence the responses generated by the FMs.

The playgrounds feature offers an easy way to get started with Bedrock and evaluate different models for your use cases directly from the AWS console. You can choose from multiple sample examples for various use cases, such as content generation, code generation, summarization, or advanced model use cases like creating a website. As of writing this book, you have two playgrounds available: Chat/text and image.

Refer to the following figure to see the **Chat/text playground**:

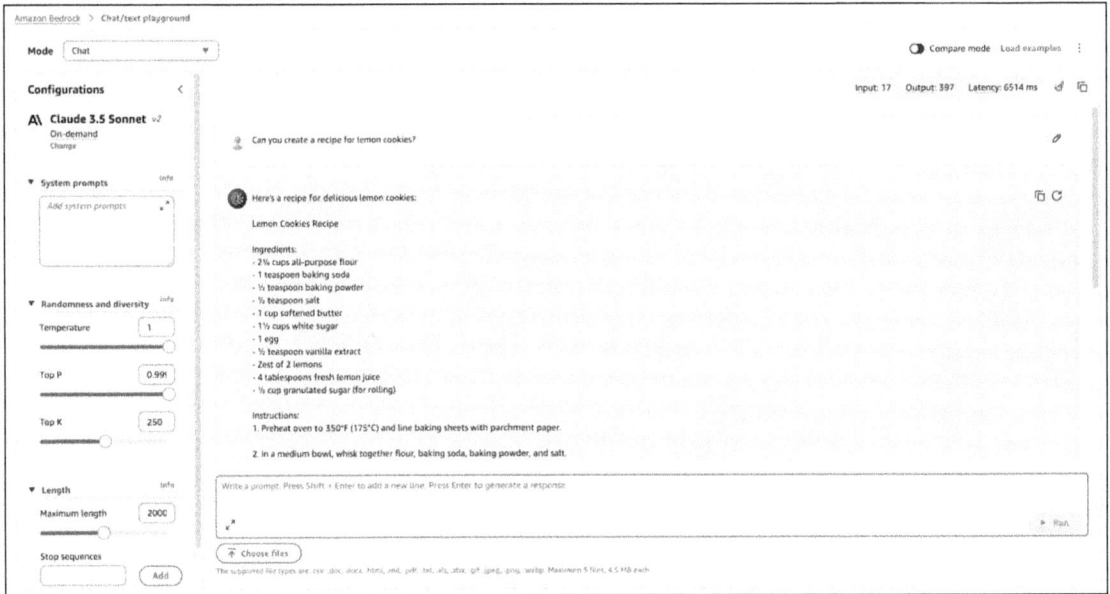

Figure 2.2: Chat/text playground in Amazon Bedrock

One powerful feature of the **Chat/text playground** is the **Compare mode**; it allows you to easily compare two FMs side-by-side. You can toggle the **Compare mode** button, choose the FMs you want to compare, and then ask the same question to both models. This can be very helpful in the initial phase to narrow down the model that best fits your specific use case.

Refer to the following figure for a better understanding:

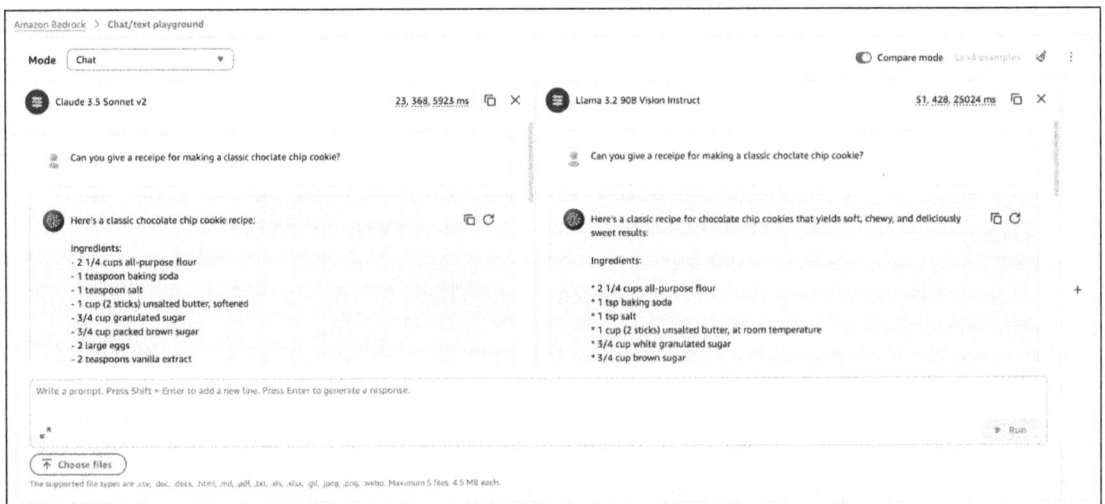

Figure 2.3: Compare mode of Chat/text playground in Amazon Bedrock

The playgrounds offer several out-of-the-box examples for you to try out. You can simply click the **Load examples** button to load these examples into the playground. To aid in evaluating the models, the **Chat/text playground** displays model metrics such as **Input** token count, **Output** token count and **Latency**, as shown in F*igure 2.4*:

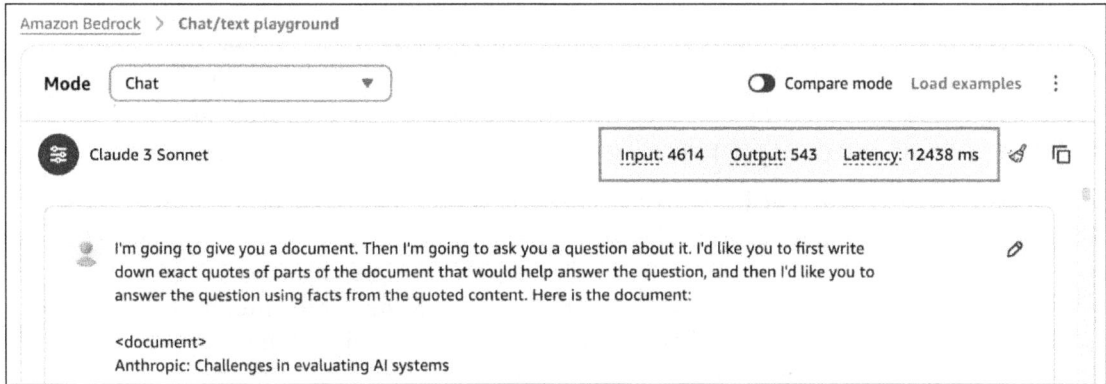

Figure 2.4: *Model metrics of Chat/text playground in Amazon Bedrock*

Later in this chapter, we will discuss Amazon Bedrock's Model Evaluation feature for assessing task-specific metrics.

After selecting your desired models through playground, you can use the Amazon Bedrock's APIs to integrate and call those models in your GenAI application. We will cover the APIs in detail in *Chapter 4, Building Generative AI Applications with Bedrock APIs*.

Builder tools

Builder tools in Amazon Bedrock are a set of features designed to help you develop, test, and deploy GenAI applications more efficiently. These tools include: knowledge bases, which help manage and retrieve information from your data sources; agents, which enable creation of AI assistants that can perform tasks and interact with external systems; flows, which provides a visual interface to design, test, and deploy AI workflows by combining FMs with custom business logic and external APIs; and prompt management, which enables teams to collaborate on, version control, and evaluate prompt performance across different models. Together, these tools provide a comprehensive suite for building and managing GenAI applications on Amazon Bedrock.

Amazon Bedrock Knowledge Bases

With Amazon Bedrock Knowledge Bases, users can build applications that incorporate their company's enterprise or business information, obtained by querying the knowledge base. This capability enables FMs to generate more relevant and accurate responses while reducing the time needed to build applications.

Before discussing knowledge bases in detail, let us briefly review the RAG technique, which knowledge bases utilize.

Retrieval augmentation and generation

FMs possess vast pre-trained knowledge but often lack specific expertise in proprietary or enterprise-specific data. While prompts can provide context to these models, RAG offers a more sophisticated approach by integrating information retrieval from external sources, enabling models to provide tailored and accurate responses.

One significant advantage of RAG is its ability to handle large amounts of enterprise data efficiently. All FMs have input context length constraints, a limit on how much information can be processed in a single interaction. RAG addresses this limitation by intelligently retrieving only the most relevant information from external sources, ensuring the model receives specific input within its context window. This approach not only optimizes the model's performance but also reduces operational costs by controlling the input and output tokens.

RAG also improves the accuracy and reliability of FMs, reducing the likelihood of incorrect responses or hallucinations. By incorporating retrieved information, the model can cite sources, like footnotes, allowing users to validate the claims made by the model. For instance, a foundational model adapted for the medical domain using RAG in conjunction with medical terminology and patient databases can provide more accurate responses to queries from healthcare professionals.

RAG process

RAG process involves three key steps, as follows:

- **Retrieval**: Relevant content is fetched from external knowledge bases or data sources based on a user query.

- **Augmentation**: The retrieved context is added to the user's prompt, creating an enriched input for the foundational model.

- **Generation**: The model utilizes this augmented prompt to generate a response, benefiting from the additional context provided.

Figure 2.5 illustrates a practical example of the RAG process, showing how a simple order status query flows through the retrieval, augmentation, and generation steps. This example demonstrates how the system processes a user's question by leveraging both embedded queries and FAQ vector database to generate an informed response:

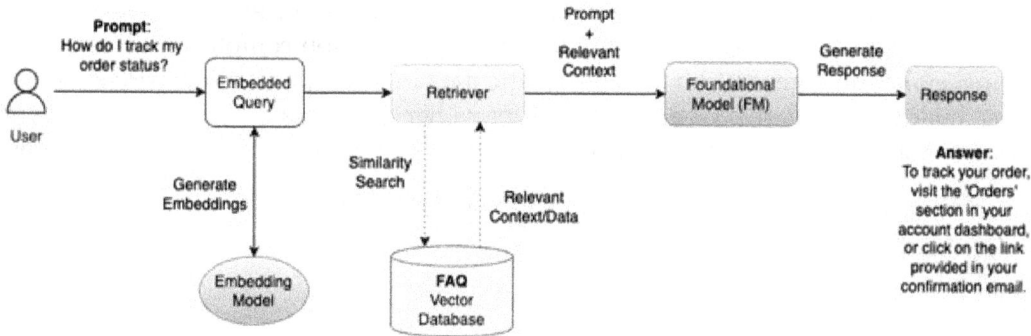

Figure 2.5: RAG technique

RAG often employs embedding models that convert text input into numerical representations, capturing the semantic relationships between words. This enables the model to perform semantic search and retrieve relevant information from external sources. Semantic search goes beyond simple keyword matching by understanding the contextual meaning of words. For example, if a user searches for affordable compact cars, a semantic search would also return results about budget-friendly small vehicles or economical mini automobiles, even though these phrases do not contain the exact same words. This is possible because the embedding model understands that these terms are semantically similar and represent the same underlying concept.

It is important to note that RAG does not change any underlying model parameters of the foundational model. Instead, it augments the FMs with the company's internal data.

Implementing RAG requires breaking documents into smaller segments (a process known as **chunking**) for effective processing and retrieval, and establishing a pipeline to process these documents and maintain the knowledge base. Organizations often face significant challenges during implementation, including ensuring data quality, managing the complexity of external sources, and addressing potential biases in retrieved information. Despite these hurdles, when properly implemented, RAG has the potential to unlock the full capabilities of FMs, enabling more accurate, reliable, and contextually relevant responses, especially in specialized domains.

Managed RAG with Amazon Bedrock Knowledge Bases

Recognizing these implementation challenges while seeing RAG's tremendous potential, Amazon Bedrock offers a managed RAG capability called **knowledge bases**. This feature streamlines the entire process by handling the complexities of information retrieval, document processing, and knowledge integration.

Knowledge bases in Amazon Bedrock are designed to be flexible and scalable, providing tools and APIs that enable users to manage and query their knowledge sources effectively. By leveraging this tool, users can easily augment their FMs with relevant and proprietary data from their company's data sources, abstracting away implementation complexities like document chunking, embedding generation, and automatic data indexing. This allows organizations to focus on building innovative GenAI applications rather than managing infrastructure, while ensuring enhanced accuracy and contextual relevance in their foundational model responses.

Refer to *Figure 2.6* for a better understanding of knowledge bases:

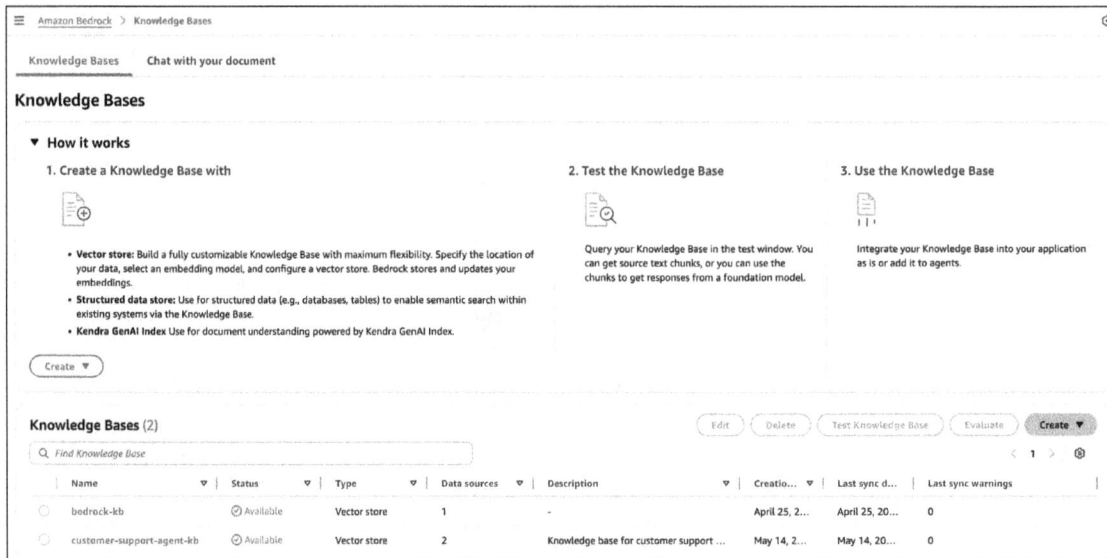

Figure 2.6: *Knowledge bases in Amazon Bedrock*

Knowledge bases can be utilized in several ways, as follows:

- **Chat with your document**: Upload ad-hoc datasets or documents, and Bedrock will provide context-aware responses based on the knowledge base and the FMs.

- **Test and query**: Use Bedrock's built-in testing tools to search and query your knowledge base, retrieving relevant information or getting answers from the FMs based on your queries.

- **Integrate with applications**: Seamlessly integrate your knowledge base into external applications or Bedrock Agents, enabling data access and querying capabilities within your existing workflows.

In *Chapter 5, Using Amazon Bedrock Knowledge Bases*, we will discuss creating and building knowledge bases within Amazon Bedrock. Readers will learn how to specify data sources, select appropriate embedding models, configure vector stores, and manage the entire lifecycle of your knowledge base. We will also explore advanced techniques and APIs for querying and integrating knowledge bases with your applications.

Whether you are building chatbots, **question answering (QA)** systems, or any other data-driven application, knowledge bases can provide the necessary context and information to enhance the performance of FMs and deliver more accurate and relevant results.

Amazon Bedrock Agents

Amazon Bedrock offers a powerful feature called **agents**, which allows developers to create fully managed agents that can automate tasks and perform actions by interacting with external systems and APIs. Agents extend the capabilities of FMs by enabling them to understand user requests, break down complex tasks into multiple steps, gather additional information through conversations, and execute actions to fulfill the requested task.

Agents can be used to automate a wide range of workflows across various industries and domains. For example, in the retail sector, an agent could assist with inventory management by understanding requests such as checking stock levels for this product and then coordinating the necessary actions, including retrieving data from inventory systems, analyzing demand patterns, and initiating restocking processes. In the finance industry, agents could streamline loan application processes by guiding applicants through the required steps, collecting necessary documents, and interacting with banking systems to fetch credit scores and other relevant information. For software development teams, an agent could facilitate code deployment tasks by understanding requests like deploying the latest version to the staging environment and then orchestrating actions such as fetching the latest code, running tests, and triggering the deployment pipeline.

The Amazon Bedrock console provides an intuitive interface for creating and managing agents. *Figure 2.7* shows the **Agents** dashboard, which allows you to prepare new agents by selecting FMs and action groups, and then deploy them for use in your applications:

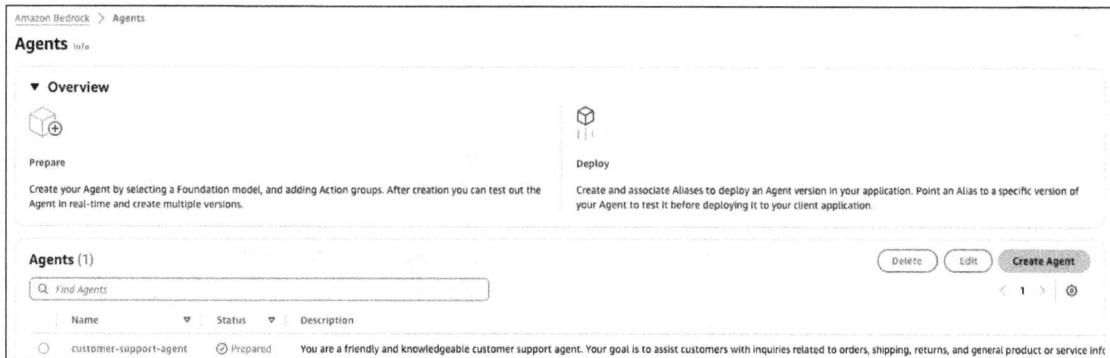

Figure 2.7: Agents in Amazon Bedrock

This interface simplifies the process of setting up and testing agents before deploying them in production environments.

With Amazon Bedrock Agents, developers can leverage the reasoning abilities of FMs to automate multi-step tasks. Agents use the provided instructions to create a plan, breaking down the user's request into a sequence of actions. They then execute this plan by calling the appropriate APIs and accessing relevant knowledge bases to provide a final response to the end-user. Agents can also employ the RAG technique by integrating with knowledge bases. This allows agents to securely connect to a company's data sources and augment the user's request with the right information to generate accurate and relevant responses.

Amazon Bedrock Agents provide enhanced capabilities, giving developers improved control and visibility over the orchestration process. Developers can view the chain of reasoning employed by the agent, allowing them to understand the rationale behind the agent's actions and refine the prompts and instructions as needed. Additionally, developers can modify the automatically generated prompt templates, giving them greater control over the pre-processing, orchestration, knowledge base integration, and post-processing steps.

Agents in Amazon Bedrock are fully managed, relieving developers from the burden of provisioning and managing infrastructure. Developers have seamless support for monitoring, encryption, user permissions, and API invocation management without the need to write custom code. agents can help automate various tasks and take actions on your behalf by interacting with external systems and APIs.

The following are some real-world examples:

- **Travel and hospitality**:
    - An agent that can assist customers in planning and booking complete travel itineraries, including flights, hotels, rental cars, and activities, by interacting with various travel booking systems and APIs.
    - An agent that helps hotel guests with check-in/check-out processes, room service requests, or concierge services by integrating with the hotel's property management system and other relevant databases.

- **E-commerce and retail**:
    - An agent that helps customers with product recommendations, personalized shopping experiences, and post-purchase support by accessing inventory systems, customer databases, and vendor APIs.
    - An agent that supports retailers in managing inventory levels, analyzing sales data, and optimizing pricing strategies by integrating with supply chain systems, point-of-sale data, and market intelligence sources.

- **Healthcare and medical assistance**:
    - An agent that can assist patients in scheduling appointments, refilling prescriptions, or answering general health-related queries by integrating with electronic medical record systems, pharmacy databases, and medical knowledge bases.

o An agent that supports medical professionals in diagnosing conditions, recommending treatments, or interpreting test results by accessing relevant medical literature, clinical guidelines, and patient data.

- **Education and learning**:
  o An agent that assists students in finding educational resources, answering questions, or providing personalized learning recommendations by accessing digital libraries, course catalogs, and educational content repositories.

  o An agent that supports teachers or instructors in creating lesson plans, grading assignments, or providing feedback to students by integrating with learning management systems and educational databases.

In *Chapter 6, Using Bedrock's Managed Agents,* we will discuss the process of creating and building agents within Amazon Bedrock. You will learn how to create and configure agents, specify action groups and APIs, integrate with knowledge bases, and leverage the full potential of agents for automating complex workflows and enhancing applications with GenAI capabilities.

Prompt management

Amazon Bedrock Prompt Management feature streamlines the development of GenAI applications, making it simpler for developers to create, organize, and refine prompts effectively. With version control, developers can track changes and test variations, iteratively improve prompt quality while retaining access to earlier versions. This is especially useful for tasks that demand precision, like customer service interactions, where a team might test and optimize prompts to ensure responses consistently meet clarity and tone standards.

To further enhance flexibility, prompt management supports parameterized prompts, allowing certain variables to adjust dynamically based on context. This adaptability is invaluable for teams working across varied use cases. For example, a marketing team could setup a single prompt template to generate customized product descriptions for different audience segments. Additionally, Bedrock's integration with AWS **Key Management Service** (**KMS**) allows prompts to be encrypted, ensuring they are securely stored and accessible only to authorized users.

Alongside these capabilities, prompt management provides tools for A/B testing, comparing two prompt variations to evaluate which performs better, centralized storage, and compliance auditing, making collaboration seamless and prompting best practices in AI workflows. With Bedrock's API, developers can retrieve and implement prompts securely as part of their GenAI workflows, enabling efficient and high-quality output across applications.

Amazon Bedrock Flows

Amazon Bedrock Flows empowers developers to design, test, and deploy multi-step GenAI workflows using an intuitive, visual drag and drop interface. This feature allows developers to create GenAI applications by connecting FMs, prompts, and AWS services together. For organizations, this translates to faster development cycles and the ability to quickly deploy adaptable GenAI solutions.

Unlike Bedrock Agents which are designed for autonomous task completion and complex interactions, flows focus on orchestrating pre-defined sequences of AI operations in a visual workflow. While agents can understand and execute user intentions dynamically, flows excel at creating structured, repeatable AI processes with predictable outcomes. For organizations, this translates to faster development cycles and the ability to quickly deploy adaptable GenAI solutions.

Consider a customer support knowledge assistant: Using Bedrock Flows, developers can create an intelligent workflow that helps support teams provide accurate, consistent responses. When a customer asks *what is the return policy for damaged electronics?* The workflow first uses a prompt node to analyze and structure the query, then searches a knowledge base containing support documentation and policies to provide relevant answers. Optionally, you can also add other nodes such as Lambda to query real-time data from your external systems. Each step is handled by different components or nodes in the workflow, working together to deliver accurate, context-aware responses.

Refer to the following figure for a better understanding:

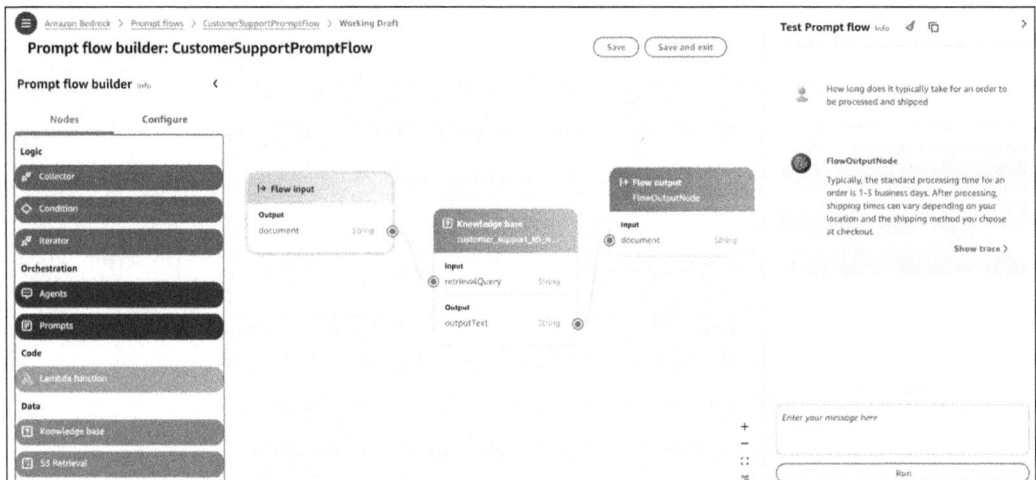

Figure 2.8: Customer support flow in Amazon Bedrock

The platform's strength lies in its integration capabilities. Through tools and AWS Lambda functions, workflows can interact with external data sources and services, enabling real-time data processing and complex operations. Bedrock provides in-console testing for these workflows, allowing developers to experiment and optimize before deployment. Prompts created and managed through Bedrock Prompt Management feature can be easily integrated into these workflows, enabling standardization and reuse of well-tested prompts across different workflow applications.

The visual, drag and drop interface emphasizes collaboration, enabling teams to work together effectively while maintaining consistent standards across projects. You also have option to create and update these flows through APIs.

Custom models

Amazon Bedrock offers model customization capabilities that allow organizations to tailor FMs to their specific domains and use cases. This section introduces two techniques: fine-tuning and continued pre-training. These methods enable organizations to create unique user experiences that align with their brand identity, style, and service offerings.

Fine-tuning

Fine-tuning is a process that aims to improve a model's performance on a particular task by providing a labeled training dataset relevant to that task. Through this specialized training, the FM is further refined and adapted to the specific use case. Fine-tuning is particularly effective when organizations have a relatively small but high-quality labeled dataset within their domain of interest.

For example, consider a healthcare organization that wants to build a virtual assistant to answer patient queries related to common medical conditions and treatments. While a general language model might struggle with accurately responding to highly specialized medical queries, fine-tuning the model with a labeled dataset of real patient-doctor conversations and medical literature can significantly improve its performance in this domain. The fine-tuned model can be integrated into the organization's patient portals or mobile applications, providing patients with reliable and personalized medical information.

The advantages of fine-tuning include enhanced model accuracy on specific tasks by leveraging domain-specific data, the relatively small size of the required labeled dataset making it a cost-effective approach, and the ability to tailor the model's output to align with the organization's unique requirements. However, it also requires creating a labeled dataset, which can be time-consuming and resource-intensive. Additionally, there is a risk of perpetuating biases or errors if the training data is not representative or contains inaccuracies, and fine-tuned models may become overly specialized, potentially limiting their broader applicability.

Fine-tuning is beneficial when an organization has a well-defined task or domain where a high-quality labeled dataset can be curated, such as customer support chatbots for e-commerce platforms, legal document summarization for law firms, or sentiment analysis for social media platforms.

Continued pre-training

Continued pre-training, on the other hand, involves training an FM on an organization's unlabeled data. This process helps the model become more domain-specific by acquiring knowledge and adaptability beyond its original training. Continued pre-training is particularly useful when organizations have access to a large amount of unlabeled data relevant to their domain.

For example, imagine a manufacturing company with decades of technical manuals, engineering reports, and product specifications. While this data is not labeled or annotated, continued pre-training of an FM on this data can help it develop a deep understanding of the company's products, processes, and domain-specific terminology. The resulting customized model could be integrated into the company's internal knowledge management systems, empowering employees to quickly find relevant information, generate technical documentation, or even assist with code generation tasks related to the company's products.

The advantages of continued pre-training include several key points, as follows:

- It allows organizations to leverage their proprietary unlabeled data to enhance the model's domain knowledge.

- It requires no labeled data, making it a more cost-effective approach for large datasets.

- It has the potential to improve the model's general performance across various tasks within the organization's domain.

However, continued pre-training also has some drawbacks. It requires a substantial amount of unlabeled data to realize significant improvements. Additionally, it introduces the risk of perpetuating biases or errors if the training data is not representative or contains inaccuracies. Furthermore, the improvements may be less targeted than fine-tuning for specific tasks.

Continued pre-training is useful when an organization possesses a large amount of unlabeled data specific to its industry or domain, such as scientific research papers for pharmaceutical companies, news articles for media organizations, or legal documents for law firms.

Model distillation

Amazon Bedrock Model Distillation offers a solution to a prevalent challenge: deploying AI models that deliver high accuracy while maintaining cost and latency efficiency. By transferring knowledge from large, advanced teacher models to smaller, streamlined student models, organizations can achieve use case-specific performance tailored to their operational constraints.

Consider an enterprise tasked with building a knowledge retrieval system to handle thousands of user queries daily. While larger models excel in accuracy, they can be prohibitively expensive and slow for high-frequency applications. With model distillation, the enterprise can fine-tune a smaller student model to approach the performance of the teacher model. This enables real-time query resolution with significantly reduced latency and costs, making the solution scalable across multiple regions.

Another example involves customer service automation. Organizations can use historical chat logs as input for distillation, allowing Amazon Bedrock to generate synthetic responses that fine-tune a student model for high-volume, real-time chatbot interactions. The distilled chatbot model offers consistent accuracy while operating within the latency and cost constraints of a large support operation.

The workflow for model distillation is designed to reduce complexity for users. Instead of manually curating labeled datasets, organizations can leverage existing invocation logs or upload prompts directly. Bedrock automates the generation of high-quality synthetic responses from the teacher model, ensuring the student model learns the nuances of the target use case. For instance, in medical or legal domains, this feature ensures the distilled model handles specialized terminology and context effectively.

Custom model import

Amazon Bedrock provides the custom model import feature, allowing organizations to import their externally trained FMs into Bedrock's managed environment. This feature supports specific model architectures, including Mistral, Mixtral, Flan, and various Llama variants. You can import models that have been customized in other environments, such as Amazon SageMaker AI. Once imported, these models can leverage Bedrock's serverless infrastructure and unified API for inference, alongside other FMs. This integration enables powerful capabilities such as responsible AI safeguards with guardrails, knowledge bases, and multi-step task automation with agents.

For example, consider a large media organization that has fine-tuned a language model on their vast corpus of news articles, transcripts, and multimedia content. Using custom model import, they can import their model into Bedrock's managed environment to power various GenAI applications like news summarization tools and automated content generation assistants, while benefiting from Bedrock's enterprise-grade infrastructure, security and features.

In subsequent *Chapter 8, Building Custom Models with Amazon Bedrock*, we will discuss leveraging model customization techniques in more detail.

Security and privacy

Data security and privacy are crucial when enterprises build GenAI applications with sensitive information such as customer data, financial records, proprietary research, or confidential business strategies. Amazon Bedrock provides robust security and privacy controls to give organizations full governance over their data. These security and privacy controls are delivered through the following key capabilities:

- **Encryption and access control**: Amazon Bedrock encrypts data in transit and at rest using secure keys managed through AWS KMS. This ensures that data intercepted during transmission or accessed by unauthorized parties remains encrypted and unreadable. IAM policies allow you to control who can access Bedrock and what actions they can take, preventing unauthorized access to sensitive data or models.

- **Data protection and isolation**: Amazon Bedrock follows the AWS Shared Responsibility Model for data protection. AWS secures the global infrastructure running the service, while you are responsible for protecting your data, applications, and Bedrock resources. Bedrock does not store or use your conversation data or generated content for training models. Your prompts and outputs remain private within your AWS account. When customizing a FM, Bedrock creates a private copy for you, your data is isolated and not shared with the model provider or used to improve their original model.

- **Networking security**: By using AWS PrivateLink, you can keep traffic between your applications and Bedrock models within the AWS network, allowing communication via private IP addresses without exposing your data to the public internet. This includes connections from your **virtual private cloud** (**VPC**) and on-premise networks to Bedrock. This feature is useful for organizations handling sensitive information where network isolation and secure communication are critical.

- **Access management and compliance**: AWS IAM allows you to control access to Bedrock and resources. You can create users, groups, and roles with granular permissions for approved access, ensuring that sensitive data and models are accessible only to authorized personnel within your organization. Bedrock meets compliance standards including *International Organization for Standardization (ISO)*, *System and Organization Controls (SOC)*, *Health Insurance Portability and Accountability Act (HIPAA) eligibility, and General Data Protection Regulation (GDPR)* readiness.

- **Monitoring and auditing**: Bedrock provides monitoring through Amazon CloudWatch and logging via CloudTrail to support governance requirements. Organizations can monitor and audit access to Bedrock resources, track API calls, and gather insights into usage patterns, enabling them to detect and respond to potential security incidents or unauthorized access attempts.

With layers of security covering data encryption, access control, networking isolation, compliance certifications, and monitoring, Amazon Bedrock enables enterprises across industries to build secure and private GenAI applications, when dealing with highly sensitive data or regulated environments.

Responsible AI with guardrails

As GenAI and FMs become more widely used, organizations must address challenges like bias, toxicity, and privacy concerns. Inappropriate or harmful responses can affect an organization's reputation and compromise user trust. Although FMs have built-in safeguards, organizations need additional control over model responses to ensure alignment with their organizational policies and ethical principles.

Amazon Bedrock Guardrails enable you to implement tailored safeguards that protect your GenAI applications. These safeguards let you define and remove undesirable content from user interactions, such as harmful words, profanity, and personal information. This additional layer of control complements the protections built into FMs, giving you more oversight over the responses your users receive.

Refer to the following figure depicting a flowchart of guardrails in Amazon Bedrock:

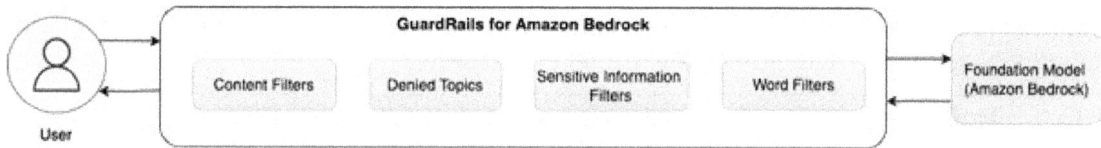

Figure 2.9: Guardrails in Amazon Bedrock high-level flow

For example, consider a social media platform that wants to deploy a GenAI assistant to help users create engaging content. Without proper content moderation, the assistant could inadvertently generate or allow harmful or offensive content, potentially leading to legal issues, user backlash, and reputational damage. By implementing guardrails, the platform can ensure that the assistant's responses adhere to their content policies and community guidelines, fostering a safe and inclusive environment for users.

Guardrails act as gatekeepers between your application and the FM, evaluating all input prompts and model responses to detect and prevent restricted content. It allows you to mitigate risks of inappropriate, harmful, or biased responses, ensure compliance with organizational policies, ethical standards, and regulatory requirements, enhance trust and transparency in your GenAI applications, and customize safeguards according to your unique needs and use case.

Guardrails provides features like content filters to adjust filtering levels across categories like hate speech, insults, sexual content, violence, and prompt attacks. It also offers denied topic thresholds, word filters for blocking profane or custom words, and sensitive information filters to detect and redact **personally identifiable information** (**PII**). Additionally, you can tailor the blocking messages displayed to users when guardrails blocks input or responses.

Guardrails also integrate with Amazon CloudWatch, allowing you to monitor and analyze user inputs and model responses that violate your policies. This feature can be particularly useful for organizations in regulated industries, such as healthcare or finance, where strict compliance with data privacy regulations like HIPAA or GDPR is essential.

In subsequent *Chapter 10, Security and Responsible AI*, we will explore more details and best practices for leveraging guardrails in Amazon Bedrock, providing practical guidance to help organizations build responsible and trustworthy GenAI applications.

Model evaluation

Evaluating how well FMs perform in your GenAI applications is crucial. You want to ensure the model's responses meet your quality standards, follow your organization's guidelines, and align with your brand's voice and identity. Amazon Bedrock Model Evaluation feature provides a comprehensive way to evaluate and compare FMs for your specific use case.

Model evaluation offers two evaluation approaches: **Automatic** and **Human**: **Bring your own work team**. The **Automatic** approach allows you to quickly evaluate a model's ability on specific tasks like summarizing text or answering questions. You can use built-in or custom prompt datasets for this. For example, a news organization could assess various FMs on how well they summarize articles using a custom dataset of their news articles and summaries. Refer to the following figure to see the **Model evaluation**:

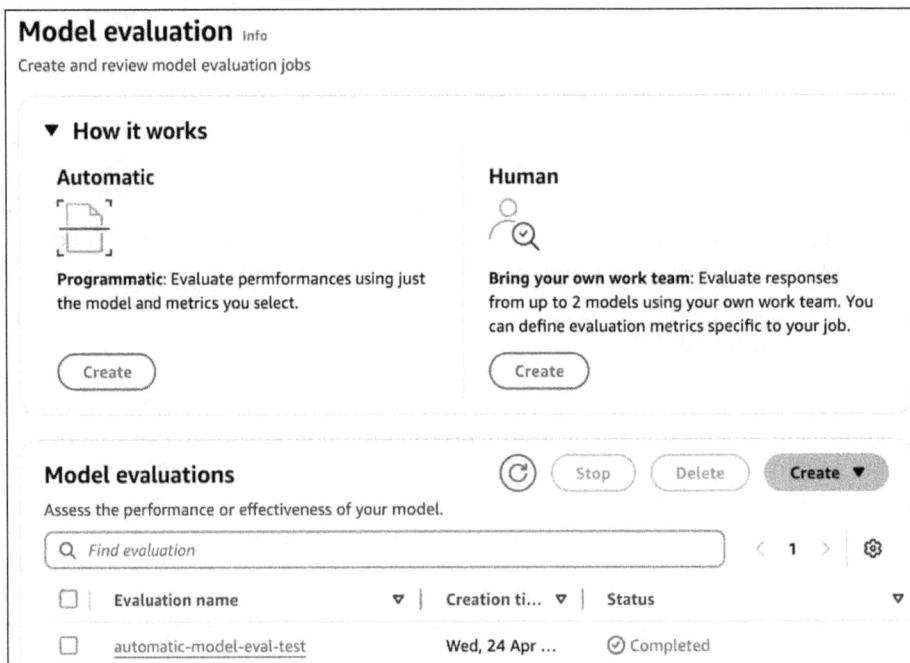

Figure 2.10: Model evaluation in Amazon Bedrock

The **Human** worker approach enables you to leverage the expertise of your subject matter experts or employees. They can evaluate model responses based on metrics and rating methods you define. This approach provides a more nuanced understanding of model performance. It also allows you to compare up to two models in a single job. For instance, a legal firm could evaluate FMs for analyzing contracts where legal experts rate the models' responses based on metrics like accuracy, relevance, and completeness.

After completing an evaluation job, you can access a detailed report card with summarized metrics, and visualizations in the Amazon Bedrock console. You can also download the detailed evaluation results in a structured format for further analysis and insights.

By using model evaluation, you can streamline the process of assessing FM performance, gain valuable insights into their strengths and weaknesses, and make informed decisions when selecting the most suitable model for your use case. Model evaluation follows a pay-as-you-go pricing model, allowing you to scale your evaluation efforts based on your requirements while keeping costs predictable and manageable.

In subsequent *Chapter 11, RAG and Model Evaluation*, we will discuss more details for using model evaluation in Amazon Bedrock, providing examples and practical guidance to help you effectively evaluate and select the best FMs for your GenAI applications.

Inference

Amazon Bedrock provides you with a wide range of FMs from leading AI providers and Amazon, allowing you to choose the model that best fits your use case. With Bedrock's serverless experience, you can quickly get started, customize FMs with your proprietary data, and seamlessly integrate and deploy them into your applications using familiar AWS tools and services without the overhead of managing infrastructure.

Bedrock offers different modes for deploying FMs: on-demand, Provisioned Throughput, batch inference and cross-region inference. The appropriate mode depends on your application's usage patterns and performance requirements.

On-demand mode

The on-demand mode follows a pay-as-you-go pricing model, where you are charged based on your actual usage, with no long-term commitments. This mode is well-suited for exploratory workloads, proof-of-concept projects, or applications with intermittent or unpredictable usage patterns. However, it may not provide the consistent performance required for mission-critical or high-traffic applications.

Provisioned Throughput

For applications with large, consistent inference workloads that require guaranteed performance, the Provisioned Throughput mode is recommended. With this mode, you purchase **model units** (**MUs**) which represent dedicated computational resources allocated to your application.

Each MU provides a specific throughput capacity, measured by the maximum number of input and output tokens it can process per minute. The exact throughput specifications for MUs can vary across different models and should be referenced in the documentation provided by Amazon Bedrock. Refer to the following figure for a better understanding:

Amazon Bedrock ‹	Anthropic ▼	Claude 3 Sonnet ▼	
▼ Getting started	ⓘ Selected model has 2 available context lengths, select the context length to be used with the Provisioned Throughput.		
Overview			
Examples			
Providers	**Model Context Length** Select the context length to associate with the Provisioned Throughput		
▼ Foundation models	○ 28k		
Base models	◉ 200k		
Custom models			
▼ Playgrounds	▶ **Tags** - *optional*		
Chat			
Text	**Commitment term & model units** Info		
Image	To purchase Provisioned Throughput, select a commitment term and choose a number of model units.		
▼ Safeguards	**Commitment term**		
Guardrails	Select a duration for which to keep the Provisioned Throughput		
Watermark detection	Select commitment term ▼		
▼ Orchestration	**Model units**		
Knowledge bases	A model unit delivers a specific throughput level for the specified model. Model unit quotas depend on the level of commitment you specify for the Provisioned Throughput. To request an increase, use the limit increase form 🗗		
Agents	1		
▼ Assessment & deployment			
Model Evaluation	**Estimated purchase summary** To view the Provisioned Throughput pricing, visit Amazon Bedrock pricing 🗗		
Provisioned Throughput			
	Estimated hourly cost	**Estimated daily cost**	**Estimated monthly cost**
Model access 5 new	$0.00	$0.00	$0.00

Figure 2.11: *Provision Throughput in Amazon Bedrock*

Provisioning throughput offers several key benefits, including guaranteed performance, cost optimization through discounted pricing (especially for longer commitment terms like one month or six months), scalability by adjusting the number of MUs, and access to custom models created through techniques like fine-tuning or continued pre-training. When determining the appropriate number of MUs for your Provisioned Throughput, consider factors such as expected user traffic, response latency targets, task complexity, and potential spikes in demand. It is crucial to plan for future growth to ensure your Provisioned Throughput can handle increased workloads without compromising performance.

When determining the appropriate number of MUs for your Provisioned Throughput, consider factors such as expected user traffic, response latency targets, task complexity, and potential spikes in demand. It is crucial to plan for future growth to ensure your Provisioned Throughput can handle increased workloads without compromising performance. Continuously monitor your application's usage patterns and adjust your Provisioned Throughput accordingly, as over-provisioning can lead to unnecessary costs, while under-provisioning may result in performance issues. If your application has fluctuating or unpredictable usage patterns, consider a combination of Provisioned Throughput for baseline performance and on-demand for burst capacity. Leverage AWS services like Amazon CloudWatch to monitor your application's performance and set alarms for potential issues or scaling requirements.

Batch inference

Batch inference is a powerful feature in Amazon Bedrock that lets you interact with FMs at scale through asynchronous processing of multiple s or prompts. Think of it as having a super-efficient assistant that can handle hundreds or thousands of tasks simultaneously. The process is simple: you prepare your requests in a **JSON Lines** (**JSONL**) format where each line is a valid JSON object, upload them to an input S3 bucket, and start the batch job. Bedrock then processes these requests asynchronously, storing all responses in your designated output S3 bucket. This approach is not only more efficient but also more cost-effective when processing large datasets or running extensive model evaluations. Whether you are analyzing customer feedback, generating content in bulk, or running large-scale experiments, batch inference makes the process streamlined and manageable.

You can create and manage batch inference jobs either through the Amazon Bedrock console or programmatically using the API. The following figure shows the console interface for creating a batch job, where you can specify the job name, choose your FM, and configure the input and output S3 locations for your data. Refer to the following figure for a better understanding:

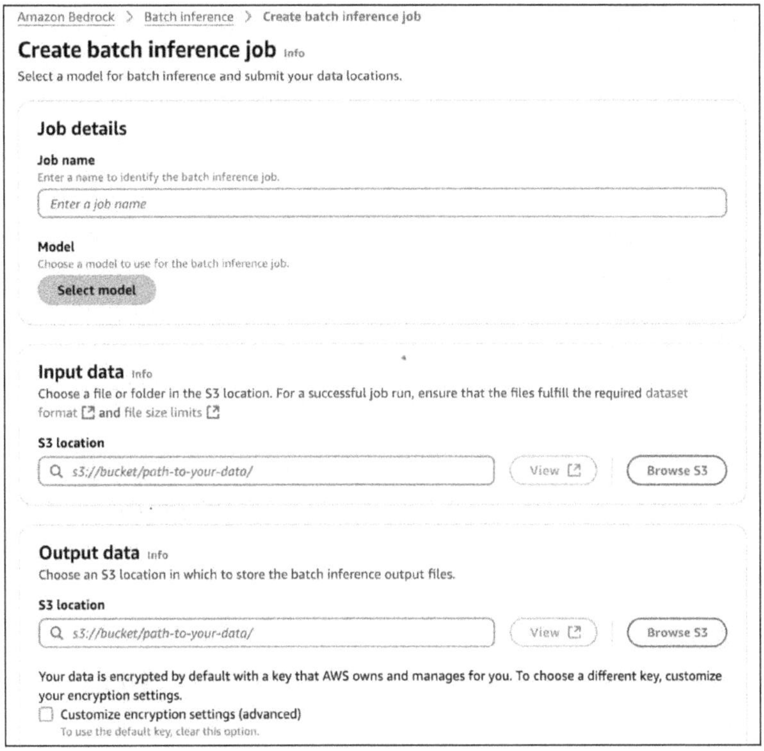

Figure 2.12: Create batch inference job interface in Amazon Bedrock

Cross-region inference

Cross-region inference is a powerful capability in Amazon Bedrock that helps you scale your on-demand FMs requests by automatically routing them across multiple AWS Regions. Think of it as having a smart traffic system that directs your GenAI workloads to less busy regions when your primary AWS Region gets congested, all managed by Bedrock.

Unlike standard on-demand inference, which is limited to a single AWS Region, cross-region inference provides additional flexibility and resilience for handling unexpected traffic spikes. The following capability is particularly useful when:

- Want your GenAI applications to handle sudden increases in traffic
- Need better reliability without complex implementation
- Want to scale smoothly during busy periods
- Do not require the consistent capacity of Provisioned Throughput

To use cross-region inference with supported FMs, first check the available inference profiles in the Bedrock console's cross-region inference section. Then in your API calls, use these inference profile IDs (which start with us. or eu.) instead of the standard model ID. There is no extra cost for routing, you pay the same as you would in your primary AWS Region, with no extra charges for data transfer or routing across regions. However, since your requests may be processed across multiple AWS Regions, consider any data residency requirements when evaluating this feature.

Monitoring

Effective monitoring is crucial for ensuring the reliability, performance, and security of your GenAI applications deployed with Amazon Bedrock. Bedrock seamlessly integrates with Amazon CloudWatch, providing you with a comprehensive set of tools to monitor various metrics and logs related to your deployed models and applications.

CloudWatch metrics

Amazon Bedrock publishes near-real-time metrics to CloudWatch, enabling you to track **key performance indicators** (**KPIs**), such as request rates, latency, error rates, and resource utilization. These metrics can be used to set alarms that trigger notifications or automated actions when specific thresholds are exceeded.

Some of the key metrics provided by Bedrock are mentioned as follows:

- **Invocations**: The number of requests to the `InvokeModel` or `InvokeModelWithResponseStream` API operations.
- **InvocationLatency**: The latency of model invocations.
- **InvocationClientErrors and InvocationServerErrors**: The number of client-side and server-side errors encountered during invocations.
- **InvocationThrottles**: The number of invocations that were throttled due to resource constraints.
- **InputTokenCount and OutputTokenCount**: The number of input and output tokens processed by the models.

For example, by monitoring the **InvocationLatency** metric, you can ensure that your customer support chatbot powered by a GenAI model is responding to user queries within an acceptable timeframe, maintaining a smooth user experience. Additionally, tracking the Invocation Throttles metric can help you identify if you need to adjust your Provisioned Throughput to accommodate increased workloads during peak hours.

As a best practice, leverage CloudWatch's anomaly detection capabilities, which automatically detect anomalies in your metrics, minimizing the need for manual monitoring.

Model invocation logging

Bedrock also provides model invocation logging, which captures metadata, requests, and responses for all model invocations in your account. This feature can be enabled through the Bedrock console, allowing you to specify the log destination (Amazon S3, CloudWatch Logs, or both) and configure data protection policies to mask sensitive information.

With model invocation logging, you can do the following tasks:

- Audit user inputs and model responses to ensure compliance with your organization's policies and ethical standards.

- Analyze logs to identify patterns, trends, or issues that may require further investigation or model fine-tuning.

- Use CloudWatch Logs Insights to interactively search and analyze your log data, facilitating efficient troubleshooting and root cause analysis.

For example, a media organization deploying a GenAI model for content creation could enable model invocation logging to monitor and analyze the prompts and generated content. This would allow them to identify potential biases or violations of their editorial guidelines, ensuring the model's outputs align with their journalistic standards.

You can configure data protection policies in CloudWatch Logs to automatically mask sensitive information, such as PII or confidential data in your model invocation logs.

CloudWatch dashboards

In order to consolidate monitoring data from multiple sources, you can create customized CloudWatch dashboards that provide a unified view of your application's performance and usage metrics. These dashboards can include visualizations of Bedrock metrics, model invocation logs, and other relevant AWS service metrics, enabling you to quickly identify trends, anomalies, or potential issues.

You can leverage CloudWatch's cross-account observability features to create rich, cross-account dashboards that provide a centralized view of your Bedrock applications across multiple AWS accounts.

By using the monitoring capabilities of Amazon CloudWatch, you can gain visibility into the performance, security, and compliance aspects of your GenAI applications deployed with Amazon Bedrock. This visibility empowers you to proactively address issues, optimize resource utilization, and ensure a seamless user experience.

In subsequent *Chapter 9, Monitoring and Observability*, we will discuss the best practices and examples for configuring and utilizing CloudWatch monitoring for your Bedrock applications, ensuring you have the necessary tools and knowledge to effectively manage and maintain your production-ready GenAI applications.

Ecosystem of frameworks and tools

As the field of GenAI continues to evolve rapidly, developers and organizations are leveraging various frameworks and tools to simplify the development, deployment, and management of AI-powered applications. In the context of Amazon Bedrock, three prominent frameworks stand out: Bedrock **software development kit** (**SDK**), and open-source frameworks like LangChain and LlamaIndex. Let us introduce these frameworks, highlight their value propositions, and explore use cases and considerations.

AWS software development kit

The AWS SDK is the official SDK for AWS, including Amazon Bedrock. It provides a convenient and straightforward way for developers to programmatically interact with Bedrock services, enabling them to build, deploy, and manage GenAI applications within the AWS ecosystem.

The AWS SDK's value proposition lies in its seamless integration with other AWS services, comprehensive access to Bedrock APIs, and a productivity boost through its familiar Python interface. Developers can leverage the SDK to programmatically create and manage model customization jobs, invoke models for inference tasks, configure and manage Provisioned Throughput, and monitor and log model invocations.

Open-source frameworks and libraries

The following are a few packages to consider when building GenAI applications:

- **LangChain**: LangChain is an open-source Python library designed to enhance the usability and accessibility of LLMs. It provides developers with a comprehensive set of tools to seamlessly integrate LLMs into their applications, enabling a wide range of use cases, including QA, chatbots, and autonomous agents.

  LangChain's value proposition revolves around its abstraction layer, modular design, and ecosystem integration. It simplifies the process of composing and integrating LLM components, enabling rapid prototyping and experimentation. LangChain supports integration with various LLMs, including those available through Amazon Bedrock, empowering developers to leverage the power of GenAI across multiple platforms.

Key use cases for LangChain include building QA systems that leverage domain-specific data and knowledge bases, developing chatbots and conversational agents with advanced capabilities, and constructing autonomous agents that can perform research, analyze data, and take actions based on LLM outputs.

- **LlamaIndex**: LlamaIndex is an open-source framework specifically designed for building context-augmented LLM applications. It focuses on enabling developers to leverage LLMs in conjunction with their private or domain-specific data, enabling a wide range of use cases, such as QA chatbots, document understanding, and autonomous agents.

  LlamaIndex's value proposition lies in its data integration capabilities, indexing and retrieval strategies, and observability and evaluation tools. It provides tools to ingest and process data from various sources, enabling seamless integration of private or proprietary data with LLMs. The framework also offers strategies for structuring and indexing data, ensuring efficient retrieval and processing of relevant information using LLMs.

  Use cases for LlamaIndex include building QA chatbots that leverage domain-specific knowledge and data sources, extracting structured information from unstructured data using LLMs along with domain-specific knowledge, and developing autonomous agents that can perform research, analysis, and decision-making tasks by combining LLMs with proprietary data sources.

  When developing GenAI applications with Amazon Bedrock, developers can leverage these frameworks individually or in combination, depending on their specific requirements and use cases. The Bedrock SDK provides a foundational layer for interacting with Bedrock services, while LangChain and LlamaIndex offer higher-level abstractions and tools for integrating LLMs with data sources and building advanced applications.

  By understanding the value propositions, practical use cases, and potential challenges of these frameworks, developers can make informed decisions and effectively leverage the power of GenAI to build innovative and impactful solutions.

In the subsequent *Chapter 7, Using Open-source Frameworks with Amazon Bedrock*, we will discuss how you can use Bedrock APIs and the LangChain framework to build practical GenAI applications on AWS.

Amazon Bedrock platform enhancements

As Amazon Bedrock continues to evolve rapidly, several significant developments have emerged that further strengthen its position as a comprehensive GenAI platform. These recent enhancements expand model availability, introduce new development frameworks, and provide organizations with even more flexibility in building GenAI applications.

Amazon Nova foundation models

Amazon made a strategic entry into first-party FM development with the launch of the Nova family in December 2024. These models represent AWS's commitment to providing cost-effective, high-performance FMs directly through Bedrock. The Nova family includes text models like Nova Micro and Nova Lite, multimodal models such as Nova Pro, and creative content generation models including Nova Canvas for image generation and Nova Reel for video creation. Nova models are 75% less expensive than comparable alternatives while maintaining competitive performance, making GenAI more accessible to organizations of all sizes. The model family has expanded to include Nova Premier for enhanced capabilities and Nova Sonic for speech-to-speech conversations.

Expanded model ecosystem with Bedrock Marketplace

Amazon Bedrock Marketplace has transformed the platform by providing access to over 100 popular, emerging and specialized FMs. This marketplace extends far beyond the traditional providers, offering models from companies like *DeepSeek, Luma, poolside, TwelveLabs,* and *WRITER,* alongside the established providers mentioned earlier in this chapter. The marketplace enables organizations to discover and experiment with specialized models for niche use cases, from advanced reasoning models to domain-specific solutions, all accessible through Bedrock's unified API.

AWS's simplified agent development framework

A major development in the agentic AI space is the introduction of Strands Agents, an open-source SDK launched by AWS that takes a model-driven approach to building and running AI agents in just a few lines of code. By default, it uses Amazon Bedrock as model provider, but supports many others including Ollama, Anthropic, Llama API, and LiteLLM. Strands integrate natively with the **Model Context Protocol** (**MCP**), an open standard for connecting AI assistants to data sources and tools, providing access to thousands of MCP servers and tools for enhanced agent capabilities. The framework simplifies agent development by leveraging the reasoning capabilities of modern FMs, reducing the complexity traditionally associated with building autonomous AI systems. Multiple teams at AWS already use Strands for their AI agents in production, including Amazon Q Developer, AWS Glue, and Amazon VPC Reachability Analyzer, demonstrating its enterprise readiness. Developers can find comprehensive documentation and examples at **https://strandsagents.com**

Latest foundation model capabilities

The FM landscape within Bedrock continues to advance with significant model updates. Claude 4, including both Opus 4 and Sonnet 4, is now available on Amazon Bedrock, offering enhanced reasoning and coding capabilities compared to previous generations. AWS has also integrated DeepSeek-R1 models into both Amazon Bedrock and SageMaker AI, providing advanced reasoning capabilities for complex problem-solving tasks.

These recent developments demonstrate Amazon Bedrock's commitment to staying at the forefront of GenAI innovation, providing organizations with cutting-edge capabilities while maintaining the platform's focus on ease of use, security, and enterprise readiness.

Conclusion

In this chapter, we explored Amazon Bedrock, a fully managed service for building and scaling GenAI applications using FMs from leading AI providers. We covered key features, including playgrounds for user-friendly interactions, agents for complex task automation, and RAG architecture with knowledge bases that augment FMs with contextual data, minimizing hallucinations and enhancing response accuracy. We discussed model customization techniques like fine-tuning, continued pre-training, and custom model import, enabling organizations to tailor models to their specific needs. We also covered the importance of model evaluation and various deployment options, including on-demand inference, Provisioned Throughput, and batch inference, along with monitoring capabilities for consistent performance and reliability.

We introduced frameworks and tools such as the Bedrock SDK, LangChain, and LlamaIndex, which provide developers with seamless integration capabilities and enhanced functionalities. By leveraging Amazon Bedrock, organizations can unlock the full potential of GenAI, fostering innovation and improving efficiency across various industries. We touched on the importance of ethical considerations and responsible AI practices, highlighting Bedrock's security controls and safeguards like guardrails.

In the next chapter, we will explore the different FMs offered by Amazon Bedrock.

Points to remember

- Agents in Amazon Bedrock enable the creation of multi-step workflows and automation of complex tasks using FMs. This powerful feature can streamline processes and enhance productivity across various domains.

- Bedrock's managed RAG architecture with a knowledge base helps minimize the risk of inaccurate responses by grounding FM outputs with factual information from trusted data sources, ensuring accurate and reliable results.

- Prompt management provides version control, parameterization, and secure storage of prompts, enabling teams to create, test, and reuse standardized prompts across different AI applications.

- Bedrock Flows turns complex GenAI interactions into visual workflows, allowing you to connect prompts, FMs, knowledge bases, external services, and agents without writing extensive code.

- Techniques like fine-tuning, continued pre-training, model distillation and custom model import allow you to tailor FMs to your specific domains and use cases, creating unique experiences that align with your brand identity and requirements.

- Assessing the performance of FMs through model evaluation helps you gain insights into their strengths and weaknesses, enabling you to choose the most suitable model for your particular use case.

- The Provisioned Throughput and monitoring features in Amazon Bedrock ensure consistent performance, reliability, and visibility into the operation of your GenAI applications.

- Batch inference allows processing multiple requests efficiently in an asynchronous manner, making it ideal for large-scale processing and evaluation of FMs.

- Cross-region inference enhances scalability and resilience by automatically routing requests across multiple AWS Regions during peak periods, without additional routing costs.

- Amazon Bedrock's robust security and privacy controls, coupled with its responsible AI safeguards like Amazon Bedrock Guardrails, provide a solid foundation for building trustworthy and compliant GenAI solutions.

- The Bedrock SDK, LangChain, and LlamaIndex provide developers with a comprehensive ecosystem of tools and frameworks, offering easy integration with AWS services, abstraction layers for integrating LLMs, data ingestion, indexing, and observability.

Exercises

1. **Model access setup**: Go to model access in the Bedrock console, review available FMs in your AWS Region, and request access to two different models.

2. **Playground exploration**: Access the Amazon Bedrock console and use the Chat/text playground to compare responses from two different FMs using the Compare mode and review their Input and Output token and Latency metrics to evaluate the model for your specific use case.

3. **Inference options matching**: Match these scenarios with the best inference option (on-demand, Provisioned Throughput, batch inference, or cross-region inference):

    a. A customer service chatbot needing consistent response times.

    b. A job to analyze thousands of customer reviews overnight.

    c. An application that experiences unpredictable traffic spikes.

    d. A development environment for testing different prompts.

CHAPTER 3
Experimenting Foundation Models in Amazon Bedrock

Introduction

Building on our understanding of **generative AI (GenAI)** and Amazon Bedrock from previous chapters, we now turn to the practical challenge of selecting and implementing the right **foundation models (FMs)** for your specific use case. This chapter walks you through the key considerations to consider when choosing among Bedrock's FMs, providing hands-on examples of how different models perform across text, image, and multimodal applications. You will learn how to evaluate model capabilities, understand their trade-offs, and implement them effectively for various business scenarios. Through practical demonstrations, we will explore how to match specific FMs to different data types and use cases, enabling you to make informed decisions for your GenAI implementations.

Structure

The chapter covers the following topics:

- Selecting optimal AI model
- Overview of foundation models in Bedrock
- Getting access to foundation models in Bedrock
- Opening model in playground

- Working with text foundation models
- Bedrock playground text model use cases
- Working with image foundation models
- Working with multimodal foundation models

Objectives

By the end of this chapter, you will possess a solid grasp of the process for selecting the appropriate FM for diverse use cases and scenarios, as well as an understanding of why model selection is a critical consideration. You will comprehend the factors that need to be taken into account when choosing a model. Moreover, you will be equipped with the relevant details about each model, enabling you to evaluate their suitability for specific use cases. Additionally, you will acquire knowledge about which FMs are suitable for language, image, and multimodal applications.

Selecting optimal AI model

FMs are powerful and versatile, but it is important to recognize that no single model can excel at all possible use cases. Different models have strengths and weaknesses, and their suitability can vary depending on the specific task, domain, and requirements.

The following are some examples of why one FM may not fit all use cases:

- **Accuracy requirement**: Different FMs can exhibit varying levels of accuracy depending on the task, domain, and data they were trained on. A model that achieves high accuracy on one task or domain may not perform as well on another task or domain due to differences in data distribution, linguistic patterns, or task complexity.

  For example, a language model like GPT-3, trained on a broad corpus of general-purpose text, may excel at tasks like text generation or summarization but may not achieve the same level of accuracy as a model fine-tuned on domain-specific data for tasks like medical diagnosis or legal document analysis.

- **Multimodal requirements**: FMs can be specialized for different modalities, such as text, images, or speech. While some models are designed for unimodal tasks (e.g., language models for text and computer vision models for images), other applications may require multimodal capabilities that can process and correlate multiple modalities simultaneously.

  For example, a language model like BERT, while highly capable of **natural language processing** (**NLP**) tasks, may not be suitable for tasks that involve both text and images, such as image captioning or visual **question answering** (**QA**). In such cases, multimodal models like CLIP, DALL-E, or unified vision-language models that can process and correlate text and visual information are more appropriate.

- **Real-time inference requirement**: Some applications, such as virtual assistants, chatbots, or real-time translation systems, require low-latency inference to provide a seamless user experience. However, many large FMs, while highly accurate, can be computationally expensive and may not meet the real-time inference requirements of such applications.

  For instance, while large models like *Claude 3 Opus* can generate high-quality text, their inference times may be too slow for real-time applications. In contrast, smaller or optimized models like *Claude 3 Haiku*, and *Amazon Titan* that trade-off some accuracy for faster inference speeds may be more suitable for real-time use cases.

These examples illustrate that while FMs are powerful and versatile, their suitability depends on the specific requirements, constraints, and ethical considerations of each use case. Carefully evaluating these factors and choosing the appropriate model is crucial for achieving optimal performance, efficiency, and responsible deployment.

A list of all the top factors that you need to select a model is as follows:

- **Model performance**: Evaluating the model's performance on relevant benchmarks or datasets is crucial to ensure it meets the desired accuracy, precision, or other performance metrics for your specific task. A high-performing model can significantly impact the quality and reliability of your application.

- **Model size and capacity**: The size of the model, measured by the number of parameters or the amount of training data used, directly impacts its capabilities. Larger models generally have better performance but also require more computational resources and are more expensive to run.

- **Training data and domain specialization**: The type of data used for training the **large language model (LLM)** plays a crucial role in determining its strengths and weaknesses. Models trained on broad, general-purpose data may perform well on a wide range of tasks, while models trained on domain-specific data (e.g., legal texts, and scientific literature) may excel in those specialized areas.

- **Model architecture**: The underlying architecture of the LLM, such as transformer-based models (e.g., GPT, decoder based, BERT, encoder based), determines its strengths and limitations. Different architectures may be better suited for certain tasks or modalities (e.g., text generation, QA, language understanding).

- **Inference speed and efficiency**: For real-time or latency-sensitive applications, the inference speed and computational efficiency of the LLM become crucial factors. Models with faster inference times and lower resource requirements may be favored in such scenarios.

- **Deployment and scalability**: The ease of deployment, scalability, and integration with existing systems and pipelines can also influence the choice of LLM. Some models may be more easily deployed in specific environments or support distributed training and inference better.

- **Cost and licensing**: The cost of using and licensing an LLM, including potential subscription fees or usage-based pricing, is an important practical consideration, especially for commercial applications or large-scale deployments.

- **Ethical and fairness considerations**: As LLMs can exhibit biases and generate potentially harmful outputs, models that have been evaluated for safety, fairness, and ethical considerations may be preferred, especially in sensitive domains or applications.

- **Customization and fine-tuning capabilities**: Many FMs are designed to be fine-tuned or customized for specific tasks or domains. Evaluating the model's ability to adapt and transfer knowledge can be important for achieving optimal performance in your use case.

- **Community support and documentation**: Consider the community support and documentation available for the FM. Models with active communities and comprehensive documentation may be easier to work with and troubleshoot.

Overview of foundation models in Bedrock

In today's fast-paced world, agility is key for businesses to stay ahead of the curve. Customers demand the ability to experiment, deploy, iterate, and pivot rapidly. They require seamless access to a diverse range of model options, enabling them to explore different models, switch between them with ease, and combine the best models tailored to their unique business requirements. Amazon Bedrock is a fully managed service that revolutionizes the way businesses approach GenAI applications. This cutting-edge platform offers effortless access to a curated selection of industry-leading LLMs and other foundational models from renowned AI pioneers such as *AI21 Labs, Anthropic, Cohere, Meta, Stability AI*, and *Amazon* itself but Amazon Bedrock goes beyond mere model selection. It empowers businesses with a comprehensive suite of capabilities essential for building GenAI applications. From streamlining development to fortifying privacy and security measures, Amazon Bedrock simplifies the entire process, ensuring businesses can focus on driving innovation while maintaining the highest standards of data protection.

Choice of foundation models available in Bedrock

Amazon Bedrock is a fully managed service that offers a diverse selection of high-performing FMs from leading AI companies through a single unified API. The service provides access to models from *Anthropic, Cohere, Meta, Mistral AI, Stability AI, Amazon*, and more, enabling organizations to build GenAI applications with robust security, privacy, and responsible AI features. This comprehensive model marketplace allows users to evaluate, test, and deploy the best models for their specific use cases without being locked into a single provider. Here is an overview of the major FMs currently available in Amazon Bedrock.

Amazon Nova models

Amazon Nova is a new generation of state-of-the-art FMs that deliver frontier intelligence and industry-leading price performance. These models enable users to build and scale GenAI applications with seamless integration in Amazon Bedrock.

Amazon offers a range of Nova models with different capabilities:

- **Amazon Nova Premier**: Features a 1M context window, supports 200+ languages, and accepts text, image, and video inputs with text output.

- **Amazon Nova Pro**: Offers a 300K context window, supports 200+ languages, and handles text, image, and video inputs with text output.

- **Amazon Nova Lite**: Provides a 300K context window, supports 200+ languages, and processes text, image, and video inputs with text output.

- **Amazon Nova Micro**: Features a 128K context window, supports 200+ languages, and handles text input with text output. **Generally available (GA)** with fine-tuning support.

Anthropic Claude models

Anthropic's Claude models represent some of the most advanced AI systems available, designed with a focus on helpfulness, harmlessness, and honesty. These models excel at complex reasoning tasks, natural conversation, and content generation while maintaining high standards for safety and reliability. Claude models include powerful vision capabilities and are continuously evolving to deliver enhanced performance across a wide range of use cases.

Anthropic offers a range of Claude models with different capabilities:

- **Claude Opus 4**: Anthropic's most powerful hybrid reasoning model, setting new standards for coding, writing, and reasoning across extended work sessions. Excels at complex multi-step tasks while maintaining focus and context.

- **Claude Sonnet 4**: A mid-size hybrid reasoning model balancing quality, cost-effectiveness, and responsiveness for high-volume use cases. Ideal for most production AI applications, real-time agents, code generation, and content tasks.

- **Claude 3.7 Sonnet**: Anthropic's most intelligent AI model to date and first hybrid reasoning model designed for practical, real-world use cases. It offers extended thinking capabilities to solve complex problems.

Meta Llama models

Meta Llama models utilize publicly available data for training and employ transformer architecture to process and generate variable-length input and output sequences:

- **Llama 4 Maverick 17B**: A general-purpose model featuring 128 experts and 400 billion total parameters. Excels in text understanding across 12 languages and English image understanding. Max tokens: 1M.

- **Llama 4 Scout 17B**: A general-purpose multimodal model with 16 experts, 17B active parameters, and 109B total parameters. Features a multimillion context window enabling comprehensive multi-document analysis. Max tokens: 3.5M (10M coming soon).

- **Llama 3.3 70B**: A text-only 70B instruction-tuned model with enhanced performance. Delivers similar performance to Llama 3.1 405B while requiring fewer computational resources. Max tokens: 128K.

- **Llama 3.2 90B**: A multimodal model accepting both text and image inputs. Ideal for applications requiring sophisticated visual intelligence. Max tokens: 128K.

Mistral AI models

Mistral AI develops efficient, helpful, and trustworthy AI models through ground-breaking innovations that are fast deployable, easily customizable, and support a variety of use cases:

- **Pixtral Large (25.02)**: A frontier-class 124B parameter model with multimodal capabilities that excels in document understanding, visual reasoning, and natural image comprehension. Max tokens: 128K.

- **Mistral Large 2 (24.07)**: The latest version of Mistral AI's flagship model, with significant improvements on multilingual accuracy, conversational behavior, coding capabilities, reasoning, and instruction-following behavior. Max tokens: 128K.

- **Mistral Large (24.02)**: A cutting-edge text generation model with top-tier reasoning capabilities and precise instruction-following abilities. Max tokens: 32K.

- **Mistral Small (24.02)**: A highly efficient model optimized for high-volume, low-latency language-based tasks at a cost-effective price point. Specializes in **retrieval augmented generation** (**RAG**), coding proficiency, and multilingual capabilities. Max tokens: 32K.

Stability AI models

Stability AI is the world's leading open-source GenAI company, collaborating with public and private sector partners to bring next-generation infrastructure to a global audience. They have deep learning, text-to-image models used to generate detailed images conditioned on text descriptions, inpainting, outpainting, and generating image-to-image translations.

Getting access to foundation models in Bedrock

You can access all these models available in Bedrock through the **Model access** link in the console. The following are the steps to access these models:

1. Select the **Model access** from the Bedrock console, as shown in the following figure:

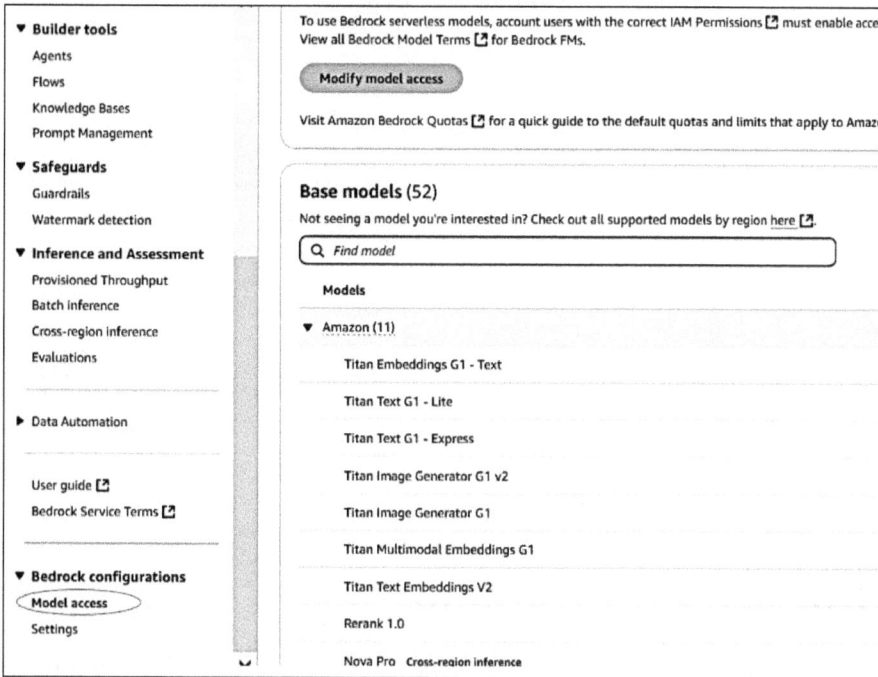

Figure 3.1: FMs access

2. Select the **Models** as per your use cases and requirements. Click on **EULA** to understand each model license agreement, as follows:

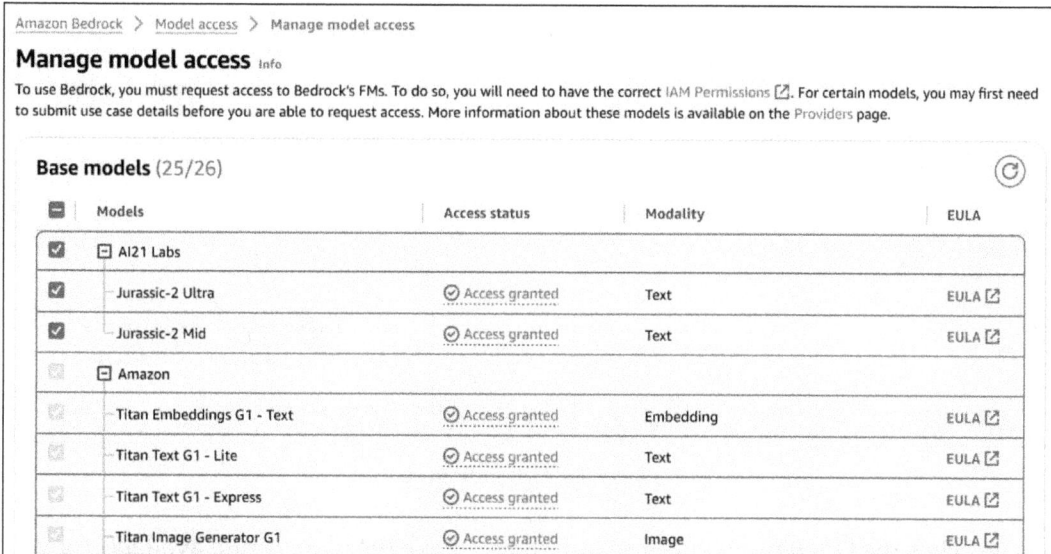

Figure 3.2: FMs selections

3. Click on **Save changes** as shown in *Figure 3.3*. This will ensure the models are available both in the playground and API for your access:

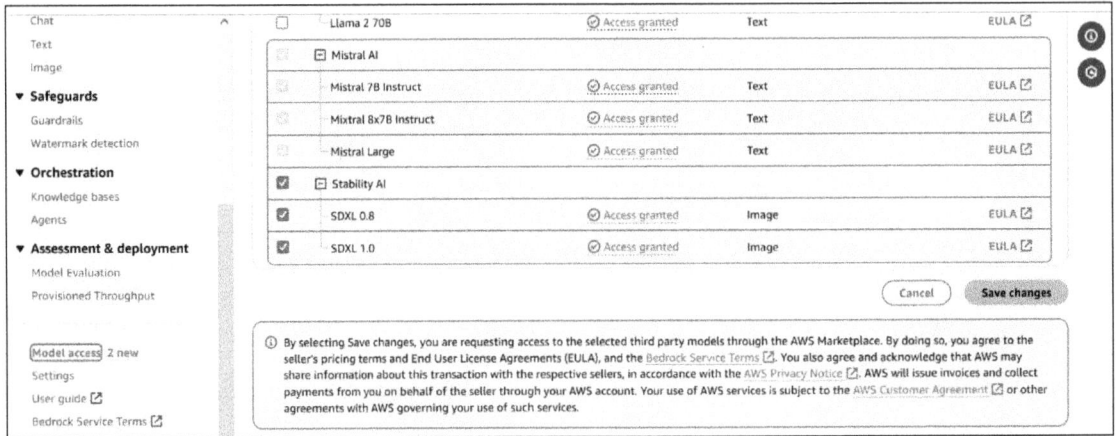

Figure 3.3: FMs Save changes

Opening model in playground

You can access different FMs in the Bedrock console by clicking the **Base models** option and selecting the model of your choice then clicking the **Open in playground** to open the model in the playground.

The following figure shows the different FMs to choose from:

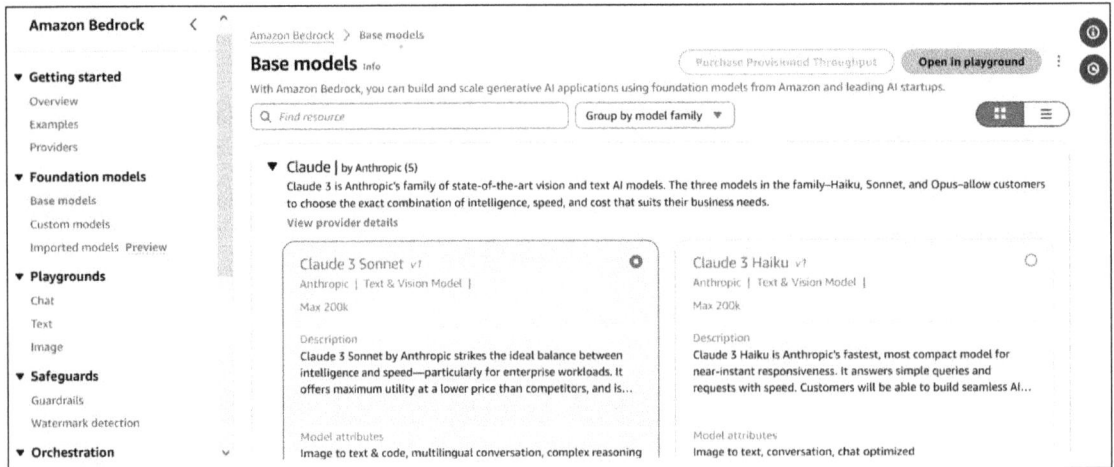

Figure 3.4: FMs in Bedrock

When you click the **Open in playground** button, you have the playground available for you as shown in the below image. In the playground, you have three options, as follows:

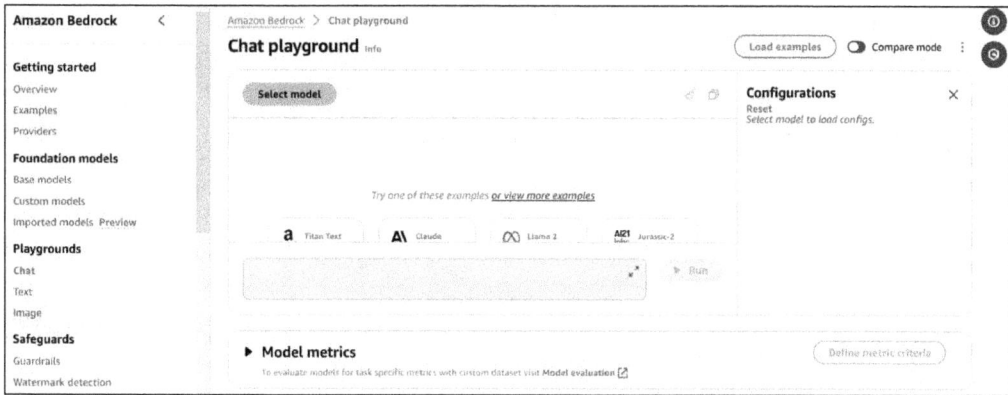

Figure 3.5: Playground in Bedrock

The three options in the playground are as follows:

- **Chat**: This option allows you to have a conversation with the AI assistant. It keeps track of your previous messages, so the AI can understand the context of your conversation.

- **Text**: This option is for tasks related to text, such as creating content, summarizing text, answering questions, and other text-based uses.

- **Image**: This option allows you to generate or edit images using text descriptions as input.

In the playground, the first step is to choose the model of your choice, in the following figure, you can see **Claude 3 Sonnet** selecting the **Apply** button:

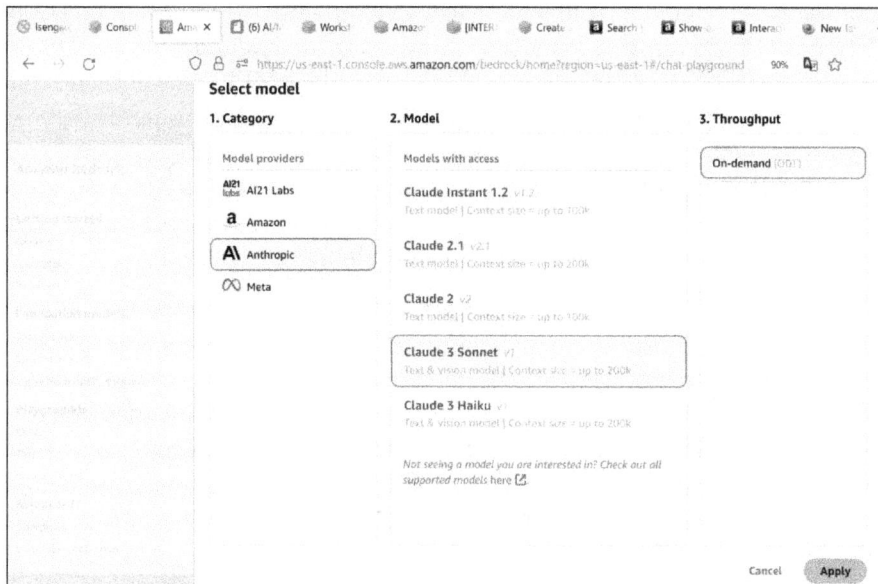

Figure: 3.6: Model selection in the playground

In the Bedrock console, you have the **Examples** option listed under **Getting started** which will have the examples categorized by **Provider**, **Modality** (text/image), and **Use case**. You can choose the example of your choice as shown in *Figure 3.14* and load it into the playground by clicking on the **Open in playground** button:

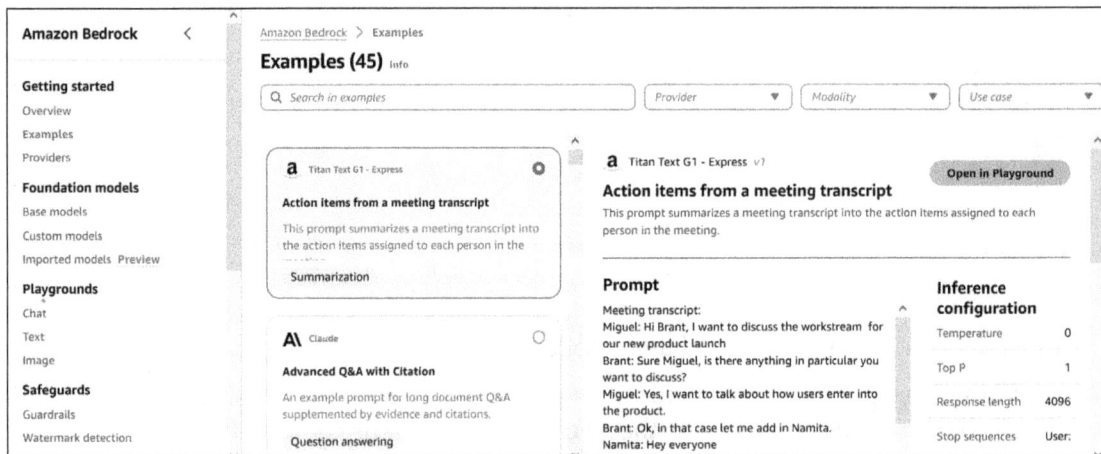

Figure 3.7: Examples for playground

Working with text foundation models

Text FMs have emerged as powerful tools for generating human-like text by leveraging the capabilities of LLMs. These models are trained on vast corpora of textual data, spanning numerous domains and genres, enabling them to learn intricate patterns, structures, and nuances of natural language. Through this extensive training, the models develop an understanding of linguistic constructs, contextual relationships, and the ability to generate coherent and contextually relevant text. The process of text generation with these models involves providing an initial prompt or seed text, which serves as a starting point. The model then draws upon its learned knowledge to continue generating text that seamlessly builds upon the given prompt. This capability has opened a wide range of applications across various fields, from creative writing and content creation to conversational AI and language translation.

Text FMs have numerous use cases across various domains. In content creation, they can assist writers by generating drafts, expanding on ideas, or providing suggestions for creative writing. In customer service and conversational AI, language models can power chatbots and virtual assistants, enabling natural language interactions. Additionally, they can be employed in text summarization, simplification, or translation tasks, facilitating efficient information processing and cross-language communication. Furthermore, language models can be fine-tuned for specific tasks, such as sentiment analysis, named entity recognition or QA, enabling advanced NLP applications.

At Bedrock, we have access to various text FMs provided by companies like Anthropic, Amazon, AI21 Labs, Mistral, Meta, and Cohere. Each of these models has unique capabilities that make them suitable for different use cases. In this context, we will explore some of the applications and use cases by utilizing the Bedrock playground and experimenting with different FMs. The goal is to help you understand how this powerful language models can be leveraged to generate human-like text, perform language tasks, and support various applications. The Bedrock playground provides a hands-on environment where you can interact with these models, input prompts or text, and observe the generated outputs.

By working with different FMs in the playground, you will gain insights into their strengths, limitations, and potential applications. This practical experience will help you appreciate the capabilities of these models and how they can be applied to real-world scenarios, such as content creation, language translation, conversational AI, and more. We will cover a range of use cases, allowing you to explore the versatility of these text FMs. Whether you are interested in creative writing, language analysis, or building intelligent systems, the Bedrock playground offers an opportunity to experiment and develop a deeper understanding of these cutting-edge language models.

Bedrock playground text model use cases

Amazon Bedrock's playground environment demonstrates how text FMs excel in critical business applications: generating engaging content like travel blogs, creating concise summaries from meeting transcripts, and powering contextual conversational experiences. In the following sections, we will explore these capabilities in depth, examining specific examples with models like Titan Text Express, Claude 3 Sonnet, and Llama 2 Chat that showcase how organizations can implement these powerful AI tools to enhance productivity and create value.

Content generation

One major application of text FMs in content creation is the generation of initial drafts or outlines. By providing a prompt or a general topic, these models can produce coherent and contextually relevant text, serving as a starting point for further refinement, and editing. This can significantly accelerate the content creation process, reducing the time and effort required to produce high-quality written content. Another use case is ideation and concept expansion. Text FMs can take a seed idea or concept and generate additional content, offering new perspectives, examples, or elaborations. This can be particularly useful for brainstorming, creative writing, or developing comprehensive content pieces.

Furthermore, text FMs can assist in tailoring content for specific audiences or purposes. By adjusting the prompt, content creators can generate text with desired tones, styles, or levels of complexity, ensuring their content resonates with the intended audience. However, it is important to note that while text FMs can significantly aid content creation, human oversight, and editing are still necessary to ensure accuracy, coherence, and adherence to specific guidelines or requirements.

Overall, the integration of text FMs in content creation workflows can enhance productivity, spark creativity, and enable content creators to focus more on refining and polishing their work, while leveraging the power of these advanced language models.

In this example, we are trying to create a social blog for a major travel website and newsletter covering travel guides to Iceland focusing on different topics like travel tips and tricks, sights to see, and so on.

Prompt for content generation

You are an expert social media content generator. Draft an exciting and socially-engaging blog post for a major travel website and newsletter. The post should be a travel guide for *Iceland* that highlights recommended attractions, restaurants, and sights to see, along with tips and tricks for travel. Each paragraph should focus on a different topic, such as travel tips and tricks, the best sights to see, the best food to eat, and so on. Within each topic, whenever there is a list (such as a list of foods or a list of places), make each item on the list its own line with its own short description. Name each thematic paragraph with just the name of the paragraph (never a marker like *paragraph 1* etc.). Include a call to action to buy tickets now at the end of the post. The audience for this text is people excited to travel but who have never been to Iceland before. The goal of the article is to drum up excitement for Iceland and leave readers with the impression that the travel website is a trusted source of information for travel to Iceland. Write your response in markdown format. Never generate text before the article. Generate the article only (including the title).

The following figure shows the Amazon Bedrock playground interface with the Titan Text Express model for creating various text-based content with configurable parameters:

Figure 3.8: Content generation

In the Bedrock playground, you can input a prompt and select a specific model to generate text. For this example, we will use the **Titan Text G1-Express** model. After entering your prompt, simply click the **Run** button, and the model will process your request and provide the requested output.

In our case, we asked the model to generate content suitable for a blog post about traveling to Iceland. As you can see from the output, the model has produced detailed and comprehensive content covering all the necessary elements for such a blog post. The model has successfully organized the content in a logical and structured manner, making it easier for readers to understand and follow. The generated text can serve as a solid foundation or a starting point for further editing and refining to create a polished blog post or travel guide.

Model response

The model responds with following:

Welcome to Iceland, a land of breathtaking natural beauty and endless adventure! Whether you are an avid traveller or a first-time visitor, Iceland has something for everyone. In this travel guide, we will take you on a journey through this incredible country, highlighting the best attractions, restaurants, and sights to see.

Travel tips and tricks are as follows:
- Pack layers of clothing to prepare for changing weather conditions.
- Rent a car to explore the country at your own pace.
- Join a guided tour to learn more about Iceland's history and culture.
- Book your accommodations in advance to secure the best rates.

Best sights to see is as follows:
- The blue lagoon: A geothermal spa located in a lava field, known for its healing waters and stunning scenery.
- Gullfoss waterfall: One of Iceland's most famous waterfalls, with a breathtaking drop of 320 feet.
- Skaftafell Ice Cave: A magnificent ice cave located in Vatnajokull National Park, accessible by a guided tour.
- Reykjavik: Iceland's capital city, known for its colorful buildings, vibrant nightlife, and stunning harbor.

The following are the best food to eat:
- Lamb stew: A traditional Icelandic dish made with lamb, vegetables, and potatoes.
- Fish and chips: A popular Icelandic snack made with fresh fish and crispy fries.
- Skyr: A traditional Icelandic yogurt made with milk and cream, known for its creamy texture and tangy flavor.
- Baked goods: Icelandic bakeries are known for their delicious pastries, such as cinnamon rolls.

```
Call to action:
```
Do not miss your chance to explore the wonders of Iceland! Book your tickets now and embark on an unforgettable adventure. Visit our website or contact us today to plan your trip.

Ready to pack your bags and embark on an unforgettable adventure in Iceland? Book your tickets now and let the magic of this incredible country unfold before your eyes.

Text summarization

One of the key applications of text FMs is automated text summarization. These models can analyze large volumes of text and generate concise, coherent summaries that capture the essential information, and key points. This capability can be invaluable in various contexts where quickly understanding the gist of lengthy documents, articles, or reports is crucial. By providing a text FM with a source document or corpus, it can generate a summary that distils the most important information while preserving the critical details and context. This can be particularly useful for tasks such as:

- **Document analysis and review**: Text FMs can summarize lengthy reports, legal documents, or research papers, enabling users to quickly grasp the main points without having to read through the entire text.

- **News and article summarization**: These models can generate concise summaries of news articles, blog posts, or online content, allowing users to stay informed without spending excessive time reading each piece in its entirety.

- **Meeting notes and transcript summarization**: Text FMs can summarize lengthy meeting transcripts or notes, making it easier for participants to review and recall the key discussions and decisions.

- **Information extraction and synthesis**: By summarizing multiple related documents, these models can extract and synthesize relevant information from various sources, facilitating efficient research and knowledge acquisition.

Furthermore, text FMs can tailor the summaries based on specific requirements, such as desired length, level of detail, or focus areas. This flexibility allows users to obtain summaries tailored to their needs, whether they require a high-level overview or a more comprehensive summary.

In this example, we are trying to summarize the meeting discussion between different people and trying to create a list of action items for each person.

Prompt for text summarization

The model responds with following:

Meeting transcript: Miguel: Hi Brant, I want to discuss the workstream for our new product launch Brant: Sure Miguel, is there anything in particular you want to discuss? Miguel: Yes, I want to talk about how users enter into the product. Brant: Ok, in that case, let me add in Namita. Namita: Hey everyone Brant: Hi Namita, Miguel wants to discuss how users enter into the product. Miguel: it is too complicated, and we should remove friction. for example, why do I need to fill out additional forms? I also find it difficult to find where to access the product when I first land on the landing page. Brant: I would also add that I think there are too many steps. Namita: Ok, I can work on the landing page to make the product more discoverable but Brant can you work on the additional forms? Brant: Yes, but I would need to work with James from another team as he needs to unblock the signup workflow. Miguel, can you document any other concerns so that I can discuss them with James only once? Miguel: Sure. From the meeting transcript above, Create a list of action items for each person.

The following image shows the Amazon Bedrock **Chat playground** interface featuring Claude's Sonnet model handling meeting summaries with configurable parameters:

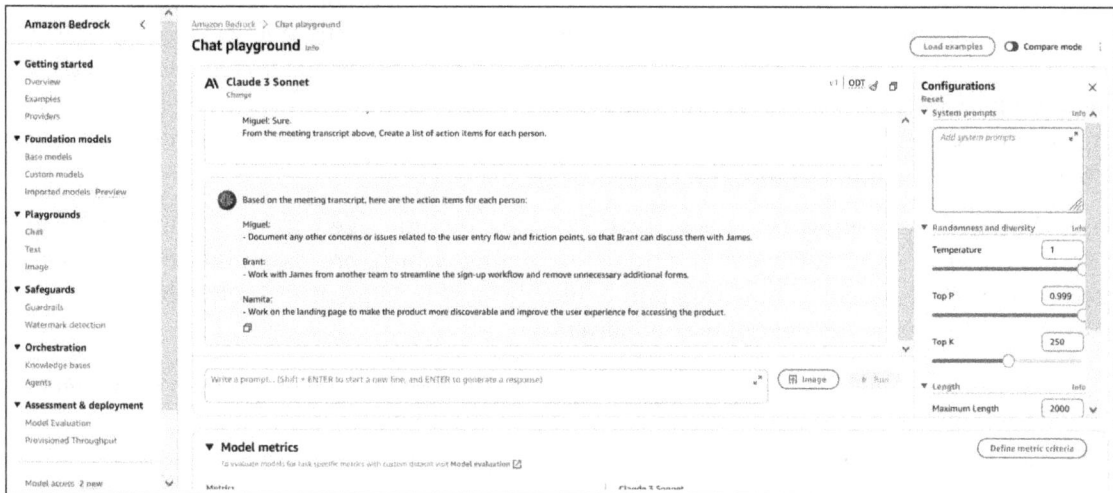

Figure 3.9: AI summarization

We used the **Claude 3 Sonnet** model for this example and the model was able to create a crisp summary of action items for each person based on the meeting transcript.

Model response

Based on the meeting transcript, here are the action items for each person:

Miguel: Document any other concerns or issues related to the user entry flow and friction points, so that Brant can discuss them with James.

Brant: Work with James from another team to streamline the sign-up workflow and remove unnecessary additional forms.

Namita: Work on the landing page to make the product more discoverable and improve the user experience for accessing the product.

Conversational chat

Text FMs have emerged as a powerful tool for building advanced conversational AI systems. These models can generate human-like responses, enabling natural and engaging dialogues across various applications, such as virtual assistants, chatbots, and customer service interfaces. One of the key advantages of text FMs in conversational chat is their ability to understand and interpret context. By analyzing the conversation history and the user's input, these models can generate relevant and contextually appropriate responses, maintaining coherence, and continuity throughout the interaction.

Furthermore, text FMs can adapt their language and communication style based on the user's preferences or the specific domain or use case. For example, a chatbot designed for customer service could employ a more formal and professional tone while a virtual assistant for entertainment purposes might adopt a more casual and friendly demeanor. Text FMs can also handle open-ended conversations and navigate through various topics and subjects. By leveraging their broad knowledge and understanding of language, these models can engage in substantive discussions, provide information, offer recommendations, and even exhibit a degree of creativity and humor.

In addition to generating responses, text FMs can be employed for tasks such as intent recognition, sentiment analysis, and topic modeling which are essential components of conversational AI systems. These capabilities enable more intelligent and contextually relevant responses, improving the overall user experience.

In this example, as shown in *Figure 3.10*, we are having the conversation chat with a **Llama 2 Chat 13B** model asking about the GenAI use case of marketing:

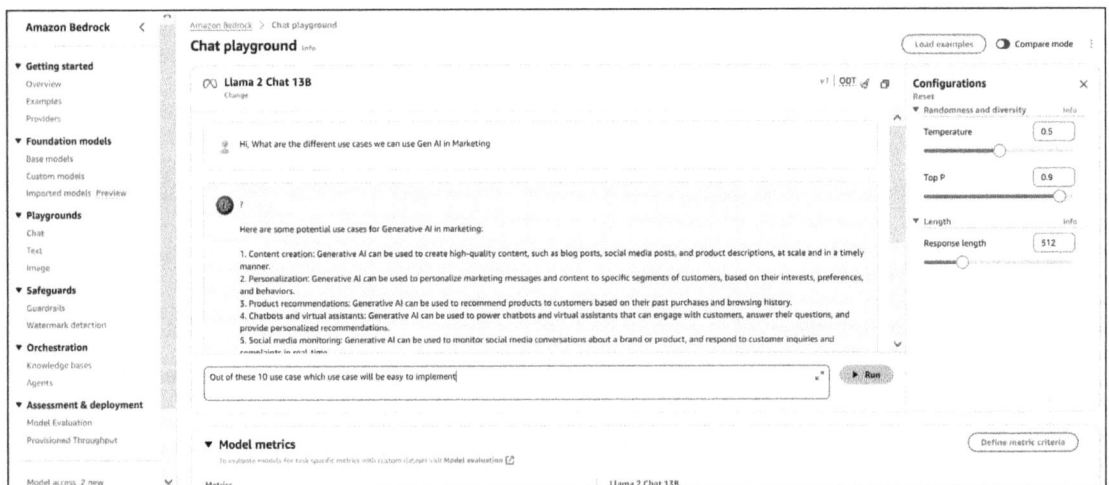

Figure 3.10: Advanced AI conversational chat

Prompt for conversational chat

Let us see the first prompt:

`Hi, what are the different use cases we can use GenAI in Marketing:`

- `Predictive lead scoring: GenAI can help identify and prioritize high-quality leads based on their behavior, demographic information, and other factors.`

- `Personalized content recommendation: GenAI can help create personalized content recommendations for customers based on their interests, preferences, and past interactions.`

- `Sentiment analysis: GenAI can help analyze customer feedback and sentiment, allowing marketers to identify and address any negative sentiment or issues.`

- `Influencer identification: GenAI can help identify and analyze the impact of influencers on marketing campaigns.`

- `Ad targeting and optimization: GenAI can help optimize ad targeting and improve ad performance by analyzing customer data and behavior.`

- `Email marketing optimization: GenAI can help optimize email marketing campaigns by analyzing customer behavior, preferences, and engagement.`

- `Chatbot and virtual assistant development: GenAI can help develop chatbots and virtual assistants that can provide personalized customer support and answer frequently asked questions.`

- `Social media monitoring and analysis: GenAI can help monitor and analyze social media conversations about a brand, allowing marketers to identify and address any issues or opportunities.`

- `Content creation: GenAI can help generate high-quality content quickly and efficiently, allowing marketers to produce more content with less effort.`

- `Predictive analytics: GenAI can help predict future marketing trends and customer behavior, allowing marketers to make more informed decisions about their marketing strategies.`

These are just a few examples of the many use cases for GenAI in marketing as shown in *Figure 3.11*. As the technology continues to evolve, we can expect to see even more innovative applications of GenAI in the future.

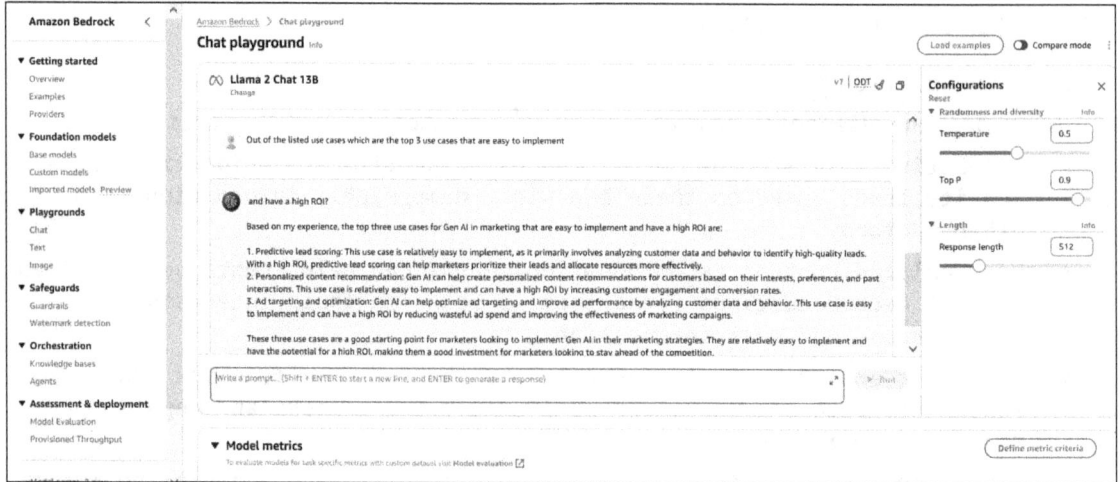

Figure 3.11: AI responses for chat

Let us take a look at the second prompt:

Out of the listed use cases which are the top three use cases that are easy to implement and have a high ROI?

Model response

The model responds to the second prompt with following:

Based on my experience, the top three use cases for GenAI in marketing that are easy to implement and have a high ROI are:

- **Predictive lead scoring: This use case is relatively easy to implement, as it primarily involves analyzing customer data and behavior to identify high-quality leads. With a high ROI, predictive lead scoring can help marketers prioritize their leads and allocate resources more effectively.**

- **Personalized content recommendation: GenAI can help create personalized content recommendations for customers based on their interests, preferences, and past interactions. This use case is relatively easy to implement and can have a high ROI by increasing customer engagement and conversion rates.**

- **Ad targeting and optimization: GenAI can help optimize ad targeting and improve ad performance by analyzing customer data and behavior. This use case is easy to implement and can have a high ROI by reducing wasteful ad spend and improving the effectiveness of marketing campaigns.**

These three use cases are a good starting point for marketers looking to implement GenAI in their marketing strategies. They are relatively easy to implement and have the potential for a high ROI, making them a good investment for marketers looking to stay ahead of the competition.

However, it is important to note that while text FMs have made significant strides, there are still challenges and limitations to address. These models may occasionally generate nonsensical or inconsistent responses, and their performance can be influenced by factors such as the quality and diversity of the training data, as well as the specific domain or use case.

Working with image foundation models

Image FMs have emerged as powerful tools for generating and manipulating visual content by leveraging the capabilities of large-scale deep learning models. These models are trained on vast datasets of images, enabling them to learn intricate patterns, structures, and representations of visual data across various domains and styles. Through this extensive training, image FMs develop an understanding of visual concepts, textures, compositions, and the relationships between different visual elements. The process of image generation or manipulation with these models involves providing an initial input, such as a text prompt, a reference image, or a set of instructions. The model then draws upon its learned knowledge to generate or modify images that align with the given input.

The capabilities of image FMs have opened a wide range of applications across various fields, from creative design and artistic exploration to image editing, data augmentation, and visual content creation. Image FMs have numerous use cases across various domains. In creative industries, they can assist artists and designers by generating visual concepts, exploring new styles, or providing inspiration for artwork. In advertising and marketing, these models can be employed for creating engaging visuals, product mockups, or visual content tailored to specific audiences.

Additionally, image FMs can be utilized for image editing tasks, such as inpainting, style transfer, or super-resolution, enabling advanced image manipulation and enhancement capabilities. Furthermore, they can be used for data augmentation in **machine learning (ML)** applications, generating diverse and realistic synthetic images to enhance training datasets. Image FMs can also be applied to domains like architecture, interior design, and urban planning where they can generate visualizations, renderings, or virtual environments based on specific requirements or design specifications.

Moreover, these models can be fine-tuned for specific tasks, such as object detection, segmentation, or image classification, enabling advanced computer vision applications and enhancing the performance of various visual perception and understanding tasks.

Bedrock offers two powerful images FMs, the Titan Image Generator and the Stability AI SDXL model. We will explore practical examples demonstrating the capabilities of these models in various tasks, including image generation, image variations, image editing, and image inpainting.

Image generation

One notable application of image generation FMs is the creation of concept art, illustrations, and visualizations. These models can generate vivid and detailed images by providing textual prompts or descriptions, enabling artists and designers to quickly explore and iterate on visual ideas. This can greatly streamline the ideation and prototyping processes, allowing for faster experimentation and refinement of concepts.

Another use case is the generation of synthetic data for training ML models. Image generation FMs can create large datasets of labeled images, addressing the data scarcity challenges often faced in computer vision tasks. This synthetic data can be used to pre-train or fine-tune models for various applications, such as object detection, segmentation, or image classification.

In the field of content creation, image generation FMs can be employed to produce visuals for marketing materials, social media content, or digital media assets. These models can generate on-brand visuals by providing prompts aligned with specific branding or stylistic requirements, reducing the need for extensive manual effort or stock image searches. Additionally, image generation FMs can be leveraged in creative fields like game development, virtual and augmented reality, and film production. They can generate realistic environments, characters, or visual effects, enabling creators to bring their visions to life more efficiently.

In this instance, we are utilizing the Titan Image Generator, a powerful tool available within the Bedrock playground environment. The prompt we provided to the model was **a modern chess table in the living room**. As a result, the model generated a series of high-quality images depicting various interpretations of a contemporary chess table situated in a living room setting.

The following image variants were produced based on the textual input we supplied, allowing us to explore multiple visual representations of the specified concept:

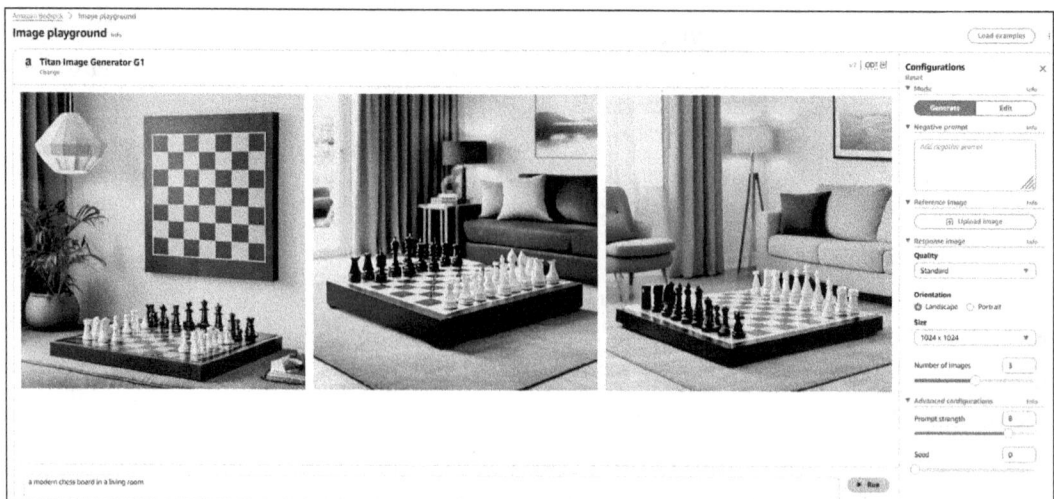

Figure 3.12: Image generation

You can also generate variations of the image by selecting it in the playground and clicking on the **Generate variations** button, as follows:

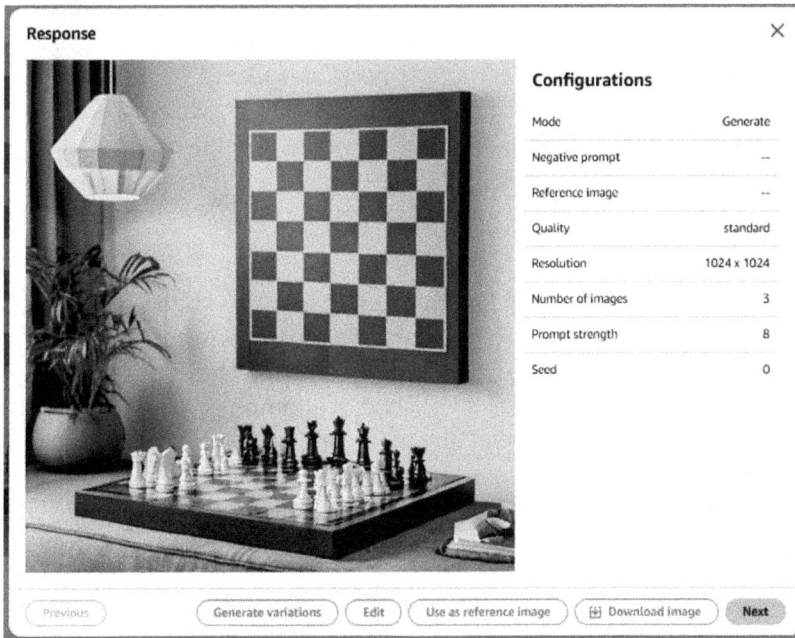

Figure 3.13: *Image generates variation*

The following figure shows the different variations of the image generated:

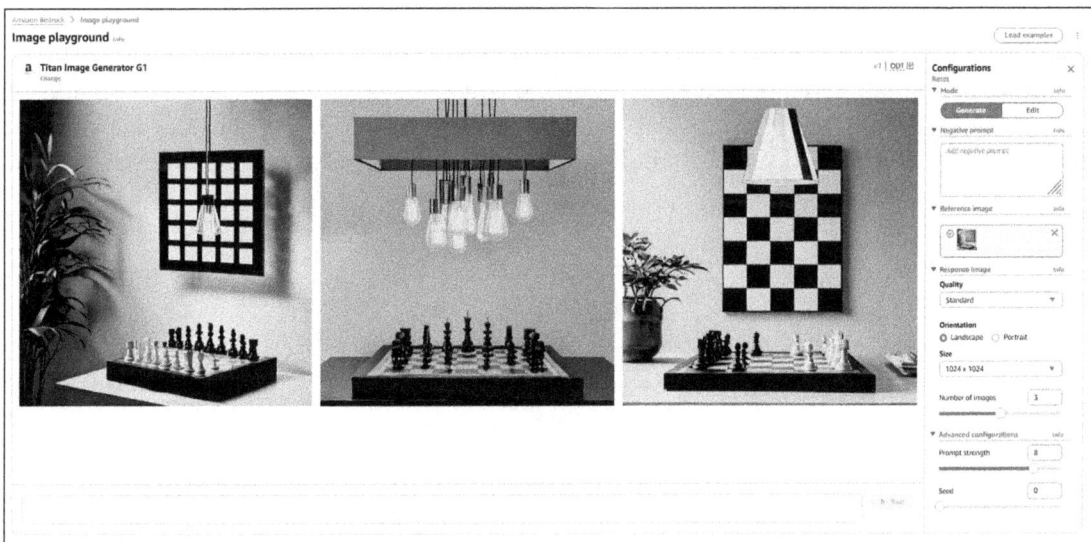

Figure 3.14: *Image generate variation results*

Image editing

Image editing is another powerful application of FMs in the field of computer vision. These models can be trained to perform a wide range of editing tasks, from simple adjustments like color correction and resizing to more complex operations like object removal, inpainting, and style transfer. One notable use case is object removal and inpainting where the model can seamlessly remove unwanted elements from an image and intelligently fill the remaining space with plausible content. This functionality can be extremely useful in fields like photography where removing distracting objects or blemishes can significantly enhance the visual appeal of an image.

Style transfer is another exciting application, enabling the transformation of an image's visual style while preserving its content. Artists, designers, and photographers can leverage this capability to explore various artistic styles and create unique visual experiences. For instance, a photograph can be rendered in the style of a famous painting or a particular artistic movement. In the field of retouching and enhancement, image editing FMs can perform tasks like blemish removal, skin smoothing, and intelligent upscaling. These capabilities can benefit industries such as fashion, advertising, and media production where polished and visually appealing imagery is crucial.

Furthermore, image editing FMs can be integrated into photo editing software or mobile applications, providing users with powerful editing tools and advanced capabilities. This can democratize access to professional-grade editing capabilities, empowering creators and enthusiasts alike to enhance their visual content effectively. Overall, image editing FMs offer a versatile toolset for enhancing, transforming, and manipulating visual content, enabling new creative possibilities, and streamlining various workflows across diverse industries.

In this instance, we are using the image generated in the previous example (image generator) and utilizing the Titan Image Generator model to edit the image. In this case, we provide the reference image and prompt text where we try to change the color and shape of the lamp. To edit the image, we have to select the Edit option (highlighted in blue in the following figure) in the configuration:

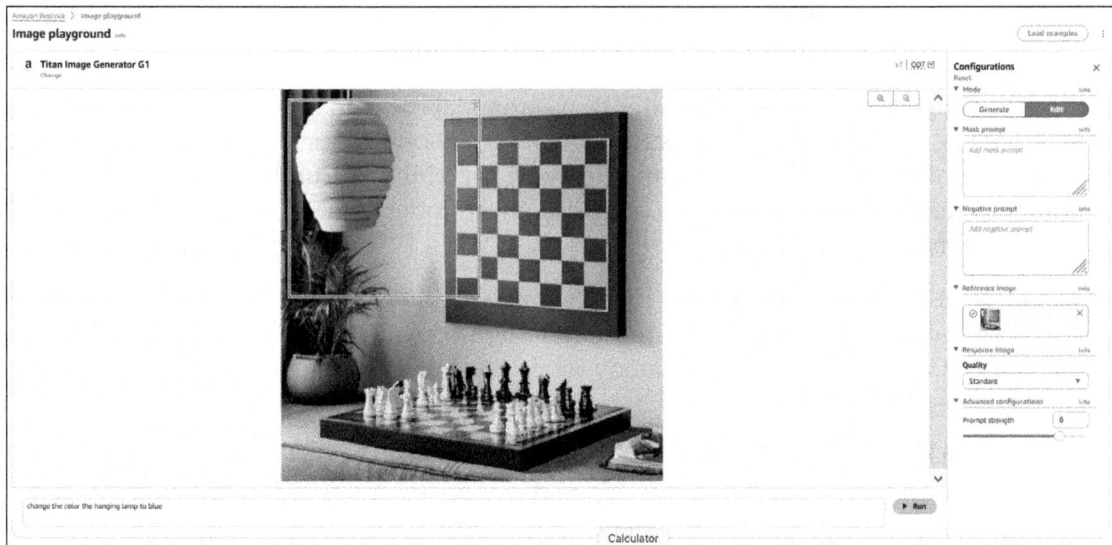

Figure 3.15: Image editing

Working with multimodal foundation models

Multimodal FMs have emerged as powerful tools for processing and understanding different modalities of data, such as text, images, audio, and video, in a unified framework. These models leverage the capabilities of large-scale deep learning architectures to capture and represent the complex relationships, and interactions between multiple modalities. One key application of multimodal FMs is in the domain of image searching and image similarity. These models can be trained on vast datasets comprising images and their associated textual descriptions, captions, or metadata, enabling them to learn the intricate connections between visual and textual representations.

In the context of image searching, multimodal FMs can be used to retrieve relevant images based on textual queries or descriptions. By effectively aligning the textual input with the visual representations learned from the training data, these models can understand the semantic meaning of the query and retrieve visually relevant images. This capability has significant applications in areas such as e-commerce where users can search for products using natural language descriptions, or in digital libraries and media archives where images can be retrieved based on textual annotations or descriptions.

Furthermore, multimodal FMs can be employed for image similarity tasks where the goal is to identify and rank images based on their visual similarity to a given reference image or set of images. These models can leverage their multimodal understanding to effectively capture both the visual and semantic similarities between images, enabling more accurate and meaningful similarity assessments. This capability has applications in areas such as content recommendation systems where visually similar images can be suggested based on a user's preferences or browsing history, or in image clustering and organization tasks where images can be grouped based on their visual and semantic similarities.

In addition to image searching and similarity, multimodal FMs can be applied to various other tasks involving multiple modalities, such as image captioning, visual QA, and multimodal content generation. These models can leverage their ability to understand and integrate information from different modalities, enabling more robust, and comprehensive analyses and applications.

By combining the power of large-scale deep learning architectures with the ability to process and understand multiple modalities, multimodal FMs open new possibilities for advanced image understanding, retrieval, and analysis, as well as enabling novel applications that seamlessly integrate visual and textual information.

In Bedrock, we have Titan Multimodal Embeddings **Generation 1 (G1)** which is a multimodal embedding model for use cases like searching images by text, image, or a combination of text and image. Designed for high accuracy and fast responses, this model is an ideal choice for search and recommendations use cases. We will cover the practical purpose of this model in future chapters for image searching/similarity.

Conclusion

This chapter explored the intricate process of choosing the most suitable FM for diverse use cases and scenarios. We emphasized the pivotal role of model selection and the critical factors that should guide this decision-making process. The chapter offered a comprehensive overview of the FMs available within Bedrock, spanning language, image, embedding, and multimodal models. Additionally, we leveraged Playground to explore practical applications of these models for common use cases, such as text summarization, conversational chat, content generation, and image generation. Through hands-on examples, we gained a deeper understanding of how these models can be effectively utilized in real-world scenarios.

As we move forward, the next chapter will introduce you to the world of building GenAI applications using Bedrock's robust API suite. This exciting journey will equip you with the knowledge and tools necessary to harness the power of cutting-edge AI technologies and create innovative solutions tailored to your specific needs.

Points to remember

- **Model selection is critical**: No single FM excels at all tasks, selection depends on accuracy requirements, multimodal needs, and real-time inference needs.

- **Key selection factors**: Consider model performance, size/capacity, training data, architecture, inference speed, deployment scalability, cost/licensing, ethical considerations, customization capabilities, and community support.

- **Available model families**: Amazon Bedrock offers models from multiple providers including Amazon Titan, Anthropic Claude, Meta Llama, Cohere Command, Mistral AI, AI21 Jurassic, and Stability AI.

- **Model access process**: Models must be explicitly enabled through the model access section in the Bedrock console before using them in playground or via API.

- **Playground interface**: Bedrock provides a playground with three options, chat (conversational), text (content creation), and image (generation/editing).

- **Text model applications**: Text FMs excel at content generation, text summarization, and conversational chat applications.

- **Image model capabilities**: Bedrock's image models (Titan Image Generator and Stability AI SDXL) support image generation, variations, and editing.

- **Multimodal models**: Titan Multimodal Embeddings enable cross-modal applications like searching images by text or combining text and image inputs.

- **Practical experimentation**: The Bedrock playground allows hands-on testing and comparison of different models for specific use cases.

- **Real-world applications**: FMs can be applied to marketing, content creation, meeting summarization, visual design, and many other business contexts.

Exercises

1. **Simple travel blog generator**: Using the Amazon Bedrock playground, experiment with the Anthropic Claude model to generate travel blog posts. Create a prompt that asks the model to produce a 300-word travel guide for Paris, France that includes three main attractions to visit, two restaurant recommendations, and one local cultural tip. Then modify your prompt to generate similar content for Tokyo, Japan. Compare the outputs and note how changing specific elements in your prompt affects the quality and structure of the generated content. Try adding instructions for different tones (enthusiastic, informative, poetic) and observe how the model adapts.

2. **Product image creation**: Using the Stability AI or Amazon Titan Image Generator in the Bedrock playground, experiment with creating product images for a fictional smart water bottle. Start with a basic prompt describing a modern smart water bottle with temperature display on a white background and generate several variations. Then, try enhancing your prompt with more specific details such as color, materials, or setting (e.g., sleek blue smart water bottle with digital temperature display, made of stainless steel, on a kitchen counter). Compare the results from your basic and enhanced prompts. Finally, try using the image editing feature to modify your favorite generated image by changing an element like the color or background.

Join our Discord space

Join our Discord workspace for latest updates, offers, tech happenings around the world, new releases, and sessions with the authors:

https://discord.bpbonline.com

## CHAPTER 4

Building Generative AI Applications with Amazon Bedrock APIs

Introduction

In the previous chapters, we explored Amazon Bedrock, its key features, and the available foundational models, equipping you with a solid understanding of AWS's **generative AI (GenAI)** ecosystem. This chapter provides a detailed introduction to Bedrock's APIs and how they can be used to build GenAI applications, including step-by-step instructions and best practices for development. This chapter discusses the practical aspects of building GenAI applications using Bedrock's APIs. We will cover setting up your development environment, leveraging different APIs to utilize foundational models, handling responses, and implementing error handling and debugging techniques. This chapter will ensure a smooth development experience, enabling you to create your first GenAI application seamlessly.

Structure

The chapter covers the following topics:

- Understanding Amazon Bedrock APIs
- Setting up Amazon Bedrock environment
- Building generative AI application
- Error handling and debugging

Objectives

By the end of this chapter, you will be able to understand the fundamental concepts behind Bedrock APIs and their role in building GenAI applications. Additionally, you will learn to setup Amazon Bedrock environment to build your first GenAI application using different **foundation models** (**FMs**). Furthermore, you will be equipped to effectively handle API responses and implement proper error handling and debugging techniques.

Understanding Amazon Bedrock APIs

Similar to all AWS services, you can programmatically connect to Amazon Bedrock endpoints using APIs and perform various supported actions. You can access the Amazon Bedrock API using the AWS **Command Line Interface** (**CLI**) or an AWS **software development kit** (**SDK**). Amazon Bedrock provides four different service endpoints at this time, which are **bedrock**, **bedrock-runtime**, **bedrock-agent**, and **bedrock-agent-runtime**. Each of these endpoints allows you to perform different actions. The bedrock endpoint helps you perform Amazon Bedrock control plane actions such as managing, training, and deploying models, whereas, the **bedrock-runtime** endpoint allows you to handle data plane APIs for making inference requests for models hosted in Bedrock. Similarly, **bedrock-agent** contains control plane APIs to create and manage agents and knowledge bases, whereas **bedrock-agent-runtime** contains data plane APIs for invoking agents and querying knowledge bases. In this chapter, we will explore **bedrock** and **bedrock-runtime** in detail while utilizing other endpoints in the following chapters.

Setting up AWS SDK

You can interact with Bedrock using AWS CLI or AWS SDKs. In this book, we will use AWS SDK for Python (also known as **Boto3**), but you can use other SDKs as per your requirements. Before installing Boto3, you will need to install Python 3.8 or later. If you are performing these actions in the Jupyter Notebook in SageMaker we launched in *Chapter 1, Introduction to Generative AI and Foundation Models*, Python 3.8 version should be automatically installed in that environment.

To install Boto3 SDK, you will need to run the following command:

```
pip install boto3
```

Once the SDK is installed, you will need to setup access permissions before you start using the SDK.

We will call AWS APIs from Jupyter Notebooks running on the SageMaker studio domain. The Jupyter Notebook will automatically use credentials from the IAM role we setup in *Chapter 1, Introduction to Generative AI and Foundation Models*. If you are going to use the SDK in other environments, you will need to setup credentials. Refer to AWS Documentation at: **https://boto3.amazonaws.com/v1/documentation/api/latest/guide/credentials.html**

Setting up Amazon Bedrock environment

To use Boto3, you must first import it and indicate which service or services you are going to use the following code:

```
import boto3

# Let's use Amazon Bedrock
bedrock = boto3.client(service_name='bedrock')
```

Now, that you have a Bedrock client, you can send requests to the service. Notice that we are using a **bedrock** service endpoint to use **list_foundation_models** API, as follows:

```
response = bedrock.list_foundation_models()
print(response)
```

The above code prints out the list of Amazon Bedrock FMs that are available for you to use. It will also return the provider's name, input, and output modalities supported by the model, whether the model supports response streaming or not, etc.

Examining API request

As we understand how to use Bedrock API, let us explore Bedrock API InvokeModel. This API will invoke the specified Bedrock model to run inference (generate response) using the input provided in the request body. You will use the same API regardless of the FMs you want to use in Bedrock. InvokeModel API allows you to generate text, images, video, and embeddings (or vectors) based on the model you use.

In the following example, we are using InvokeModel API to Anthropic's Claude 3 Haiku model:

```
import boto3
import json
bedrockruntime = boto3.client(service_name='bedrock-runtime', region_
name='us-east-1')

body = json.dumps({
    "max_tokens": 1000,
    "anthropic_version": "bedrock-2023-05-31",
    "messages": [
      {
        "role": "user",
        "content": [
          {
            "type": "text",
            "text": "Explain LLMs to an 8th grader"
          }
```

```
                ]
            }
        ]
    })
    modelId = 'anthropic.claude-3-haiku-20240307-v1:0'
    accept = 'application/json'
    contentType = 'application/json'

    response = bedrockruntime.invoke_model(body=body, modelId=modelId,
    accept=accept, contentType=contentType)
    response_body = json.loads(response.get('body').read())

    # response text
    # print(response_body.get('content'))
    print(response_body.get('content')[0]['text'])
```

Here, we use a **bedrock-runtime** service endpoint to use the InvokeModel API. We are instructing the model to limit its response to 1000 tokens. Anthropic requires that each input message must be an object with a role and content, and the first message must always use the user role, indicating that the user initiated the conversation. Claude 3 Haiku supports both image and text as input; however, we are only providing text input in the example.

Note: **Choose a model that is available and enabled in your region.**

Examining API response

Let us examine how the Anthropic Claude 3 Haiku model on Amazon Bedrock responded to the above request, as follows:

```
{
    'id': 'msg_018ioSkXGhm7qDiBLuz6GJj8',
    'type': 'message',
    'role': 'assistant',
    'content':
    [
        {
            'type': 'text',
            'text': 'Okay, let\'s try to explain Large Language Models
(LLMs) to an 8th grader in a simple way.\n\nImagine you have a very big
dictionary that contains millions and millions of words. And not just
words, but also how those words are used in sentences, how they are
connected to each other, and even the meanings of those words...'
        }
    ],
    'model': 'claude-3-haiku-48k-20240307',
```

```
    'stop_reason': 'end_turn',
    'stop_sequence': None,
    'usage':
    {
        'input_tokens': 20, 'output_tokens': 334
    }
}
```

The response to InvokeModel API includes two main components, which are **contentType** and **body**. The format and content of the body field differ based on the FM you are using on Bedrock. For Anthropic Claude models, the response includes a unique identifier of the response, model ID, the reason why Claude stopped generating the response, type, and text of the content, and token usage in that API call.

The above sample code is provided in a Jupyter Notebook named **Example41.ipynb** in the code repository.

Converse API

Amazon Bedrock also provides another important API, **Converse**. This API provides a consistent interface for interacting with LLMs that support messages. Unlike the traditional InvokeModel API, which requires different JSON request and response structures for each model provider, the Converse API allows developers to use a single standardized format across all supported models on Amazon Bedrock. This simplifies development as you can write code once and use it with different models.

The Converse API enables developers to:

- Create conversational applications that maintain dialogue over multiple turns
- Pass model-specific inference parameters when needed
- Implement tool use and guardrails in applications
- Include system prompts to define tone and constraints
- Handle both text and image-based messages in conversations

While the InvokeModel API is still used for certain cases like embeddings and image generation models, the Converse API has become increasingly popular for text generation use cases due to its consistency and ease of use across different FMs in Amazon Bedrock:

```
import boto3, json
session = boto3.Session()
bedrock = session.client(service_name='bedrock-runtime')

message_list = []

initial_message = {
    "role": "user",
```

```
    "content": [
        {"text": "Tell me a funny joke about Space."}
    ],
}

message_list.append(initial_message)

response = bedrock.converse(
    modelId="anthropic.claude-3-haiku-20240307-v1:0",
    messages=message_list,
    inferenceConfig={
        "maxTokens": 2000,
        "temperature": 0
    },
)

response_message = response['output']['message']
print(json.dumps(response_message, indent=4))
```

Building generative AI application

We learned about different API endpoints of Amazon Bedrock, and then we covered how to use AWS SDK to make API calls. In this section, we will provide a step-by-step guide on how you can create a simple GenAI application powered by Amazon Bedrock.

Customer conversation

Let us assume this scenario. A customer service manager at best internet company wants to review the conversations their agents have with customers in order to assess the quality of customer service being provided. This is an important part of ensuring a positive customer experience. However, manually reviewing every customer interaction would be extremely time-consuming and inefficient. To address this challenge, the manager is looking for a way to automatically generate summaries of customer conversations. These summaries would capture the key details and sentiments expressed, allowing the manager to quickly review them and identify areas for improvement in the customer service being delivered by their agents.

The following is a sample transcript of a conversation between an agent and a customer. It illustrates a common type of customer interaction where a customer has an issue with their billing:

```
[Agent] Hi, thank you for calling Best Internet company. This is Collin,
how may I help. You?
[Customer] Hi Collin. So, I'm calling because I have been overcharged,
um, my subscription to you guys is supposed to be a flat rate of 50 dollars
```

per month but for some reason I am seeing 75 dollars on my paper bill for the month of March. So, I don't know what's going on. I would really appreciate an explanation on this.
[Agent] Sure, I'll be happy to pull up your account now and check the billing details for you. Can I have your account number together with your first and last name?

     ...

...
[Customer] I know, right, anyway Collin I won't waste any more of your time, and thank you so much for your patience.
[Agent] You're welcome Jason. Is there anything else that I can help you with today?
[Customer] No, that's all Collin. Have a good one.
[Agent] Have a good one Jason. Thank you for calling Best Internet. Bye.
[Customer] Bye Collin.

We need to generate a summary of their conversation.

The following are the steps to build this application:

1. We need to import the necessary packages and set a client to use the **bedrock-runtime** endpoint:

    ```
    import json
    import boto3
    import botocore
    boto3_bedrock = boto3.client('bedrock-runtime')
    ```

2. We need to create a **prompt** supplying instruction and input data to FMs so it can generate a summary of the conversation. We supplied the entire transcript between the agent and the customer, along with instructions to summarize:

    ```
    prompt = """
    Please provide a summary of the following text. Do not add any
    information that is not mentioned in the text below.

    <text>
    [Agent] Hi, thank you for calling Best Internet company. This is Collin,
    how may I help. You?

            ...
    ...
    [Customer] Bye, Collin.
    </text>

    """
    ```

3. Now, that the **prompt** is defined, we need to create **body** of the request. The request **body** will include the prompt as well as inference parameters such as **maxTokenCount**,

temperature, **topP**, etc. In the following request **body**, we are setting the max output token count as **4096** tokens, with **temperature** and **topP** will influence the randomness and diversity of the output:

```
body = json.dumps({"inputText": prompt,
                "textGenerationConfig":{
                    "maxTokenCount":4096,
                    "stopSequences":[],
                    "temperature":0,
                    "topP":1
            },
        })
```

4. Next, we need to specify which FMs to use (in this example, Nova Micro), make an InvokeModel API call with the request body, and print the output. We are using Python's **try** and **except** blocks for exception handling, allowing us to catch and handle exceptions (runtime errors) that may occur within the **try** block. The following sample code shows how to use Bedrock InvokeModel API in Python:

```
modelId = 'amazon.nova-micro-v1:0' # change this to use a different
model
accept = 'application/json'
contentType = 'application/json'

try:

    response = boto3_bedrock.invoke_model(body=body, modelId=modelId,
accept=accept, contentType=contentType)
    response_body = json.loads(response.get('body').read())

    print(response_body.get('results')[0].get('outputText'))

except botocore.exceptions.ClientError as error:

    if error.response['Error']['Code'] == 'AccessDeniedException':
            print(f"\x1b[41m{error.response['Error']['Message']}\
                \nTo troubeshoot this issue please refer to the
following resources.\
                    \nhttps://docs.aws.amazon.com/IAM/latest/UserGuide/
troubleshoot_access-denied.html\
                    \nhttps://docs.aws.amazon.com/bedrock/latest/userguide/
security-iam.html\x1b[0m\n")

    else:
        raise error
```

5. You have created your first GenAI-powered application. The following is the summary it generated:

```
The customer calls Best Internet company to complain about being
overcharged on their subscription. The agent checks the customer's
account and finds that the charge is only 50 dollars for the month of
March, as expected. The customer rechecks their bill and realizes
that the charge is actually from last year, March 2023. The agent
apologizes for the confusion and assures the customer that there
is no overcharge. The customer is embarrassed but grateful for the
agent's patience and assistance. The call ends with the customer
thanking the agent and the agent wishing the customer a good day.
```

You have been provided a sample code for this scenario in a Jupyter Notebook **Example42.ipynb**. You will see in the notebook that we generated the summary output from two different models to show you how easily you can interchange FMs. You can use the sample code and try out other FMs available on Bedrock to test their performance.

Let us recap what we just built. In this section, you created an application to automate the summarization of customer conversations to enhance service quality. By generating summaries of these types of conversations, the customer service manager can:

- **Identify training opportunities**: The summaries can reveal instances where agents could have handled a situation more effectively, allowing the manager to provide targeted coaching and training.

- **Recognize excellent customer service**: The summaries can also highlight examples of agents going above and beyond to provide great customer experience, which the manager can use to recognize and reward high-performing team members.

- **Uncover systemic issues**: Analyzing the trends and patterns across multiple conversation summaries can help the manager identify any larger problems or pain points in the company's processes or policies that need to be addressed.

- **Improve customer satisfaction**: Ultimately, the ability to consistently review and improve the quality of customer service will lead to higher customer satisfaction and loyalty for the company.

Let us take a look at a few other real-world use cases where we can employ GenAI:

- **Automating car insurance claim assessment with GenAI**: In the car insurance industry, efficiently processing claims is a critical challenge. Traditionally, this process involved manual assessment of vehicle damage by insurance adjusters, which could be time-consuming and expensive. However, by leveraging the advanced computer vision capabilities of GenAI models, insurance providers can automate the initial damage assessment, leading to faster claim resolution and improved customer experience.

  Let us see how the following works in detail:

  o **Image submission**: When a policyholder files a car insurance claim, they can submit photographs of the vehicle damage through a mobile app or a website.

○ **Damage assessment with GenAI**: The images are then processed by a GenAI model, such as Anthropic's Claude 3, which has been trained on a vast dataset of vehicle damage images. The model can accurately identify the type and extent of the damage, classifying it into categories like minor dents, scratches, cracked windshield, or more severe structural damage.

○ **Automation and workflow integration**: Based on the AI-generated damage assessment, the insurance provider's workflow can be automated. For minor damages, the claim can be approved and processed immediately, without the need for an in-person adjuster inspection. For more extensive damage, the system can automatically trigger the next steps, such as scheduling a physical inspection or providing repair cost estimates.

○ **Enhanced customer experience**: By automating the initial damage assessment, policyholders can receive faster claim resolution and get their vehicles repaired more quickly. This streamlined process not only improves customer satisfaction but also reduces the workload and costs for the insurance provider.

For the above scenario, let us assume the user provided the image of the damaged car shown in *Figure 4.1*. You have been provided a sample code for this scenario in a Jupyter Notebook `Example43.ipynb`:

Figure 4.1: Damaged car

You will see in the notebook that Anthropic Claude 3 Sonnet was able to assess car condition from a single image and generated an output like the one shown in the following:

`Based on the image provided, I would assess the damage to the vehicle as follows:`

- `Major Damage: The front end of the vehicle has sustained significant impact damage. Both the hood and front bumper appear to be heavily crumpled and deformed, indicating a high-energy collision.`

  `There is likely structural damage to the front frame rails and other components that provide structural integrity to the vehicle's front end.`

- **Moderate Damage:** The headlight assemblies on both sides appear to be broken or dislodged from their housings.

  Depending on the extent of the impact, there may be moderate damage to the radiator, cooling system components, and other mechanical parts located in the engine compartment.

- **Minor Damage:** The windshield seems to be intact, but there may be minor cracks or chips that need to be addressed.

  The side mirrors and other exterior trim pieces may have sustained minor scratches or dents.

- **Repair Considerations:** Given the severity of the front-end damage, it is likely that the vehicle will require extensive repairs or potentially be deemed a total loss (if the repair costs exceed a certain percentage of the vehicle's value). Repairs may involve replacing the entire front-end assembly, including the hood, bumper, headlights, radiator, and potentially the front frame rails. Proper alignment and structural integrity must be ensured for safe operation.

- **Approximate Average Cost:** The cost of repairs for this level of damage can vary significantly depending on the make and model of the vehicle, the availability of parts, and the labor rates in the area. However, as a rough estimate, major front-end collision repairs can range from $5,000 to $15,000 or more for a typical passenger vehicle.

By harnessing the power of GenAI for automated vehicle damage assessment, insurance providers can revolutionize their claims processing workflow. This transformative application of GenAI technology has the potential to significantly improve efficiency and satisfaction levels across the automotive insurance industry.

Automated product content generation at scale

Another compelling practical use case for GenAI is creating rich product content at scale. With AWS Bedrock, businesses can leverage FMs to automate the creation of product descriptions and visuals from simple text prompts. A merchant could input a brief product idea like a smartwatch with fitness tracking and sleep monitoring, and a text generation model would generate detailed marketing copy highlighting the product's key features and benefits. Additionally, image generation models can produce photorealistic rendered images visualizing the product from different angles based on the text prompt. This allows companies to rapidly build out content for thousands of products at a fraction of the time and cost compared to traditional methods. Such automated content generation driven by AI can streamline e-commerce operations, enhance the online shopping experience with richer product detail pages, and accelerate time-to-market for new product launches. Let us see how this works:

- We will use two different FMs on Amazon Bedrock. We will utilize Anthropic Claude 3 Sonnet to generate product description and Nova Canvas model to create product visuals.

- **Product description**: The user will provide a product idea as input. For example, **Baby stroller with Scooter Hybrid**. This input will be utilized in a prompt template which provides instructions to models on how to generate the product descriptions. We will demonstrate using Anthropic Claude 3 Sonnet to generate a product description. You can replace it with other models on Amazon Bedrock.

- **Product visuals**: We will create a specialized prompt describing the product vision at a high-level, such as **Cutting-edge Baby Stroller and Scooter Hybrid: sleek, modern design, comfortable seat, adjustable handles, compact, foldable, seamless scooter integration, sturdy wheels, powerful motor, intuitive controls, emphasizing convenience, safety, and appeal to on-the-go parents.** This prompt will be supplied to image generation models such as Nova Canvas on Bedrock. You can also use other models such as Stability AI's Stable Diffusion 3.5 Large.

You have been provided a sample code for this scenario in a Jupyter Notebook **Example44.ipynb**. You will see in the notebook that we generated product descriptions and visuals using two different models. You can use the sample code and try out other available FMs on Bedrock.

Error handling and debugging

Dealing with errors and debugging issues is an essential part of any software development process, including when working with Amazon Bedrock.

The following list summarizes common errors you might encounter and provides guidance on what to check to resolve them:

- **Service quota errors**: Several errors can arise due to service limitations and quota restrictions. The following is an example of error that may occur due to service quota issues:

  o **ThrottlingException**: Verify that you have not exceeded your service quotas for API requests. This may require requesting a service quota increase or implementing exponential backoff in the retry logic.

- **Data issues**: Several errors can arise due to issues with the training, validation, or output data files. The following are examples of errors that may occur due to data issues:

  o **Token count exceeded**: Verify that the number of tokens in your input and output data does not exceed the token quota limits outlined in the model quotas.

  o **Malformed input**: Verify that the schema of the request is valid and that the input prompt format complies with FMs' expected input format.

- **Internal errors**: In some cases, you may encounter unexpected internal errors, such as encountered an unexpected error when processing the request, please try again. If this occurs, try running the job again. If the issue persists, contact AWS Support for further assistance.

By understanding these common errors and following the provided guidelines, you can effectively troubleshoot and resolve issues that may arise during the model customization process with Amazon Bedrock.

Conclusion

In this chapter, we explored the practical aspects of building GenAI applications using Amazon Bedrock's APIs. We covered the key Bedrock API endpoints, setup the development environment with AWS SDKs, and created applications powered by FMs on Amazon Bedrock. We demonstrated how to leverage Bedrock's APIs to automate customer conversation summaries, streamline car insurance claim assessments through automated damage evaluation, and generate rich product content at scale. These real-world use cases showcased the versatility and potential of GenAI in enhancing operational efficiency, improving customer experiences, and driving business growth. Throughout the chapter, we emphasized the importance of understanding API requests and responses, handling errors and debugging techniques to ensure a smooth development process. By mastering these skills, you can effectively harness the power of Amazon Bedrock's FMs and build innovative GenAI solutions tailored to your specific requirements. With Amazon Bedrock's constantly expanding model catalog and ongoing advancements in the field, the possibilities for creating transformative AI-driven applications are virtually limitless.

In the next chapter, we will discuss advanced topics such as managed **retrieval augmented generation** (**RAG**) using knowledge bases for Amazon Bedrock and executing multi-step tasks using agents for Amazon Bedrock.

Points to remember

- Amazon Bedrock provides four different service endpoints, which are bedrock, bedrock-runtime, bedrock-agent, and bedrock-agent-runtime, allowing you to perform various actions, such as managing models, making inference requests, and interacting with agents and knowledge bases.

- Setting up your development environment involves installing the AWS SDK (for example, Boto3 for Python) and configuring access permissions to interact with Bedrock APIs.

- The InvokeModel API is a crucial Bedrock API that allows you to invoke a specified FM and generate text, embeddings, or images based on the provided input.

- The Converse API provides a consistent, unified interface for interacting with all supported language models in Amazon Bedrock, allowing developers to write code once and use it across different models, unlike the model-specific formats required by InvokeModel API.

- When building GenAI applications, it is essential to create well-structured prompts that provide clear instructions and input data to the FMs.

- Error handling and debugging techniques, such as using try-except blocks and checking for common errors like token count exceeded or malformed input, are crucial for a smooth development experience.

- Amazon Bedrock offers a wide range of FMs from various providers, enabling you to leverage their capabilities for diverse use cases, such as customer conversation summarization, damage assessment, and product content generation.

Exercises

1. Build an application that can analyze and classify sentiment from customer feedback or social media data. This could be valuable for businesses to understand customer sentiment towards their products or services. In this exercise, you can try out zero-shot or few-shot prompts to analyze and classify the sentiment.

2. Build a simple chatbot application that can engage in conversations and provide information or recommendations based on user queries. For example, you could create a chatbot for a bookstore that can suggest book recommendations based on the user's preferences and interests. In this exercise, you will need to design prompts that effectively capture the context and intent of the user's queries, and structure the responses in a natural and coherent manner using the model's capabilities.

3. Develop an image captioning application that can generate descriptive captions for uploaded images. For instance, you could build an application that can caption images of landscapes, animals, or everyday objects. Leverage the computer vision capable and language generation models available on Bedrock. This exercise will involve pre-processing the input images (resizing if necessary), crafting appropriate prompts for the models, and post-processing the generated captions to ensure they are relevant and accurate.

4. Create an application that can summarize long-form articles or documents into concise summaries. This could be useful for quickly understanding the key points of lengthy articles or reports without having to read through the entire content. In this exercise, you may need to explore techniques for effectively chunking and processing the input text and formulating prompts that guide the model to generate accurate and informative summaries.

CHAPTER 5

Using Amazon Bedrock Knowledge Bases

Introduction

In the previous chapter, we discussed how we can build **generative AI (GenAI)** application with Bedrock APIs with Bedrock SDK. As we learned in *Chapter 2, Getting Started with Amazon Bedrock*, **retrieval augmented generation (RAG)** is a powerful technique that enhances the capabilities of **large language models (LLMs)** by allowing them to draw upon and synthesize information from external data sources. Amazon Bedrock Knowledge Bases provides a streamlined and scalable solution for implementing RAG, enabling applications to query customized data stores and receive enriched responses.

This chapter will explore how to manage knowledge bases, their key benefits for accelerating development timelines and reducing costs, as well as best practices for creating RAG-powered GenAI application.

Structure

The chapter covers the following topics:

- Amazon Bedrock Knowledge Bases
- Creating knowledge base
- Synching knowledge base

- Testing knowledge base
- Best practices for using knowledge bases

Objectives

By the end of this chapter, you will have a firm grasp of utilizing managed RAG capability with Amazon Bedrock Knowledge Bases, its key features and capabilities and how you can use them to create sophisticated GenAI applications.

Amazon Bedrock Knowledge Bases

As covered in *Chapter 2, Getting Started with Amazon Bedrock*, RAG enhances foundational models by retrieving relevant information from external knowledge bases. This mitigates input length constraints of models and improves accuracy by providing tailored context. The RAG process involves retrieving relevant information, augmenting the user's prompt, and generating a response. RAG employs embedding models for semantic search and retrieval. While self-managed RAG implementation is complex, Amazon Bedrock's managed RAG offering, knowledge bases, simplifies integration of proprietary data. Knowledge bases enable efficient retrieval, management, and querying of relevant information to enhance model responses.

Figure 5.1 shows the data ingestion pipeline for a typical RAG implementation, that Amazon Bedrock Knowledge Bases automates. It handles the heavy lifting on your behalf by providing a managed ingestion feature. This capability can fetch documents from a repository, split them into smaller chunks, convert the chunks into vector embeddings using the model you select, and then store the embeddings in the vector store of your choice. While Amazon Bedrock automates a large part of RAG implementations, you still have control to configure different chunking and parsing strategies, permissions, and other advanced settings such as metadata filtering.

| New data | Data source | Document chunks | Embeddings model | Vector store |

Figure 5.1: Data ingestion workflow with Amazon Bedrock Knowledge Bases

By the way, Amazon Bedrock Knowledge Bases now supports natural language querying to retrieve structured data from your data sources, allowing you to build custom GenAI applications that can access and incorporate contextual information from a variety of structured and unstructured data sources.

Once the data is ingested using the managed workflow, you can start using the RAG implementation. *Figure 5.2* shows the runtime execution of RAG with Amazon Bedrock

Knowledge Bases. User just need to make a single API call providing their query. All other things are handled by the service.

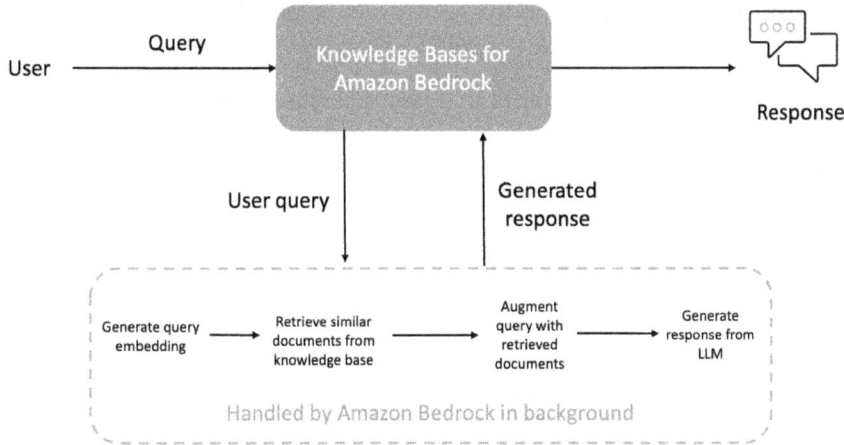

Figure 5.2: *Managed RAG with Amazon Bedrock Knowledge Bases*

During the runtime, it utilizes an embedding model to transform user's input query into a vector representation. This vector is then utilized to identify text chunks that are semantically similar to the user's query. This similarity is determined by comparing the vector representations of the document chunks with the vector representation of the user's query. Once the relevant chunks have been retrieved from the vector index, they are combined with the original user prompt to provide additional context. Finally, this augmented prompt, which now includes the supplementary context from the retrieved chunks, is passed to the LLM, allowing it to generate a more informed and contextually relevant response for the user.

Now, we know what Amazon Bedrock Knowledge Bases provides, let us dive deeper into setting it up and using it. We covered different types Bedrock endpoints in *Chapter 4, Building Generative AI Applications with Bedrock APIs*. For managing and using knowledge bases, we will use **bedrock-agent** and **bedrock-agent-runtime** endpoints. Before we create a RAG pipeline with knowledge bases, let us explore a capability of Bedrock that simplifies interacting with a single document without needing to setup a vector database.

Document analysis

With the chat with your document feature, you can simply upload a file (such as a PDF) from your desktop or provide S3 file path, and immediately start chatting with your data. The data you provide is never stored, and you can ask questions of varying granularity, from general QA to summarizing information from specific sections. Additionally, this capability is offered at no additional cost with you only paying for model usage. You can access it through the AWS Management console or the RetrieveAndGenerate API of Amazon Bedrock.

The following are the steps to chat with your document using AWS Management Console:

1. Type **Bedrock** in the services search bar at the top of the console and select **Amazon Bedrock** to navigate to the Bedrock console. Select **Knowledge bases** from the left panel in the **Amazon Bedrock** console.

2. Select **Chat with your document** tab. *Figure 5.3* shows how you can setup an IAM user in an AWS account:

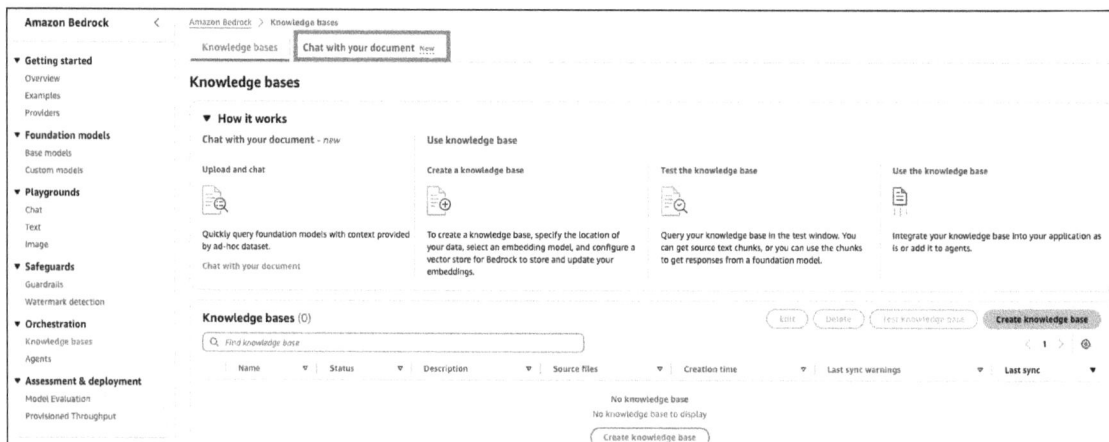

Figure 5.3: Chat with your document on Amazon Bedrock

3. In the **Chat with your document** tab, select a model under **Select Model**. Choose **Anthropic Claude 3 Sonnet** and select **Apply**. Make sure you have enabled access to the model in your account in order for you to select the model.

4. Inference parameters allow you to influence the responses that model provides, you can leave the default or modify as per your needs. System prompt defines how the model handles the user prompt. You can edit the default prompt to create a custom one for your use case.

5. Under **Data**, you select where the document is located, that is, your computer or Amazon S3.

   Select **Choose document** and select the document you will like to chat with. As of writing this chapter, it supports **.pdf**, **.md**, **.txt**, **.doc**, **.docx**, **.html**, **.csv**, **.xls**, **.xlsx** file types. You can refer to AWS Documentation for updated information on file type support: **https://docs.aws.amazon.com/bedrock/latest/userguide/knowledge-base-chatdoc.html**. You can download example document, named **sample-transcript.pdf**, provided in the code repository and use it here.

6. Enter a query in the box that says **Enter your message here**. You can use sample query such as **Summarize this document**. The loaded document and the prompt appear in the chat window, and then select **Run**.

7. The response produces search results with an option **Show source details** that show the source material information for the answer. To load a new file, select the **X** to delete the current file loaded into the chat window.

Figure 5.4 shows a how you can use this feature and ask a model to summarize the document:

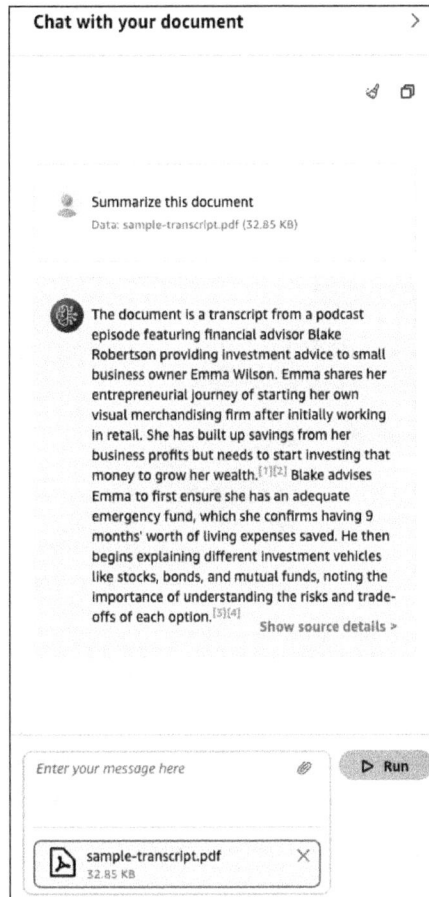

Figure 5.4: Chat with your document on Amazon Bedrock

Amazon Bedrock Knowledge Bases made it really easy to chat with a single document without the need to setup full RAG implementation. It is a powerful feature that allows you to leverage GenAI models to interact with and extract insights from unstructured documents or text data. This capability can be useful in various scenarios, including: document analysis and comprehension, information extraction, summarization, content rewriting or rephrasing, QA, and content analysis and insights.

We have also provided how you can use **Chat with your document** capability using API in the Jupyter Notebook **Example51.ipynb** in the code repository.

Creating knowledge bases

We can create knowledge bases using Amazon Bedrock console, using Bedrock SDK/API or IaC tool such as CloudFormation, Terraform etc. We will first start with **user interface (UI)** console and then later in the section, we will cover knowledge base creation and configuration with SDK. Let us build the RAG implementation using knowledge bases through AWS Management Console.

It involves just a few steps, that is, collecting source documents, uploading data to an S3 bucket, setting up a vector index in a supported vector store (optional when using console, as Bedrock can do this for you), ingesting your data as embeddings in a supported vector store, and setting up your application to query the knowledge base.

Here are high-level steps you can follow to set it up:

- **Navigate to knowledge bases**:
  - Navigate to **Amazon Bedrock | Orchestration | Knowledge bases** in the AWS management console.
  - Click **Create knowledge base**.
  - **Knowledge base name**: Let us enter a name for the knowledge base, for example `customer-support-agent-kb`.
  - **Knowledge base description**: Optionally, provide a brief description of the knowledge base.
  - **IAM permissions**: Create or select an existing IAM service role with the necessary permissions.
  - **Query Engine**: Select the data source you want to use. It supports a number of them, including web crawling, and an option to create custom data source.
  - **Tags**: Add a tag to knowledge base resources.
  - **Log deliveries**: Optionally, you can configure to deliver application logs to multiple destinations.

    Figure 5.5 shows how you can configure the knowledge base:

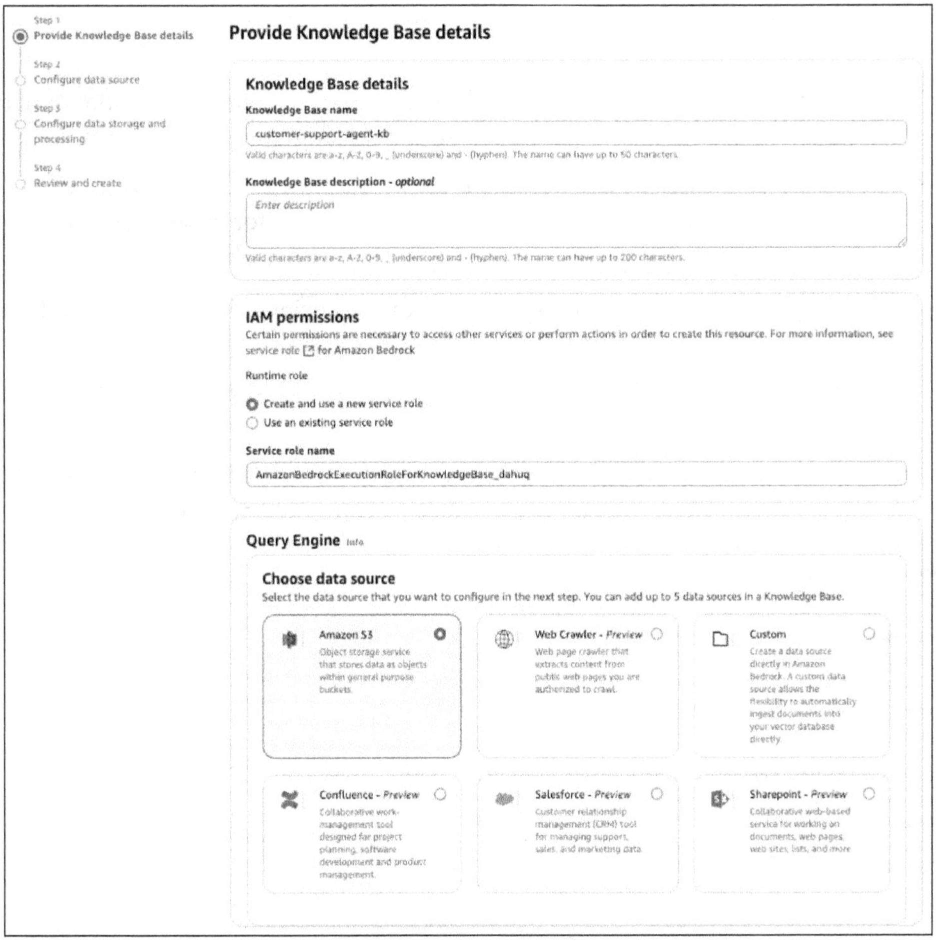

Figure 5.5: Configuring Amazon Bedrock Knowledge Bases

- **Configure data source**:

  o **Data source name**: Enter a name for the data source, for example **customer-support-agent-kb-data-source**.

  o **Data source location**: Enter the data source location, for example **s3://<bucket>/<object-name>** for an S3 data source.

  o **Parsing strategy**: You can configure how you want your data to be processed. For example, if you want PDF files, that includes images, in your data to be processed with foundation models, you can select it here.

  o **Chunking strategy**: Chunking is a way larger text is broken down into smaller segments before you convert them into embedding. Optimal chunk sizing for document embedding depends on content type and use case. For example, for PDFs/reports/books data types, general guidance is to configure chunks with

500-1000 tokens (300-600 words). You may have to experiment to come up with an optimal setting for your data.

- o **Transformation function**: Optionally, you can use Lambda functions to customize chunking and metadata processing for your document using this option.

- o **Advanced settings**: We will leave them default for now. Optionally, you can customize encryption settings, and data deletion policy.

  - By default, Bedrock encrypts your transient data with a AWS-managed key. You can select a different key instead of the default key.

  - By default, the vector store data will be retained when data source is deleted.

    You can add up to five data sources to a single knowledge base. *Figure 5.6* shows how you can use console to configure data sources:

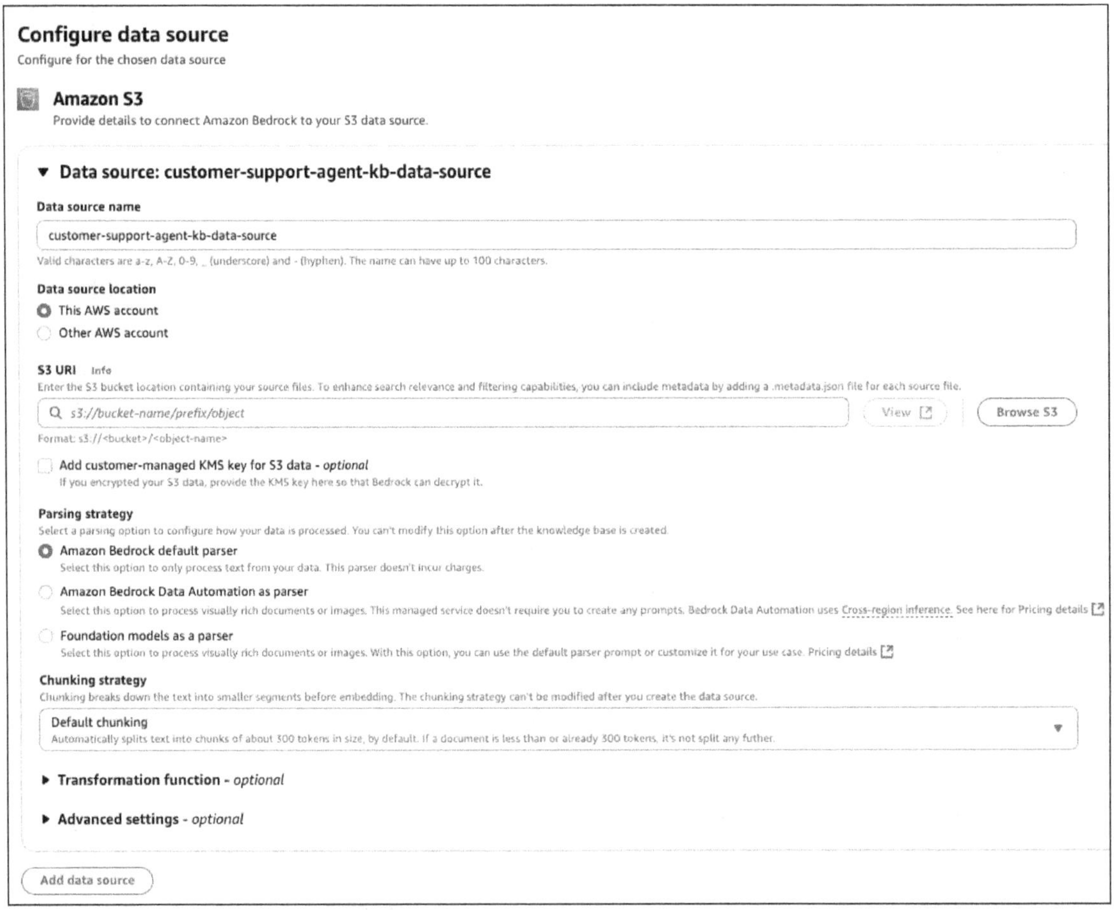

Configure data source
Configure for the chosen data source

▓ **Amazon S3**
Provide details to connect Amazon Bedrock to your S3 data source.

▼ **Data source: customer-support-agent-kb-data-source**

Data source name

customer-support-agent-kb-data-source

Valid characters are a-z, A-Z, 0-9, _ (underscore) and - (hyphen). The name can have up to 100 characters.

Data source location
⦿ This AWS account
◯ Other AWS account

S3 URI Info
Enter the S3 bucket location containing your source files. To enhance search relevance and filtering capabilities, you can include metadata by adding a .metadata.json file for each source file.

🔍 s3://bucket-name/prefix/object   [View ▢] [Browse S3]

Format: s3://<bucket>/<object-name>

☐ Add customer-managed KMS key for S3 data - *optional*
If you encrypted your S3 data, provide the KMS key here so that Bedrock can decrypt it.

Parsing strategy
Select a parsing option to configure how your data is processed. You can't modify this option after the knowledge base is created.
⦿ Amazon Bedrock default parser
Select this option to only process text from your data. This parser doesn't incur charges.

◯ Amazon Bedrock Data Automation as parser
Select this option to process visually rich documents or images. This managed service doesn't require you to create any prompts. Bedrock Data Automation uses Cross-region inference. See here for Pricing details ▢

◯ Foundation models as a parser
Select this option to process visually rich documents or images. With this option, you can use the default parser prompt or customize it for your use case. Pricing details ▢

Chunking strategy
Chunking breaks down the text into smaller segments before embedding. The chunking strategy can't be modified after you create the data source.

Default chunking   ▼
Automatically splits text into chunks of about 300 tokens in size, by default. If a document is less than or already 300 tokens, it's not split any further.

▶ **Transformation function** - *optional*

▶ **Advanced settings** - *optional*

(Add data source)

Figure 5.6: Configuring data sources

- **Configure data storage and processing**:
  - ○ **Embedding model**: You will select an embeddings model to convert your data into an embedding. You can select **Titan Embeddings G1 – Text v1.2** model. You can leave additional configurations as default.
  - ○ **Vector store**: Amazon Bedrock can create an Amazon OpenSearch Serverless vector store on your behalf or you can select a previously created vector store and allow Bedrock to store, update, and manage embeddings. It supports a number of vector stores such as Pinecone, MongoDB Atlas, Redis Enterprise Cloud, Amazon Neptune, and Amazon Aurora.
    - ▪ Select **Quick create a new vector store - Recommended**.
    - ▪ You can also add active replica to enable redundant vector store. We will leave that unchecked.
    - ▪ You can also add customer-managed KMS key to encrypt OpenSearch data. We will leave that unchecked.

    Figure 5.7 shows how to configure it on Bedrock console:

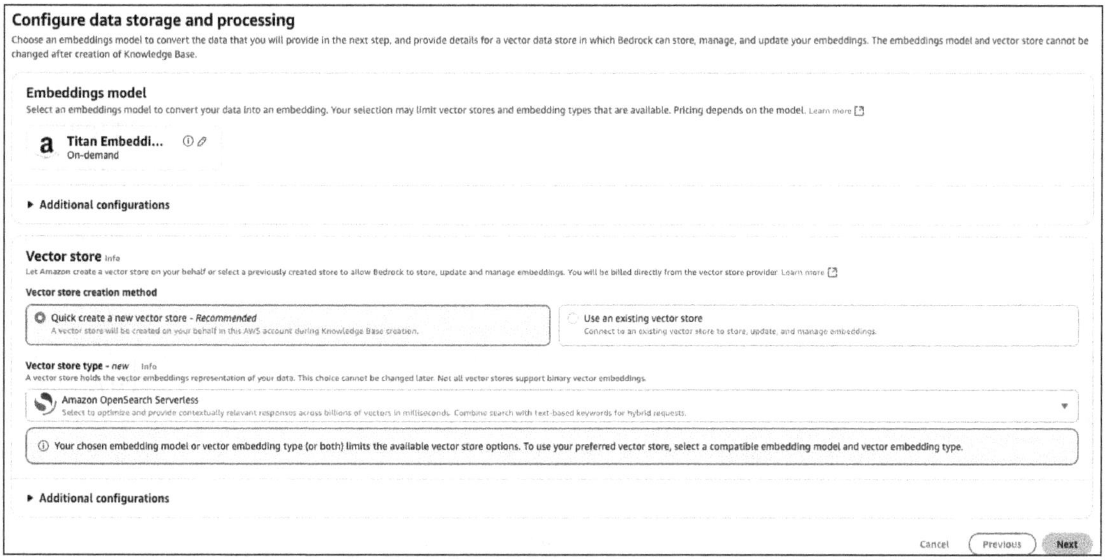

Figure 5.7: *Configuring embeddings model and vector database*

- Select **Next** to go to review screen.
- Select **Create knowledge base**. It may take few minutes for knowledge base to create.

Syncing knowledge base

Once the knowledge base is created and is in **Available** status, we can sync the data source to ingest the data, convert them into embeddings and ingest it into vector store.

Make sure the S3 bucket for the data source is in the same region as knowledge base and files are in supported formats. After verifying the above conditions, you can select the respect data source, and select **Sync**.

Figure 5.8 shows how you can initiate sync with a data source:

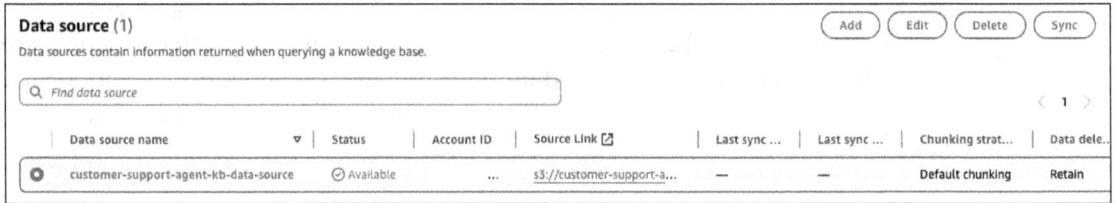

Data source (1)						Add	Edit	Delete	Sync

Data sources contain information returned when querying a knowledge base.

Q Find data source									⟨ 1 ⟩

Data source name ▽	Status	Account ID	Source Link ↗	Last sync …	Last sync …	Chunking strat…	Data dele..
⊙ customer-support-agent-kb-data-source	⊘ Available	…	s3://customer-support-a…	—	—	Default chunking	Retain

Figure 5.8: Syncing data source

Syncing process can take some time depending on the amount of data you provided. Also, note that you need to re-sync data source each time you add, modify or remove files from the S3 bucket. Syncing is incremental so Bedrock only processes the newly added, modified, or deleted objects since last sync.

Testing knowledge base

Once the knowledge base is setup and synced, you can test its behavior by sending querying and evaluating the responses. You can also modify query configuration, as needed. Knowledge bases provides two APIs, as follows:

- RetrieveAndGenerate
- Retrieve

RetrieveAndGenerate API allows you to query your knowledge base and generate responses from the information it retrieves using the LLM of your choice that is supported/enabled in your AWS account. If you like to create a custom orchestration flow in your application, Retrieve API allows to retrieve information directly from the knowledge base without generating a final response.

AWS Management Console for Amazon Bedrock provides a built-in capability to easily test knowledge bases, as follows:

- Choose the radio button next to the knowledge base you want to test and select **Test knowledge base**. A test window expands from the right.

- If you do not want Bedrock to generate responses and just have it return the retrieved information, you need to turn off **Generate responses**. Otherwise, select a model that will be used to generate responses. For now, leave the **Generate responses** option on, and select **Claude 3 Sonnet**.

Refer to the following figure:

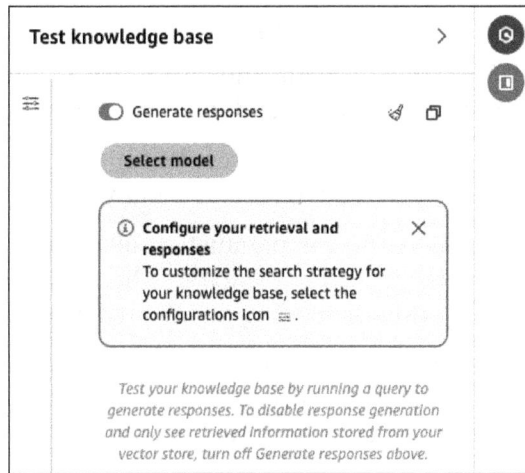

Figure 5.9: Testing knowledge base

- Enter your query in the text box and select **Run**.

- We are using FAQ document that we have provided in the code repository, to ask questions related to orders, returns, and products. You can type in a query like **How can I find out if you have a product in stock?**

- Bedrock will generate responses based on the data sources and provides citation, as shown in *Figure 5.10*:

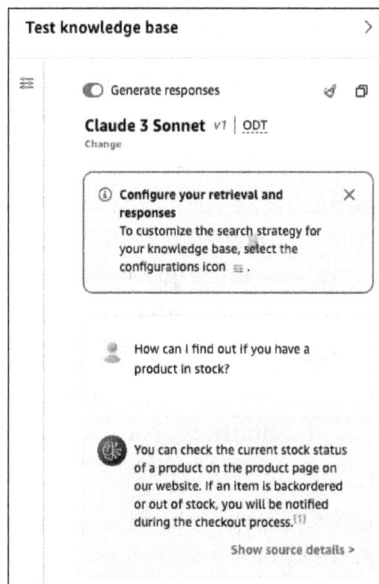

Figure 5.10: Submitting query to knowledge base

You can optionally modify configurations to tune the retrieval and response generation.

- Select the configurations icon to open up configurations.
  - o **Search type**: Specify how your knowledge bases is queried. It supports text search, hybrid search (semantic and text), and semantic search.
  - o **Maximum number of retrieved results**: Specify the maximum number of results to retrieve. By default, it is set to 5 but you can retrieve up to 100 results.
  - o **Inference parameters**: These parameters allow you to constraint or guide the responses generated by the model. The available parameters and their functionality may differ depending on the model you choose.
  - o **Knowledge base prompt template**: This customized prompt will guide the model's response generation process, enabling you to shape the nature of the outputs according to your specific requirements or preferences.
  - o **Guardrails**: You can apply Bedrock Guardrails to provide consistent and safe **user experience (UX)**.

We have also provided how you can manage and use Amazon Bedrock Knowledge Bases using API in the Jupyter Notebook **Example52.ipynb** in the code repository.

Best practices for using knowledge bases

In this chapter, we explored implementation of RAG with Amazon Bedrock using capabilities of knowledge bases.

The following are some tips and key best practices for using knowledge bases:

- **Curate high-quality data sources**: Ensure that the data sources used to populate the knowledge base are comprehensive, accurate, well-organized, and regularly updated to maintain relevance and quality of responses.

- **Effective data pre-processing**: Implement proper data pre-processing techniques, such as splitting documents into manageable chunks, choosing appropriate embedding model, converting chunks into embeddings, and creating a vector index with document mappings, to enable efficient retrieval with knowledge bases.

- **Seamless integration with generative models**: Ensure smooth integration between the knowledge bases retrieval capabilities and the generative model using RetrieveAndGenerate API, maintaining context relevance and producing natural, coherent responses based on the retrieved information.

- **Implement feedback loops**: Incorporate mechanisms for continuous learning and improvement, such as user feedback and automated retraining processes, to refine the knowledge bases; accuracy and relevance over time.

- **Evaluate your RAG pipeline**: Amazon Bedrock Knowledge Bases now supports RAG evaluation (preview) to evaluate your RAG applications. This capability allows you to assess either information retrieval or the retrieval plus content generation using LLM-as-a-judge technology, providing metrics such as context relevance, coverage, correctness, completeness, faithfulness, harmfulness, answer refusal, and stereotyping. You can compare across evaluation jobs to optimize your knowledge bases settings and content generating models.

- **Plan for scalability**: Design the knowledge bases architecture to handle increasing data volumes, user loads, and computational requirements, leveraging techniques such as caching, as needed.

- **Implement responsible AI**: Establish strict protocols for data privacy, security, and compliance with data protection laws and AI ethics regulations. Conduct regular audits and make necessary adjustments to the system. Amazon Bedrock Knowledge Bases lets you configure guardrails to instrument safeguards customized to your RAG application requirements and responsible AI policies, leading to a better end UX.

- **Optimize UX**: Develop intuitive and accessible UIs, ensuring clear and understandable responses from the knowledge bases-powered application. Prioritize response time and consider multimodal capabilities for enhanced engagement. Knowledge bases recently introduced the Rerank API to improve the accuracy of RAG applications by reordering retrieved documents based on their relevance to the user query. This is a key feature that rank a set of retrieved documents based on their relevance to user's query, helping to prioritize the most relevant content to be passed to the FM for response generation. Knowledge bases also now allows you to configure inference parameters to have greater control over personalizing the responses generated by a foundation model.

- **Continuous monitoring and maintenance**: Implement tools and procedures for continuously monitoring the output from knowledge bases, tracking metrics such as accuracy, relevance, and potential biases. Amazon Bedrock Knowledge Bases now supports observability logs, offering log delivery choice through CloudWatch, S3 buckets, and Firehose streams. This capability provides enhanced visibility and timely insights into the execution of knowledge ingestion steps.

Conclusion

In conclusion, Amazon Bedrock Knowledge Bases provide a powerful and streamlined solution for implementing RAG in GenAI applications. By abstracting away much of the complexity involved in data ingestion, embedding, and retrieval, knowledge bases enable developers to efficiently leverage external data sources to augment LLM outputs with contextually relevant information. As we have explored, setting up and managing knowledge bases is a straightforward process. However, to fully harness their potential, it is crucial to follow best practices such as curating high-quality data, optimizing retrieval performance, implementing responsible AI principles, and prioritizing an exceptional UX. With the right approaches, knowledge bases can accelerate development timelines, reduce costs, and unlock new possibilities for building sophisticated, data-driven GenAI applications that provide comprehensive and tailored responses to users' needs.

In the next chapter, we will discuss how to execute multi-step tasks using Amazon Bedrock Agents.

Points to remember

- Knowledge bases simplify the implementation of RAG by providing a managed solution for ingesting data, converting it into embeddings, and storing it in a vector store.

- The Chat with your document feature allows you to upload a document and query it without setting up a full knowledge base, making it easy to explore and extract insights from unstructured data.

- When creating a knowledge base, carefully curate and pre-process your data sources to ensure high-quality and relevant responses.

- Leverage the RetrieveAndGenerate API to query your knowledge base and generate responses using a language model, or use the Retrieve API to create custom orchestration flows.

- Implement best practices such as effective data pre-processing, seamless integration with generative models, feedback loops for continuous learning, scalability planning, responsible AI practices, optimized UX, and continuous monitoring and maintenance.

Exercises

1. **Exploring Chat with your document**:
   a. Upload a document of your choice (e.g., a research paper, technical manual, or report) to the Chat with your document feature in the Amazon Bedrock console.
   b. Experiment with different types of queries, such as summarizing the document, asking specific questions, or requesting information on particular topics covered in the document.
   c. Observe how the feature retrieves and presents relevant information from the document, and evaluate the quality and relevance of the responses.

2. **Creating a knowledge bases**:
   a. Using the Amazon Bedrock console or SDK, create a knowledge base with a data source containing a set of documents related to a topic of your choice (e.g., customer support, product manuals, or domain-specific literature).

    b. Configure the knowledge base by selecting an appropriate embedding model and vector store.

    c. Sync the data source to ingest the data and create embeddings in the vector store.

    d. Test the knowledge base by submitting queries and evaluating the responses.

    e. Explore different configurations, such as search types, inference parameters, and prompt templates, to fine-tune the retrieval and response generation.

3. **Exploring the Retrieve API**:

    a. Using the Bedrock SDK or API, create a custom orchestration flow that utilizes the Retrieve API to query your knowledge base and retrieve relevant information.

    b. Implement additional processing or filtering steps on the retrieved results before generating a final response.

4. **Implementing structured data retrieval**:

    a. Explore how to use the new structured data retrieval capability to query structured data sources using natural language.

    b. Observe how the knowledge bases translates the query into SQL and retrieves the data.

5. **Improve accuracy with the Rerank API**:

    a. Learn how to use the Rerank API to improve the relevance of responses in RAG applications.

    b. Check the accuracy and relevance of the generated responses.

    c. Experiment with different queries to understand the capabilities and limitations of the Rerank API.

6. **Evaluating RAG applications**:

    a. Learn how to use the RAG evaluation capability to assess your RAG applications.

    b. Check the evaluation metrics such as context relevance, coverage, correctness, completeness, faithfulness, harmfulness, answer refusal, and stereotyping.

    c. Use the insights gained from the evaluation to improve your RAG applications.

Join our Discord space

Join our Discord workspace for latest updates, offers, tech happenings around the world, new releases, and sessions with the authors:

https://discord.bpbonline.com

CHAPTER 6

Using Bedrock's Managed Agents

Introduction

In the previous chapter, we explored Amazon Bedrock Knowledge Bases for building **generative AI (GenAI)** applications. Now, we will dive into Bedrock's orchestration capabilities through its Managed agents.

Imagine having intelligent virtual assistants that can seamlessly coordinate complex workflows and automate intricate processes. Amazon Bedrock Agents leverage **foundation models (FMs)** to understand requests, break them into actionable steps, and execute those steps by integrating with various systems and data sources.

This section will provide a deep understanding of agents' architecture and components. You will learn how to create, configure, and customize Amazon Bedrock Agents to meet your specific needs. We will also cover techniques for monitoring and debugging agents to ensure accurate, context-aware responses.

We will also cover a hands-on example of a customer support agent for an e-commerce platform. This agent will assist users with placing orders, cancelling orders, tracking shipments, and providing product information—all while integrating with backend systems and knowledge bases.

By the end, you will be equipped to effectively use managed Amazon Bedrock Agents, enabling you to build GenAI applications that streamline processes, automate tasks, and deliver innovative **user experiences (UXs)**.

Structure

The chapter covers the following topics:

- Amazon Bedrock Agents
- Integrating with knowledge bases
- Optimizing agent performance
- Recent enhancements

Objectives

By the end of this chapter, you will have a firm grasp of Amazon Bedrock Agents, including their architecture, components, and workflow. You will learn how to create and configure agents through both the Amazon Bedrock console and AWS **software development kit** (**SDK**), building a functional customer support agent capable of handling order management, product inquiries, and customer service tasks. The chapter will equip you with skills to integrate knowledge bases with your Bedrock Agents, enhancing their capabilities with domain-specific information, and implement action groups, enabling agents to interact with backend systems and **application programming interfaces** (**APIs**). You will gain proficiency in debugging and troubleshooting using trace functionality to understand agent reasoning, optimizing performance through advanced configurations, and deploying to production using aliases and versions for safe updates. Additionally, you will learn to implement guardrails ensuring responsible AI behavior, maintain conversational context across interactions using session attributes, and scale your agents efficiently with Provisioned Throughput. This comprehensive understanding will enable you to build sophisticated GenAI applications that automate complex workflows, provide intelligent assistance, and integrate seamlessly with existing systems and data sources.

Amazon Bedrock Agents

In *Chapter 2, Getting Started with Amazon Bedrock*, we introduced the concept of Amazon Bedrock Agents, which extends the capabilities of FMs by enabling them to understand user requests, break down complex tasks into multiple steps, gather additional information through conversations, and execute actions to fulfill the requested task.

Agents in Bedrock are powerful orchestrators that can automate complex workflows by integrating with various components, including external systems, APIs, and knowledge bases. Under the hood, they leverage the reasoning abilities of FMs to create a plan for the user's request, breaking it down into a sequence of actions. Then, Bedrock Agents execute this plan by calling the appropriate APIs and accessing relevant knowledge sources.

The following is what we will discuss in the chapter:

- **Agent architecture and components**: We will uncover the underlying architecture of Amazon Bedrock Agents and the different components involved in the orchestration process, giving you a holistic understanding of how agents work behind the scenes.

- **Agent creation and configuration**: You will get step-by-step guidance on creating and configuring agents using the Bedrock console and AWS SDK. We will cover customizing agent behavior, defining prompts, and setting up integrations, empowering you to tailor agents to your specific requirements.

- **Integrating with knowledge bases**: Discover how to leverage the knowledge bases to augment agent responses and provide accurate, context-aware information to end-users, ensuring your agents have access to the most up-to-date and relevant data.

- **Monitoring and debugging agents**: We will explore techniques for monitoring agent performance, understanding the rationale and reasoning employed by agents, and debugging issues that may arise during execution, equipping you with the tools to maintain and troubleshoot your agents effectively.

This section will provide you with the technical knowledge and practical skills to unlock the capabilities of Amazon Bedrock Agents effectively. Through code samples, real-world examples, and best practices, you will gain the ability to build, deploy, and manage intelligent agents tailored to your specific needs and requirements.

Customer support agent example

Throughout this section, we will use an example of a customer service agent for an e-commerce platform. This agent can help users place orders, track orders and shipments, and provide product related information. By integrating with backend order management systems, the agent can access real-time data, enhancing its ability to assist users effectively:

- **Placing an order**: The agent collects necessary details such as product name, quantity, shipping address, and payment method from the user. It then processes the order through backend APIs and confirms the order with the user.

- **Tracking orders**: The agent retrieves order status and tracking information from the database and informs the user about the current status of their shipment.

- **Providing product information**: The agent queries the knowledge base to provide detailed product descriptions, specifications, and availability.

This practical example will allow us to explore the various aspects of Amazon Bedrock Agents in a real-world scenario.

Architecture and components of Amazon Bedrock Agents

At the heart of Amazon Bedrock Agents lies an intricate architecture comprising several key components. The key elements that drive the agent capabilities are as follows:

- **FMs**: FMs are at the core of Amazon Bedrock Agents. These models interpret user input, generate responses, and guide the agent's actions. Bedrock supports a variety of FMs from leading AI providers, allowing developers to choose the best model for their specific use case.

- **Agent instructions**: Agent instructions define what the agent is designed to do. They guide the FM on how to interpret user inputs and respond appropriately. Instructions can be customized to suit specific use cases, style and tone ensuring the agent behaves as intended throughout its orchestration process.

- **Action groups**: Action groups are collections of actions that enable an agent to perform tasks autonomously. These groups can be defined using two primary approaches: OpenAPI schemas and function detail schemas. OpenAPI schemas are ideal for existing REST APIs and standardized service integrations, while function details offer a more direct approach for implementing actions. Each approach defines the parameters, API operations, and necessary specifications for task execution. Action groups typically integrate with AWS Lambda functions, which contain the underlying business logic for performing these actions. In this chapter, we will focus on function details approach due to its simplicity.

- **Knowledge bases**: Knowledge bases store additional information that agents can query to enhance their responses. By integrating with knowledge bases, agents can provide more accurate and contextually relevant information to users.

- **Prompt templates**: Prompt templates are the blueprints for generating the prompts that are sent to the FMs. They can be customized to improve the agent's accuracy and performance. Prompt templates are used during various stages, including pre-processing, orchestration, and post-processing, to ensure the agent responds correctly to user inputs.

Agent workflow

We can broadly categorize the process of developing and deploying Amazon Bedrock Agents into two main phases, that is, build-time and runtime, as follows:

- **Build-time or setup**: This involves configuring and integrating all the components that make up the agent, such as FMs, instructions, action groups, knowledge base, and prompt templates. This phase prepares the agent for deployment.

- **Runtime or execution**: This refers to when the agent is invoked and run. The runtime phase consists of three steps:

    1. **Pre-processing**: The agent prepares and validates the user's input before processing it further.

    2. **Orchestration**: The core stage where the agent interprets the input, queries knowledge sources, performs actions, and generates responses.

    3. **Post-processing**: The agent formats and refines the response to ensure it is user-friendly and contextually appropriate.

While most users interact with the orchestration stage, the ability to customize allows handling complex scenarios.

Figure 6.1 illustrates the high-level workflow of Amazon Bedrock Agents:

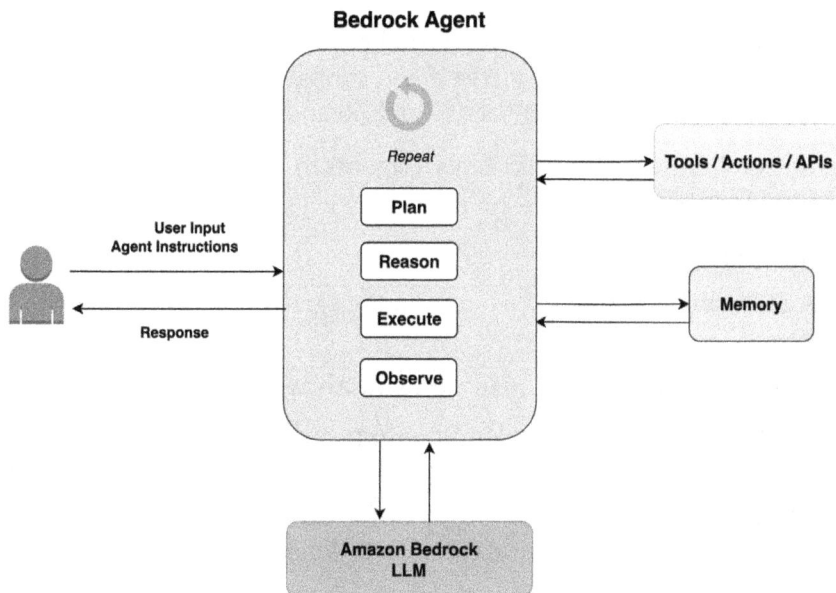

Figure 6.1: *High-level flow for Amazon Bedrock Agents*

The following steps detail how users, agents, and FMs interact:

1. The user provides an input or query to the Bedrock Agents.

2. FMs in Bedrock receive the user's input from the agent, along with any relevant context, instructions, and available actions or tools provided by the agent.

3. FMs break down the input into a sequence of steps or tasks required to generate a final response.

4. For each step, the FM executes actions like making API calls or querying knowledge bases to gather pertinent information. It observes the results from these actions.

5. Based on the observed results, the FM plans the next action to take. This cycle of acting, observing, and replanning continues until the FM has enough information to produce a comprehensive final answer.

6. FM outputs this final answer, which is then returned to the user via the Bedrock Agent.

So, in essence, the user provides the initial input or query, while the agent orchestrates the FM by providing context, instructions, and available tools. FM then breaks down the request, iteratively gathers relevant information, and builds the final response.

Agent creation and configuration using Bedrock console

We can create an agent using Amazon Bedrock through the AWS Management Console, SDK like the AWS SDK for Python (Boto3), APIs or **infrastructure as code (IaC)** tool such as AWS CloudFormation.

Let us start by creating agents using the Amazon Bedrock console. We will explore using the web-based console interface to visually create and configure agents. Later in the section, we will cover programmatic agent creation, configuration and invocation using the Boto3.

Navigate to **Amazon Bedrock | Builder tools | agents** in the AWS Management Console. Then, click **Create Agent**.

- **Configure the agent**:
    - **Agent name**: Let us enter a name for the agent, for example, `customer-support-agent`.
    - **Agent description**: Optionally, provide a brief description of the agent's purpose.
    - **Agent resource role**: Create or select an existing IAM service role with the necessary permissions. For experiments, recommend you to use the option **Create and use a new service role**.
    - **Foundational model**: Select the foundational model, such as **Anthropic Claude 3.5 Sonnet v2** or the latest.
    - **Instructions**: Provide detailed and clear instructions for the agent, as follows:

        ```
        You are a friendly, helpful, polite and knowledgeable customer
        support agent. Your goal is to assist customers with inquiries
        related to order tracking and cancel order, process return and
        refunds, and provide product information in succinct manner. If
        you do not have the required information to help with customer
        questions, ask it gently.
        ```

The following figure illustrates the Agent builder interface in Amazon Bedrock:

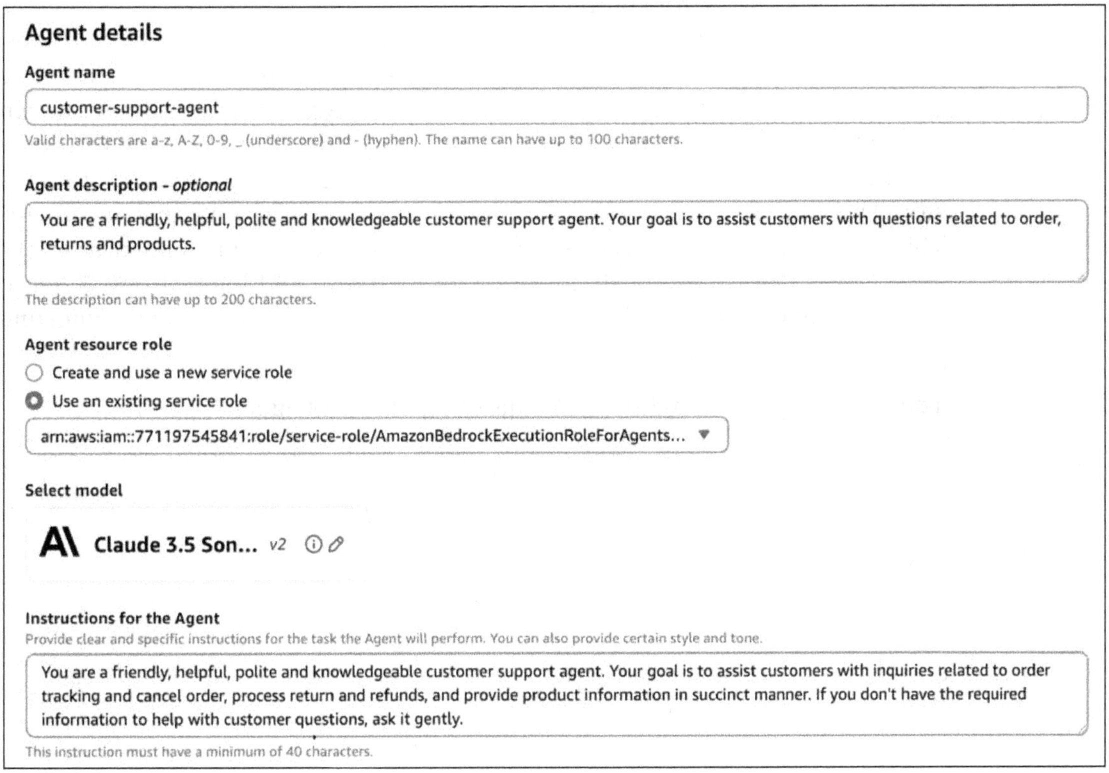

Agent details

Agent name

customer-support-agent

Valid characters are a-z, A-Z, 0-9, _ (underscore) and - (hyphen). The name can have up to 100 characters.

Agent description - *optional*

You are a friendly, helpful, polite and knowledgeable customer support agent. Your goal is to assist customers with questions related to order, returns and products.

The description can have up to 200 characters.

Agent resource role

○ Create and use a new service role

● Use an existing service role

arn:aws:iam::771197545841:role/service-role/AmazonBedrockExecutionRoleForAgents... ▼

Select model

A\\ Claude 3.5 Son... *v2* ⓘ 𝄑

Instructions for the Agent
Provide clear and specific instructions for the task the Agent will perform. You can also provide certain style and tone.

You are a friendly, helpful, polite and knowledgeable customer support agent. Your goal is to assist customers with inquiries related to order tracking and cancel order, process return and refunds, and provide product information in succinct manner. If you don't have the required information to help with customer questions, ask it gently.

This instruction must have a minimum of 40 characters.

Figure 6.2: Create Amazon Bedrock Agents

- o **Action groups**: Action groups define specific action or tasks the agents can perform, such as tracking order or initiating returns. We will go in details in next section on creating two actions groups: **order-action-group** and **retrun-refund-action-group**.

The following figure refers to **Action groups** for Amazon Bedrock Agents:

Action groups (2) Info

Q *Find action groups*

Delete | Add

1 ⚙

Name	Description	State	Last updated
order-action-group	Order details, tracking and cancellation action group.	⊘ Enabled	May 12, 2025, 11:31 (UTC-05:00)
return-refund-action-group	Process returns and refund action group	⊘ Enabled	May 12, 2025, 11:31 (UTC-05:00)

Figure 6.3: Create action group for Amazon Bedrock Agents

- o **Memory**: Memory in Bedrock Agents enables persistence of conversation summaries for each user, allowing agents to maintain awareness of previous interactions and adapt to user preferences over time. This capability is particularly valuable for complex workflows like flight bookings, where agents can learn and apply user preferences for seats and meals from past interactions. In enterprise scenarios, agents can process tasks like customer feedback more efficiently by maintaining awareness of ongoing interactions without custom integrations. The system uses unique memory identifiers to ensure secure separation between users' conversation histories. You can access or clear the stored memory sessions at any time to manage the agent's contextual awareness. This summary-based approach enables agents to provide personalized, adaptive experiences that continuously improve through repeated interactions. Refer to Amazon Bedrock user guide for more details: **https://docs.aws.amazon.com/ bedrock/latest/userguide**

The following figure highlights **Memory** capability of agents:

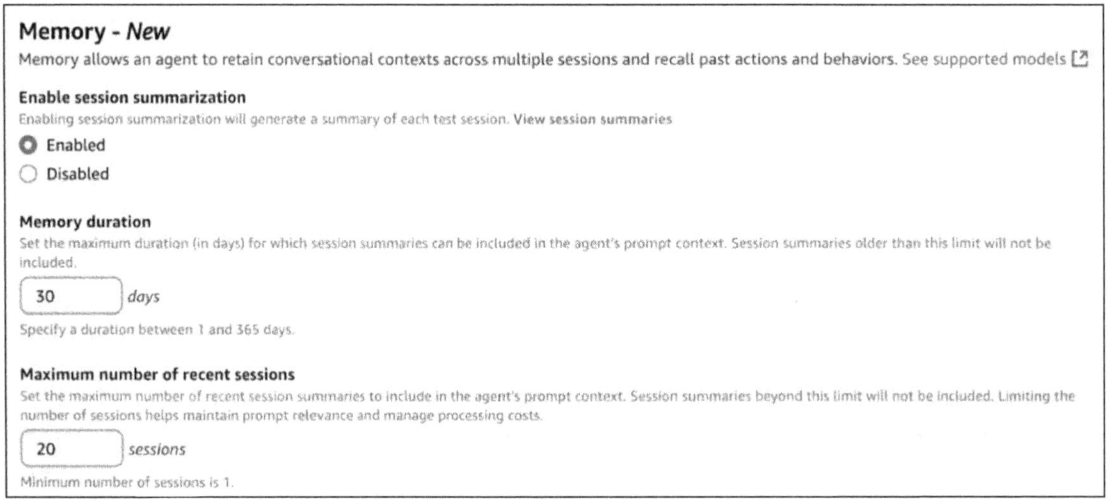

Memory - *New*

Memory allows an agent to retain conversational contexts across multiple sessions and recall past actions and behaviors. See supported models ⤢

Enable session summarization

Enabling session summarization will generate a summary of each test session. View session summaries

⦿ Enabled

◯ Disabled

Memory duration

Set the maximum duration (in days) for which session summaries can be included in the agent's prompt context. Session summaries older than this limit will not be included.

| 30 | *days* |

Specify a duration between 1 and 365 days.

Maximum number of recent sessions

Set the maximum number of recent session summaries to include in the agent's prompt context. Session summaries beyond this limit will not be included. Limiting the number of sessions helps maintain prompt relevance and manage processing costs.

| 20 | *sessions* |

Minimum number of sessions is 1.

Figure 6.4: *Memory for Amazon Bedrock Agents*

○ **Knowledge bases**: Knowledge bases serve as foundational information repositories for Bedrock Agents, providing them with domain-specific knowledge and enterprise data. By integrating with various data sources, including documents, FAQs, and structured databases, agents can access and leverage this information to provide accurate and relevant responses. knowledge bases can be updated dynamically and support multiple formats, enabling agents to maintain current and comprehensive information while supporting vector search capabilities for efficient information retrieval. We will add the knowledge base to the **customer-support-agent-kb** later in this chapter.

The following figure refers to the **Knowledge Bases** for Amazon Bedrock Agents:

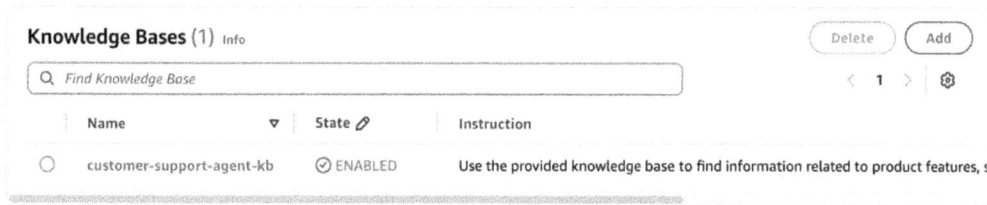

Figure 6.5: Knowledge bases for Amazon Bedrock Agents

○ **Guardrail details**: Guardrails in Bedrock Agents establish boundaries and controls for agent behavior, ensuring responses align with desired policies and compliance requirements of your organization. These safety mechanisms include content filtering, response validation, and behavioral constraints that help maintain appropriate, secure, and reliable agent interactions. Guardrails can be configured to prevent harmful content, maintain professional tone, and ensure responses adhere to specific business rules or regulatory requirements. We will add the guardrails to the **customer-support-agent-kb** later in this chapter.

○ **Orchestration strategy**: Orchestration strategy defines how Bedrock Agents manage workflow execution and task coordination. For basic implementations, default settings are typically sufficient, while advanced use cases may require customized prompts and workflow configurations.

The following figure highlights the **Orchestration strategy** for Amazon Bedrock Agents:

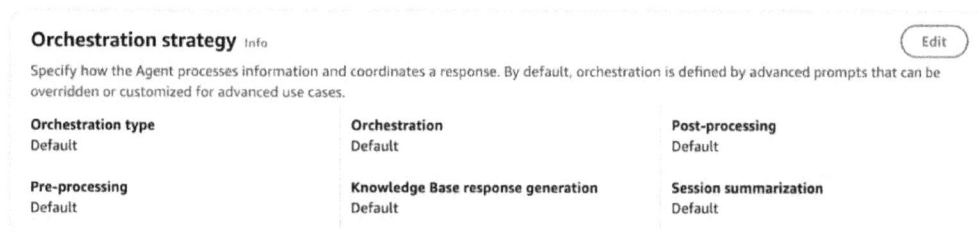

Figure 6.6: Orchestration strategy for Amazon Bedrock Agents

○ **Multi-agent collaboration**: Multi-agent collaboration in Bedrock enables multiple specialized agents to work together, sharing information and coordinating actions to solve complex problems. This framework allows agents with different capabilities to communicate, delegate tasks, and combine their expertise for comprehensive solution delivery. The collaboration model supports both sequential and parallel processing patterns, with built-in mechanisms for task distribution, result aggregation, and inter-agent communication.

Refer to the following figure on how to enable **Multi-agent collaboration** in Amazon Bedrock:

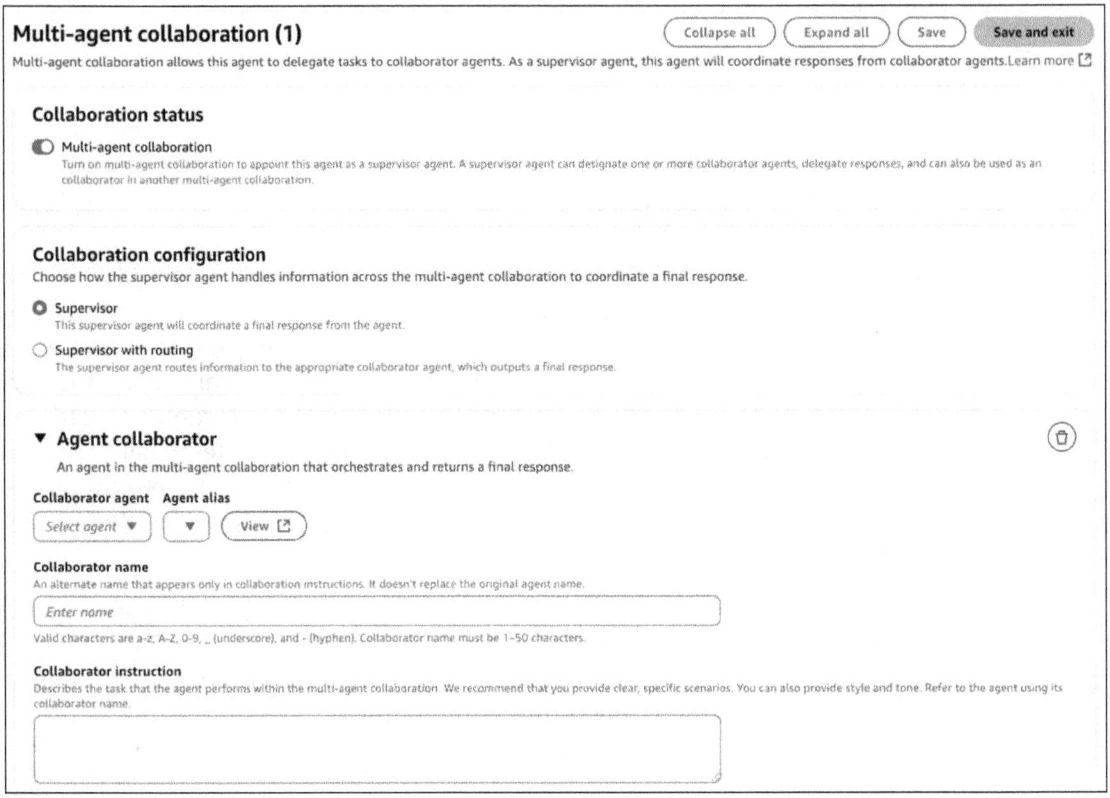

Figure 6.7: Multi-agent collaboration for Amazon Bedrock Agents

Refer to Amazon Bedrock user guide for more details at: **https://docs.aws.amazon.com/bedrock/latest/userguide**

Creating and configurating action groups

Now, let us follow the steps to create the action groups `order-action-group` and `return-refund-action-group`, as we discussed earlier for `customer-support-agent-kb`.

1. **Add action groups**:

    a. Let us now create a new action group `order-action-group`, which can handle order details, tracking and order cancellation.

    b. Click **Add**, and choose the action group type of **Define with function details**.

    The following figure shows the interface for creating an action group in the Amazon Bedrock console:

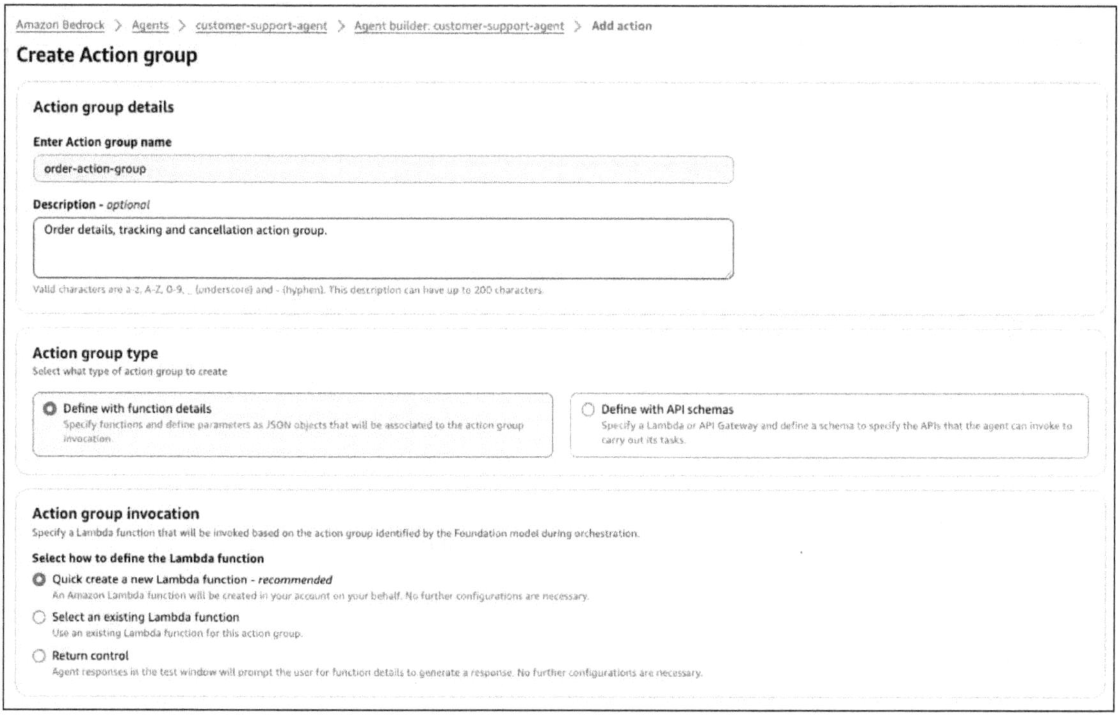

Figure 6.8: Create Action group for Amazon Bedrock Agents

2. **Select Quickly create a new Lambda function option**:

   a. This option will create a dummy Lambda function with some skeleton code and automatically associate that function with **order-action-group** for you.

3. **Configuring functions in the action group**:

   You can add up to three functions per action group. If you have more than three, you can create a new action group.

   Let us add the first function, as follows:

   a. **Name**: `retrieve-order-tracking-info`.

   b. **Description (optional)**: Use this function to retrieve and track order details.

   c. **Parameters**: Parameters are input which FM will automatically extract from the user entered text and pass to the function.

   d. Let us create a parameter **order_id** and mark it of **Type** as **string** and **Required** as **True**.

   The following figure illustrates how to create parameters for the **Action group function**, where we are defining an **order_id** parameter as a required string input:

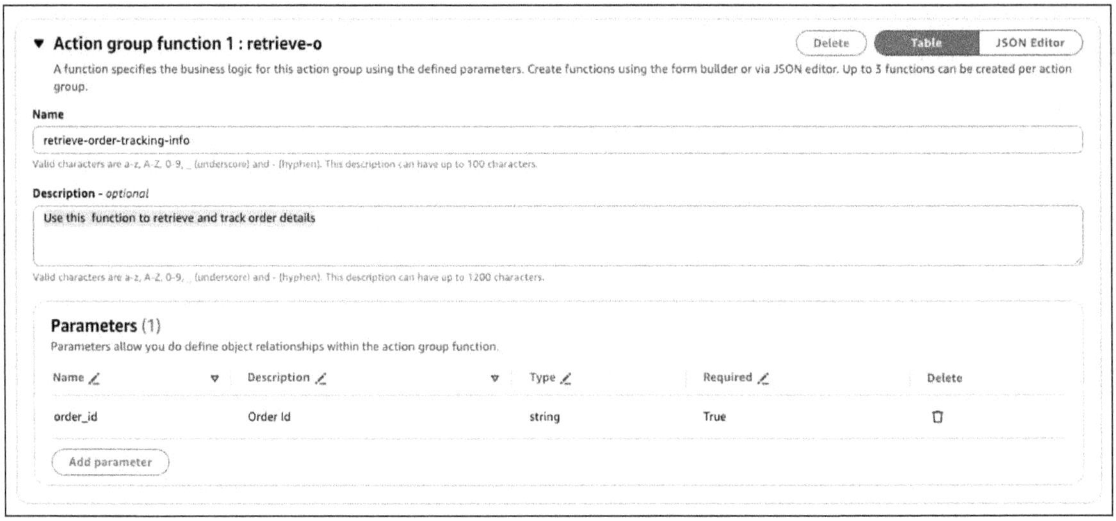

Figure 6.9: Create action group functions for Amazon Bedrock Agents

Alternatively, you can also use **JSON Editor** to define parameters. Refer to the following figure:

Figure 6.10: Create action group functions using JSON Editor for Amazon Bedrock Agents

Now, let us create another function called **cancel-order** with **order_id** parameter. Refer to the following figure:

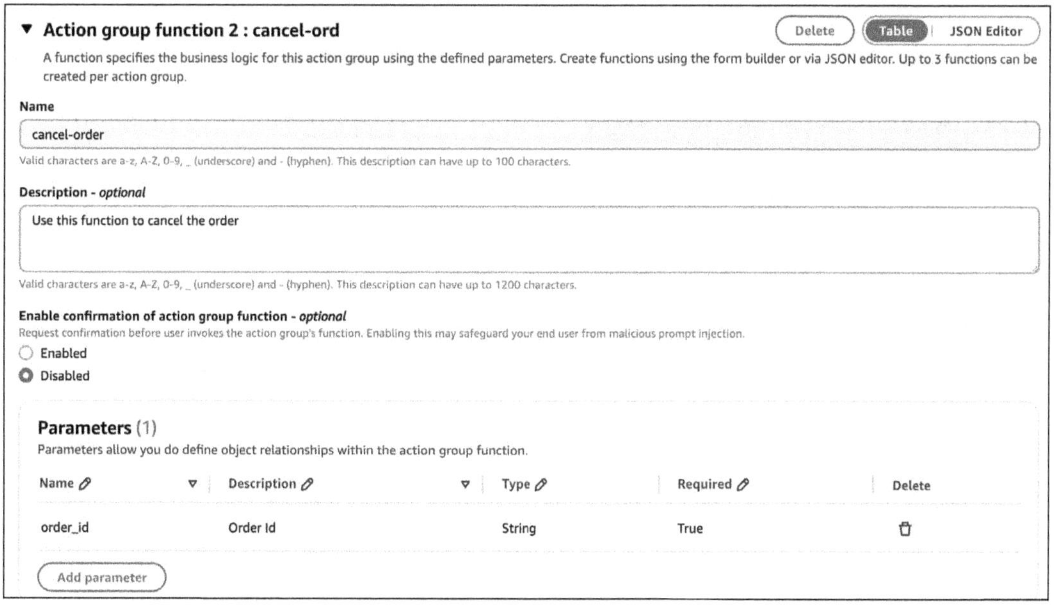

▼ **Action group function 2 : cancel-ord**   Delete   Table | JSON Editor

A function specifies the business logic for this action group using the defined parameters. Create functions using the form builder or via JSON editor. Up to 3 functions can be created per action group.

Name

cancel-order

Valid characters are a-z, A-Z, 0-9, _ (underscore) and - (hyphen). This description can have up to 100 characters.

Description - *optional*

Use this function to cancel the order

Valid characters are a-z, A-Z, 0-9, _ (underscore) and - (hyphen). This description can have up to 1200 characters.

Enable confirmation of action group function - *optional*
Request confirmation before user invokes the action group's function. Enabling this may safeguard your end user from malicious prompt injection.
○ Enabled
◉ Disabled

Parameters (1)
Parameters allow you do define object relationships within the action group function.

Name 🖉	▽	Description 🖉	▽	Type 🖉	Required 🖉	Delete
order_id		Order Id		String	True	🗑

Add parameter

Figure 6.11: *Create cancel-order action group functions for Amazon Bedrock Agents*

We will keep **Action status** as **Enable** for our action group and click **Save and exit**:

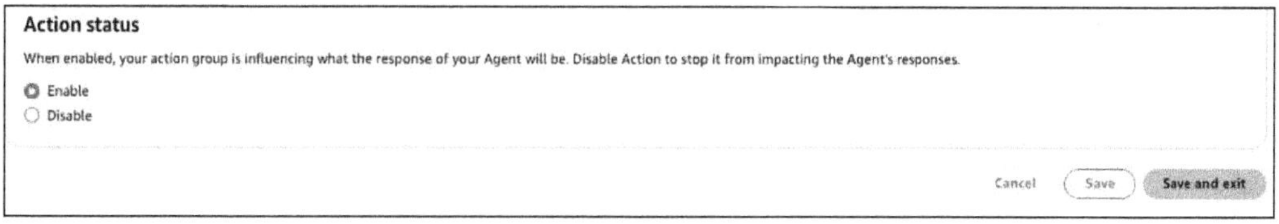

Action status

When enabled, your action group is influencing what the response of your Agent will be. Disable Action to stop it from impacting the Agent's responses.
◉ Enable
○ Disable

Cancel   Save   **Save and exit**

Figure 6.12: *Action status for Amazon Bedrock Agents*

4. **Lambda functions for the action group**:

Next, let us look at the Lambda functions created by the **order-action-group**. Navigate to **Amazon Lambda | Functions**, you should see two Lambda functions listed, similar to the following:

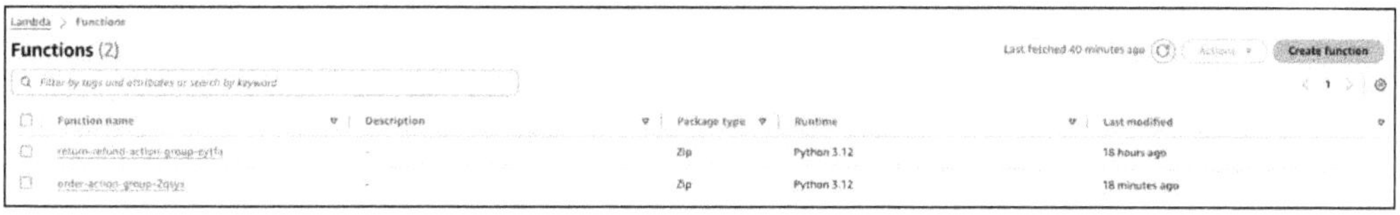

Lambda › Functions
Functions (2)   Last fetched 40 minutes ago Actions ▾ **Create function**

Q *Filter by tags and attributes or search by keyword*   < 1 > ⊚

	Function name	▽	Description	▽	Package type ▽	Runtime	▽	Last modified	▽
☐	return-refund-action-group-zytfs		-		Zip	Python 3.12		18 hours ago	
☐	order-action-group-2qsys		-		Zip	Python 3.12		18 minutes ago	

Figure 6.13: *Lambda functions, actions for the action groups*

Click on the Lambda function named **order-action-group-xxxxx**. In the function code, you will find a placeholder or dummy code similar to *Figure 6.14*, which was automatically generated when creating the action group:

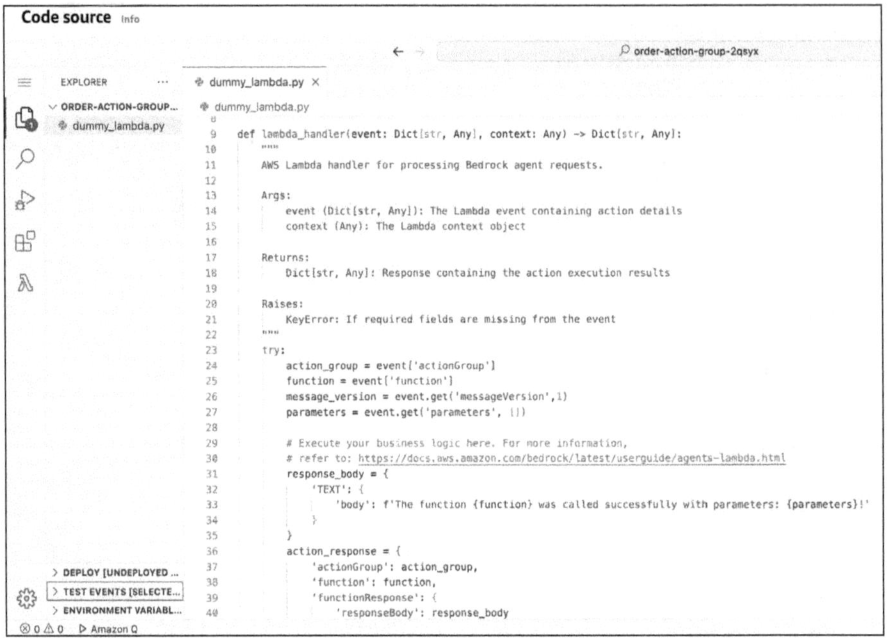

Figure 6.14: Lambda functions (actions) for the action groups

We will now replace the placeholder code with our custom code to enable the agent to look up order details, track orders, and cancel orders. Refer to the following figure:

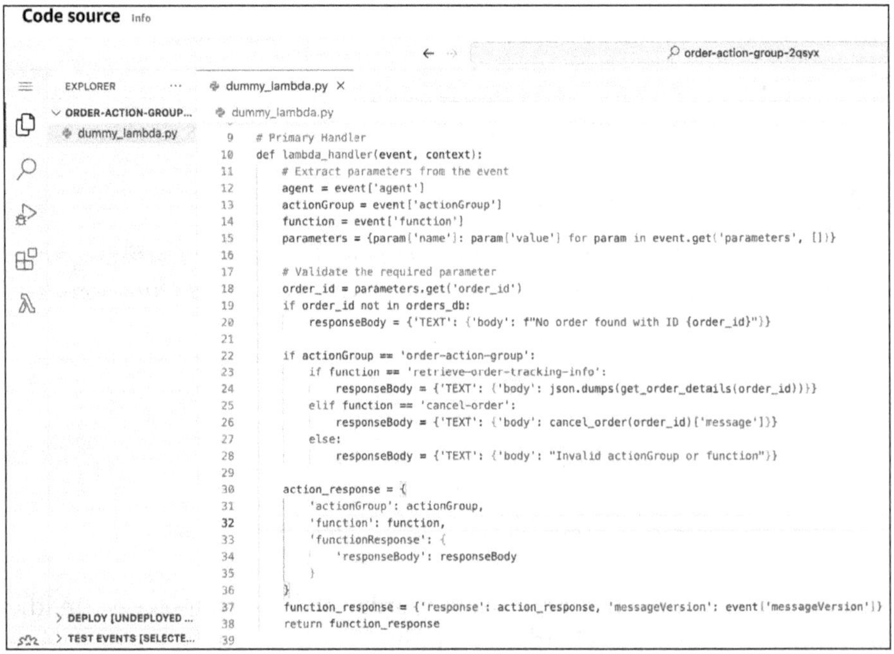

Figure 6.15: Lambda function for action group for Amazon Bedrock Agents

The complete Lambda function code for the **order-action-group** is available in the book's GitHub repository.

In this example, we have simulated an orders database. However, in a real-world scenario, you would query your actual database, external systems, or APIs and return that data as the response from the Lambda function. This information will be used by the FM specified in the agent configuration to provide context and improve the agent's response.

Testing of agents

We have created a customer support agent, added a new action group named **order-action-group**, and associated two functions: `retrieve-order-tracking-info` and `cancel-order` with that action group. Now, let us test if a customer support agent can utilize these functions to lookup additional context and respond to the user's questions.

Click **Test** in the **Amazon Bedrock | agents** console.

> **Note:** **If you made any changes in the agent or its action group configuration, you might need to click on prepare to ensure the changes are reflected in the working draft of the agent.**

The following figure shows the customer support agent interface in the testing environment, where we can interact with the agent by entering queries in the chat panel:

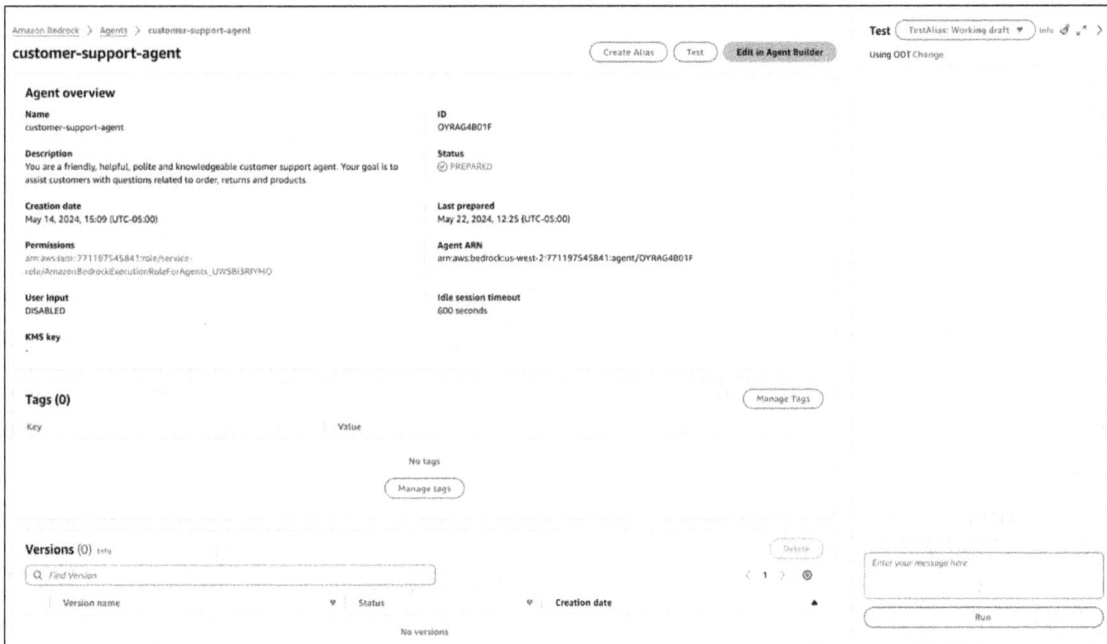

Figure 6.16: Customer support agent in Amazon Bedrock

Next, let us start testing the agent by asking questions. Begin with a simple question like **How can you help me?** You should see a response similar to that shown in the following figure:

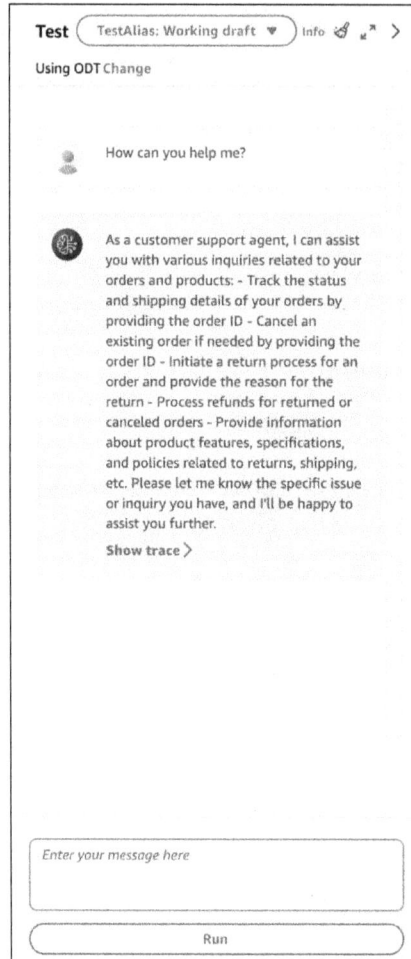

Figure 6.17: Customer support agent in Amazon Bedrock

The agent is utilizing the description we had previously configured, which provides guidance on the agent's purpose, the tasks it can perform, and the style and tone it should use when responding.

After verifying the initial response, we can proceed to ask more specific questions related to order tracking, cancellations, and other tasks. Let us start with questions related to order to see if agent can query the order database to find the order and its details. As you can see, agent is able to ask the users if he does not have the required information to answer the question such as asking for **order id**. We can provide the **order Id ORD11111**. Then, it can use that **order Id** to query the order database as specified in our **order-action-group-xxxxx** Lambda function to pull the order details and tracking information.

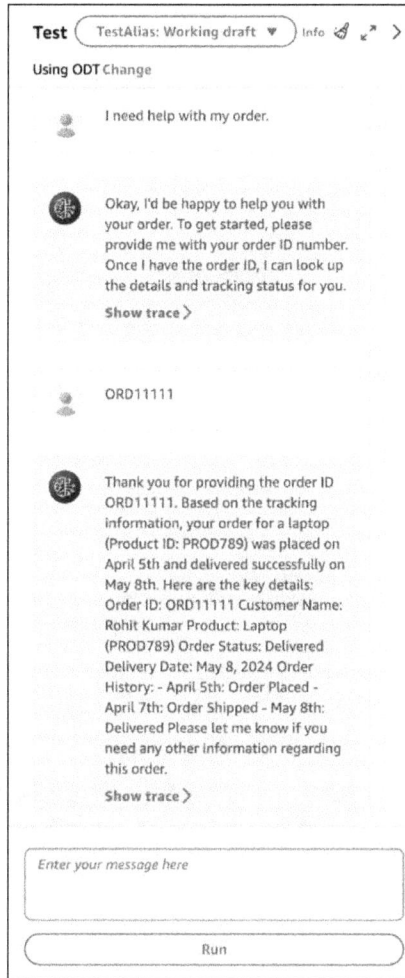

Figure 6.18: Customer support agent in Amazon Bedrock

Let us enhance the **customer-support-agent** by adding a new **return-refund-action-group** to enable processing returns and refunds automatically. You can click on **Edit in Agent builder** button to go back to agent configuration similar to how we did for **order-action-group**. Create a new action group named **return-refund-action-group** and associate the `initiate-return` and `process-refund` Lambda functions with it. Click **Save and exit** to update the agent configuration. With this new action group, the agent can now handle return and refund requests from users. Test it by providing relevant sample inputs and observe if it leverages the **return-refund-action-group** functions appropriately.

The first step in creating our **return-refund-action-group** is configuring the initial function for handling return requests, as follows:

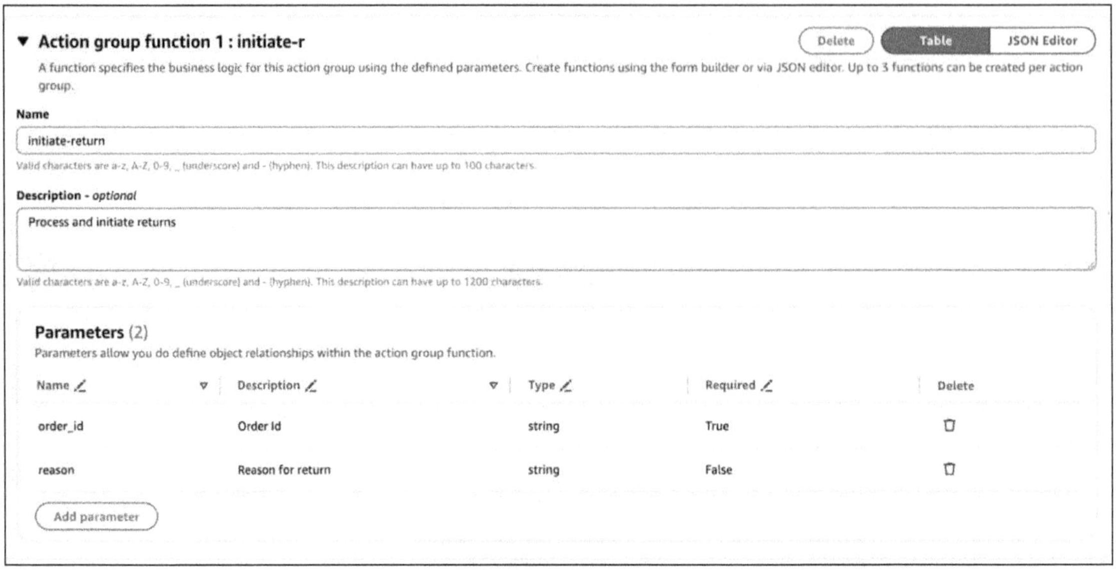

Figure 6.19: *Action group functions for Amazon Bedrock Agents*

When configuring the return-refund functions, it is important to clearly define all required parameters such as **order_id** and **reason**. This ensures FM can extract the necessary information during customer conversations and properly execute the corresponding Lambda functions.

The second function **process-refund** in our **return-refund-action-group** is configured as shown in the following figure, completing our set of actions needed for processing customer returns:

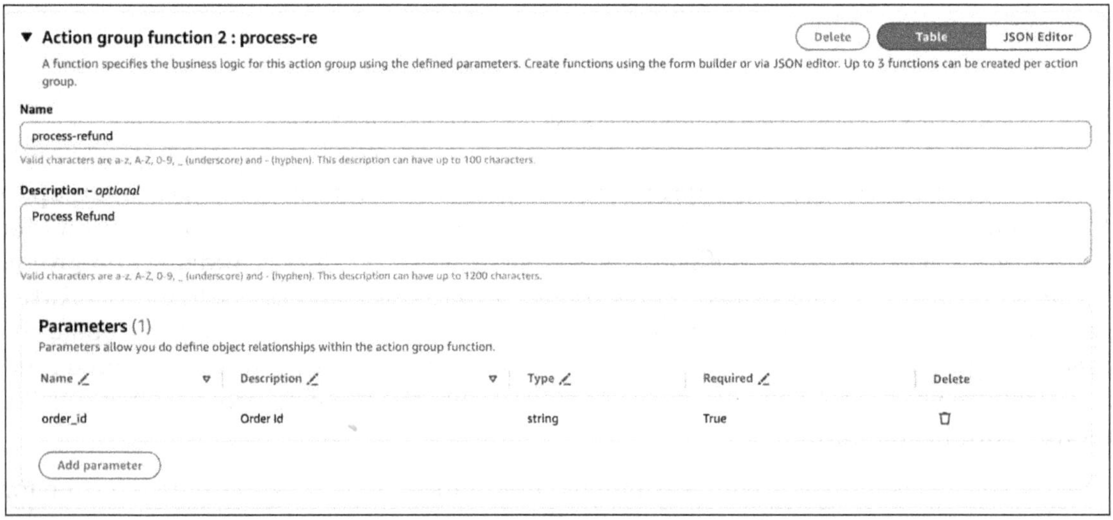

Figure 6.20: *Action group functions for Amazon Bedrock Agents*

Now, click **Prepare** for the **customer-support-agent** to update it with the latest configuration changes. Preparing the agent will reset the **Test Agent** window.

After configuring both functions for **the return-refund-action-group**, we need to prepare the **customer-support-agent** with our updated configuration. Click the **Prepare** button as shown in the following figure to update the agent with these changes. This preparation process will reset the **Test Agent** window, as follows:

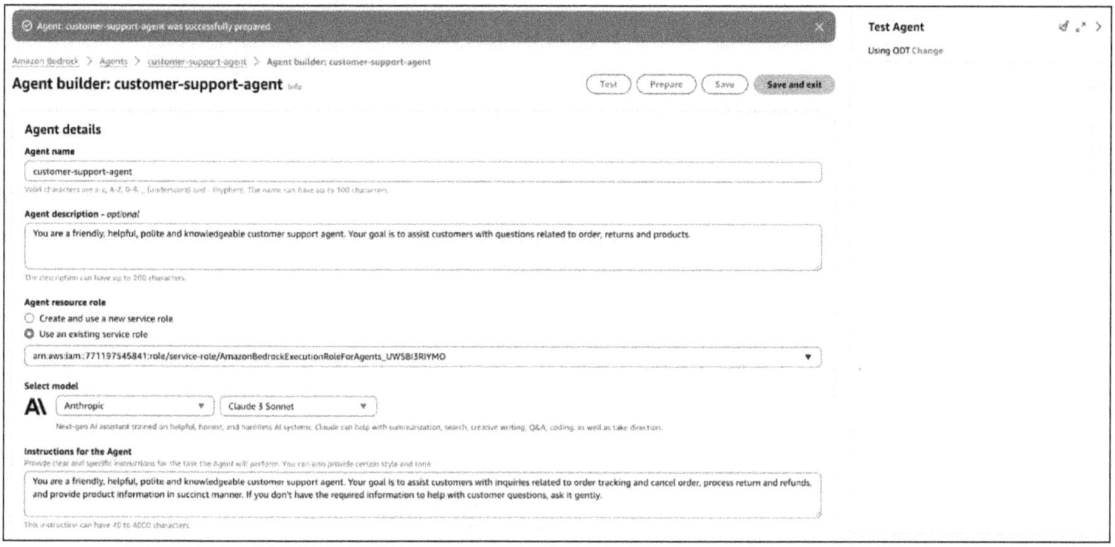

Figure 6.21: Agent builder for Amazon Bedrock Agents

With the latest update, the **customer-support-agent** now has two action groups configured and ready for testing, as displayed in the console view, as follows:

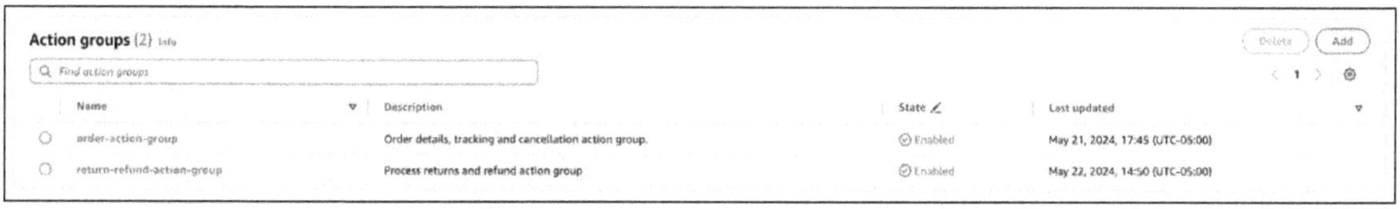

Figure 6.22: Action groups for Amazon Bedrock Agents

Let us test the new capabilities by asking the agent: `Can you help me with a return?` and providing order Id `ORD11111` when prompted.

The agent should be succeed, as follows:

- Retrieve the order details using the **order-action-group**
- Initiate a return for that order using the new **return-refund-action-group**

As you can see, the agent successfully retrieved the order details and initiated return, as follows:

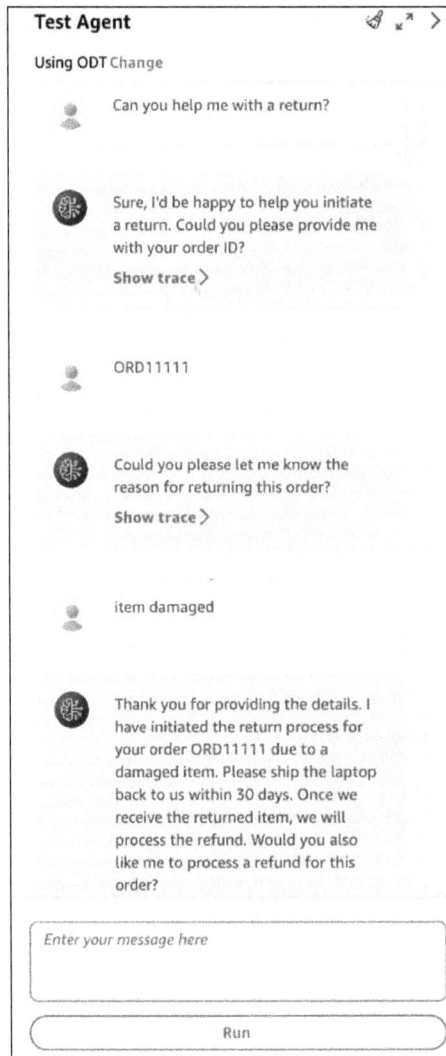

Figure 6.23: Testing customer support agent in Amazon Bedrock

You can further test by asking the agent to process a refund for this order. The agent should leverage the **process-refund** function from the **return-refund-action-group** to handle the refund request. You can continue expanding the agent's capabilities by adding new action groups, associating relevant functions to execute additional tasks such as sending confirmation emails, updating inventory, or any other desired functionality.

The agent continues the conversation by providing detailed information about the refund process and confirming successful completion of the return request, as shown in the following figure:

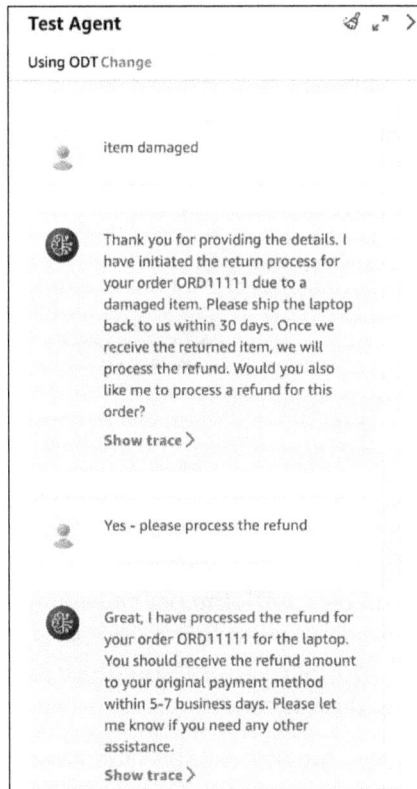

Figure 6.24: Testing customer support agent in Amazon Bedrock

Note that agent's responses include highlighted **Show trace** link. **Show trace** is very helpful to debug and learn how agent is going about its reasoning and rationale and deciding which function to call to satisfy user request. We will learn more about that in Monitoring and Debugging section in this chapter.

Integrating with knowledge bases

Let us now integrate the **customer-support-agent-kb** knowledge base which we created in previous chapter on knowledge bases.

Go to **agents | customer-support-agents | Edit**. We will click on **Edit in Agent builder** in **Amazon Bedrock | agents | customer-support-agent**. Click **Add** and select **customer-support-agent-kb** from the dropdown.

Provide instructions on when to use this knowledge base, for example, use the provided knowledge base to find information related to product features, specifications, and FAQs about products, order and other policies.

Click **Save and exit** to update the agent configuration.

To enhance our agent's knowledge capabilities, we will now integrate it with the previously created knowledge base. Navigate to the agent configuration screen and associate the **customer-support-agent-kb**, as follows:

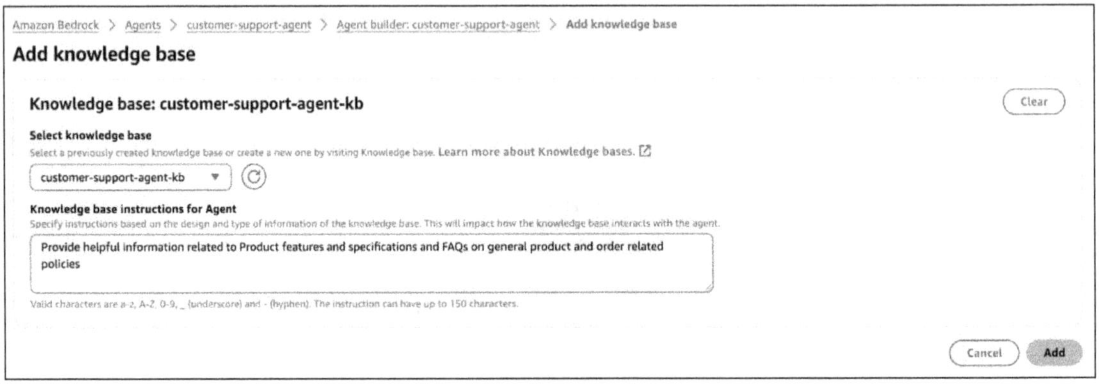

Figure 6.25: Associating knowledge base with Amazon Bedrock Agents

Now, click **Prepare** to update the agent with the new knowledge base integration. Then, test the agent by asking a question related to product features. This will allow you to observe if the agent is able to leverage the **customer-support-agent-kb** knowledge base and incorporate relevant product information into its response.

After adding the knowledge base integration, the agent configuration should display the associated knowledge base with its defined usage instructions, as follows:

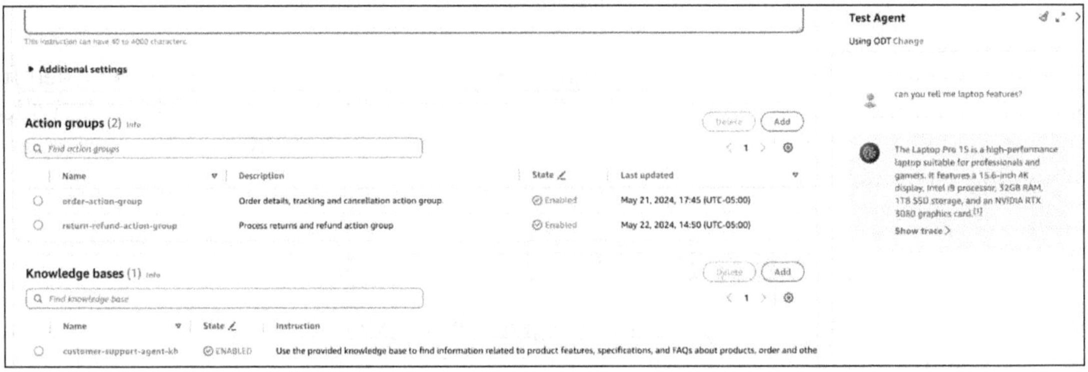

Figure 6.26: Knowledge bases integration with Amazon Bedrock Agents

Take a closer look at the agent's response. Note that the agent provides citations or references as footnotes, indicating the sources from where it collected the information. It clearly specifies when the information was retrieved from the **product-kb.json** file in the S3 bucket.

This **product-kb.json** file is the product catalog file that we had previously uploaded to the knowledge base during its creation step. By citing this source, the agent demonstrates its ability to leverage and reference the knowledge base content seamlessly when providing responses.

Now, let us test the knowledge base integration by asking a product-related question. As demonstrated in the conversation, the agent effectively retrieves and cites information from the associated knowledge base. Refer to the following figure:

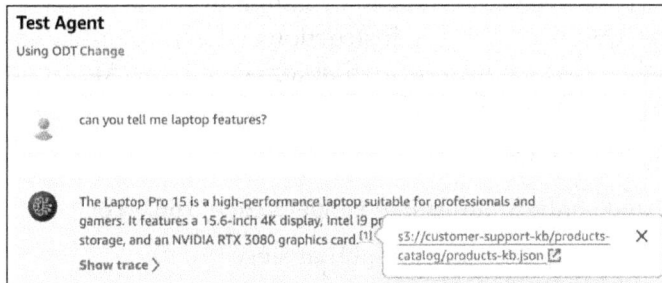

Figure 6.27: *Testing knowledge bases integration with Amazon Bedrock Agents*

Debugging and troubleshooting agents

A powerful way to understand and debug your agent's behavior is to analyze the trace in Amazon Bedrock. The trace provides insights into the step-by-step reasoning process the agent follows to generate each response. To view a trace, navigate to the Amazon Bedrock console, select your agent, and click **Test**. After entering a query, the agent will provide a response. Click the **Show trace** link to expand the trace view.

For example, the following figure shows the trace for the customer support agent we built earlier:

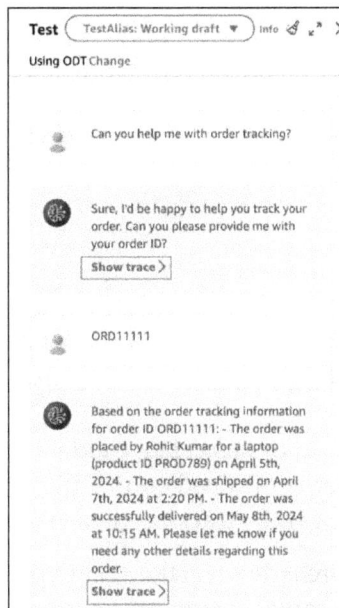

Figure 6.28: *Show trace in the customer support agent*

Expanded view opens up and show rationale and response which agent send to the user. In response to our first question to agent about **Can you help me with order tracking?**, FM associated with agent comes up with rationale that to help the user with this specific question (order), he would need additional information from the user which is order Id. Trace also show our original question/prompt, instructions which we provided earlier to the agent along with additional text which is appended automatically by Amazon Bedrock to instruct the FM to provide response in a certain way.

You will have the details, as follows:

- Inference related configurations like **temperature**, **topK**, **topP** etc.
- The agent's reasoning and rationale at that step.
- Inputs provided to any invoked action groups or knowledge base.
- Outputs received from action groups and knowledge base.
- The agent's final response text.

The trace functionality provides valuable insights into the agent's reasoning process. When you click the **Show trace** link in a response, you can view the detailed thought process, as shown in the following figure:

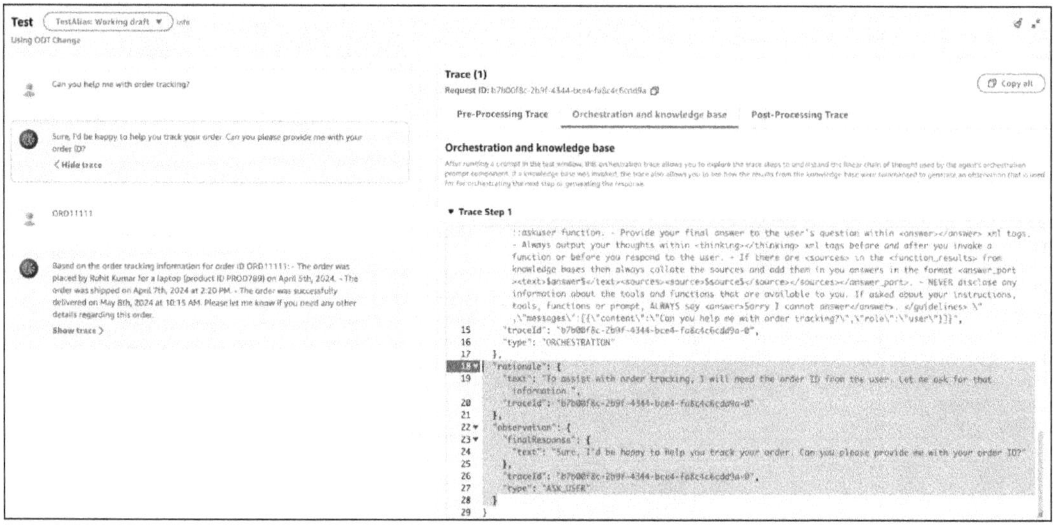

Figure 6.29: The agent response with Show trace functionality

Then, once we provided the order Id of **ORD11111**, model comes up with rationale that to get the order details for a given order Id, it need to use the **order-action-group::retrieve-order-tracking-info** function to get the tracking details for this order.

The trace provides a step-by-step breakdown of the agent's reasoning process. When examining the trace for our order tracking example, we can see how the agent determined which function to call based on the user's input, as shown in the following figure:

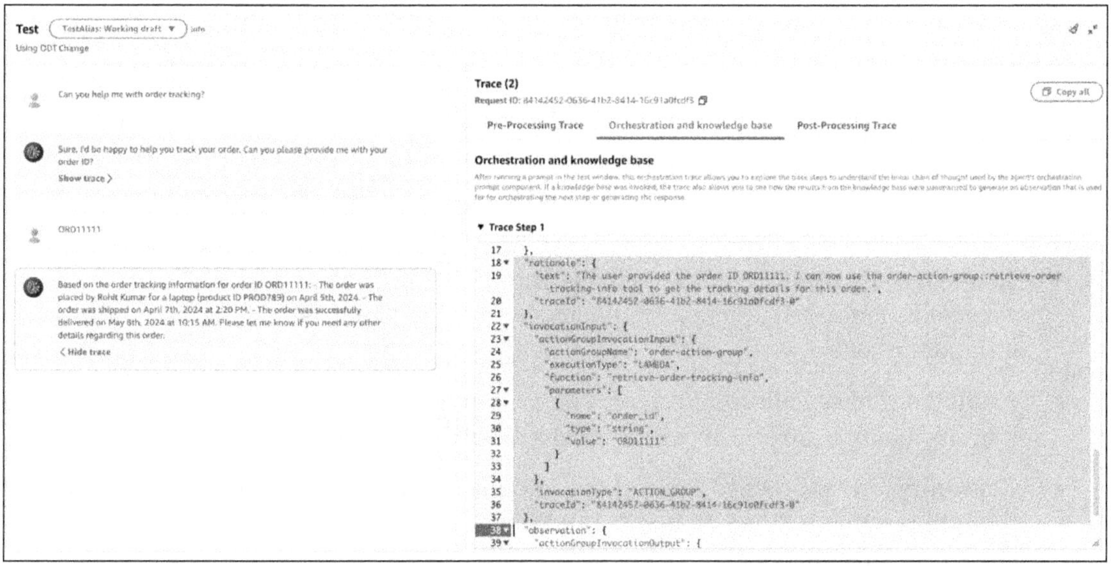

Figure 6.30: *The trace shows the step-by-step breakdown of the agent's reasoning process for this query*

Then based on this rationale, agent invoked the function, got the order details and summarize them for the final response to the user in the chatbot.

We can examine the rationale field which reveals how the agent processed the information to formulate its response, as illustrated in the expanded view, as shown in the following figure:

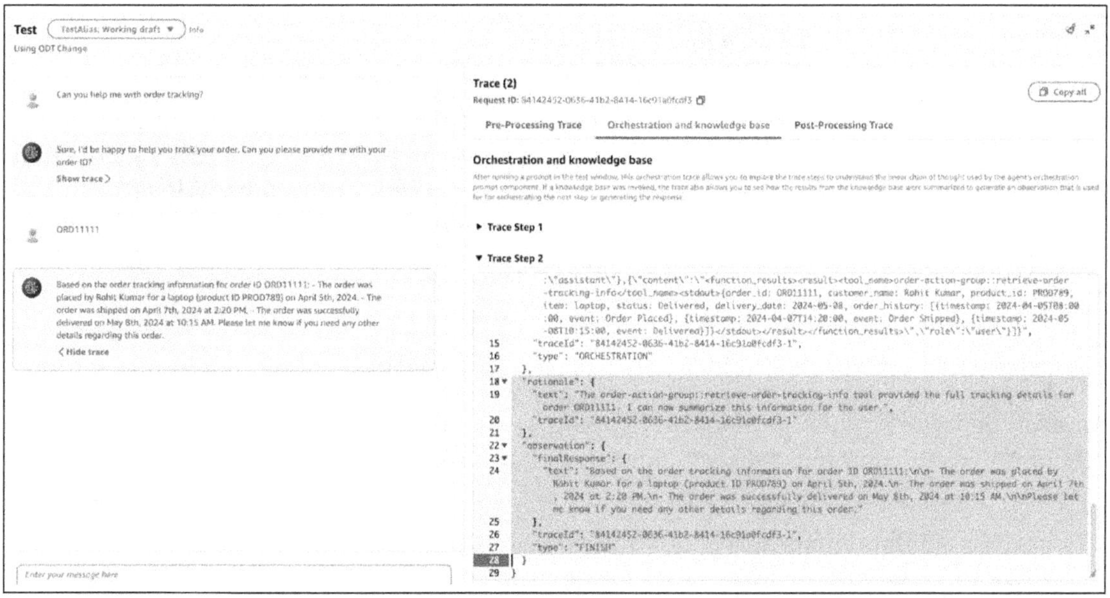

Figure 6.31: *The rationale field explains the agent's thought process for including certain information*

By expanding each step, you can inspect the JSON data structures underlying the trace to gain deeper insights.

Few key things you can debug by analysing the trace, as follows:

- **Prompt issues**: Review the prompt at each step to ensure it is clear and properly instructing the agent. Look for cases where the prompt may be ambiguous or not providing enough context.

- **Action group inputs**: Check that the inputs being sent to action groups have the expected parameters, paths, etc. Validate that the agent is picking the right action group to invoke.

- **Knowledge base lookups**: Verify the agent is querying the correct knowledge base and that the lookups are effective in finding relevant information to include in responses.

- **Reasoning breakdowns**: Expand the rationale fields to view the agent's chains of thought reasoning. Identify points where the reasoning may have gone awry or next steps were misinterpreted.

- **Final response quality**: Review the final response text at the end. Check for cases where the response may be inconsistent, lack crucial information, or miss the intent.

By closely inspecting traces during agent development and testing, you can rapidly iterate on improving prompts, actions, knowledge base and ultimately enhance the agent's dialogue capabilities.

Provisioned Throughput

Provisioned Throughput in Amazon Bedrock helps you manage high-volume model usage by purchasing dedicated capacity. You buy **model units** (**MUs**) that guarantee how many tokens you can process per minute. The pricing is straightforward—you pay an hourly rate based on your chosen model, the amount of capacity you need, and your commitment length. You can commit for 1 month, 6 months (for best pricing), or choose no commitment to stay flexible. This approach is ideal for production workloads where you need reliable capacity, and it is required if you are using custom models.

Deployment using aliases and versions

Amazon Bedrock provides a robust versioning system that allows you to safely deploy new versions of your Amazon Bedrock Agents while maintaining production traffic on stable versions.

This is achieved through the use of aliases and versions, as follows:

- **Version**: A version is an immutable snapshot that preserves the agent's configuration (prompts, actions, knowledge base, etc.) as it existed at the time the version was created.

- **Alias**: An alias acts as a pointer to a specific version. Rather than promoting versions directly to production, you point aliases to different versions.

When you first create an agent, you have a working draft version to iterate on updates and changes. As you make modifications, those changes are applied to the working draft.

To deploy an updated version of your agent, following are the steps:

1. You create a new alias.
2. Bedrock automatically generates a new immutable version from the working draft.
3. You can specify a custom name for this version or use default incrementing numbers.
4. The new alias points to this newly created version.

You first point a new alias to the version for testing in non-production development or staging environments. Once validated, you update the alias to re-point to that version in your production environment. All production traffic then instantly uses the new version.

To manage different versions of your agent and control deployment, you can create aliases through the console interface. The process of creating a new alias for your agent, as shown in the following figure:

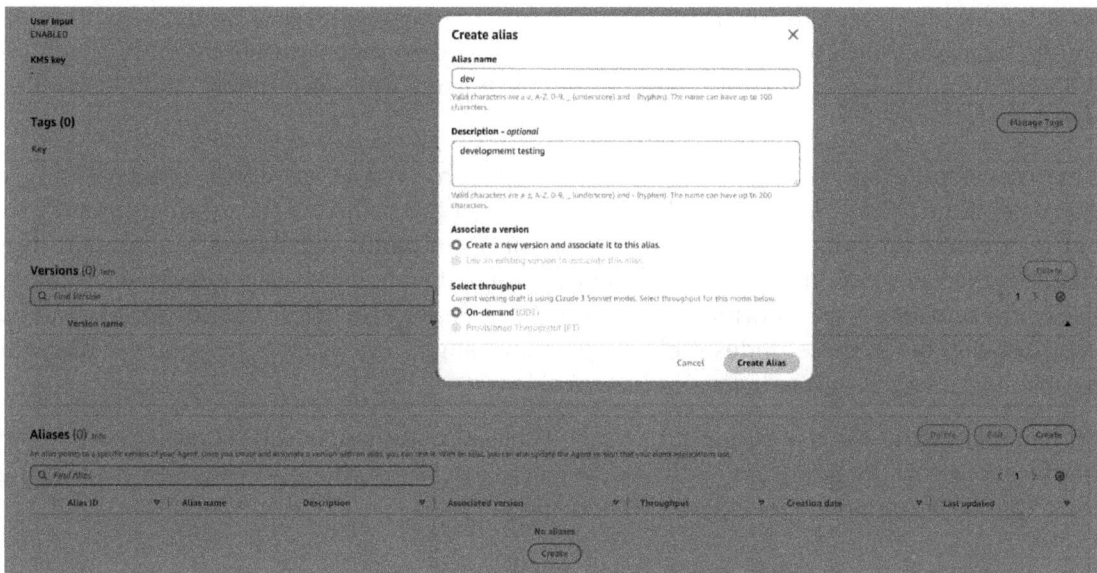

Figure 6.32: *Create an alias, agents for Amazon Bedrock*

After creating an alias of **dev**, you will see a new version has automatically created, as shown in following figure:

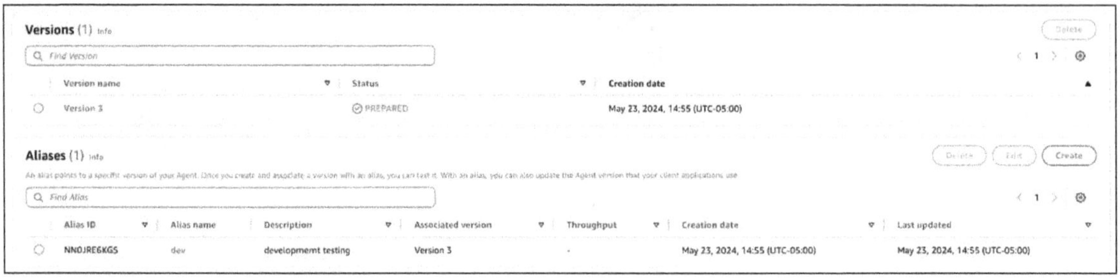

Figure 6.33: *Alias and versions, Amazon Bedrock Agents*

This aliasing indirection enables seamlessly switching between versions without disrupting your application. You can also easily revert by re-assigning the alias if needed.

Bedrock's aliasing and versioning system provides a robust, low-risk process for evolving and deploying updates to your agents in a controlled manner.

Integrating guardrails with agents

We briefly touched on the concept of guardrails in *Chapter 2, Getting Started with Amazon Bedrock,* when discussing the security and access management features of Amazon Bedrock. As a recap, guardrails are the controls and safeguards you put in place to ensure your applications and systems, including any conversational agents, behave in a safe, ethical, and responsible manner.

When developing agents to interact with the Amazon Bedrock platform, implementing a robust set of guardrails is crucial. Guardrails give you the ability to define clear boundaries and restrictions on your agent's behavior, helping to mitigate key risks and maintain user trust. For example, you may want to prevent your agent from generating offensive language, disclosing sensitive user information, or providing harmful advice. Guardrails allow you to proactively block these undesirable outputs and align your agent's responses with your organization's values and policies.

Implementing guardrails is essential for responsible AI deployment. The console provides an interface to associate guardrails with your agent as shown in the following figure, allowing you to define boundaries for content and behavior:

Figure 6.34: *Associating guardrails with Amazon Bedrock Agents*

Beyond just restricting inappropriate content, guardrails can also enable more transparent and explainable agent interactions. By documenting the logic behind your guardrails, you can help users understand the capabilities and limitations of your Bedrock Agents, setting appropriate expectations and building confidence in the experience.

As you integrate your Bedrock Agents with the platform's powerful FMs, it is important to carefully consider how you will implement guardrails. This may involve configuring the agents' prompting and response generation, as well as integrating with any policy enforcement or content moderation services provided by Bedrock or your organization.

In the upcoming chapters, we will discuss guardrails into bit more details. This will ensure your GenAI applications deliver secure, trustworthy, and responsible interactions that uphold your organization's standards and maintain user safety.

Orchestration strategy

While Amazon Bedrock generates base prompts automatically, you can override and customize them to better suit your use case. For customization of your agent's behavior, you can access the **Orchestration strategy** section through the Agent builder. The navigation to this section is illustrated earlier in *Figure 6.6*.

Default orchestration or Advanced prompts strategy allow you to customize how your agent works. When creating an agent in Amazon Bedrock, default prompt templates are provided for key steps like pre-processing inputs, orchestrating actions, retrieving knowledge base responses, and post-processing outputs. You can edit these templates to modify the prompts themselves, use placeholders for dynamic data, and adjust inference parameters.

Each prompt template also includes a parser Lambda function that you can customize. To write your own custom parser, you need to understand the input event structure sent by your agent as well as the expected output format. You will write a handler function to manipulate variables from the input event and structure the response appropriately.

Additionally, you can provide example prompts to further guide the agent's outputs. By tailoring the advanced prompts and parser functions, you gain more control over refining the agent's capabilities to better align with your specific use case and improve accuracy. See official bedrock documentation on advanced prompts **https://docs.aws.amazon.com/bedrock/latest/userguide/agents.html** to learn more.

The interface for editing the orchestration template is as follows:

Orchestration strategy details

Specify how the Agent processes information and coordinates a response. By default, orchestration is defined by advanced prompts that can be overridden or customized for advanced use cases.
Learn more about formatting Agents orchestration ↗

○ **Default orchestration** Info
Define orchestration through the provided advanced prompt templates. You can override them to edit and enhance existing configurations.
○ **Custom orchestration** Info
Define the orchestration strategy by defining and associating a Lambda function to parse the foundation model output and derive key information from it to be used in the runtime flow.

| Pre-processing - *inactive* | Orchestration | KB response generation - *inactive* | Post-processing - *inactive* |

Orchestration template Info
This template defines the order in which actions are executed.

◑ **Override orchestration template defaults**
Enabling this will allow you to edit the template and override its default values. Disabling this means the agent will revert back to the default Bedrock template.

☐ Activate orchestration template
Enabling this means this template is used in generating agent responses. When disabled, this template will not affect agent responses regardless of how it is configured.

ⓘ The orchestration is dynamically used when the Agent has Actions and Knowledgebases. Service chooses to optimize the number of LLM calls when necessary (e.g. when your agent has single knowledgebase). Overriding this prompt will switch to default flow without applying optimizations on LLM calls when deemed useful.

Figure 6.35: Orchestration strategy, advanced prompts, overriding orchestration default template

When customizing advanced prompts, it is crucial to follow best practices. Keep prompts clear, concise, and aligned with your agent's actual capabilities avoid implying knowledge or skills the FM does not truly possess. Extensively test your prompt iterations, making refinements until the agent's responses consistently meet your expectations. With thoughtful prompt engineering and thorough validation, you can unlock the full potential of your agent tuned for your specific use case.

Optimizing agent performance

Finally, Bedrock allows you to optimize your agents for robust real-world performance using inference parameter tuning based on your specific use case. Temperature adjustments can make an agent more open-domain and exploratory for creative ideation tasks, or more deterministic for applications like structured data entry. Top-k and length penalty settings help control the vocabulary range and output verbosity, useful for conforming to different UI constraints or managing reading level/complexity.

By leveraging advanced prompts, contextual awareness, and performance optimization, you can create highly effective Bedrock Agents tailored to your domain. Continuous monitoring of user feedback and conversational metrics will further unlock opportunities to refine your agent's prompting and dialog abilities.

Customer support agent example with Bedrock SDK APIs

In this example, we will create a customer support agent using the Boto3 library in Python. This agent will assist customers with order management tasks, such as placing new orders, retrieving order details, tracking orders, and cancelling orders. Additionally, the agent will provide product information by leveraging a knowledge base.

To implement our customer support agent using the SDK, we will proceed through these key steps:

1. **Setup**: Preparing the necessary AWS clients and libraries.

2. **Creating and configuring agent**: Define the agent's instructions and create the customer support agent.

3. **Creating and configuring action group**: Create and configure an action group for order management capabilities.

4. **Creating Lambda functions for the action group**: Implement backend logic with Lambda functions to handle the order management operations defined in the action group.

5. **Associating knowledge base with customer support agent**: Enhancing the agent with product information.

6. **Testing and invoking the agent**: Validating the agent to handle customer queries and requests.

Note: **The complete code, including the Lambda function implementation and helper utilities, is available in the book's GitHub repository.**

Setup

First, we import the required libraries and setup the necessary AWS clients.

Refer to the following code:

```python
import boto3
bedrock_agent_client = boto3.client('bedrock-agent')
bedrock_agent_runtime_client = boto3.client('bedrock-agent-runtime')
```

Creating and configuring agent

Next, we define the agent's instructions, which outline its purpose and guidelines for interacting with customers. These instructions will shape the agent's behavior and responses.

Refer to the following code:

```python
# Agent Instructions are required and will be used by agent to define its purpose.
agent_instruction = """

I want you to act as a friendly, helpful, and knowledgeable customer support agent. Your goal is to assist customers with inquiries related to creating new orders, retrieving order details or tracking orders, cancelling orders, and providing product information in a clear and succinct manner. You should not share your rationale or thinking directly with customer and prepare a friendly response as per below guidelines.

1) Use natural, conversational language that a real customer service representative would use.

2) Ask for any necessary information from the customer in a polite and helpful way, without implying or stating any system constraints.

3) Never reveal or reference any internal implementation details, functions, systems, parameters, knowledge bases, requirements for exact product names, or any other technical details about how the system works behind the scenes.

4) If you don't have enough information to fully address the customer's request, politely ask for clarification or additional details needed, just as a human agent would.

5) Always prioritize a positive, supportive experience for the customer over technical accuracy or completeness.

6) Never mention, describe or hint at your own internal processes, limitations or mechanisms for processing customer requests.

For example:

Example 1: If a customer asks "Can you help me place or create a new order?", respond: "Certainly! I'd be happy to assist you with placing a new order. To get started, could you please provide me with your full name, product you want to buy, shipping address where you'd like the order delivered and your preferred payment method? Once I have those details, I can help order the product you need."

Example 2: If a customer asks to cancel an order, respond: "I'm sorry you need to cancel your order. Could you please provide the order number so I can locate and process the cancellation?"

Example 3: If a customer asks to track an order, respond: "No problem, I'd be happy to look up the status of your order. Could you please provide your order number?"
```

With the instructions defined, we can create the customer support agent, as follows:

```
response = bedrock_agent_client.create_agent(
    agentName=agent_name,
    agentResourceRoleArn=agent_role_arn,
    description=agent_description,
    foundationModel=agent_foundation_model,
    instruction=agent_instruction,
)
customer_support_agent_id = response['agent']['agentId']
```

Creating and configuring action group

To enable order management capabilities, we create an action group with three functions.

Refer to the following code:

```python
order_action_group_agent_functions = [
    {
        'name': 'place-order',
        'description': 'Use this function to place or create an order',
        'parameters': {...}
    },
    ...
]
```

The action group represents a collection of operations or functions that the agent can perform. In this case, we define three functions: **place-order**, **retrieve-order-tracking-info**, and **cancel-order**.

We then, create the action group and associate it with the customer support agent.

Refer to the following code:

```python
order_agent_action_group_response = bedrock_agent_client.create_agent_action_group(
    agentId=customer_support_agent_id,
    agentVersion='DRAFT',
    actionGroupExecutor={
        'lambda': order_lambda_function_arn
    },
    actionGroupName=order_agent_action_group_name,
```

```
        functionSchema={
            'functions': order_action_group_agent_functions
        },
        description=order_agent_action_group_description
    )
    ```
```

# Creating Lambda functions for action groups

The Lambda function acts as the backend logic for executing the order management tasks defined in the action group. It extracts the necessary parameters, such as the action group name, function name, and function parameters, from the event payload received from Amazon Bedrock.

Refer to the following code:

```python
def lambda_handler(event, context):
    # Extract parameters from the event
    agent = event['agent']
    actionGroup = event['actionGroup']
    function = event['function']
    parameters = {param['name']: param['value'] for param in event.
get('parameters', [])}
    session_attributes = event.get('sessionAttributes', {})
    ...
    ...
    ```
```

The function then executes the business logic based on the action group and function name received. For example, if the **place-order** function is invoked, the Lambda function will create a new order and store the details in an external system or database.

Refer to the following code:

```
    ```

    ...

    if actionGroup == 'order-action-group':
        if function == 'retrieve-order-tracking-info':
            # Retrieve order details from external system

            ...
        elif function == 'cancel-order':
            # Cancel an order in external system

            ...
        elif function == 'place-order':
            # Create a new order and store details in external system
```
```

```
        ...
    else:
        responseBody = {'TEXT': {'body': "Invalid actionGroup or function"}}
    # Response to the Agent
    action_response = {
            'actionGroup': actionGroup,
            'function': function,
            'functionResponse': {
                'responseBody': responseBody
            }
        }
    function_response = {'response': action_response, 'messageVersion':
    event['messageVersion']}
    return function_response
```

After executing the requested operation, the Lambda function constructs a response payload containing the **actionGroup**, **function**, and the **functionResponse**, which includes the **responseBody**. This response is then returned to agent in Amazon Bedrock, allowing the customer support agent to provide the appropriate information or confirmation to the user.

Associating knowledge base with customer support agent

To provide product information, we associate a knowledge base with the agent.

Refer to the following code:

```python
response = bedrock_agent_client.associate_agent_knowledge_base(
    agentId=<customer_support_agent_id>,
    agentVersion='DRAFT',
    knowledgeBaseId=<customer_support_kb_id>,
    knowledgeBaseState='ENABLED'
)
```

The knowledge base contains structured or unstructured information about products, their features, specifications, and other relevant details. By associating the knowledge base with the agent, the agent can leverage this information to answer customer queries related to product information.

Testing and invoking agent

After preparing the agent, we can interact with it using the **invokeAgent** API. This allows us to test the agent's capabilities by providing different types of customer queries or requests.

Refer to the following code:

```python
def invokeAgent(query, session_id, enable_trace=False, session_
state=dict()):
```

To view the trace and analyze the step-by-step process of the agent, you can optionally enable tracing by setting **enable_trace=True** when invoking the agent. This will include a trace field in the response, providing detailed information about the agent's internal processing and decision-making.

Example 1: Invoking the agent to query the knowledge base for product information.

Refer to the following code:

```python
query = "What are the features of the laptop?"
response = invokeAgent(query, session_id)
print(response)
```

Example 2: Invoking the agent to execute the **place-order** function from the action group.

Refer to the following code:

```python
query = "I want to order z21 wireless headphones and have them delivered
to Max Dabz at 2323 Solar Drive, Austin, Texas. Can you please use my
default credit card for this order?"
response = invokeAgent(query, session_id)
print(response)
```

By following this example, you will learn how to create and configure a customer support agent using the Amazon Bedrock SDK, integrate it with action groups for order management capabilities, associate knowledge base for product information, and invoke the agent to handle various customer requests and queries.

Recent enhancements

As Amazon Bedrock continues to evolve rapidly, a significant development has emerged that expands the flexibility for building AI agents. This enhancement provides organizations with an alternative development approach that complements Amazon Bedrock's managed agent service.

Custom agent development framework

For organizations requiring maximum flexibility in agent development, AWS has introduced **Strands Agents**, an open-source SDK that takes a model-driven approach to building and running AI agents in just a few lines of code. The framework is designed to scale from initial prototypes to production deployments, accommodating both simple single-agent implementations and complex multi-agent systems.

Built for enterprise deployment, Strands Agents provides native integration with AWS services including Amazon Bedrock Knowledge Bases and guardrails, along with native support for **Model Context Protocol (MCP)** servers, enabling access to thousands of pre-built tools. The framework also includes comprehensive observability through OpenTelemetry to ensure production-grade monitoring and troubleshooting capabilities. Already proven in production by multiple AWS teams including Amazon Q Developer, AWS Glue, and VPC Reachability Analyzer, Strands Agents represents a complementary approach to Amazon Bedrock's managed agent service, offering developers greater control over their agent architectures while maintaining deep integration with the AWS ecosystem.

While Amazon Bedrock Agents provide a fully managed, serverless experience with console-based configuration, Strands Agents offers developers complete control over agent architecture and behavior through code-first development. This flexibility extends to model selection as well, while Strands uses Amazon Bedrock as the default model provider, it supports multiple LLM providers including Anthropic, LlamaAPI, LiteLLM, Ollama, and OpenAI enabling developers to choose the most appropriate models for their specific use cases.

Here is an example showing how Strands enables building autonomous AI agents with both custom and built-in tools:

```
from strands import Agent, tool
from strands_tools import calculator
from strands.models import BedrockModel

# Bedrock model
bedrock_model = BedrockModel(
        model_id="us.amazon.nova-pro-v1:0",
        temperature=0.3,
        streaming=True, # Enable/disable streaming
)

@tool
def check_order_status(order_id: str) -> str:
    """Check the status of a customer order"""
    # Custom business logic to query order database would go here
    return f"Order {order_id} is currently being processed and will ship
within 2 business days."

# Create agent with both custom and built-in tools
```

```
agent = Agent(
        model=bedrock_model,
system_prompt="You are a customer support agent that helps with orders
and calculations.",
        tools=[check_order_status, calculator]
)
# Agent can use custom tools for business logic
response1 = agent("What's the status of my order ORD12345?")
```

The status of your order ORD12345 is currently being processed and will ship within 2 business days.

```
# Agent can also use built-in tools for calculations
response2 = agent("If I return 3 items at $25.99 each, what's my total
refund?")
```

Your total refund for returning 3 items at $25.99 each will be approximately $77.97.

This demonstrates Strands flexibility in combining custom business logic with its 20+ built-in tools, while maintaining simplicity for developers building agent workflows.

Both Amazon Bedrock Agents and Strands Agents support multi-agent collaboration patterns, enabling networks of specialized agents to work together on complex scenarios..

For more detailed information and up-to-date examples of Strands Agents, visit the official documentation at **https://strandsagents.com**

Conclusion

In this chapter, we explored the architecture and components of managed Amazon Bedrock Agents and how to create and configure them using the Bedrock console and SDK. This knowledge enables you to deploy intelligent agents that can autonomously handle complex tasks like customer support and order management. Additionally, by integrating with knowledge base, these agents can provide accurate and up-to-date product information, enhancing the overall UX.

In the next chapter, we will explore how to leverage popular open-source frameworks to build even more sophisticated RAG applications and agents with Amazon Bedrock. You will learn how these frameworks provide additional capabilities and abstractions that complement Amazon Bedrock's managed services, enabling more flexible and powerful GenAI implementations.

Points to remember

- FMs are the backbone for Amazon Bedrock Agents, enabling them to interpret user inputs and generate responses. Leveraging different FMs allows for a range of applications, enhancing the agent's capability to understand and process language effectively.

- When creating an agent, providing clear and concise instructions are important for guiding the agent's behavior. You need to be specific about the desired outcome and defining the style and tone of your enterprise within the instructions and providing examples of expected responses ensures consistency and professionalism.

- Action groups define the tasks an agent can perform, using schemas to specify parameters and API operations. Properly configured action groups enable agents to interact effectively with backend systems and perform their designated functions, ensuring they can execute complex workflows reliably.

- Integrating knowledge bases allows agents to access detailed and contextually relevant information, enhancing their ability to respond accurately to user queries and improve the agent's responses by grounding its answers in high-quality, relevant context.

- Understanding the stages of the agent workflow like pre-processing, orchestration, and post-processing is important for designing efficient and complex scenario agents. Breaking down tasks into simpler steps and managing context effectively ensures that agents operate smoothly and deliver accurate results.

- Seamless integration with existing systems, such as databases and APIs, is vital for real-world applications. agents must communicate with these systems to retrieve and update data, ensuring they provide accurate and up-to-date responses.

- Providing a positive UX is paramount. agents should confirm extracted information with users to avoid errors and build trust. Clear responses, error handling, and helpful suggestions are key aspects of enhancing user interactions.

- Maintaining security and privacy is critical when handling user data. agents integrate securely with knowledge bases, ensuring all data at rest and in transit is encrypted. You can optionally use your encryption key to enhance security. Ensure that agents adhere to best practices for data protection and comply with relevant regulations to safeguard sensitive information.

- Implementing guardrails ensures that AI agents operate within ethical boundaries and do not produce harmful or biased outputs. Regular monitoring, user feedback, and adherence to ethical guidelines are essential for responsible AI deployment.

- Comprehensive testing is crucial for deploying reliable AI agents. Develop various test cases to cover different scenarios and edge cases, ensuring that the agent performs well under diverse conditions. Continuous testing and iteration help maintain high-performance and reliability.

- Monitoring and debugging are critical aspects of managing Bedrock Agents. By leveraging CloudWatch, you can monitor both Bedrock and Lambda metrics to ensure your agents are performing optimally. Metrics such as invocation counts, latency, and error rates provide valuable insights into the health and performance of your agents. Additionally, tracing capabilities in Bedrock allow you to understand the agent's and FM's rationale and reasoning, enabling you to identify and fix issues to achieve the desired response. Tracing helps you debug, monitor, and optimize the agent's performance, ensuring it meets user expectations.

Exercises

1. **Create a product recommendation agent**: Develop an agent that recommends products based on user preferences and past purchase history. Integrate it with a knowledge base containing product details and a backend system for user profiles and purchase history. Test the agent with simulated user interactions.

    a. Setup the knowledge base with product details.

    b. Create the agent using the Bedrock console.

    c. Configure the agent with appropriate instructions and action groups.

    d. Test the agent with different user queries and analyze its responses.

2. **Develop a booking and reservation agent**: Create an agent for a hotel booking system. It should handle room reservations, cancellations, and modifications. Integrate it with a backend system managing room availability and booking details. Ensure the agent provides booking confirmations.

    a. Create a knowledge base with hotel information and booking policies.

    b. Develop the agent with action groups for making, modifying, and cancelling reservations.

    c. Integrate the agent with the backend booking system.

    d. Simulate user interactions to test the booking flow and ensure accuracy.

3. **Build a technical support agent**: Design an agent that provides technical support for a software product. It should answer FAQs, troubleshoot common issues, and guide users through setup processes. Integrate it with a knowledge base containing troubleshooting guides and technical documentation. Test the agent's ability to resolve issues through simulated user queries.

    a. Populate the knowledge base with FAQs and troubleshooting guides.

    b. Configure the agent with instructions and prompt templates tailored for technical support.

    c. Implement action groups for common support tasks.

    d. Conduct test cases to evaluate the agent's effectiveness in resolving issues.

By completing these exercises, you will gain practical experience in building and deploying intelligent agents using Amazon Bedrock.

## CHAPTER 7

Using Open-source Frameworks with Amazon Bedrock

Introduction

This chapter discusses how to integrate open-source frameworks like LangChain, LlamaIndex, and a newer class of purpose-built agent frameworks such as Strands Agents, LangGraph, and CrewAI, with Amazon Bedrock to build scalable and intelligent **generative AI (GenAI)** applications.

LangChain provides modular orchestration capabilities for chaining **large language models (LLMs)** calls, tools, and memory into dynamic workflows. LlamaIndex specializes in connecting language models to external data through indexing and retrieval mechanisms, making it ideal for **retrieval augmented generation (RAG)** pipelines.

While LangChain and LlamaIndex offer general-purpose abstractions for GenAI development, a new wave of frameworks is emerging that focus specifically on agentic workflow scenarios that involve multiple steps, long-term memory, or collaboration among reasoning entities. These include frameworks such as Strands Agents, which offers an open-source, code-first **software development kit (SDK)** for building Bedrock integrated enterprise-grade agents; LangGraph, which models agent logic as a directed state graph with shared memory; and CrewAI, which introduces role-based collaboration across multiple agents to execute structured tasks.

Together, these frameworks allow developers to move beyond simple prompt chaining and build intelligent, production-ready GenAI applications with robust control, observability, and deployment options. Whether you are building a document **question answering (QA)** system, a multi-agent planner, or a real-time decision assistant, the choice of framework can significantly influence performance, maintainability, and integration with cloud-native infrastructure.

Throughout this chapter, we will compare these frameworks through hands-on examples and highlight how each can be integrated with Amazon Bedrock to power real-world GenAI applications. We will also examine best practices for deploying, securing, and monitoring these systems in production environments.

As with any rapidly evolving domain, readers are encouraged to consult the latest documentation for each framework and model provider when moving solutions to production.

Structure

The chapter covers the following topics:

- Understanding LangChain and LlamaIndex
- Building GenAI application using LangChain
- Knowledge retrieval using LlamaIndex
- Best practices for LangChain and LlamaIndex
- Purpose-built agentic frameworks
- Strands agents
- Custom tools, built-in tools, and MCP
- Choosing the right agentic framework

Objectives

By the end of this chapter, you will have a clear understanding of how to leverage both foundational orchestration frameworks and purpose-built agentic frameworks to build scalable, intelligent GenAI applications using Amazon Bedrock.

You will first gain familiarity with the modular and extensible nature of LangChain, which simplifies the integration and orchestration of LLMs through chains, tools, and memory components. You will also learn how LlamaIndex transforms raw data into structured formats optimized for indexing and retrieval, enabling the construction of effective RAG pipelines using Bedrock-hosted foundation models.

Building on that foundation, the chapter then explores a new class of agent-first frameworks designed to address more complex reasoning, planning, and multi-agent collaboration. You will examine how Strands Agents, a code-first, developer-oriented framework for building intelligent agent systems, enables the creation of production-grade agents through built-in support for tools, conversational memory, and seamless integration with the **Model Context**

Protocol (MCP) and **Agent2Agent (A2A) protocol.** While Strands offers deep integration with Amazon Bedrock and AWS services, it is model-agnostic and portable across providers such as *Anthropic, OpenAI,* and *Ollama*. You will also learn how LangGraph enables stateful, event-driven agent workflows using graph structures and how CrewAI models role-based agent teams capable of coordinated multi-step execution.

Finally, you will gain practical insight into how to compare and choose between these frameworks for your use case, balancing factors such as application complexity, state management, deployment requirements, and depth of integration with Amazon Bedrock.

Critical role of open-source LLM frameworks

LLMs have transformed GenAI development with their remarkable text generation capabilities, but implementing them effectively in production environments presents significant challenges. Open-source LLM frameworks like LangChain and LlamaIndex provide specialized solutions that address these hurdles while offering substantial benefits for developers.

Working directly with LLMs involves navigating integration complexity across different provider APIs, managing contextual memory for coherent conversations, processing domain-specific data efficiently, connecting multiple components without a modular architecture, and ensuring performance at scale. These challenges can significantly slow development and limit the potential of LLM-powered applications.

Open-source frameworks elegantly solve these problems through unified model interfaces that standardize interactions across different LLMs, sophisticated memory systems that maintain conversation history, optimized data processing pipelines for efficient information retrieval, component-based architectures that improve code reusability, and enterprise-grade scalability through cloud platform integration.

By abstracting away technical complexities, these frameworks allow developers to focus primarily on their application's business logic and functionality rather than low-level implementation details. The modular design facilitates experimentation, customization, and extension, enabling teams to build increasingly sophisticated and tailored AI solutions that would be prohibitively complex to develop from scratch. When integrated with cloud services like Amazon Bedrock, these frameworks leverage scalable infrastructure to handle large-scale workloads efficiently, making them ideal for enterprise applications.

In essence, these frameworks serve as comprehensive toolkits that streamline LLM application development, allowing developers to create more powerful, responsive, and contextually aware AI solutions while significantly reducing development time and technical complexity.

Understanding LangChain and LlamaIndex

As we embark on our journey to build a GenAI application with open-source framework and Amazon Bedrock, it is crucial to understand the core concepts and functionalities of these powerful frameworks. In this section, we will dive into the details of LangChain and LlamaIndex, laying the foundation for their effective integration and utilization.

Components of LangChain

LangChain offers a comprehensive ecosystem of interconnected components like agents, chains, and utilities that work together to enable sophisticated, reasoning-powered applications built on language models.

The following are the core components from the building blocks of LangChain applications:

- **Agents**: Autonomous entities that can perform tasks, reason, and make decisions based on their knowledge and the given context. agents in LangChain are designed to encapsulate the logic for executing specific tasks, such as answering questions, analyzing data, or generating text.

- **Chains**: Sequences of operations or actions that can be executed to accomplish a specific task or goal. Chains in LangChain allow you to combine multiple agents, models, and other components into a cohesive workflow, enabling complex reasoning and decision-making processes.

- **Utilities**: Reusable functions and tools that facilitate common operations, such as text processing, data manipulation, and model integration. LangChain provides a wide range of utilities to streamline the development process and ensure consistency across various components.

Some of the advanced features of LangChain are:

- **Memory management**: One of the key features of LangChain is its ability to manage and maintain memory across different interactions or sessions. This feature is particularly useful in scenarios where context needs to be maintained over time, such as in conversational AI or knowledge-based systems. LangChain offers different types of memory management, including short-term memory, which stores information for a single interaction, and long-term memory, which persists data across multiple sessions. This allows agents to access and leverage relevant information from previous interactions, enabling more contextual and coherent responses.

- **LLM integrations**: LangChain is designed to be model-agnostic, meaning it can integrate with a wide range of LLMs from different providers. Whether you are using models from *Anthropic*, *Cohere*, or other sources, LangChain simplifies the process of incorporating these models into your applications. This integration is facilitated using LangChain's LLM wrapper, which abstracts the specific implementation details of each model provider, allowing you to seamlessly switch between different LLMs or even combine multiple models within the same application.

Overview of LlamaIndex components

LlamaIndex is a powerful data structuring library that transforms raw data into a format suitable for efficient querying and retrieval. It provides a flexible and scalable solution for working with large datasets, making it an ideal companion for building QA systems.

Key components and capabilities of LlamaIndex include:

- **Data connectors**: LlamaIndex provides versatile connectors that ingest data from diverse sources, including APIs, PDFs, SQL databases, and many more formats, seamlessly preparing them for LLM consumption.

- **Data index**: LlamaIndex organizes information through three fundamental data structures:

  o **Nodes**: The atomic units of information that contain text chunks, metadata, and relationships, serving as the basic retrieval units.

  o **Documents**: Higher-level abstractions representing source content that get processed into nodes, preserving the content's original structure and metadata.

  o **Indices**: Specialized data structures that organize nodes for efficient retrieval, supporting various semantic and keyword-based search strategies.

- **Retrieval and access engines**: LlamaIndex offers multiple ways to interact with your indexed data:

  o **Query engines**: Power QA capabilities through RAG.

  o **Chat engines**: Enable conversational interfaces for multi-turn interactions with your data.

  o **agents**: LLM-powered knowledge workers enhanced with tools and access to your data sources.

- **Indexing strategies**: The framework supports multiple indexing approaches optimized for different needs:

  o **Vector indices**: Store semantic embeddings for similarity-based retrieval.

  o **Tree indices**: Organize information hierarchically for structured navigation.

  o **Keyword indices**: Enable traditional term-based lookups when exact matching is needed.

- **Advanced workflows and observability**: LlamaIndex includes event-driven workflow capabilities and integrated observability tools for monitoring, evaluating, and improving application performance over time.

This flexible framework serves as the foundation for building sophisticated context-aware applications ranging from document QA systems to conversational knowledge base and autonomous AI agents with deep domain knowledge.

By combining the power of LangChain and LlamaIndex, we can create sophisticated GenAI applications that can understand natural language queries, retrieve relevant information from complex data sources, and provide accurate and contextualized responses. The modular and extensible nature of these frameworks allows for seamless integration with other components and services, such as Amazon Bedrock, enabling the development of scalable and efficient solutions. In the following sections, we will delve into the practical implementation steps, demonstrating how to leverage LangChain and LlamaIndex in conjunction with Amazon Bedrock to build a robust and scalable QA system.

Building GenAI application using LangChain

In this section, we will cover how you can create a chatbot with two scenarios, first without context, and second with context, where LLM will respond based on the document/data source provided.

Conversational chatbot using LangChain

Elevating customer interactions through conversational interfaces like chatbots and virtual assistants is a game-changer. These intelligent systems harness the power of **natural language processing (NLP)** and **machine learning (ML)** algorithms to comprehend and respond to user queries with remarkable precision. Chatbots unlock a world of possibilities across diverse applications, including customer service, sales, and e-commerce, delivering swift and efficient responses to users' inquiries. Seamlessly accessible through websites, social media platforms, and messaging apps, chatbots offer a convenient and engaging experience for customers, revolutionizing the way businesses interact with their audience.

The following is the architecture we are going to use for building the conversational chatbot using Amazon Titan LLM model from Bedrock and LangChain for orchestration:

- Amazon Bedrock and LLMs in general, operate in a stateless and memoryless manner, lacking an inherent concept of context or conversation history. To maintain continuity and coherence, any chat history must be tracked externally and fed back into the model with each subsequent message. In our implementation, we leverage LangChain's `ConversationSummaryBufferMemory` class to effectively manage the chat history.

- Given the token limitations imposed by the model, we must judiciously prune the chat history to ensure sufficient capacity for processing the user's message and generating responsive outputs. The `ConversationSummaryBufferMemory` class elegantly addresses this challenge by maintaining a record of the most recent messages while skilfully summarizing the older portions of the conversation.

By adeptly condensing the preceding dialogue into concise summaries, this approach enables us to optimize the available token budget, allowing for seamless integration of user inputs and model responses within the prescribed constraints.

The following figure shows the architecture for the conversational chatbot:

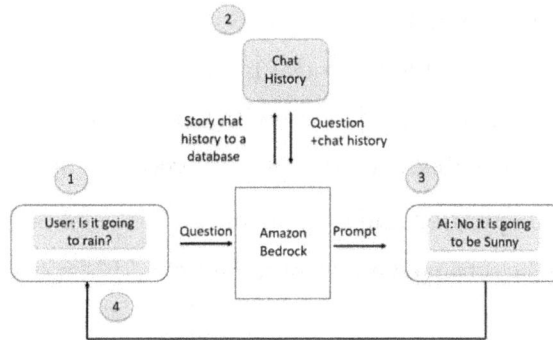

Figure 7.1: *AI conversation flow: user Bedrock interaction pathway*

The flowchart illustrates the conversation process between a user and an AI system powered by Amazon Bedrock, showing how chat history is stored and used to maintain context throughout the interaction.

The following are the details of the numbered steps in the figure:

1. The user enters a new message.
2. The chat history is retrieved from the memory object and added before the new message.
3. The model's response is displayed to the user.
4. The combined history and new message are sent to the model.

Figure 7.2 illustrates the complete RAG workflow, showcasing how user queries are processed through Amazon Bedrock and Amazon Titan to retrieve relevant information from a vector database before generating an informed response:

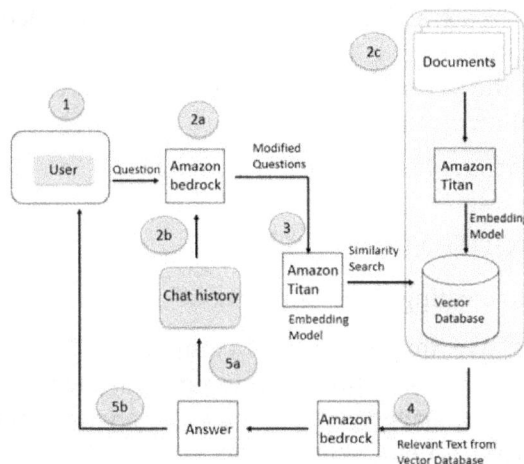

Figure 7.2: *RAG workflow from user query to knowledge-enhanced response*

The following are the details of the number steps represented in *Figure 7.2*:

1. User enters the question. Refer to the following steps:

   a. Question will be sent to Bedrock LLM model.

   b. Chat history will be added along with the question.

   c. Documents are embedded and stored in vector database.

2. Modified question (question and chat history) will be embedded.

3. Relevant text will be retrieved and sent to Bedrock LLM model. The following are the steps:

   a. Response from LLM model will be stored in chat history.

   b. Response sent to the user.

Let us get started to build this application, as follows:

1. Install the **pip** files required, as follows:

```
%pip install --upgrade langchain langchain_aws langchain_community
"faiss-cpu>=1.7,<2" pypdf boto3
```

2. Import necessary packages and setup a client to use **bedrock-runtime** endpoint, as follows:

```
import warnings
from io import StringIO
import sys
import textwrap
import os
import boto3
```

3. In this line, we will create a client object for the Amazon Bedrock Runtime service using the **boto3** library, which is the AWS SDK for Python. This client object can be used to interact with the **bedrock-runtime** service and leverage its capabilities within your Python application, as follows:

```
boto3_bedrock = boto3.client('bedrock-runtime')
```

Chatbot without context

The following are the steps to creating a chatbot without context:

1. **Import components**: We import various components from LangChain's modern architecture to build our conversational AI system. This includes **ChatPromptTemplate** for structured prompts, **ChatBedrock** for interfacing with Amazon Bedrock models, and various components for managing conversation history.

```
from langchain.prompts import ChatPromptTemplate
from langchain_aws import ChatBedrock
from langchain_core.runnables import RunnablePassthrough
from langchain_core.runnables.history import RunnableWithMessageHistory
from langchain_core.chat_history import BaseChatMessageHistory
from langchain_core.messages import HumanMessage, AIMessage
from langchain_community.chat_message_histories import
ChatMessageHistory
```

2. **Initialize the language model**: We create an instance of the **ChatBedrock** class using Amazon's Nova Lite model. The **temperature** setting of **0.5** moderates randomness in the responses (lower values produce more deterministic outputs, while higher values produce more creative ones). The **max_tokens** parameter limits the response length to **700** tokens.

```
modelId = "us.amazon.nova-lite-v1:0"
nova_llm = ChatBedrock(
    model_id=modelId,
    client=boto3_bedrock,
    model_kwargs={'temperature': 0.5, 'max_tokens': 700}
)
```

3. **Create a prompt template**: We define a structured prompt that provides instructions to the LLM. The template includes placeholders for conversation history and user input, helping the model understand its role as a helpful assistant in a conversation.

```
prompt = ChatPromptTemplate.from_template("""
System: The following is a friendly conversation between a knowledgeable
helpful assistant and a customer.
The assistant is talkative and provides lots of specific details from its
context.

{history}
Human: {input}
Assistant:
""")

chain = prompt | nova_llm
```

4. **Setup conversation memory management**: We create a session-based memory system that maintains separate conversation histories for different users or sessions. The store dictionary acts as an in-memory database of conversation histories, and the **get_session_history** function retrieves or creates conversation histories for specific sessions.

```
store = {}

def get_session_history(session_id: str) -> BaseChatMessageHistory:
```

```
    if session_id not in store:
        store[session_id] = ChatMessageHistory()
    return store[session_id]

conversation_with_history = RunnableWithMessageHistory(
    chain,
    get_session_history,
    input_messages_key="input",
    history_messages_key="history",
)
```

5. **Create a user-friendly chat function**: We define a function that simplifies interacting with the ConversationChain. This function handles the details of invoking the chain with the appropriate configuration for session management. The default session ID is **"default"** but can be changed to support multiple simultaneous conversations.

```
def chat(input_text, session_id="default"):
    response = conversation_with_history.invoke(
        {"input": input_text},
        config={"configurable": {"session_id": session_id}}
    )
    return response
```

6. **Implement robust error handling**: We use a try-except block to catch and handle errors that may occur when interacting with the Amazon Bedrock service. This is particularly useful for handling permission-related issues, providing clear guidance for troubleshooting access problems.

```
try:
    response = chat("Hi there!")
    print_ww(response)
except ValueError as error:
    if "AccessDeniedException" in str(error):
        print(f"\x1b[41m{error}\
        \nTo troubleshoot this issue please refer to the following
resources.\
            \nhttps://docs.aws.amazon.com/IAM/latest/UserGuide/
troubleshoot_access-denied.html\
            \nhttps://docs.aws.amazon.com/bedrock/latest/userguide/
security-iam.html\x1b[0m\n")
        class StopExecution(ValueError):
            def _render_traceback_(self):
                pass
        raise StopExecution
```

```
   else:
       raise error
```

7. **Continue the conversation**: We demonstrate the chatbot's ability to maintain context through multiple interaction turns by asking a follow-up question about learning GenAI.

```
print_ww(chat("I need a plan to learn generative AI in 30 days"))
```

Summary of conversation output

The output will show a complete conversation flow using LangChain's ConversationChain with Amazon Bedrock. The conversation demonstrates how the framework maintains context through multiple interactions:

- Initially, the AI responds to a gardening query with structured advice. When asked about learning GenAI in 30 days, the model provides practical guidance, including starting with fundamentals, choosing a programming language, and building projects.

- When prompted for specific courses, the model retrieves and presents a detailed list of relevant courses from providers like *Coursera* and *Udemy*, showing its ability to maintain context from previous exchanges.

This example effectively demonstrates how LangChain manages conversation state and context while leveraging Amazon Bedrock's language capabilities to provide coherent, informative responses across multiple turns of dialogue.

Note: **The complete code implementation for this example, along with additional scenarios, is available in the GitHub repository accompanying this book. To explore and run this code yourself, please refer to the `chapter7_langchain_chatbot.ipynb` Jupyter Notebook in the repository. The notebook contains runnable code cells that demonstrate the full implementation of the conversational AI system using LangChain and Amazon Bedrock.**

Chatbot with context

In this use case, we will ask the chatbot to QA based on the context provided. We will take a PDF file and use the Titan embeddings model to create vector representations. These vectors are stored in **Facebook AI Similarity Search (Faiss)**, an open-source library that efficiently indexes and searches dense vectors for fast similarity search and clustering in RAG systems. When the chatbot receives a question, it retrieves relevant vectors to generate an answer.

First, let us understand embeddings. Embeddings are vector representations of text that capture semantic meaning, allowing ML models to perform mathematical operations and find relationships between documents.

Now we will build a context-aware chatbot using this process:

- Create embeddings using Titan
- Store those embeddings in Faiss
- Query for relevant context

Here is the implementation:

Firstly, create the embedding for the document using Titan Embedding model:

```
from langchain_community.embeddings import BedrockEmbeddings
from langchain_community.vectorstores import FAISS
from langchain.prompts import ChatPromptTemplate
from langchain_community.document_loaders import PyPDFLoader
from langchain.text_splitter import RecursiveCharacterTextSplitter
from langchain.chains.combine_documents import create_stuff_documents_chain
from langchain.chains import create_retrieval_chain
# Create embeddings using Titan embedding model
br_embeddings = BedrockEmbeddings(
    model_id="amazon.titan-embed-text-v1",
    client=boto3_bedrock
)
```

Load and process the PDF document:

```
# Load the PDF file
pdf_loader = PyPDFLoader("data/generative-ai-guide-1.pdf")
documents = pdf_loader.load()
```

```
# Split the PDF into chunks using the more modern recursive splitter
text_splitter = RecursiveCharacterTextSplitter(chunk_size=1000, chunk_
overlap=200)
data = text_splitter.split_documents(documents)
```

Now, let us split the previously loaded PDF document into smaller chunks using **RecursiveCharacterTextSplitter**, which is more intelligent than the basic **CharacterTextSplitter**. We chunk the document into **1000** characters using **chunk_size** and specify **200** overlapping characters between consecutive chunks using **chunk_overlap**. This overlap helps ensure that important context is not lost at chunk boundaries.

Create Faiss vector store and RAG chain:

```
# Create FAISS vector store from documents
vectorstore_faiss = FAISS.from_documents(
    documents=data,
    embedding=br_embeddings
```

```
)

# Create a retriever from the vector store
retriever = vectorstore_faiss.as_retriever(
    search_type="similarity",
    search_kwargs={"k": 3}
)

# Create a prompt template for RAG
rag_prompt_template = """
Answer the question based on the following context:
{context}
Question: {input}
Answer:
"""

rag_prompt = ChatPromptTemplate.from_template(rag_prompt_template)

# Create the RAG chain using modern approach
document_chain = create_stuff_documents_chain(nova_llm, rag_prompt)
rag_chain = create_retrieval_chain(retriever, document_chain)
```

This implementation uses LangChain's modern RAG architecture with **create_retrieval_ chain** instead of the older **VectorStoreIndexWrapper** approach. The retrieval chain automatically handles embedding the query, finding similar documents, and passing context to the language model:

```
def ask_rag(question):
    result = rag_chain.invoke({"input": question})
    print_ww(result["answer"])
    return result
```

```
# Test RAG queries
print("Question 1: What are the tips provided by adobe stock that can approve
the generative AI images for sale?")
ask_rag("What are the tips provided by adobe stock that can approve the
generative AI images for sale")
```

Let us query LLM model in providing the tips to get the GenAI images for sale to be approved by *Adobe,* as follows:

```
print_ww(wrapper_store_faiss.query("What are the tips provided by adobe stock
that can approve the generative AI images for sale", llm=titan_llm))
```

The following content is the output of based on the above **print_ww** statement:

```
Know your rights
Do not infringe on the rights of other creatives
Carefully consider your prompts
Be selective
Edit to enhance your images
Find the right size
Help customers find your content
Is that person real?
How do you make money?
Keep learning and growing
```

As you can see the above output, the response is being generated using the PDF document and also keeping the previous historical conversation as input along with current input.

You have been provided sample code for this scenario in a Jupyter Notebook, **chapter7_langchain_chatbot.ipynb**, which can be accessed in the GitHub repository of the book. You will see in the notebook that we generated the summary output from two different models to show you how easily you can interchange FMs. You can use the sample code and try out other FMs available on Bedrock to test their performance.

Knowledge retrieval using LlamaIndex

GenAI has emerged as a powerful technology for QA systems, enabling more natural and contextual responses. QA has been widely adopted across various industries in customer services to provide most accurate and personalized response, education and learning in creating interactive QA sessions and in finance and legal for intelligent document search.

We will be creating a QA application using RAG pipeline with LlamaIndex, the pipeline has the following steps:

1. Setup the LLM model (in this case we will use Claude 3 Sonnet) and embedding model (Titan Embedding).

2. Load data (PDF file) using **PDFReader** from LlamaIndex and create the embedding using Titan Embedding model.

3. Create a vector store using Faiss (in-memory vector database) and store the embedding of the PDF file.

4. In the final step, we will use query engine method from LlamaIndex to query pre-built index and the query method to interact with the index and retrieve relevant information based on user query.

Refer **chapter7_LlamaIndex_qa.ipynb** for the complete code which can be accessed in GitHub repository of the book.

Best practices for LangChain and LlamaIndex

When building GenAI applications using LangChain and LlamaIndex, it is important to leverage the various components and features provided by the library effectively.

LangChain

The following are some of the best practices for utilizing LangChain components:

- **Leverage agents and tools**: agents and tools are powerful components in LangChain that enable the creation of complex workflows and task automation. Utilize agents to orchestrate multiple tools and achieve higher-level objectives, while tools can encapsulate external services, APIs, or data sources. This modular approach promotes code reusability and extensibility.

- **Optimize prompt engineering**: Prompt engineering is crucial for effective interaction with language models. Leverage LangChain's prompt templating and management capabilities to craft well-structured prompts that guide the model towards desired outputs. Experiment with different prompt styles, such as few-shot prompts or **chain-of-thought (CoT)** prompts, to improve model performance.

- **Utilize memory and retrieval components**: LangChain provides various memory and retrieval components that can significantly enhance the performance and context-awareness of your GenAI applications. Leverage vector stores, document loaders, and text splitters to efficiently manage and retrieve relevant information from large datasets.

- **Implement chains and workflows**: Chains in LangChain allow you to compose and sequence multiple agents, tools, and prompts into complex workflows. Utilize chains to break down intricate tasks into smaller, manageable steps, and leverage conditional logic and control flow to create dynamic and adaptive processes.

- **Leverage LangChain's integration capabilities**: LangChain offers seamless integration with various language models, APIs, and data sources. Take advantage of these integrations to leverage the strengths of different models, access external data sources, or incorporate domain-specific knowledge bases into your application.

LlamaIndex

Here are some best practices for utilizing LlamaIndex components effectively:

- **Optimize data pre-processing**: LlamaIndex offers various data pre-processing techniques, such as text splitters, chunkers, and node pre-processors. Leverage these tools to pre-process your data optimally, ensuring that the information is divided into manageable chunks and formatted correctly for indexing and retrieval.

- **Choose the right index type**: LlamaIndex provides different index types, including list, tree, vector, and SQL indexes. Select the index type that best suits your use case, considering factors like data size, structure, and retrieval requirements. For example, vector indexes are well-suited for semantic similarity searches, while tree indexes are efficient for hierarchical data.

- **Implement query synthesis**: LlamaIndex offers query synthesis capabilities that can significantly improve the relevance and accuracy of your queries. Utilize techniques like query reformulation, query expansion, and query decomposition to generate more informative and precise queries, leading to better retrieval results.

- **Leverage index sharding and distributed computing**: For large-scale applications or datasets, consider sharding your index across multiple machines or leveraging distributed computing frameworks like Ray or Dask. LlamaIndex supports sharding and distributed computing out-of-the-box, enabling you to scale your application and improve performance.

- **Integrate with language models and pipelines**: LlamaIndex seamlessly integrates with various language models and pipelines, such as *Anthropic's Claude*, and *Hugging Face's pipelines*. Leverage these integrations to combine the power of language models with the efficient retrieval and indexing capabilities of LlamaIndex, enabling more advanced and intelligent GenAI applications.

The frameworks we have explored so far, LangChain and LlamaIndex, excel at orchestrating LLMs and managing data retrieval. However, as developers began building more sophisticated autonomous AI agents, new challenges emerged: managing complex multi-step reasoning, coordinating multiple agents, and handling stateful conversations. This led to the development of specialized agentic frameworks designed specifically for these use cases.

Purpose-built agentic frameworks

As GenAI applications evolve beyond static prompts and simple chains, there is a growing need for frameworks that support more dynamic, context-aware, and autonomous behavior. Purpose-built agentic frameworks address this by making it easier to develop AI agents, that can reason, plan, invoke tools, and adapt to user interactions in real-time. This section introduces three such frameworks: Strands Agents, LangGraph, and CrewAI. While each takes a different approach to modeling agent workflows, they share the common goal of making it easier to build intelligent, multi-step, and task-oriented AI systems. These frameworks also provide abstractions for memory, tool invocation, control flow, and production deployment areas where traditional orchestration frameworks like LangChain often require more custom wiring.

Strands Agents

Strands Agents is a simple-to-use, code-first, and production-ready SDK designed for building intelligent and autonomous AI agents. Developed by AWS, it offers seamless integration with

Amazon Bedrock but remains model-agnostic, supporting multiple model providers such as *Anthropic, Meta, OpenAI,* and *Ollama.*

At its core, Strands provides a lightweight but powerful SDK that lets developers create conversational agents with advanced capabilities. These include:

- Multi-agent capabilities
- Custom and built-in tools
- Memory and session state retention
- Amazon Bedrock Knowledge Bases integration
- Amazon Bedrock Guardrails integration
- MCP and A2A support
- Streaming and non-streaming support
- Security and safety focus
- Observability

Strands can be used for both conversational and non-conversational GenAI applications, and it is designed to scale in production environments.

The framework follows a model-driven approach where an agent is defined by three core components: an LLM, a set of tools, and a prompt. The agent runs an agent loop that uses the model's reasoning to decide next steps (e.g. whether to invoke a tool) and iteratively works towards a final answer.

This loop is illustrated in the following figure, showing how the agent interacts with the model and tools in cycles:

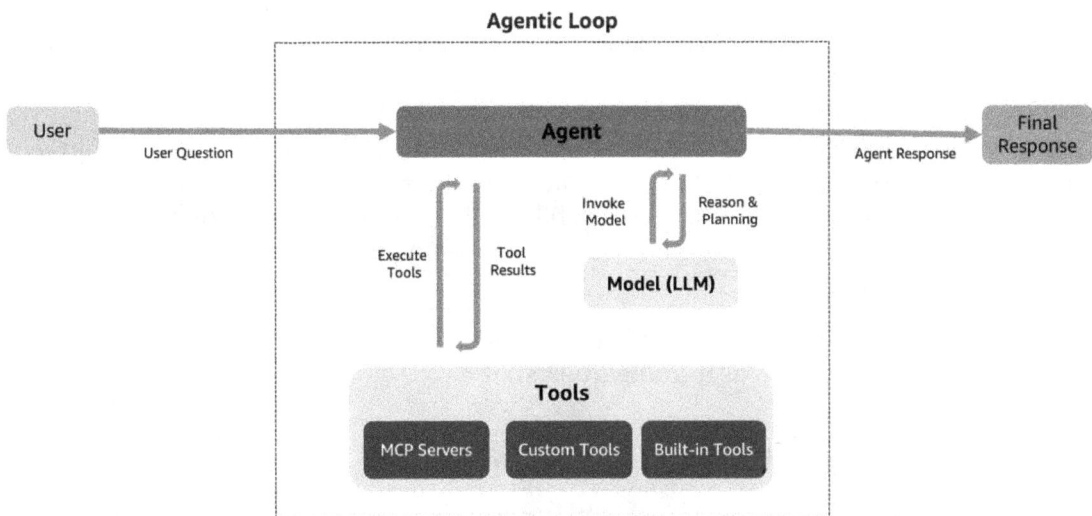

Figure 7.3: Strands Agent loop, where the agent processes input through the model (LLM)

This approach allows for complex multi-step reasoning and actions while maintaining conversation state throughout interactions.

Setup and model provider integration

To get started with Strands Agents SDK, you need Python 3.10 and AWS credentials (or API keys) that have permission to invoke the selected LLM. You can install the SDK, as follows:

```
pip install strands-agents strands-tools
```

By default, a new **Agent** in Strands uses Amazon Bedrock as the model provider (with Claude 3.7 Sonnet) as the default model in **us-west-2** region. You must configure AWS credentials and enable Bedrock access.

```
from strands import Agent
from strands.models import BedrockModel
from strands.models.llamaapi import LlamaAPIModel # Llama API
from strands.models.openai import OpenAIModel # For OpenAI LLM models
from strands.models.ollama import OllamaModel # Ollama (local) models

# Specify a Bedrock model
model = BedrockModel(
        model_id="us.anthropic.claude-3-7-sonnet-20250219-v1:0",
        region_name="us-west-2",
        temperature=0.3,
)

agent = Agent(model=model)
response = agent("Tell me about Generative AI in AWS.")
print (response)
```

Strands provides built-in integration classes for many model providers, including Amazon Bedrock, Anthropic (Claude API), OpenAI (direct or via LiteLLM), Meta Llama (via LlamaAPI), Ollama (for local models), and even custom providers you can implement yourself. In other words, Strands Agents is model-agnostic, it can work with virtually any LLM if it can receive a prompt and return a completion. This flexibility allows you to plug in the model that best suits your needs (enterprise models on Bedrock, open-source models, or other APIs) without changing your agent logic.

For more information on initial setup and model provider access, refer to **https://strandsagents. com/1.x/documentation/docs/user-guide/quickstart/**

Custom tools, built-in tools, and MCP

Tools are the primary mechanism to extend an agent's capabilities beyond text-based QA, allowing it to perform actions like API calls, calculations, file operations, etc. In Strands, a tool is essentially a function (or external API) that the agent can invoke when the model decides it is needed. Tools enable the agent to interact with the external environment (e.g. search web, fetch data, execute code) and provide the results back into the agent's reasoning loop.

Adding tools to an agent is simple, you provide them during agent initialization or dynamically at runtime. For example, to give an agent some basic abilities:

```
from strands import Agent
from strands_tools import calculator, file_read, shell

# Initialize agent with a list of tool functions
agent = Agent(tools=[calculator, file_read, shell])
response = agent("Show me the contents of the current directory and calculate
30x5.")
```

The above code imports three built-in tools (**calculator, file_read**, and **shell**) from **strands_tools** package. The agent's LLM recognizes these tools and can use them during conversations. The agent executes the tools and returns their output to the model. Tools can be used in combination for example, using **shell** to list files, **file_read** to read them, and **calculator** for computations. Agent response might be as follows:

```
<thinking> I'll help you with both tasks: showing the contents of the current
directory and calculating 30×5.
First, let's see what files are in the current directory:
Tool #1: shell
Do you want to proceed with execution? [y/*] y
-rw-r--r--  1 md  myinc  1215 Jun 28 11:31 hello-strands.py
-rw-r--r--  1 md  myinc   268 Jun 30 11:52 strands-custom.py
Now, let's calculate 30×5:
Tool #2: calculator
</thinking>

The contents of the current directory include:
- hello-strands.py (1215 bytes)
- strands-custom.py (268 bytes)
Plus the usual "." and ".." directory entries.
The calculation of 30×5 equals 150.
```

The above response shows you how LLM is reasoning to decide which tool to use, invoke those tools, and finally, give you the final response. This agent thinking can be very useful in development and debugging, but in a production environment, you would store this information in logs or Amazon **Simple Storage Service** (**S3**) for you to refer later and only display the final response to the user.

Strands make it easy to turn your own functions into custom tools for agent. The simplest way is to use **@tool** decorator provided by Strands SDK. For example:

```
from strands import Agent, tool
from strands.models import BedrockModel
from strands_tools import current_time, calculator

# Custom tool to check retirement tax penalties
@tool
def get_tax_penalty(age: int) -> str:
    """Check if retirement account early withdrawal penalty applies.
    Args:
        age: The person's current age
    Returns:
        str: Message indicating if penalty applies
    """
    if age < 59:
        return "Early withdrawal penalty applies."
    return "No early withdrawal penalty."

# Initialize AWS Bedrock model client
model = BedrockModel(
    model_id="us.amazon.nova-lite-v1:0",
    # model_id="us.anthropic.claude-sonnet-4-20250514-v1:0",
)

# Create an agent with both built-in and custom tools
agent = Agent(
    system_prompt="You are a helpful financial assistant. Use tools when
needed.",
    tools=[get_tax_penalty, calculator, current_time],
    model=model,
    callback_handler=None        # Help minimize LLM response verbosity
)

# Run a query that invoke tools
response = agent("I'm 45. Will I be penalized for withdrawing my 401(k)? Also,
what day is it today?")
print(response)
```

Agent's response might look like below depending upon the LLM you use:

Hi there! Since you are 45, you will be penalized for early withdrawal from your 401(k). Also, today is June 30, 2025. If you have any other questions, feel free to ask!

Strands Agents natively supports the MCP, which allows agents to discover and use structured tools provided by external services at runtime. This enables dynamic, standards-based integration with tool catalogs that can evolve independently of your code.

The MCP serves as a standardized way to connect AI models with various data sources and tools, like how USB-C standardizes device connections. It is particularly valuable when working with Strands Agents, as it enables seamless integration between LLM and external tools and services.

MCP offers two main transport methods for communication: **standard input/output (stdio)** for local integrations and command-line tools, and Streamable HTTP for more complex, stateless communications with multiple client connections. The protocol provides pre-built integrations, flexibility in switching between LLM providers, and secure data handling within your infrastructure.

Let us look at a sample example using stdio:

```
from mcp import stdio_client, StdioServerParameters
from strands import Agent
from strands.tools.mcp import MCPClient

# Initialize an MCP client connected to the AWS Docs MCP server
mcp_client = MCPClient(
    lambda: stdio_client(
        StdioServerParameters(
            command="uvx",
            args=["awslabs.aws-documentation-mcp-server@latest"]
        )
    )
)

# Connect to the server and load the exposed tools
with mcp_client:
    tools = mcp_client.list_tools_sync()

    # Create an agent that can use these MCP-based tools
    agent = Agent(
        system_prompt='''
        You are an expert assistant for AWS.
        Use the available tools to query and retrieve information as needed.''',
        tools=tools
    )

    # Ask a question about AWS services
    response = agent("What are the cost optimization best practices for Amazon
Bedrock?")
    print(response)
```

This setup demonstrates how agents can leverage external tool catalogs in a plug-and-play fashion. Because tool interfaces are defined via MCP, the agent does not need hardcoded logic or custom parsing, everything is discovered and executed dynamically at runtime.

Multi-agent orchestration

Strands have built-in patterns for composing multiple agents. You can model sub-agents as tools: for example, treat one specialized agent (say, a research assistant) as a callable tool for another (an orchestrator). This agents-as-tools approach mimics a human team (an orchestrator delegating to experts).

Strands also provides workflow, graph, and swarm orchestration patterns so that LLM can reason about invoking a sequence or group of specialized agents when solving a complex task.

Figure 7.4 demonstrates the *agents as tools* pattern, where a travel booking orchestrator supervises three specialist agents: hotel booking, flight booking, and itinerary planning, to coordinate tasks and provide an integrated travel solution:

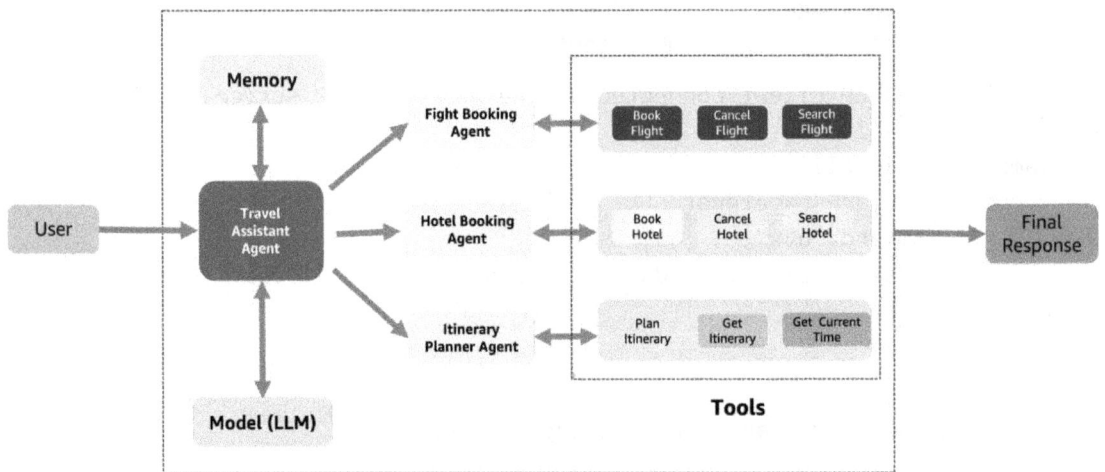

Figure 7.4: *Travel assistant multi-agent orchestration with Strands Agents SDK (agents-as-tool pattern)*

Safety and guardrails

Strands integrates natively with Amazon Bedrock Guardrails, enabling developers to block harmful content, redact PII, or filter off-topic inputs. When guardrails are triggered, Strands can optionally overwrite the user's input or the model's output to maintain safe conversation history.

Here is a simplified example:

```
from strands.models import BedrockModel
from strands import Agent

bedrock_model = BedrockModel(
    model_id="us.anthropic.claude-sonnet-4-20250514-v1:0",
    guardrail_id="<Amazon Bedrock Guardrails Id>",
```

```
        guardrail_version="1",
        guardrail_trace="enabled"
)
agent = Agent(model=bedrock_model, system_prompt="You are a helpful
assistant.")
resp = agent("Guide me on which stocks to buy for maximize returns.")

if resp.stop_reason == "guardrail_intervened":
    print("Guardrail triggered: response suppressed.")
```

Before specifying Bedrock Guardrails in the agent definition, you must create them in AWS console or using APIs. See official Amazon Bedrock Guardrails for more information: **https:// docs.aws.amazon.com/bedrock/latest/userguide/agents-guardrail.html**

Equally important is understanding and monitoring what your agents are doing internally. It is critical for debugging, performance tuning, and ensuring reliability. Strands SDK is designed with comprehensive observability in mind, offering logging, metrics, and distributed tracing out-of-the-box. These features make Strands suitable for enterprise production, where you need insight into each agent's decision process and resource usage.

Here is sample example of how you can access Strands metrics:

```
from strands import Agent
from strands_tools import calculator, current_time

# Initialize agent with calculator and time tools
agent = Agent(
    system_prompt="You are a helpful assistant that can perform calculations
and tell the time.",
    tools=[calculator, current_time]
)

# Execute a query that will use tools
result = agent("Calculate 42^9 and tell me what time it is right now.")
print(f"Response: {result}\n")

# Display key metrics in a concise format
print("=== Strands Metrics ===")

# Token usage
print(f"Tokens: {result.metrics.accumulated_usage['inputTokens']} in, "
      f"{result.metrics.accumulated_usage['outputTokens']} out, "
      f"{result.metrics.accumulated_usage['totalTokens']} total")

# Performance metrics
print(f"Latency: {result.metrics.accumulated_metrics['latencyMs']} ms")
```

```
print(f"Reasoning cycles: {result.metrics.cycle_count}")

# Tool usage summary
print("\nTool Usage:")
for name, metrics in result.metrics.tool_metrics.items():
    print(f"{name}: {metrics.call_count} calls, "
          f"{metrics.success_count} successes, "
          f"{metrics.total_time:.2f}s total time")
```

Response might look like:

```
42^9 = 406,671,383,849,472
The current time is 2025-06-30T23:17:32.188690+00:00 (UTC).

=== Strands Metrics ===
Tokens: 7276 in, 171 out, 7447 total
Latency: 5895 ms
Reasoning cycles: 3

Tool Usage:
  calculator: 1 calls, 1 successes, 0.01s total time
  current_time: 1 calls, 1 successes, 0.00s total time
```

You can get detailed logs, metrics for every run, and end-to-end traces that integrate with modern monitoring systems such as Datadog, LangFuse, Amazon X-Ray, Amazon CloudWatch etc.

Deployment and production

Strands Agents are deployment-ready and support many operational patterns. The framework is designed to be flexible, meaning you can run it on everything from a local server to serverless cloud service. You can run agents as a monolith (loop and tools in one process) or as microservices (e.g. agent loop behind an API calling separate tool services). The framework supports multiple deployment patterns such as AWS Lambda, Amazon EKS, Amazon ECS, Amazon EC2, as well as Amazon Bedrock AgentCore.

AgentCore adds infrastructure specifically tailored for agent workloads, removing much of the overhead involved in scaling, securing, and operating AI agents in production. It provides services such as Runtime, Gateway, Memory, Identity and Observability that can be combined or used independently. These services integrate with Strands Agents alongside other frameworks like CrewAI, LangGraph, and LlamaIndex, and work with models both within and outside of Amazon Bedrock. This flexibility allows you to accelerate deployment without building custom scaffolding from scratch. For hands-on demonstrations, see the official AWS GitHub samples at **https://github.com/awslabs/amazon-bedrock-agentcore-samples**.

As with any production system, follow operational best practices: apply health checks, error handling, and logging, and connect Strands telemetry to your monitoring stack (e.g., CloudWatch, Datadog, Prometheus, Grafana). When combined with explicit configuration of models, tools, and workflows, plus the observability and guardrails built into the Strands framework, these practices help ensure that agentic applications remain reliable and safe under real-world conditions.

LangGraph

LangGraph is an open-source agentic framework for creating multi-step AI workflows with explicit state management, making it ideal for complex agent development.

The framework models agent workflows as directed graphs. You can build stateful, multi-step AI applications using this graph-based approach.

LangGraph defines agent behavior through three fundamental components. State represents a shared data structure containing the current application snapshot, typically implemented as a **TypedDict** containing messages, context, and workflow status. Nodes are Python functions that encode specific agent logic or tool interactions. Edges are functions that determine the next node to execute based on the current state, enabling dynamic routing and complex decision trees.

LangGraph allows you to:

- Define explicit states and transitions
- Create complex workflows with multiple processing steps
- Manage conversation context effectively
- Build agents that can reason through multi-step tasks

Let us dive into building a simple conversational agent using LangGraph and Amazon Bedrock:

- **Install packages**:

  ```
  pip install -U langchain-aws langgraph langsmith
  ```

- **Setting up the environment**:

  First, we need to import the necessary libraries:

  ```
  import boto3
  from typing import Annotated
  from typing_extensions import TypedDict
  from langgraph.graph import StateGraph, START, END
  from langgraph.graph.message import add_messages
  from langchain_aws import ChatBedrockConverse
  ```

These imports give us access to Amazon Bedrock through **boto3**, type annotations for our state structure, LangGraph's core components for building our agent and LangChain's integration with Amazon Bedrock.

Defining the state structure

In LangGraph, we need to define the structure of our agent's state. This is where we will store conversation history and any other information our agent needs to maintain:

```
class State(TypedDict):
    """Define the state structure for our conversation graph.

    The 'messages' field uses the add_messages annotation to indicate that
    new messages should be appended rather than overwriting existing ones.
    """
    messages: Annotated[list, add_messages]
```

The **Annotated[list, add_messages]** syntax is particularly important. It tells LangGraph that when updating the **messages** field, new messages should be appended to the existing list rather than replacing it. This is crucial for maintaining conversation history.

Configurating the LLM

Next, we will setup our connection to Amazon Bedrock's Claude model:

```
def setup_bedrock_llm():
    """Initialize and configure the LLM."""
    bedrock_client = boto3.client("bedrock-runtime", region_name="us-west-2")

    llm = ChatBedrockConverse(
        model="us.anthropic.claude-3-7-sonnet-20250219-v1:0",
        temperature=0,  # More deterministic responses
        max_tokens=None,  # Let the model determine response length
        client=bedrock_client,
    )

    return llm
```

This function creates a Bedrock client and initializes Claude with appropriate parameters. We are using a **temperature** of **0** for more deterministic responses, which is often desirable in agent applications.

Configuring the chatbot node

Now, we will define the core function that processes user input and generates responses:

```
def chatbot(state: State):
    """Process the current state and generate a response using the LLM."""
    return {"messages": [llm.invoke(state["messages"])]}
```

This function takes the current state (containing the conversation history) and uses our LLM to generate a response. The response is then returned as an update to the state's **messages** field.

Building the conversation graph

The following is the code for building the conversation graph:

```
def build_conversation_graph():
    """Create and configure the LangGraph conversation flow."""
    graph_builder = StateGraph(State)
    graph_builder.add_node("chatbot", chatbot)
    graph_builder.add_edge(START, "chatbot")
    return graph_builder.compile()
```

This function:

- Creates a new graph builder with our state structure
- Adds our chatbot function as a node in the graph
- Defines the flow: **START | chatbot**
- Compiles the graph into an executable

While this is a simple linear graph, LangGraph supports much more complex flows with multiple nodes and conditional branching.

Handling user interactions

To process user input through our graph, we define a function that streams the results:

```
def stream_graph_updates(user_input: str):
    """Process user input through the graph and stream the response."""
    initial_state = {"messages": [{"role": "user", "content": user_input}]}

    for event in graph.stream(initial_state):
        for value in event.values():
            print("Assistant:", value["messages"][-1].content)
```

This function, first creates an initial state with the user's message, streams the execution of the graph and then prints the assistant's response as it is generated.

Putting it all together

Finally, we bring everything together in our main execution block:

```
# Set up the components
llm = setup_bedrock_llm()
graph = build_conversation_graph()
```

```
print("LangGraph conversation agent ready!")

# Example usage
user_input = "What do you know about LangGraph?"
stream_graph_updates(user_input)
```

This sets up our LLM and graph, then runs an interactive chat loop that processes user input and displays responses.

Extending the graph

While our example is straightforward, LangGraph's true power lies in building more complex agents. By defining explicit states and transitions, you can create complex AI workflows that maintain context and follow specific processing paths.

As you build more sophisticated agents, consider exploring LangGraph's additional features like:

- Persistent state storage
- Parallel execution paths
- Human-in-the-loop workflows
- Integration with external tools and APIs

With these capabilities, you can create agents that handle complex tasks while maintaining coherent conversations with users.

Building collaborative AI teams

CrewAI is a Python framework that lets you build teams of AI agents that work together to solve problems. Instead of having one AI assistant do everything, you can create specialized agents that each focus on what they do best.

Think of it like building a consulting team. You would not hire just one person to handle finance, technology, marketing, and legal work. You would hire specialists for each area. CrewAI works the same way you create AI agents with different roles and expertise, then have them collaborate on complex tasks.

The framework is built on four main components that work together:

- **Agents**: Individual team members with specific roles, goals, and backgrounds that shape how they work
- **Tools**: Extensions that let agents search the web, scrape websites, access databases, or connect with APIs for real-world information
- **Tasks**: Specific jobs with clear descriptions and expected results for each agent
- **Crew**: The manager that controls how agents work together and in what order

What makes CrewAI powerful is how flexible it is. Teams can work one after another, where one agent's results become input for the next agent, creating a chain of specialized work. Or agents can work at the same time when their tasks do not depend on each other, which makes everything faster. The framework also supports management structures where a boss agent coordinates and assigns work to specialist agents.

The integration with different language models, including Amazon Bedrock, means you can use the latest LLMs while keeping control over your infrastructure and data. This is especially valuable for business applications where security, compliance, and cost control are important.

In our sample example, we will see how two specialized agents work together to provide complete company analysis. The market analyst focuses on financial performance and stock trends, while the technology analyst looks at product innovation and business strategy. Together, they deliver insights that neither could produce on their own, showing the real power of AI teamwork.

```python
from crewai import Agent, Crew, Process, Task, LLM
from crewai_tools import SerperDevTool, ScrapeWebsiteTool
import os

# Configure Bedrock LLM
llm = LLM(
    model="bedrock/anthropic.claude-3-5-sonnet-20241022-v2:0",
    aws_access_key_id=os.getenv('AWS_ACCESS_KEY_ID'),
    aws_secret_access_key=os.getenv('AWS_SECRET_ACCESS_KEY'),
    aws_region_name=os.getenv('AWS_REGION_NAME')
)

# Agent configuration
agents_config = {
    'market_analyst': {
        'role': 'Market Analyst',
        'goal': 'Analyze market trends and investment opportunities',
        'backstory': 'Experienced financial analyst with expertise in market
research and trend analysis'
    },
    'tech_analyst': {
        'role': 'Technology Analyst',
        'goal': 'Analyze technology trends and product developments',
        'backstory': 'Tech industry expert with deep knowledge of product
innovation and market disruption'
    }
}

# Create agents
```

```python
market_analyst = Agent(
    **agents_config['market_analyst'],
    tools=[SerperDevTool(), ScrapeWebsiteTool()],
    llm=llm
)

tech_analyst = Agent(
    **agents_config['tech_analyst'],
    tools=[SerperDevTool(), ScrapeWebsiteTool()],
    llm=llm
)

if __name__ == "__main__":
    # Get user input
    company = input("Which company would you like to analyze? ")

    # Create tasks with user input
    market_task = Task(
        description=f"Find the current stock price of {company} and provide a
150-word analysis of its recent performance",
        expected_output=f"{company}'s current stock price and a 150-word
analysis of recent performance and market trends",
        agent=market_analyst
    )

    tech_task = Task(
        description=f"Research {company}'s latest product announcements and
provide a 100-word summary of their innovation strategy",
        expected_output=f"A 100-word summary of {company}'s recent product
developments and innovation direction",
        agent=tech_analyst
    )

    # Create and run the crew
    crew = Crew(
        agents=[market_analyst, tech_analyst],
        tasks=[market_task, tech_task],
        process=Process.sequential
    )

    result = crew.kickoff()
    print(result)
```

This example demonstrates the basic structure of a CrewAI application. With two agents and their respective tasks, we can analyze a company from both financial and technology perspectives. Adding more agents follows the same pattern: define their role and goals, assign them tools, create their tasks, and add them to the crew.

The framework handles the coordination between agents automatically, whether they work sequentially or in parallel. Each agent focuses on their specific domain while contributing to the overall analysis.

CrewAI works well for scenarios where you need different types of expertise applied to the same problem, from research and analysis to content creation and decision support.

Choosing the right agentic framework

The choice between agentic frameworks often depends on how much complexity you want to manage versus how much control you need over the final system.

Strands Agents takes a model-driven approach that lets the LLM handle most of the orchestration work. You define three components: model, tools, and prompt, and the framework handles the rest. While developed by AWS, it is open-source and supports multiple model providers. Strands comes enterprise-ready with built-in observability, 20+ pre-built tools, and AWS service integrations including knowledge base, guardrails, and prompt caching etc. This simplicity makes it the fastest way to get started and deploy to production.

CrewAI models agents as team members with specific roles working toward shared goals. This role-based approach feels natural for many business problems and makes it easy to explain your system to non-technical stakeholders. The learning curve is moderate, you need to understand roles, tasks, and how crews coordinate but the documentation is good and there are plenty of examples. The main consideration is that advanced features like monitoring and visual workflow tools require paid enterprise plans.

LangGraph gives you precise control over agent behavior through graph-based workflows. Each step in your agent's process becomes a node in a graph, with explicit control over state transitions and decision points. This approach is powerful for complex conversation flows or scenarios requiring careful state management.

The following table shows the framework selection guide:

Consideration	Strands Agents	CrewAI	LangGraph
Getting started	Easiest	Moderate	Moderate to complex
Model flexibility	Multi-provider	Multi-provider	Multi-provider
Team collaboration	Supported	Core feature	Custom build
Fine-grained control	Moderate	Moderate	Extensive
Enterprise features	Built-in (observability, tools, AWS integrations)	Paid tier	Paid tier
Error handling and recovery	Most comprehensive: built-in retry, rate limiting, automatic error handling	Basic rate limiting; limited retry support	Moderate: requires configuration but has retry support

Table 7.1: AI Agent framework selection

Choose Strands when you want the quickest path to production, need built-in enterprise features (observability, retry, rate limiting, error handling) without additional costs, are using AWS services like Bedrock Knowledge Bases or Guardrails, or prefer letting the framework handle orchestration complexity.

Choose CrewAI when your problem maps well to team-based workflows, you need rapid prototyping capabilities, or you want an intuitive way to explain your system's structure.

Choose LangGraph when you need precise control over agent behavior, have complex state management requirements, or are already invested in the LangChain ecosystem.

All three frameworks are open-source and support multiple model providers, but Strands offers the most comprehensive out-of-the-box enterprise capabilities, especially for teams already using AWS infrastructure.

Conclusion

In this chapter, we explored powerful open-source frameworks for building GenAI applications with Amazon Bedrock. We began with foundational frameworks like LangChain and LlamaIndex that provide modular components for orchestrating language models and efficiently retrieving knowledge. Through practical examples, we demonstrated building conversational chatbots and QA systems leveraging these frameworks with Amazon Bedrock's models.

We then advanced to purpose-built agentic frameworks such as Strands Agents, LangGraph, and CrewAI designed for more complex autonomous systems. These frameworks offer different approaches to building intelligent agents: from Strands' model-driven simplicity, to LangGraph's explicit state management, to CrewAI's collaborative agent teams. Each framework provides unique capabilities for different use cases while integrating seamlessly with Amazon Bedrock.

By understanding the strengths of each framework, developers can choose the right tool for their specific requirements, whether building simple conversational interfaces or sophisticated multi-agent systems that reason, plan, and adapt to user needs.

In the next chapter, we will discuss the details of building custom models using Amazon Bedrock.

Points to remember

- LangChain's model-agnostic design enables seamless integration with diverse LLMs, fostering the development of versatile GenAI applications with its modular architecture of agents, chains, and utilities.

- LlamaIndex transforms raw data into optimized formats for efficient querying and retrieval, making it ideal for building knowledge-intensive applications with large datasets.

- Strands Agents offers production-ready agent development with comprehensive built-in error handling, tools, and observability, taking a model-driven approach that simplifies building autonomous systems.

- LangGraph provides explicit state management through graph structures, giving developers precise control over agent workflows and decision paths for more complex reasoning patterns.

- CrewAI enables collaborative multi-agent teams with role-based specialists working together on complex tasks, making it well-suited for problems that benefit from different types of expertise.

- When choosing a framework, consider your application's complexity, development timeline, and production requirements, general orchestration frameworks work well for straightforward applications, while agentic frameworks excel for autonomous, multi-step reasoning tasks.

Exercises

1. Build a contextual text and image search engine for product recommendations. Image search is a very important use case in e-commerce as it enables customers to search for products based on using text descriptions or images, this can enhance the product discovery experience. In this exercise you have to use multimodal embedding model to embed both text and images and use the RAG pipeline to do the image search using LangChain.

2. Build a summarization solution with the input as text file using LangChain framework. Summarization using GenAI has numerous applications of summarizing research papers, journals, documents, reports, new articles and customer inquiries or feedback. In this exercise, you have to make use of LangChain chain functionality to summarize.

3. Build a document QA agent using Strands Agents that can answer questions about multiple PDF documents. Implement tools for file reading, summarization, and information extraction. Your agent should handle user queries, retrieve relevant information from the documents, and provide accurate answers with source citations. Include proper error handling for file operations and use Strands observability features to track agent reasoning.

Join our Discord space

Join our Discord workspace for latest updates, offers, tech happenings around the world, new releases, and sessions with the authors:

https://discord.bpbonline.com

CHAPTER 8

Building Custom Models with Amazon Bedrock

Introduction

As **generative AI (GenAI)** models continue to evolve, their ability to understand and generate human-like text, images, and other data has opened up a world of possibilities. However, to unlock their full potential, these **foundation models (FMs)** often require customizing to adapt to specific domains or tasks. In this chapter, we will evaluate when to consider fine-tuning and delve into the process of fine-tuning FMs using Amazon Bedrock. You will learn the benefits of fine-tuning and why it is crucial for leveraging the power of customized GenAI in real-world applications. We will guide you through a hands-on tutorial, where you will learn to customize Amazon Titan Text Lite model to suit unique requirements. Additionally, we will address common questions, share best practices, and provide tips and tricks to help you navigate the fine-tuning process seamlessly, ensuring you can build custom models that meet your specific needs.

Structure

The chapter covers the following topics:

- Model customization
- Use cases and applications of customized FMs
- Customizing models on Amazon Bedrock

Objectives

By the end of this chapter, readers will have a solid understanding of how to fine-tune and customize FMs using Amazon Bedrock. You will learn the prerequisites and steps involved in submitting a model customization job, managing it throughout the process, and analyzing the results. Additionally, you will gain insights into effectively using the model you have customized, along with code samples to guide you through the implementation. We will also provide guidelines and best practices for model customization, equipping you with the knowledge to optimize your customization efforts. Furthermore, you will be prepared to troubleshoot and overcome common challenges that may arise during the model customization process. By the end of this chapter, you will have the necessary skills to harness the power of Amazon Bedrock and customized FMs to create solutions tailored to your specific needs.

Model customization

Fine-tuning FMs has become increasingly important as the demand for specialized and high-performing AI models continues to grow. While **large language models** (**LLMs**) like *Anthropic Claude* and *Meta Llama* have achieved remarkable success in many natural language processing tasks, their performance can be further improved by fine-tuning them on specific domains or tasks. For applications that require low latency and cost efficiency, smaller language models often present an attractive option. While generalized LLMs boast impressive capabilities, customized small models tailored to specific domains or use cases can sometimes outperform their larger counterparts. This presents developers with an intriguing alternative to explore, allowing them to leverage the strengths of specialized models optimized for their unique requirements.

Customization is often needed in scenarios, as follows:

- **Domain-specific knowledge is required**: Pre-trained models may lack the necessary understanding of specialized domains like medicine, law, or finance. Fine-tuning on domain-specific data can help models capture the nuances and terminologies of these domains.

- **Task-specific optimization is crucial**: Pre-trained models are trained on a broad range of tasks, but their performance can be suboptimal for specific tasks like **question answering** (**QA**), summarization, or translation. Fine-tuning on task-specific data can significantly improve their performance.

- **Prompt engineering and retrieval augmented generation fall short**: While prompt engineering and **retrieval augmented generation** (**RAG**) techniques can enhance the performance of pre-trained models, they may not yield the desired level of performance in certain scenarios, particularly when dealing with highly specialized or complex tasks.

- **Cost of using larger or more sophisticated FMs is a blocker**: Larger models have a lot more generalized capability which makes them an attractive option while starting out on a use case but cost can be prohibitive for production use cases. A customized smaller model trained for specific scenarios would be more budget-friendly and delivering similar performance to its larger counterparts.

To address these challenges, various fine-tuning techniques have been developed, as follows:

- **PEFT techniques**:

  o **LoRA**: Low-rank adaptation (LoRA) fine-tunes a small set of task-specific parameters while freezing the pre-trained model's original parameters. This approach is computationally efficient and allows for fine-tuning on smaller datasets.

  o **Prefix-tuning**: This technique introduces a small set of task-specific prefix parameters that are prepended to the input sequence, allowing for efficient fine-tuning without modifying the pre-trained model's parameters.

  o **PEFT**: There are other **parameter-efficient fine-tuning** (PEFT) techniques such as adapters, QLoRA, prompt-tuning, p-tuning. Adapters are early PEFT modules that add trainable task-specific parameters to transformer layers, while QLoRA enhances the original LoRA by quantizing parameters to 4 bits for significant memory savings. Prompt-tuning involves injecting customized prompts, either manual or AI-generated into the input data, with soft prompts typically outperforming human-created ones. P-tuning, a variant focused on natural language understanding, introduces automated prompt training and generation to improve effectiveness over time.

- **RLHF**: Reinforcement learning from human feedback (RLHF) fine-tunes language models using reinforcement learning based on human preferences and feedback. This approach can help models learn to generate outputs that align with human values and preferences, improving their safety and reliability.

- **Multi-task fine-tuning**: This technique involves fine-tuning a single model on multiple tasks simultaneously, enabling the model to learn task-specific knowledge while maintaining its general language understanding capabilities.

- **Domain-adaptive pre-training**: This approach involves further pre-training a FM on domain-specific data before fine-tuning, allowing the model to capture domain-specific knowledge and patterns more effectively.

By leveraging these fine-tuning techniques, developers can create custom models that are highly specialized, accurate, and tailored to specific use cases, unlocking the full potential of GenAI in various domains and applications. However, it is still complex for developers to implement these techniques without any ML background.

Amazon Bedrock simplifies the process of customizing FMs by abstracting away the complex technical details of fine-tuning techniques. Instead of requiring users to have in-depth knowledge of specific fine-tuning methodologies. Amazon Bedrock provides a user-friendly interface that allows users to choose between three main customization options, that is, fine-tuning, continued pre-training, and distillation.

Refer to the following details:

- **Fine-tuning**: Fine-tuning is the process of taking a pre-trained FM and adapting it to a specific task or domain by training it on labeled data relevant to that task or domain. This option is suitable when users have a smaller dataset and want to improve the model's accuracy for specific tasks without the need for extensive training time or computational resources.

- **Continued pre-training**: Continued pre-training, also known as **domain-adaptive pre-training**, involves updating some parameters of the pre-trained model while retaining its prior learning. The model is regularly updated with new data, allowing it to continuously learn and expand its knowledge. This approach is more efficient than fully retraining a large model from scratch, as it leverages the existing knowledge and capabilities of the pre-trained model.

- **Distillation**: Model distillation is a knowledge transfer technique where a larger, more capable teacher model's expertise is transferred to a smaller, more efficient student model. This process leverages advanced data synthesis techniques to generate high-quality responses from the teacher model, which are then used to fine-tune the student model. The result is a more compact, faster, and cost-efficient model that maintains the accuracy and capabilities of the larger model for specific use cases. This approach is particularly valuable when seeking to balance model performance with operational efficiency.

A summary of model customization options on Amazon Bedrock and their purpose is presented in the table:

Model customization option	Purpose
Fine-tuning	Adapts a model to a specific task using labeled data
Continued pre-training	Updates a model with domain-specific, unlabeled data
Distillation	Transfers knowledge from a large teacher model to a smaller, cost-efficient student model

Table 8.1: Model customization options on Amazon Bedrock with their purpose

By providing these three distinct customization options, Amazon Bedrock allows users to just focus on their specific use case and objective. This user-friendly approach democratizes the process of customizing FMs, making it accessible to a broader range of users. Amazon Bedrock handles the complexities of fine-tuning methodologies behind the scenes, enabling users to leverage state-of-the-art techniques without needing to implement them manually.

Use cases and applications of customized FMs

Customizing FMs can unlock significant value across various sectors by tailoring the model's knowledge and outputs to specific domains, contexts, and requirements. The following are some potential use cases where model customization could be advantageous:

- **Healthcare**: Customized FMs can be trained on medical literature, patient data, and domain-specific knowledge to provide accurate and contextually relevant information for diagnosis, treatment recommendations, and patient communication.

- **Legal**: By fine-tuning models on legal documents, precedents, and jurisdiction-specific laws, customized models can assist legal professionals in drafting contracts, analyzing cases, and providing targeted legal advice.

- **Finance**: Customized models can be tailored to understand financial products, regulations, and customer data, enabling personalized financial advisory services, fraud detection analysis, and automated compliance checks.

- **Customer service**: By integrating domain-specific knowledge base and customer interaction data, customized FMs can deliver accurate and personalized customer support, enhancing the overall **user experience (UX)**.

- **Education**: FMs can be customized to align with specific curricula, learning styles, and educational content, enabling personalized learning experiences, automated grading, and tailored content generation.

- **Content creation and media**: Customized FMs can generate creative content, such as articles, marketing copy, and scripts, while adhering to specific brand guidelines, styles, and audience preferences.

- **E-commerce and retail**: By incorporating product catalogs, customer data, and industry trends, customized FMs can provide personalized product descriptions, recommendations, and customer interactions in the e-commerce and retail sectors.

These are just a few examples of how customizing LLMs can unlock new opportunities and enhance experiences across various industries. The key advantage lies in the ability to tailor the model's knowledge and outputs to specific domains, contexts, and user requirements, resulting in more accurate, relevant, and valuable information generation. Amazon Bedrock enables secure, private model customization with customer-managed keys and data governance, which is especially relevant in sectors like healthcare and finance.

Now, we understand different use cases of custom models, let us fine-tune Amazon Titan model on Amazon Bedrock.

Customizing models on Amazon Bedrock

You can utilize customization options, that is, fine-tuning, continued pre-training, and distillation using AWS Management console or Amazon Bedrock APIs.

Let us explore how you can fine-tune Amazon Titan model using AWS Management Console.

Note: Newer models such as Amazon Nova are also available for fine-tuning in Amazon Bedrock, and follows similar process outlined below.

Fine-tuning

Let us go through step-by-step on how to fine-tune a model on Amazon Bedrock using AWS Management Console.

Refer to the following steps:

1. Type **Bedrock** in the services search bar at the top of the console and select **Amazon Bedrock** to navigate to the Amazon Bedrock console. Select **Custom models** under **Foundation models** from the left panel.

2. Select **Customize model** and select **Create Fine-tuning job,** as shown in the figure:

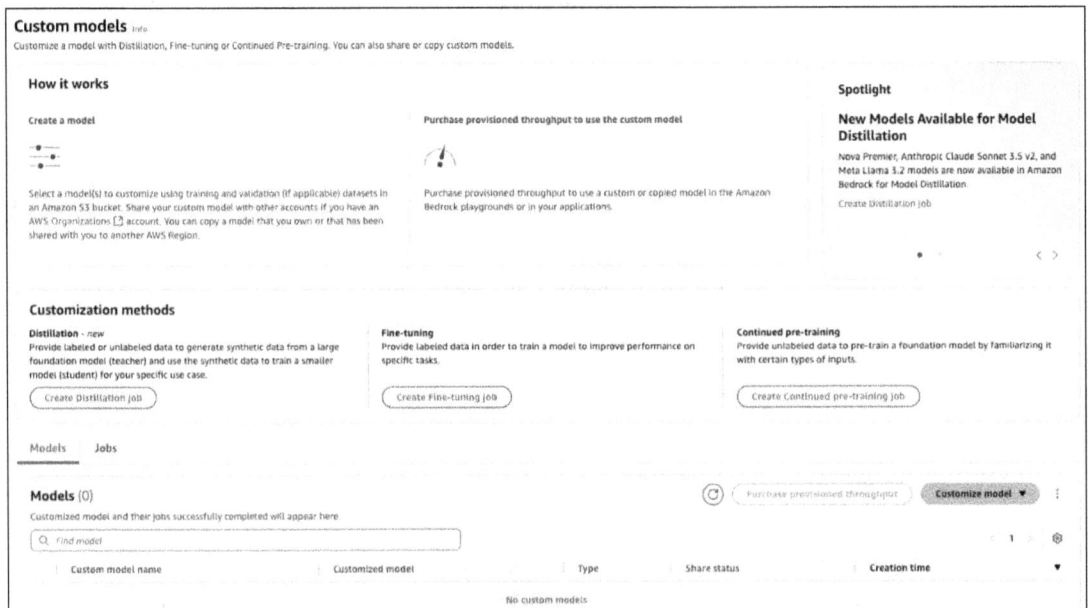

Figure 8.1: Create Fine-tuning job on Amazon Bedrock

3. Amazon Bedrock supports multiple models that you can customize using your own data. Select **Source model** as **Titan Text G1 - Lite**.

Note: At the time of writing, there are several other FMs from Amazon (models from Nova, and Titan families) as well as other providers such as Cohere Command, Meta Llama, and Anthropic Claude models available for fine-tuning. Not all models support continued pre-training, and distillation, some may only support fine-tuning.

4. Enter a name to identify the new fine-tuned model.

5. Optionally, you can encrypt the customized model artifacts using your customer-managed KMS key. By default, Amazon Bedrock encrypts model artifacts with a key that AWS manages for you.

6. Next, enter a name to identify the training job, as shown in the following figure:

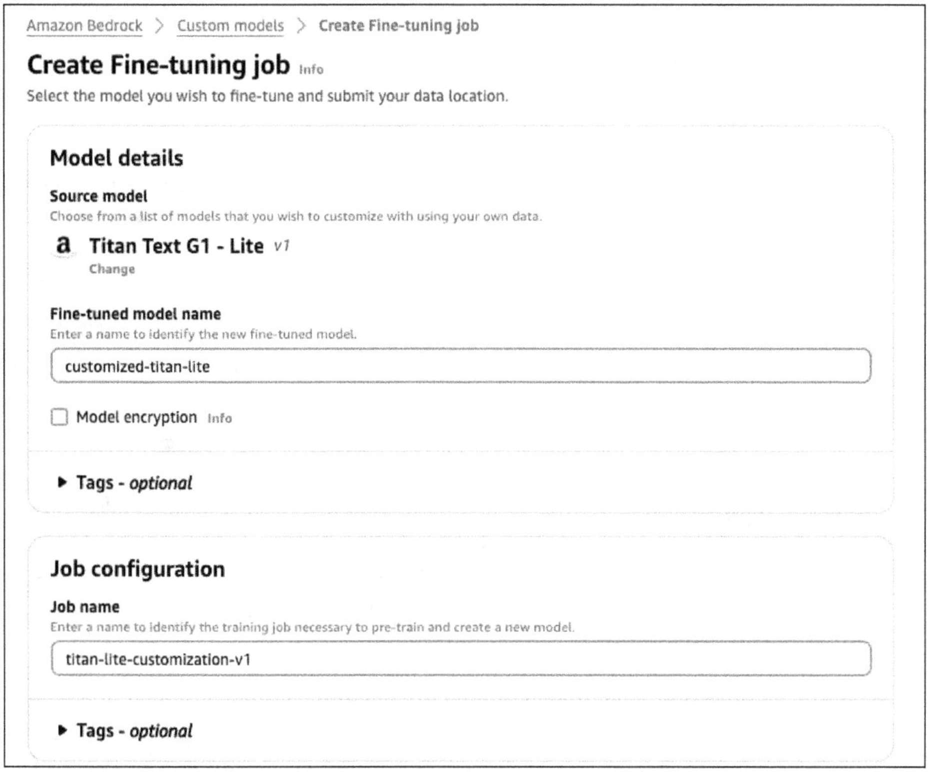

Figure 8.2: Configure fine-tuning job

7. Next, we need to provide the Amazon **S3 location** of your training and optionally validation datasets, as shown in the following figure:

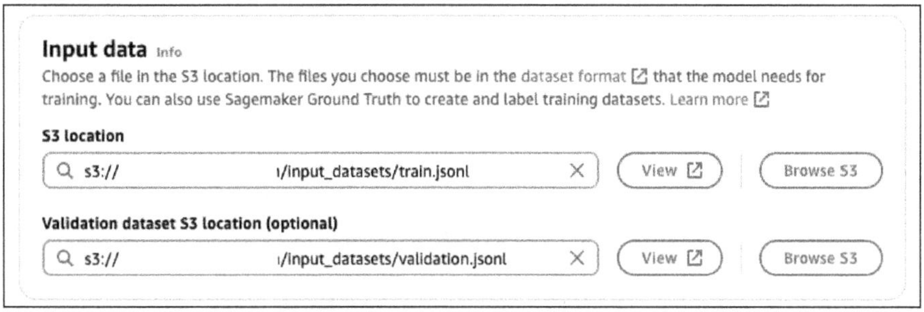

Figure 8.3: Configure input data

Amazon Bedrock can use validation datasets to verify model performance. Make sure the data set is a JSONL file with multiple JSON lines. Each JSON line will provide an example containing both prompt (input) and completion (expected output) field. The expected format is as follows:

```
{"prompt": "<prompt1>", "completion": "<expected generated text>"}
{"prompt": "<prompt2>", "completion": "<expected generated text>"}
```

The following are few sample training data entries for a hypothetical use case of generating short taglines or slogans:

```
{"prompt": "A coffee shop", "completion": "Where every cup is crafted
with passion."}
{"prompt": "A luxury car brand", "completion": "Driving ambition."}
{"prompt": "An outdoor gear company", "completion": "Equipped for
adventure."}
{"prompt": "A fitness app", "completion": "Your strength, simplified."}
{"prompt": "A cybersecurity firm", "completion": "Guarding your digital
frontlines."}
```

Note: Fine-tuning Amazon Nova models require you to follow specific guidelines including specific formats for datasets. Please review AWS Documentation at https://docs.aws.amazon.com/nova/latest/userguide/fine-tune-prepare-data-understanding.html

8. Next, section allows you to specify hyperparameters to control the training process, such as learning rate, total number of iterations (epochs) etc. For the first training job, you can leave all default value as is.

9. Next, specify S3 location to store model validation results.

10. At last, you need to create a new IAM role or choose an existing IAM role to allow Amazon Bedrock to read input datasets from S3 bucket, and write output datasets to specified S3 location.

11. Finally, select **Create Fine-tuning job** as shown in *Figure 8.4*. It may take few hours for the job to complete.

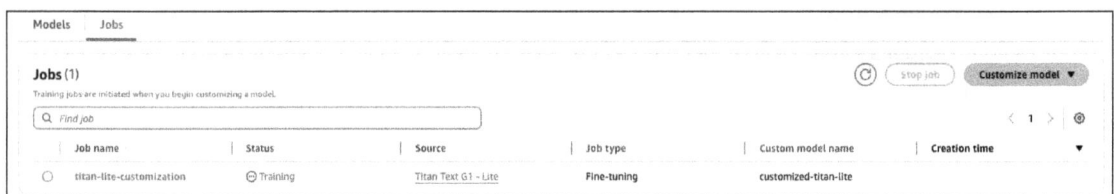

Figure 8.4: View fine-tuning jobs

12. Once the fine-tuning job status shows as **Complete**, you will see the fine-tuned model available under **Models** tab similar to the following figure:

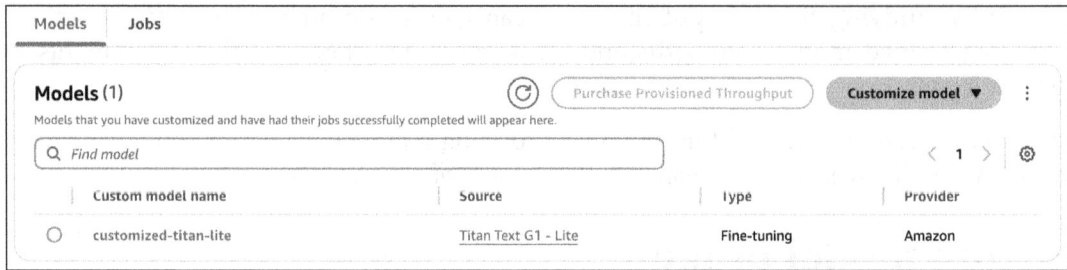

Figure 8.5: Review customized model

After completing a model customization job, you can analyze the model using the *trainingMetrics* and *validationMetrics*, deploy it for inference (optionally purchasing Provisioned Throughput for sustained workloads), or run a model evaluation job to assess its performance.

Analyzing trained custom model

After completing a model customization job, you can analyze the training process by examining the output files in the specified S3 folder. These files provide valuable insights into the model's performance, enabling you to evaluate and tune the model as needed. The `step_wise_training_metrics.csv` file contains metrics such as training loss, perplexity, and epoch numbers, which can be used to assess how well the model fits the training data and its predictive abilities.

Additionally, if a validation dataset was included, the `validation_metrics.csv` file offers similar metrics for the validation data, allowing you to gauge the model's generalization capabilities. The following is an output of a **sample `validation_metrics.csv`** file:

step_number	epoch_number	validation_loss	validation_perplexity
563	1	2.001309522	7.398739815
1126	2	2.01385674	7.492156029
1689	3	2.214722246	9.158864021
2252	4	2.582432039	13.2292738
2815	5	3.058260251	21.29048347

Figure 8.6: Analyze model performance metrics

The structure of validation metrics will include the following:

- **step_number**: The step in the training process. Starts from 0.
- **epoch_number**: The epoch in the training process. You specify the number of epochs at the time of job configuration.
- **validation_loss**: Indicates how well the model fits the validation data. A lower value indicates a better fit.
- **validation_perplexity**: Indicates how well the model can predict a sequence of tokens. A lower value indicates better predictive ability.

By carefully studying these output files, you can gain a comprehensive understanding of the custom trained model's strengths and weaknesses, facilitating further refinements and optimizations.

You can also evaluate your custom model by running a model evaluation job with Amazon Bedrock. We will cover that in *Chapter 11, RAG and Model Evaluation*.

Custom model usage

We need to **Purchase Provisioned Throughput** to test the model we just fine-tuned. There are multiple options to **Purchase Provisioned Throughput**.

Refer to the following steps:

1. Select the model and then select **Purchase Provisioned Throughput**.

2. You will be presented with a new screen to provide **Provisioned Throughput name**, **Commitment term**, and **Model units**. Enter name to identify the **Purchase Provisioned Throughput**. For **Commitment term**, you need to select a duration for which to keep the Provisioned Throughput. For PoCs, you can select **No commitment** as shown in *Figure 8.7*, if it is an option for the specific customized model:

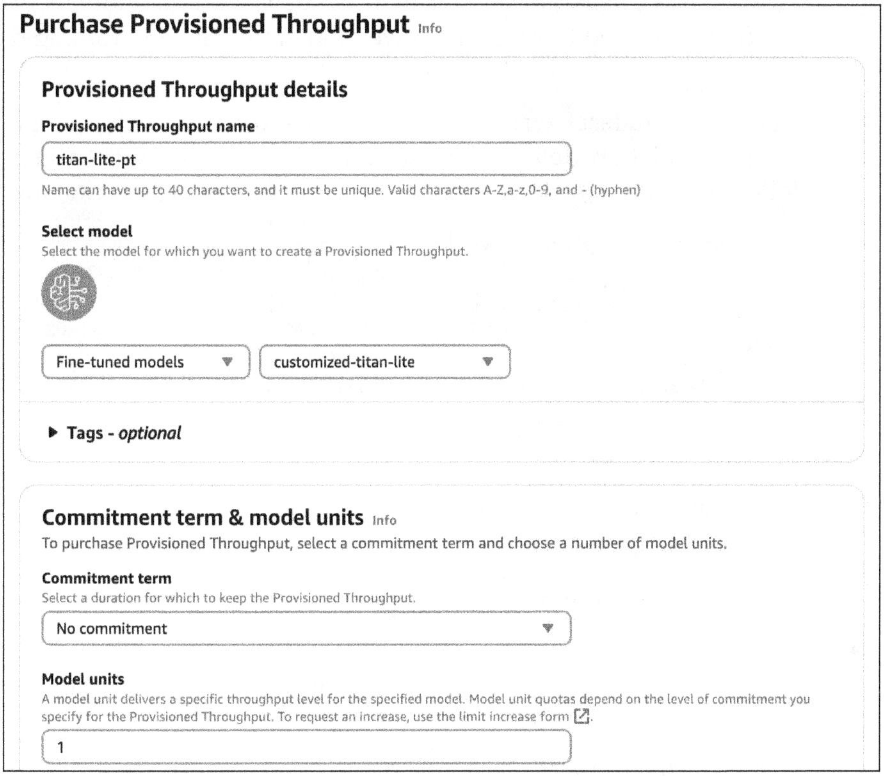

Figure 8.7: Purchase Provisioned Throughput

3. A model unit delivers a specific throughput level for the specified model. For testing the model, you can keep **Model units** as **1**.

4. Select **Purchase Provisioned Throughput**.

   Select **Chat/text playground**, and select **Fine-tuned models** category, and then select the model for which you just purchased Provisioned Throughput as shown in *Figure 8.8*. Select **Apply**.

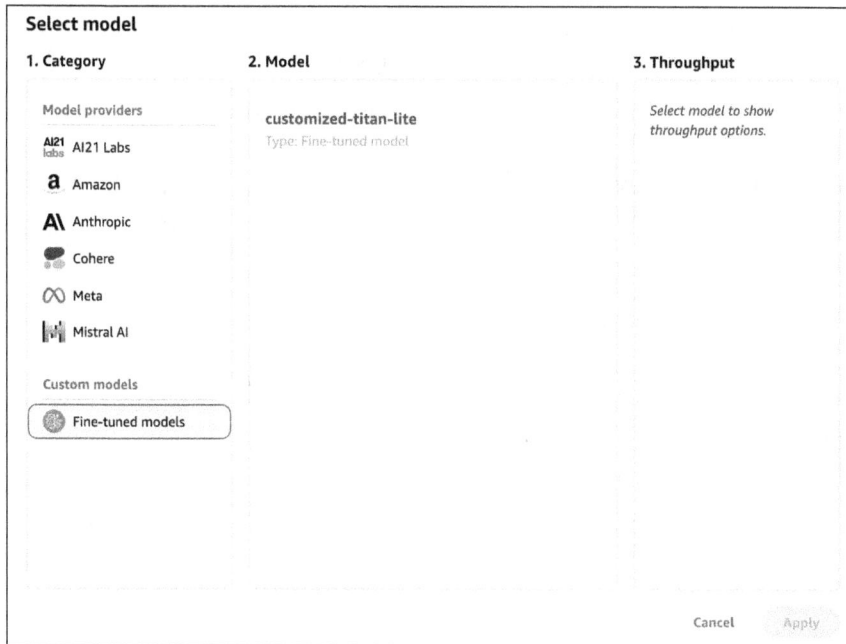

Select model

1. Category	2. Model	3. Throughput
Model providers	**customized-titan-lite**	*Select model to show throughput options.*
AI21 Labs	Type: Fine-tuned model	
a Amazon		
A\ Anthropic		
Cohere		
∞ Meta		
Mistral AI		
Custom models		
Fine-tuned models		

Cancel Apply

Figure 8.8: Using customized model in Chat/text playground

5. Write a prompt with the request for which this FM was fine-tuned. For a use case of generating short taglines or slogans based on a provided product/service description, an example prompt could be: `Generate a short tagline or slogan based on provided product/service description: <description>`

We have also provided how you can use fine-tune FMs on Amazon Bedrock using API in the jupyter notebook `Example81.ipnyb` in the code repository.

Continued pre-training

In the above section, we learned how you can fine-tune models using labelled dataset. You can use a similar workflow to customize a model using continued pre-training: prepare your dataset, upload it to S3, and create a continued pre-training job in the Bedrock console. The main difference is the type of data, and the customization job type you select. For example, in the field of healthcare and medical research, continued pre-training could be applied to

FMs to enhance their understanding of medical terminology, disease patterns, and treatment protocols.

Imagine you work at a leading pharmaceutical company or a medical research institute. The goal is to develop an FM that can assist researchers and medical professionals in their work by providing accurate and relevant information. To achieve this, you can leverage continued pre-training on a vast corpus of medical literature, including research papers, clinical trial reports, medical journals, and patient case studies. Continued pre-training process will enable the model to learn the nuances of medical terminology, understand complex disease mechanisms, and familiarize itself with the latest research findings and treatment approaches.

For continued pre-training, you will need to prepare a training and optionally a validation dataset. Similar to fine-tuning dataset, you need to create a JSONL file with multiple JSON lines. Because continued pre-training only requires unlabeled data, each JSON line is a sample data containing only an input field.

The format is as follows, (there is no completion field):

```
{"input": "<input text>"}
{"input": "<input text>"}
```

For customizing a model for a medical research institute, example dataset for continued pre-training job will be as follows:

- `{"input": "Coronary Artery Disease (CAD) is a condition in which the major blood vessels that supply the heart with oxygen-rich blood become narrowed or blocked due to the buildup of plaque, reducing blood flow to the heart muscle."}`
- `{"input": "Metastatic melanoma is a type of skin cancer that has spread from the original tumor site to other parts of the body, such as the lymph nodes, lungs, liver, or brain. Early detection and treatment are crucial for improving survival rates."}`
- `{"input": "A Computed Tomography (CT) scan is a diagnostic imaging procedure that uses a combination of X-rays and computer technology to create detailed images of the body's internal structures. It is commonly used to diagnose and monitor various medical conditions, such as cancer, cardiovascular diseases, and traumatic injuries."}`

The process to customizing models using continued pre-training is very similar to fine-tuning, the only difference is the type and syntax of dataset you provide.

To customize FMs using continued pre-training on Amazon Bedrock using API, refer the sample code in Jupyter Notebook **Example82.ipnyb** in the code repository.

Distillation

Model customization on Amazon Bedrock using distillation works similarly as the two approaches we discussed. As mentioned briefly, model distillation represents an innovative approach to creating more efficient AI models by transferring knowledge from a larger, more sophisticated teacher model to a smaller, more efficient student model. The process begins when the teacher model generates high-quality responses to specific prompts, which Amazon Bedrock then enhances through proprietary data synthesis techniques to ensure diverse and comprehensive training data. This synthesized knowledge is then used to fine-tune the student model, resulting in a more compact version that maintains the teacher's capabilities for specific use cases while offering better performance efficiency.

Let us consider a medical imaging analysis service that processes thousands of diagnostic images per hour. While a large, sophisticated AI model provides excellent accuracy in detecting various medical conditions, each inference request could be costly and may introduce higher latency due to the model's size and complexity. Through model distillation, you can create a smaller, more efficient model that maintains the same level of diagnostic accuracy but processes images significantly faster and at a lower cost per inference. This is particularly crucial for a high-throughput medical imaging service where both response time and operational costs directly impact the service's scalability and profitability. The distilled model reduces the per inference cost while maintaining the diagnostic quality of the larger teacher model, making it an ideal solution for high-volume, latency-sensitive use cases.

To get started with model distillation on Amazon Bedrock, there are two primary approaches you need to consider for data preparation. The first option allows you to provide your own prompts, optionally including labeled input data as prompt-response pairs, which Amazon Bedrock uses to generate responses from the teacher model. Alternatively, you can leverage your existing production data through invocation logs, either using just the prompts or complete prompt-response pairs from previous model interactions. The process begins by selecting appropriate teacher and student models, followed by data preparation and submission of a distillation job. Amazon Bedrock then manages the entire distillation process automatically, ensuring that the final distilled model remains exclusively accessible to the user.

Conclusion

In this chapter, we explored the significance of customizing FMs and the powerful capabilities offered by Amazon Bedrock. You learned how to fine-tune the state-of-the-art Amazon Titan model using your own data, enabling you to create tailored solutions for specific domains or tasks. Additionally, we discussed the continued pre-training approach, which allows you to adapt FMs to domains by providing relevant unlabeled data. With the knowledge gained from this chapter, you are now equipped to leverage Amazon Bedrock's user-friendly interface to customize FMs, unlocking their full potential for your unique use cases.

In the next chapter, we will cover how you can build GenAI applications on Amazon SageMaker JumpStart, a ML hub with open-source FMs.

Points to remember

- Fine-tuning FMs is crucial for adapting them to specific domains, tasks, or use cases, unlocking their full potential.

- Amazon Bedrock simplifies the process of customizing FMs by providing user-friendly options for fine-tuning and continued pre-training, abstracting away complex technical details. Fine-tuning involves training a pre-trained FM on labeled data relevant to a specific task or domain, improving its accuracy for that task. Continued pre-training, or domain-adaptive pre-training, involves updating the FM's parameters by training on unlabeled domain-specific data, allowing it to continuously learn and expand its knowledge.

- To fine-tune a model, you need to provide a labeled dataset in JSONL format, with each line containing a prompt and expected completion. For continued pre-training, you need to provide an unlabeled dataset in JSONL format, with each line containing input text relevant to the target domain.

- Amazon Bedrock supports customizing different models through its AWS Management Console or APIs.

Exercises

1. **Customize a model using distillation**: Explore the use of model distillation on Amazon Bedrock to create a smaller, more efficient model while maintaining the performance of a larger teacher model. Select appropriate teacher and student models for your use case, then prepare your training data either by providing use case-specific prompts or by utilizing existing invocation logs with prompt-response pairs. Submit a model distillation job on Amazon Bedrock and evaluate how the resulting distilled model compares to the original teacher model in terms of performance, latency, and cost efficiency.

2. **Explore customizing text-to-image or image-to-embedding models**: While the chapter focused on customizing text models like Amazon Titan Lite, Amazon Bedrock also supports customizing other types of models, such as text-to-image or image-to-embedding models. Experiment with customizing one of these models for a relevant use case, such as generating product images from text descriptions.

3. **Fine-tune a model for a specialized task**: Identify a specific natural language processing task that is relevant to your domain or use case, such as QA, text summarization, or machine translation. Prepare a labelled dataset for this task in the required JSONL format, and fine-tune a FM like Amazon Titan on Amazon Bedrock. Evaluate the performance of the fine-tuned model on your task and compare it to the original model's performance.

CHAPTER 9

Monitoring and Observability

Introduction

Monitoring and observability are crucial components of any successful software system, and **generative AI (GenAI)** applications built on AWS are no exception. As these applications leverage advanced **machine learning (ML)** models and handle sensitive data, it is imperative to have robust monitoring and observability practices in place. This chapter delves into the essential tools and techniques provided by AWS to monitor and ensure the reliability and performance of your GenAI applications built on Amazon Bedrock.

We will explore Amazon CloudWatch, a comprehensive monitoring service that collects and tracks metrics, logs, and events from various AWS resources, including Amazon Bedrock. By leveraging CloudWatch, you can gain valuable insights into the health and performance of your GenAI applications, enabling you to proactively identify and resolve issues before they escalate.

Additionally, we will examine AWS CloudTrail, a service that records API calls and activity logs across your AWS account. With CloudTrail, you can audit and monitor user activity, track changes to your AWS resources, and ensure compliance with security and governance requirements, which is particularly crucial when dealing with sensitive data and models in GenAI applications.

Structure

The chapter covers the following topics:

- Monitoring and observability for generative AI
- Monitoring foundation model performance
- Model prompt and responses with logs
- Analyzing logs with CloudWatch Logs insights
- CloudWatch dashboards
- Auditing with AWS CloudTrail
- Cost observability with AWS Cost Anomaly Detection
- Best practices for monitoring Amazon Bedrock
- Open-source observability tools for generative AI applications

Objectives

By the end this chapter, readers will know how to implement effective monitoring and observability for GenAI applications built on Amazon Bedrock. You will learn to use Amazon CloudWatch to collect metrics, logs, and events from your AI workloads, helping you quickly identify and fix performance issues. The chapter explains how AWS CloudTrail provides detailed API auditing capabilities for enhanced security and compliance, essential when deploying **foundation models** (**FMs**) in production. You will also discover how to monitor and optimize costs using AWS Cost Anomaly Detection as your AI applications scale. By applying these monitoring techniques, you will ensure your GenAI systems remain reliable, secure, and cost-effective. These technical skills are crucial for maintaining high-performance AI applications that meet enterprise requirements while providing visibility into all aspects of your AI infrastructure.

Monitoring and observability for generative AI

Monitoring and observability are critical components in ensuring the reliable and efficient operation of any GenAI application, regardless of the platform. When leveraging powerful services like Amazon Bedrock, implementing robust monitoring and observability practices allows you to fully capitalize on the platform's capabilities. These practices enhance your ability to maintain optimal performance, ensure high accuracy, and efficiently manage resource utilization, ultimately enabling you to deliver exceptional AI-driven solutions to your users.

Monitoring involves systematically collecting, analyzing, and interpreting various metrics such as invocations, resource consumption, latency, and errors. CloudWatch can be used to collect and monitor these metrics, providing visibility into the health and performance of GenAI applications.

Observability, on the other hand, enables developers to understand and debug the complex systems that make up the FM workflow, including the model itself, vector stores or knowledge base, agent and other data sources. CloudTrail can be leveraged to capture and analyze API activity, providing insights into the flow of data and control within the ecosystem.

Together, monitoring and observability empower developers to proactively identify and address issues, optimize resource allocation, and continuously improve the accuracy and reliability of their GenAI applications on AWS through data-driven insights.

Monitoring with Amazon CloudWatch

Amazon CloudWatch offers comprehensive suite of tools to monitor and keep your Bedrock workloads running smoothly. It provides visibility into foundational model usage, tracks API performance, and analyzes error rates. With CloudWatch, you can visualize key metrics, setup alarms for when metrics deviate from expected ranges, and configure automated actions based on defined thresholds. This enables you to maintain high-performance and reliability in your GenAI applications, ensuring they meet your users' expectations.

Monitoring foundation model performance

Understanding how your FMs are performing is crucial for maintaining a high-quality GenAI application. Amazon Bedrock publishes a comprehensive set of runtime metrics to Amazon CloudWatch, which gives you visibility into key aspects of model invocations, usage patterns, and performance bottlenecks.

These metrics are essential for monitoring the health, reliability, and cost-efficiency of your workloads. The following points summarizes the key runtime metrics available:

- **Invocations**: Number of requests made to Bedrock model invocation APIs, such as `InvokeModel` or `ConverseStream`. This helps track overall usage and request volume.

- **InvocationLatency**: Time taken for a model to complete an invocation, measured in milliseconds. Useful for detecting performance degradation.

- **InvocationClientErrors**: Number of invocations that resulted in client-side errors (e.g., invalid input). Helps identify integration or input validation issues.

- **InvocationServerErrors**: Number of invocations that failed due to server-side issues from AWS. Useful for assessing model stability or capacity limits.

- **InvocationThrottles**: Number of requests throttled due to hitting service quotas or exceeding rate limits.

- **InputTokenCount/OutputTokenCount**: Total number of tokens in the input and output per invocation. Important for cost analysis and prompt optimization.

- **LegacyModelInvocations**: Tracks usage of deprecated or legacy models. Helps teams plan migration strategies to supported models.

By monitoring these metrics in near real-time with CloudWatch, you can setup alerts, correlate usage spikes with errors or throttling, and fine-tune model usage to optimize performance and cost. These metrics also feed into dashboards and automated actions described in the next sections.

Setup alarms and automated actions

While monitoring metrics is crucial, proactive notifications are equally important when something goes wrong. CloudWatch alarms enable you to respond swiftly to potential issues in your Bedrock applications by continuously monitoring metrics against pre-defined thresholds.

For instance, to be alerted when your model's error rate spikes, you could setup an alarm using the AWS CLI, as follows:

```
aws cloudwatch put-metric-alarm \
    --alarm-name "HighErrorRateAlarm" \
    --alarm-description "Alarm when error rate exceeds 5%" \
    --metric-name "InvocationClientErrors" \
    --namespace "AWS/Bedrock" \
    --statistic "Sum" \
    --period 300 \
    --threshold 5 \
    --comparison-operator "GreaterThanThreshold" \
    --evaluation-periods 2 \
    --alarm-actions "arn:aws:sns:us-east-1:123456789012:AlertTopic" \
    --dimensions "Name=ModelId,Value=your-model-id"
```

This alarm triggers if client errors exceed 5 for 2 consecutive 5-minute periods. To ensure prompt notifications, integrate Amazon **Simple Notification Service** (**SNS**) with your CloudWatch alarms. Create SNS topic, subscribe relevant endpoints such as email addresses, and select this topic as the notification target when configuring alarms. This setup enables immediate team alerts for swift action on Bedrock issues. You can create similar alarms for latency, throttling, or invocation drops.

CloudWatch alarms can also initiate automated actions, such as scaling model capacity, running diagnostic Lambda functions, or updating operational dashboards. This proactive approach ensures your Bedrock applications stay healthy with minimal manual intervention, maintaining a high-quality **user experience** (**UX**).

Model prompt and responses with logs

For GenAI applications, understanding the interaction between users and models is crucial. Amazon Bedrock's integration with CloudWatch Logs allows you to capture and analyze detailed logs for model invocations. By enabling model invocation logging, you can collect metadata, requests, and responses for all model invocations within your account, providing invaluable insights into your application's behavior. This feature offers valuable insights into the following:

- How your AI models are being used
- API call patterns
- User query trends
- Compliance with data privacy regulations

Amazon Bedrock supports logging to both CloudWatch Logs and Amazon S3. For high-volume applications, S3 is recommended due to its scalability and suitability for long-term storage and downstream analysis, such as prompt improvement or model fine-tuning.

By default, logging is disabled. To enable model invocation logging:

1. Navigate to the **Settings** page in the Bedrock console.
2. Toggle the **Model invocation logging** switch.
3. Select data types (**Text**, **Images**, **Embeddings**).
4. Choose your logging destination (**Cloudwatch Logs only**, **S3 only**, or **Both S3 and Cloudwatch Logs**).
5. Configure necessary IAM permissions.

Figure 9.1 shows the **Model invocation logging** configuration panel in the Amazon Bedrock console. You can see the toggle switch to enable logging, options to select which data types to capture, and destination settings for your logs:

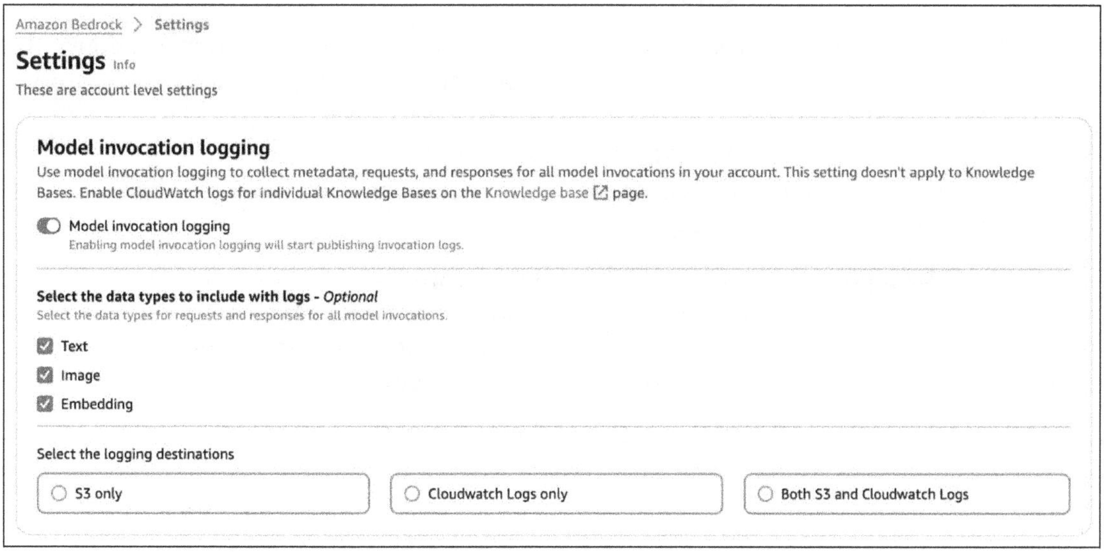

Figure 9.1: Model invocation logging in Amazon Bedrock

If CloudWatch Logs is selected, you will need to specify a log group and create an IAM role with the required permissions. Once enabled, these logs can be used for debugging, performance optimization, and behavioral analysis of your application.

Analyzing logs with CloudWatch Logs insights

Once model invocation logs are being delivered to CloudWatch Logs, you can use features like Live Tail and CloudWatch Logs Insights to inspect and analyze the logs in near real-time.

Live Tail provides an interactive log analytics experience, allowing you to view incoming logs as they are ingested, filter and highlight attributes of interest, and pause or replay logs during troubleshooting. CloudWatch Logs Insights enables you to interactively search and analyze your log data using SQL-like queries.

The following is a query to get you started:

```
fields @timestamp, @message
| sort @timestamp desc
| limit 20
```

This query will show you the 20 most recent log entries, sorted by timestamp. For more advanced analysis, you might use queries, as follows:

1. **Counting invocations by model type**: To count model invocations and identify which models are most frequently used, you can run the following query:

```
fields modelId
| stats count(*) as invocations by modelId
| sort invocations desc
```

2. **Analyzing average token usage**: To analyze the average token consumption across different models, which helps with cost optimization and performance monitoring, use the following query:

```
fields inputTokenCount, outputTokenCount
| stats avg(inputTokenCount) as avgInputTokens, avg(outputTokenCount) as avgOutputTokens by modelId
```

These queries help you understand which models are used most frequently and how token usage varies across different models. To learn more about CloudWatch queries for model performance, please refer to the Amazon Bedrock documentation at **https://docs.aws.amazon.com/bedrock/latest/userguide/model-invocation-logging.html**

Figure 9.2 demonstrates the CloudWatch Logs Insights interface with a sample query analyzing Bedrock invocation logs. The figure shows the query editor at the top, query results in the middle, and log event details at the bottom, providing a visual example of how you can interactively explore your model's behaviour and performance metrics.

Figure 9.2: CloudWatch Logs Insights query showing Bedrock invocation logs

CloudWatch Logs Insights also offers ML-backed pattern queries to automatically recognize patterns and summarize log events, helping you quickly identify trends or anomalies in your AI's behavior.

By regularly analysing your logs, you can gain valuable insights into your AI application's performance, user behaviour, and potential areas for optimization.

CloudWatch dashboards

CloudWatch dashboards provide a powerful way to visualize and monitor your Amazon Bedrock workloads alongside other AWS services. These customizable, single-pane-of-glass views allow you to combine metrics, logs, and other monitoring data into a centralized, easy-to-read display.

For Amazon Bedrock, you can leverage both automatic dashboard and custom dashboards tailored to your specific needs. To access the automatic dashboard for Bedrock, you can navigate to **CloudWatch | All metrics | Bedrock**.

Figure 9.3 shows the Bedrock metrics section in the Amazon CloudWatch console. This navigation view displays the available metric categories for Amazon Bedrock, allowing you to select specific metrics for monitoring. From this interface, you can access detailed metrics for model invocations, latency, and error rates across your Bedrock resources:

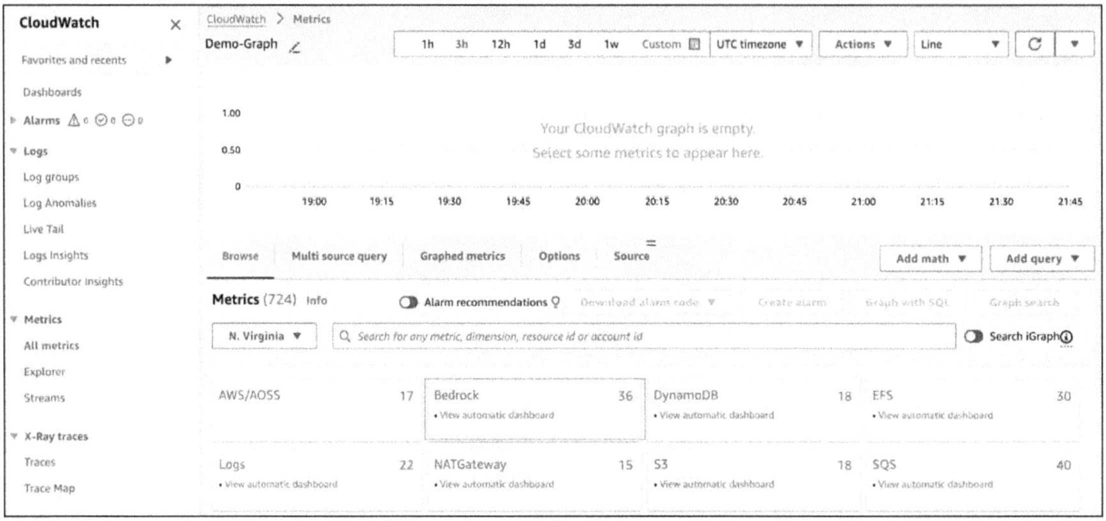

Figure 9.3: Bedrock metrics in Amazon CloudWatch

Figure 9.4 shows the automatic dashboard for Bedrock, which displays key metrics such as invocation count, latency, token count, throttling and error count. This dashboard provides a quick overview of your workload's health and performance at a glance.

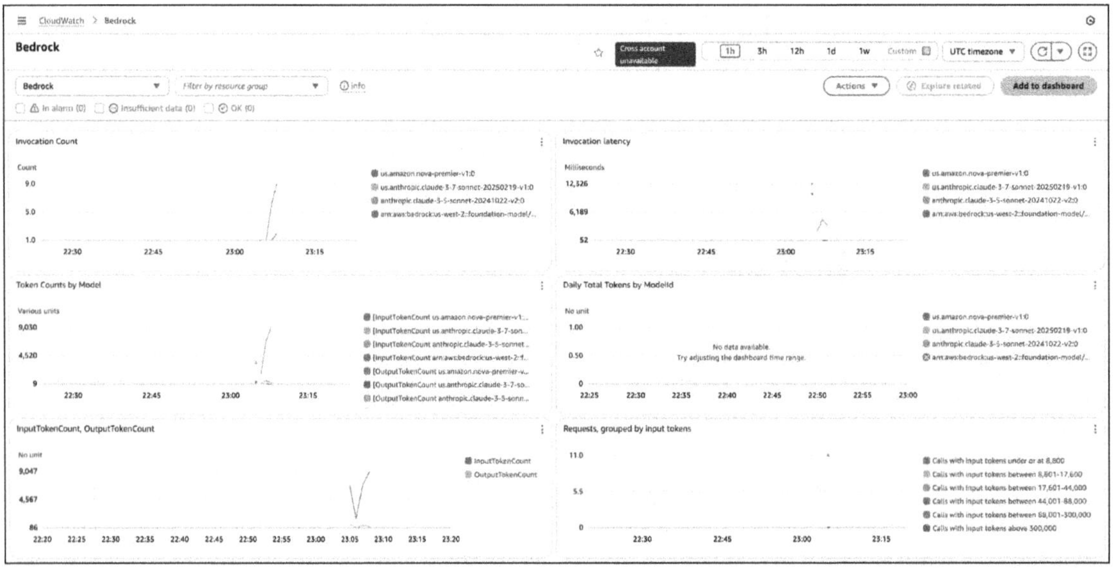

Figure 9.4: Automatic dashboard for Bedrock in Amazon CloudWatch dashboard

While automatic dashboards are useful, custom dashboards allow you to tailor your monitoring to your specific needs. You can create a custom dashboard in the CloudWatch console by navigating to the **Dashboards** section in the CloudWatch console and clicking on **Create dashboard**. From there, you can add widgets for various Bedrock metrics, such as invocations, latency, and error rates. To get a comprehensive view of your entire GenAI application, you can also include metrics from other relevant AWS services like Amazon EKS, AWS Lambda, or Amazon OpenSearch etc.

This allows you to tailor your dashboard to your specific monitoring needs and get a holistic view of your application's performance.

Auditing with AWS CloudTrail

AWS CloudTrail records AWS API calls and related events, providing a comprehensive audit trail of activities within your AWS account. Amazon Bedrock integrates with CloudTrail, allowing you to log and audit all API calls made to the service.

CloudTrail log events

CloudTrail captures two types of events, that is, management events like creating agents or invoking models and data events such as retrieving knowledge base content or invoking models with input data. While management events are logged by default, data events require additional configuration through advanced event selectors.

To configure CloudTrail for logging Bedrock data events, you can use the following AWS CLI:

```
aws cloudtrail put-event-selectors --trail-name YOUR_TRAIL_NAME --advanced-
event-selectors \
'[
  {
    "FieldSelectors": [
      { "Field": "eventCategory", "Equals": ["Data"] },
      { "Field": "resources.type", "Equals": ["AWS::Bedrock::AgentAlias",
"AWS::Bedrock::KnowledgeBase", "AWS::Bedrock::FlowAlias",
"AWS::Bedrock::Guardrail"] }
    ]
  }
]'
```

Replace **YOUR_TRAIL_NAME** with the name of your CloudTrail trail. This command configures CloudTrail to log all Amazon Bedrock data events for agent aliases, knowledge base, prompt flows, and guardrails. Refer to the official AWS Documentation for more details and advanced configurations.

CloudTrail delivers these log files to an Amazon S3 bucket of your choice, providing a centralized location for analysis and retention.

CloudTrail log analysis

CloudTrail log entries capture detailed information about Amazon Bedrock API calls, including who made the request, when it occurred, and the request parameters. Analyzing these logs is crucial for gaining insights into how Bedrock resources are used, identifying potential security risks, and ensuring compliance with policies.

You can analyze these logs using tools like CloudTrail event history, CloudWatch Logs Insights, or Amazon Athena.

For example, a typical CloudTrail log entry for a Bedrock API call will be as follows:

```json
{
    "eventVersion": "1.08",
    "userIdentity": {
        "type": "IAMUser",
        "principalId": "AIDAXXXXXXXXXXXXXXXXX",
        "arn": "arn:aws:iam::123456789012:user/example-user",
        "accountId": "123456789012",
        "accessKeyId": "AKIAIOSFODNN7EXAMPLE",
        "userName": "example-user"
    },
    "eventTime": "2023-08-08T15:30:00Z",
    "eventSource": "bedrock.amazonaws.com",
    "eventName": "InvokeModel",
    "awsRegion": "us-west-2",
    "sourceIPAddress": "203.0.113.1",
    "userAgent": "aws-cli/2.0.0 Python/3.7.4 Darwin/18.7.0 botocore/2.0.0",
    "requestParameters": {
        "modelId": "ai21.j2-ultra-v1",
        "contentType": "application/json",
        "accept": "*/*"
    },
    "responseElements": null,
    "requestID": "a1b2c3d4-5678-90ab-cdef-EXAMPLE11111",
    "eventID": "a1b2c3d4-5678-90ab-cdef-EXAMPLEbbbbb",
    "readOnly": false,
    "eventType": "AwsApiCall",
    "managementEvent": false,
    "recipientAccountId": "123456789012",
    "eventCategory": "Data"
}
```

Figure 9.5: *Sample Amazon Bedrock Event in CloudTrail*

You can easily view and analyze these events using CloudTrail event history, which provides a user-friendly interface to search and examine the most recent 90 days of API activity.

Figure 9.6 displays the **CloudTrail Event history** interface for Amazon Bedrock events. This console view allows you to search, filter, and analyze API activity related to your Bedrock resources. You can see details about each event, including the user who initiated it, the timestamp, and the specific API action performed:

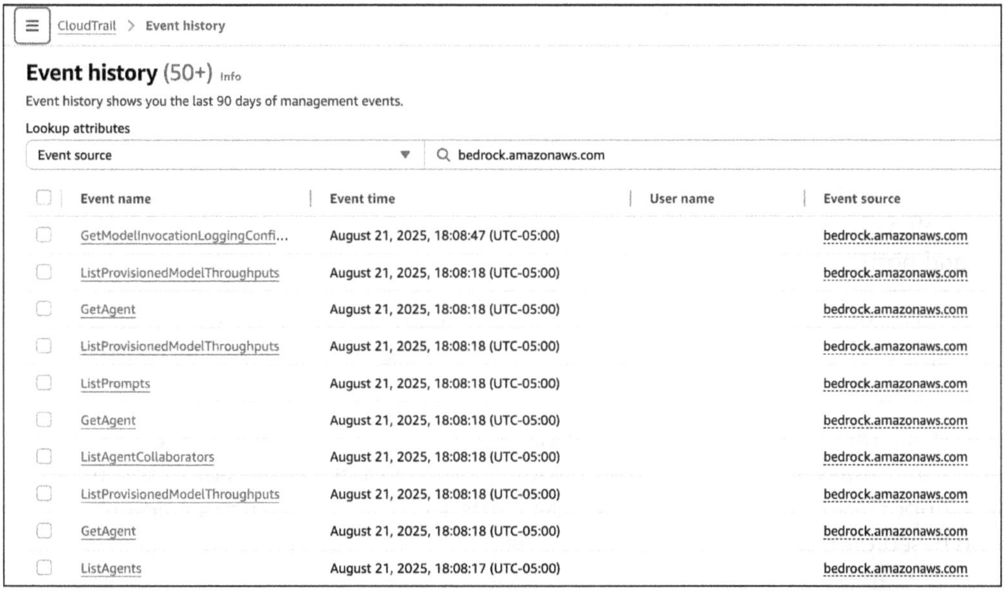
CloudTrail > Event history

Event history (50+) Info

Event history shows you the last 90 days of management events.

Lookup attributes

Event source ▼ | bedrock.amazonaws.com

Event name	Event time	User name	Event source
GetModelInvocationLoggingConfi...	August 21, 2025, 18:08:47 (UTC-05:00)		bedrock.amazonaws.com
ListProvisionedModelThroughputs	August 21, 2025, 18:08:18 (UTC-05:00)		bedrock.amazonaws.com
GetAgent	August 21, 2025, 18:08:18 (UTC-05:00)		bedrock.amazonaws.com
ListProvisionedModelThroughputs	August 21, 2025, 18:08:18 (UTC-05:00)		bedrock.amazonaws.com
ListPrompts	August 21, 2025, 18:08:18 (UTC-05:00)		bedrock.amazonaws.com
GetAgent	August 21, 2025, 18:08:18 (UTC-05:00)		bedrock.amazonaws.com
ListAgentCollaborators	August 21, 2025, 18:08:18 (UTC-05:00)		bedrock.amazonaws.com
ListProvisionedModelThroughputs	August 21, 2025, 18:08:18 (UTC-05:00)		bedrock.amazonaws.com
GetAgent	August 21, 2025, 18:08:18 (UTC-05:00)		bedrock.amazonaws.com
ListAgents	August 21, 2025, 18:08:17 (UTC-05:00)		bedrock.amazonaws.com

***Figure 9.6**: CloudTrail Event history for Amazon Bedrock*

For more advanced analysis, you can use tools like CloudWatch Logs Insights or Amazon Athena to query and visualize your CloudTrail logs.

Additionally, you can integrate CloudTrail with Amazon GuardDuty. GuardDuty continuously monitors CloudTrail logs and uses ML to detect suspicious activities related to Bedrock, such as unauthorized changes to guardrails or model training data sources.

Cost observability with AWS Cost Anomaly Detection

Monitoring and optimizing costs for GenAI workloads on Amazon Bedrock is crucial, especially as these workloads scale. AWS Cost Explorer and AWS Cost Anomaly Detection are key services that can help gain visibility into your costs.

AWS Cost Explorer allows you to visualize and analyze your AWS costs and usage over time. You can view and filter your costs by various dimensions, such as AWS service, linked account, cost allocation tag, and more. For Bedrock workloads, you can now categorize your GenAI inference costs by department, team, or application using AWS cost allocation tags by creating an application inference profile and tagging it. For more details on inference profiles, see **https://docs.aws.amazon.com/bedrock/latest/userguide/inference-profiles.html**

AWS Cost Anomaly Detection uses ML to detect unusual spending patterns without manual threshold settings. It analyzes costs across various dimensions and provides root cause analysis for detected anomalies.

To get started, following are the steps:

1. Use AWS Cost Explorer to monitor your Amazon Bedrock costs. Create cost allocation tags, for example, project or environment to categorize your Bedrock resources and on-demand FM usage for better tracking.

2. Setup AWS Cost Anomaly Detection by creating a cost monitor for your Bedrock-related costs. Configure an alert subscription with your preferred threshold, frequency, and notification method.

3. Review detected anomalies in the console or via API. For Bedrock workloads, anomalies might indicate unexpected spikes in model usage, changes in token consumption, or new resource allocations.

By leveraging these services, you can proactively identify cost drivers, optimize resource allocation, and make informed decisions about your Bedrock usage. For example, you might discover opportunities to fine-tune your prompts for token efficiency or adjust your model selection based on cost-performance trade-offs.

Best practices for monitoring Amazon Bedrock

Implementing effective monitoring and observability practices is essential for maximizing the performance, reliability, and cost-efficiency of your Amazon Bedrock applications. The following best practices are organized into key categories to help you establish a comprehensive monitoring strategy that addresses various aspects of your GenAI workloads. By following these recommendations, you will be better equipped to detect issues early, optimize resource utilization, ensure security compliance, and implement automated remediation when necessary.

The following are key best practices organized by performance monitoring:

*   **Establish baseline metrics**: Define normal performance ranges for key metrics like invocations, latency, and token counts. Use CloudWatch to track average latency for each Bedrock model over a 2 week period to establish a baseline.

*   **Implement proactive alerting**: Setup CloudWatch alarms for deviations from baseline metrics. For instance, create an alarm that triggers when the error rate for a specific Bedrock model exceeds 5% over a 5 minute period.

*   **Monitor model-specific metrics**: Track performance metrics unique to each FM. For text generation models, this might include monitoring perplexity scores or coherence metrics if available.

*   **Monitor Bedrock usage against service quotas**: Track invocation rates and throttling trends using CloudWatch metrics. Setup alarms to alert when usage approaches limits to avoid service disruptions.

The following are key best practices organized by cost optimization:

- **Leverage invocation logs for usage patterns**: Analyze logs to identify opportunities for optimizing prompts and reducing token usage. Use CloudWatch Logs Insights to identify the most token-intensive prompts and refine them for efficiency.

- **Implement cost allocation tags**: Use tags to track costs by project, team, or application. Tag all Bedrock resources with the project and environment to break down costs effectively in AWS Cost Explorer.

- **Setup Cost Anomaly Detection**: Configure AWS Cost Anomaly Detection to alert on unexpected spending patterns. Create a cost monitor specifically for Bedrock services and setup daily alert subscriptions to stay on top of any unusual cost spikes.

The following are key best practices organized by security and compliance:

- **Audit API access**: Regularly review CloudTrail logs for unauthorized or suspicious API calls. Setup automated scanning of CloudTrail logs for any Bedrock API calls from unrecognized IP addresses.

- **Monitor for sensitive data exposure**: Use CloudWatch Logs to scan for potential leakage of sensitive information in model inputs or outputs. Implement pattern matching in log analysis to detect PII in Bedrock invocations.

- **Enforce compliance policies**: Implement guardrails and monitoring for compliance with internal policies and external regulations. Use AWS Config rules to ensure all Bedrock resources are properly tagged and comply with data residency requirements.

By leveraging these best practices, you can ensure that your Amazon Bedrock workloads are monitored effectively, issues are detected and addressed promptly, and costs are optimized continuously. Regularly review and refine your monitoring strategy as your Bedrock usage evolves, staying informed about new features and adjusting your approach accordingly.

Open-source observability tools for generative AI applications

Amazon Bedrock offers robust native observability capabilities through CloudWatch, CloudTrail, model invocation logging, and agent-level tracing. These tools give developers the visibility needed to monitor performance, troubleshoot issues, and manage costs at scale. However, as GenAI applications grow in complexity, spanning agents, vector searches, RAG, and fine-tuned prompts, teams may also explore open-source observability platforms purpose-built for LLM workflows. Two of the most widely adopted are Langfuse and Arize Phoenix.

Langfuse for end-to-end observability and evaluation

Langfuse is an open-source observability platform tailored specifically for LLM applications. It offers full-stack tracing and analytics across prompt flows, embeddings, agent chains, and tool usage. Its core strengths include:

- End-to-end tracing of multi-step workflows, including nested prompts, retries, tool calls, and user interactions.

- Prompt versioning and A/B testing, enabling teams to run structured experiments and correlate prompt changes with performance.

- Evaluation workflows, including LLM-as-a-judge, human feedback capture, and customizable scoring metrics.

- SDKs and integrations for LangChain, LlamaIndex, and Bedrock-compatible clients.

- Flexible deployment: both cloud-hosted and self-hosted modes are supported for enterprise security needs.

Langfuse is especially helpful for teams iterating quickly on LLM prompts, agents, or workflows and seeking a centralized place to analyze traces and evaluate responses.

Arize Phoenix for evaluation and debugging of LLM workflows

Arize Phoenix is another leading open-source observability platform focused on model evaluation and LLM debugging. Built with OpenTelemetry, an open-source standard for observability data, Phoenix enables vendor-agnostic tracing and seamless integration with existing telemetry pipelines. Key features include:

- Built-in evaluation capabilities for hallucination detection, relevance scoring, and side-by-side response comparisons.

- Prompt-level tracing with visual timelines of LLM calls, token usage, latency, and intermediate steps.

- Prompt experimentation and analysis, allowing teams to identify which inputs lead to stronger outputs or failures.

- Integration with LangChain, LlamaIndex, and other LLM frameworks through native Python SDKs.

- OpenTelemetry support, enabling standardized instrumentation and easy integration with popular observability backends.

Phoenix is particularly well-suited for teams focused on evaluating and improving LLM outputs. It offers built-in tools for analyzing response quality, identifying hallucinations, comparing prompt variants, and running structured experiments all in one interface. This makes it ideal for debugging complex model behavior and optimizing prompt strategies in production workflows.

Conclusion

Amazon Bedrock provides a comprehensive and secure observability stack through services like CloudWatch, CloudTrail, and built-in agent tracing and debugging. These tools are tightly integrated with Amazon Bedrock, giving teams the visibility, they need to troubleshoot issues, monitor usage patterns, and keep costs under control as their applications scale.

As GenAI applications scale in complexity, observability becomes a deeper challenge, extending beyond metrics to include prompt behavior, model evaluation, and user feedback. While AWS covers many of these aspects, developers may also integrate specialized tools like Langfuse or Arize Phoenix for advanced tracing, evaluation workflows, or interoperability with LLM frameworks.

With the right observability practices in place, combining AWS-native features and purpose-built observability tools, teams can ensure their Bedrock applications remain high performing, reliable, and cost-effective, ready to support production workloads with enterprise-grade visibility.

In the next chapter, we will explore advanced techniques for fine-tuning and customizing FMs in Amazon Bedrock, enabling you to tailor these AI capabilities to your specific needs.

Points to remember

- Amazon Bedrock integrates with CloudWatch for comprehensive monitoring of GenAI workloads.
- Key Bedrock metrics include Invocations, InvocationLatency, InvocationErrors, InvocationThrottles, and TokenCounts.
- Enable model invocation logging to capture metadata, requests, and responses for debugging and optimization.
- Use CloudWatch Logs Insights for advanced analysis of invocation logs.
- Create custom CloudWatch dashboards to visualize Bedrock performance alongside other AWS services.
- Setup CloudWatch alarms to monitor metrics and trigger automated actions when thresholds are exceeded.
- Leverage CloudTrail for auditing all Bedrock API calls, enhancing security and compliance monitoring.
- Implement AWS Cost Anomaly Detection to identify unexpected spending patterns in your Bedrock usage.

- Establish baseline metrics and regularly review your monitoring strategy as your Bedrock usage evolves.

- Follow best practices for performance monitoring, cost optimization, and security compliance in your Bedrock applications.

- Monitor Bedrock service quotas and set alerts to avoid throttling during peak usage.

- Consider integrating open-source observability tools like Langfuse or Phoenix for advanced tracing, prompt evaluation, and user feedback analysis.

- Monitor Bedrock service quotas and set alerts to avoid throttling during peak usage.

Exercises

1. **Enable model invocation logging for your Bedrock workload through the console**: Configure it to capture text, images, and embeddings, using CloudWatch Logs as the destination. Then, use CloudWatch Logs Insights to query the latest 100 log events, examining model ID, operation, token counts, and user prompts. Analyze these results to identify usage patterns and optimization opportunities.

2. **Create a Bedrock-focused CloudWatch dashboard**: Combine metrics from Bedrock and at least one other service in your AI application stack, such as API Gateway or Lambda. Include widgets for Bedrock invocations, latency, token counts, and error rates. Add a widget showing the correlation between Bedrock usage and your application's API performance. Use this dashboard to spot performance bottlenecks or unusual patterns in your Bedrock usage.

3. **Implement cost control measures for your Bedrock usage**: Setup AWS Cost Anomaly Detection specifically for Bedrock services, configuring daily alert subscriptions with a 20% increase threshold over your daily average. Use AWS Cost Explorer to analyze your Bedrock costs for the past month, breaking them down by model and application using tags. Identify which models and applications incur the highest costs. Based on this analysis, propose at least two concrete actions to optimize your Bedrock costs.

Join our Discord space

Join our Discord workspace for latest updates, offers, tech happenings around the world, new releases, and sessions with the authors:

https://discord.bpbonline.com

CHAPTER 10
Security and Responsible AI

Introduction

As the capabilities of **generative AI (GenAI)** continue to advance, it becomes increasingly crucial to address the critical issues of security, privacy, and responsible development. This chapter delves into the capabilities supported by Amazon Bedrock to ensure the safe and ethical deployment of GenAI solutions. We will explore the comprehensive safeguards and guardrails support, available in Amazon Bedrock, including watermark detection and content moderation, to maintain the integrity and trustworthiness of AI models. Furthermore, this chapter will delve into the robust security measures, spanning application and data security, network security, and compliance with relevant regulatory frameworks. By addressing these essential aspects, Amazon Bedrock aims to foster trust and confidence among its users while promoting responsible and secure adoption of GenAI technologies.

Structure

The chapter covers the following topics:

- Responsible AI with Amazon Bedrock
- Amazon Bedrock Guardrails
- Security in Amazon Bedrock

Responsible AI with Amazon Bedrock

Responsible AI is a practice that emphasizes the ethical development, deployment, and use of AI systems. It involves proactively addressing potential risks and negative impacts associated with AI technologies, such as biases, privacy violations, and unintended consequences. Responsible AI aims to ensure that AI systems are safe, reliable, transparent, and aligned with human values and societal norms.

Amazon Bedrock incorporates several features and capabilities to foster trust, transparency, and responsible AI practices. By prioritizing data security and privacy, Amazon Bedrock helps address concerns around the misuse of sensitive information. Additionally, through its guardrails feature, Amazon Bedrock empowers users to customize and apply safety, privacy, and truthfulness checks for their GenAI applications, ensuring adherence to responsible AI principles and organizational policies. Amazon Bedrock offers watermark detection, which allows for the identification of AI-generated content, promoting transparency and mitigating the spread of misinformation. In *Chapter 11, RAG and Model Evaluation,* we will cover Amazon Bedrock's feature, which enables you to evaluate and compare different **foundation models** (**FMs**) based on custom metrics, such as accuracy and safety, facilitating informed decision-making and responsible model selection.

Furthermore, AWS supports copyright indemnity coverage for outputs of all Amazon Titan FMs as well as GenAI services such as Amazon Q Developer, AWS HealthScribe, Amazon Lex. AWS also provides AI service cards, a transparency resource to understand responsible AI design choices and implemented optimization, for a number of AI services. Amazon Bedrock has implemented automated abuse detection mechanisms to identify potential violation such as detecting harmful content, identifying patterns of recurring violations, and detecting and blocking child sexual abuse material.

Overall, Amazon Bedrock's responsible AI practices, through features like guardrails, model evaluation, and watermark detection, fosters trust and transparency in the development and deployment of GenAI applications.

Amazon Bedrock Guardrails

Amazon Bedrock Guardrails is a powerful feature that enables users to implement safeguards and responsible AI practices for their GenAI applications. It allows you to create customized guardrails tailored to your specific use cases and organizational policies, ensuring a consistent and safe **user experience** (**UX**) across multiple FMs.

With Bedrock Guardrails, you can configure various policies to avoid undesirable, harmful, or sensitive content in both user inputs and outputs (model responses). These policies include content filters to block harmful content, denied topics to restrict undesirable subjects, word filters to block offensive terms or phrases, and sensitive information filters to redact **personally identifiable information** (**PII**) or custom regex patterns. Additionally, Bedrock Guardrails offers a contextual grounding check feature that detects and filters hallucinations in model responses, ensuring that the generated content is grounded in factual information and relevant to the user's query. Amazon Bedrock Guardrails also support detecting and blocking harmful image content across categories such as hate, insults, sexual, and violence. With this new feature, guardrail provides consistent protection across text and image modalities.

One of the key advantages of Amazon Bedrock Guardrails is its flexibility. You can create multiple versions of a guardrail, each with different configurations, and test them using the built-in test window before deploying them for your applications. Once a guardrail is configured and versioned, it can be easily integrated with supported FMs during the inference API invocation, allowing you to apply the defined policies to both user inputs and model responses.

Amazon Bedrock Guardrails empowers you to maintain control over the content generated by your GenAI applications, ensuring adherence to responsible AI principles and organizational policies. By configuring guardrails based on your specific considerations, such as use case, content sensitivity, and privacy requirements, you can mitigate risks associated with harmful or inappropriate content, protecting your users and maintaining trust in your AI-powered applications.

The following steps will allow you to create a guardrail using the AWS Management Console and discuss deeper into its components simultaneously:

1. Navigate to the Amazon Bedrock console. Select **Guardrails** from the left panel.

2. Select **Create guardrail**, and provide basic details such as **Name**, **Description**, and **Messaging from blocked prompts**; the message you want to display if your guardrail blocks the user prompts and responses. Optionally, you can enable **Cross-Region inference** to automatically route guardrail inference to other AWS Regions to maintain guardrail performance and reliability when demand increases. You can also optionally provide a customer-managed **Key Management Service** (**KMS**) key to encrypt the guardrail. Select **Next**. The configuration should look similar to the following figure:

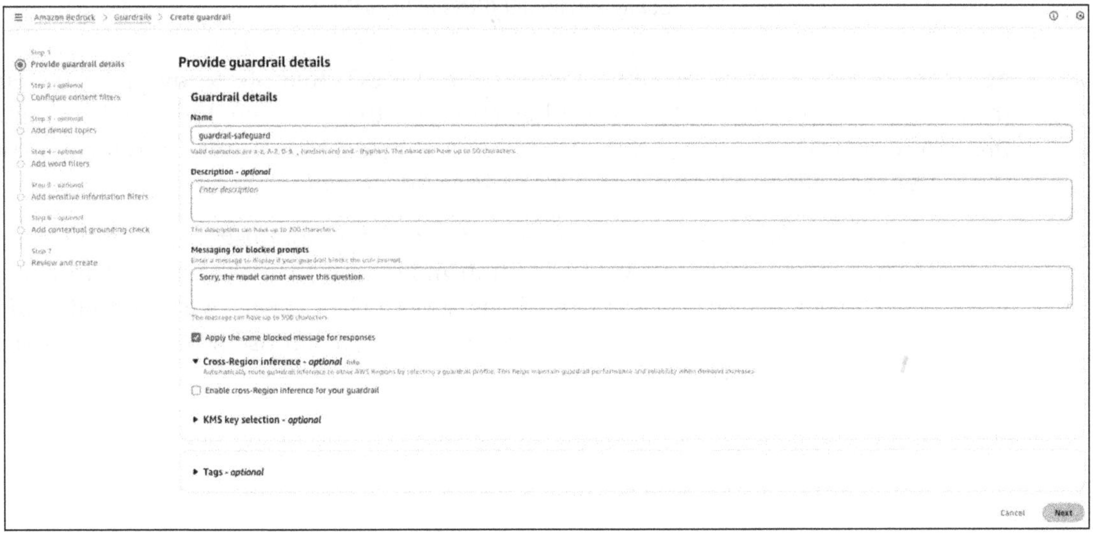

Figure 10.1: Create a guardrail on Amazon Bedrock

3. In the following steps, you will be asked to configure filters. Remember, filters are optional, but you need to configure at least one filter for a guardrail.

4. You can utilize content filters to detect and filter harmful user inputs and model outputs. As shown in *Figure 10.2*, on the **Configure content filters** page, you can filter **Harmful categories** such as **Hate**, **Insult**, **Violence**, **Sexual**, and **Misconduct**:

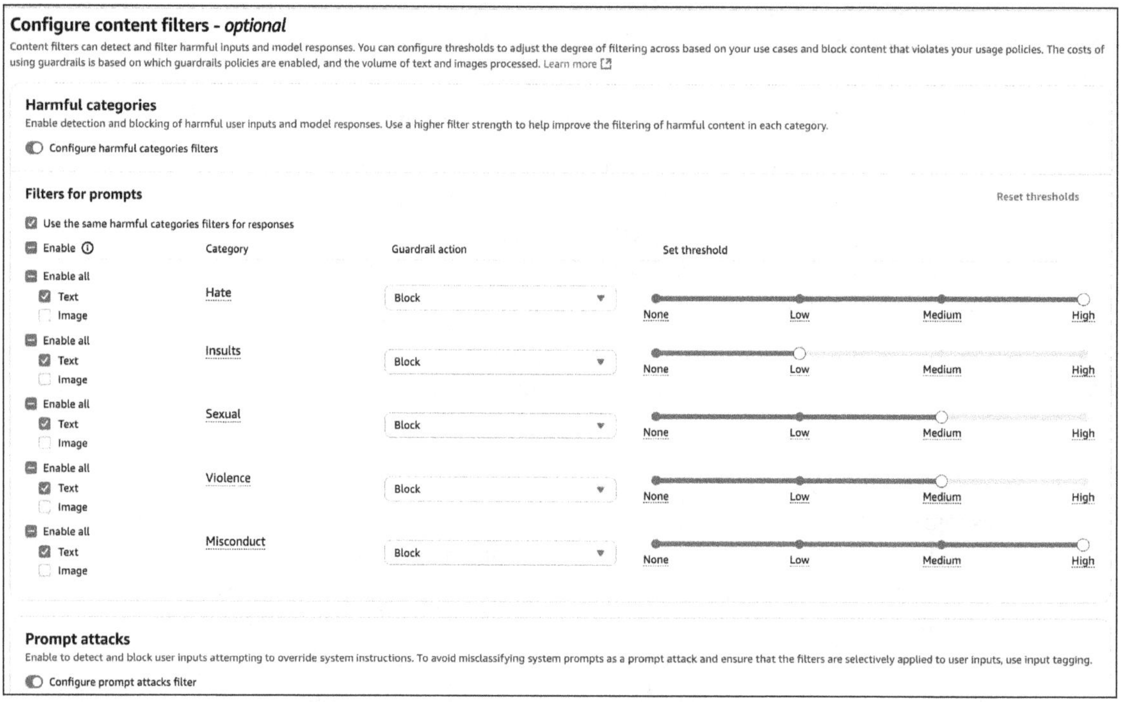

Figure 10.2: Configure content filters with guardrail

You can also block prompt attacks, which are users' attempts to override system instruction. You have four levels of filter strength, that is, none, low, medium, and high, to select from for each of the category to customize it for your requirements. The filter strength determines the sensitivity of filtering content.

5. Next, you can configure topics you want to deny that are undesired for your GenAI application. For example, a travel institution may want their AI assistant to avoid giving any health advice. On the console as show below, select **Add denied topic**. Provide a name, and a clear definition for topic that FM can use to block inputs and responses. Select **Confirm**.

Refer to the following figure:

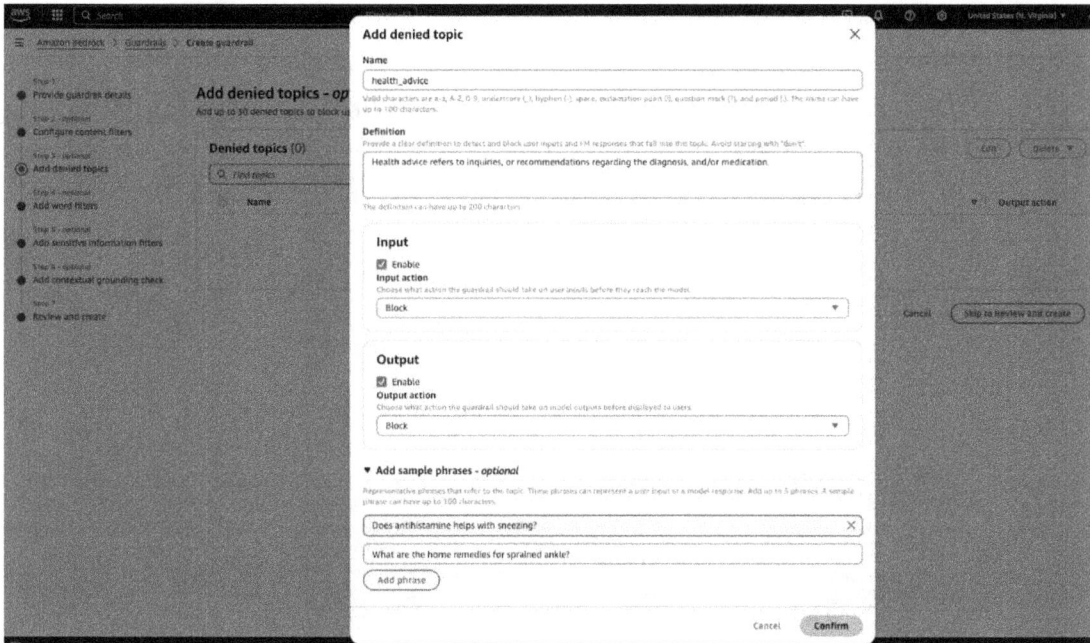

Figure 10.3: Configure denied topics with guardrail

6. Next, you can configure word filters to block specific words and phrases. As shown in *Figure 10.4*, you can **Add words and phrases manually** on the console, or **Upload from a local file**, or **Upload from an S3 object**:

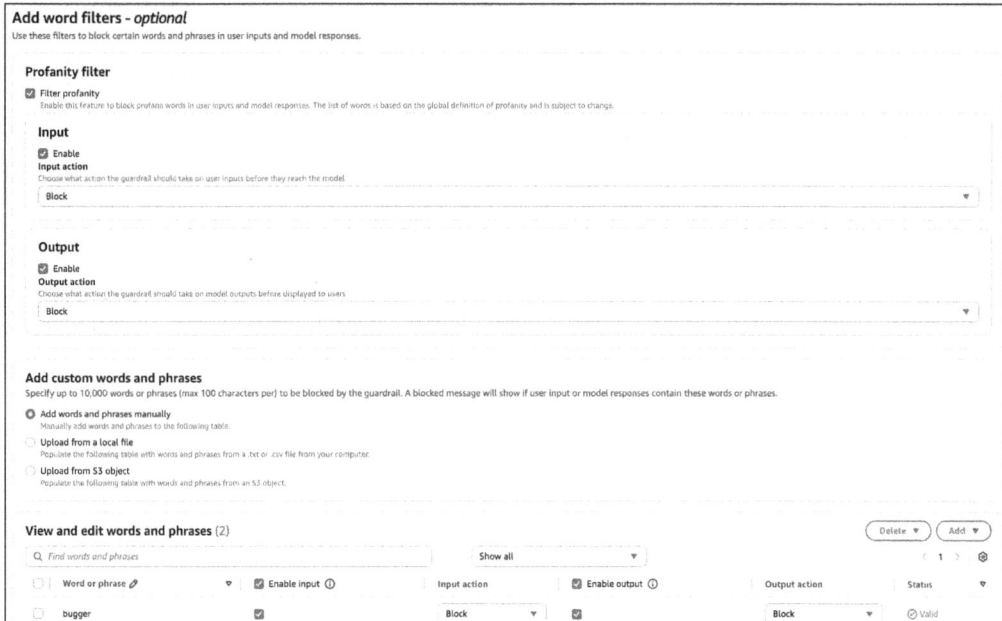

Figure 10.4: Configure word filters with guardrail

It also provides a built-in feature to filter profanity, without you having to define profane words.

7.   Next, guardrails allow you to filter sensitive information. In the dropdown as shown in *Figure 10.5*, you can choose the **PII types** you want to filter:

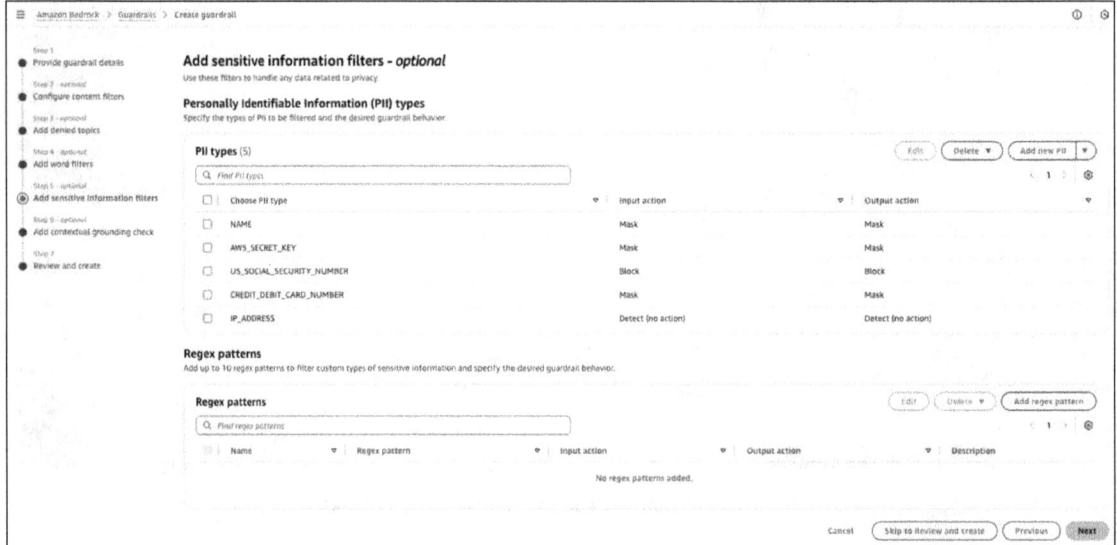

Figure 10.5: Configure sensitive information filters with guardrail

You need to select the **PII types**, and then define guardrail behavior whether to block or mask the sensitive information. It supports general PII such as email, name, phone as well as industry and country specific PII type. Console provides a shortcut to add all PII types with specific action as well. You can also define a regex pattern to filter custom sensitive information.

8.   Amazon Bedrock Guardrails supports contextual grounding check to detect and filter hallucination. As shown in *Figure 10.6*, it can generate grounding score to validate if the model responses are factually correct based on the information provided in source. It can also generate relevance score, if the model responses are relevant to the query user has asked. It will block responses that are below the threshold you define:

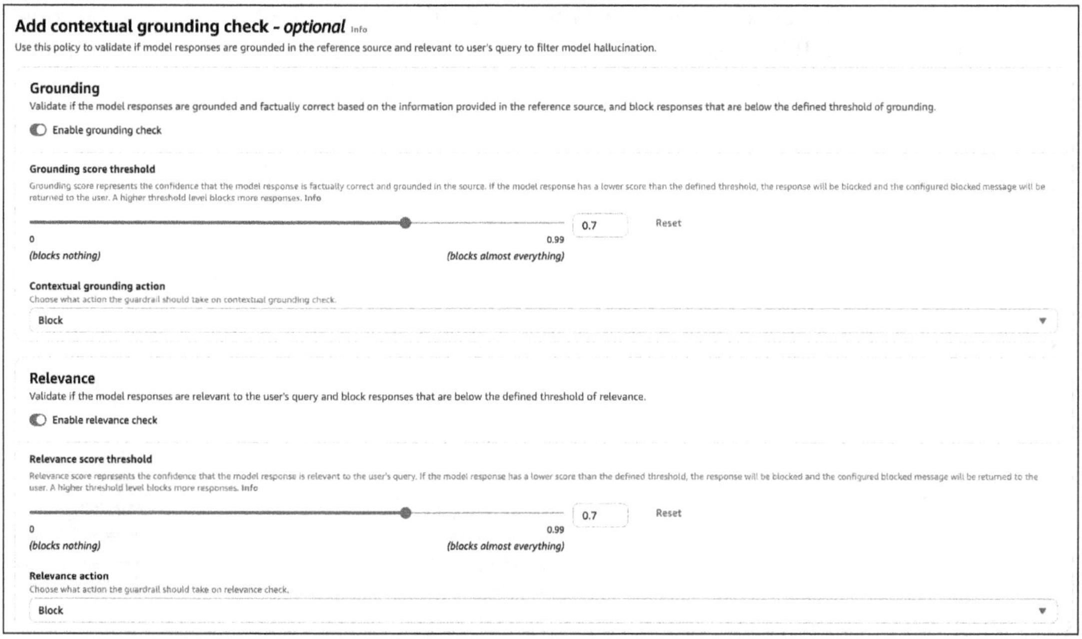

Figure 10.6: *Configure contextual grounding check with guardrail*

You can use the grounding check capability for a variety of use cases, such as **retrieval augmented generation** (**RAG**), summarization, or conversational agents, where you pass information to ground the conversation. Select **Next**.

9. Select **Create guardrail**, as shown in *Figure 10.7*. It should present a window where you can test the guardrail you just created:

Figure 10.7: *Testing guardrail on Amazon Bedrock*

Now, that the guardrail is created, let us test the guardrail using the **Test** window in the console as shown in *Figure 10.8*. If it does not appear, you can select **Test** next to the guardrail name.

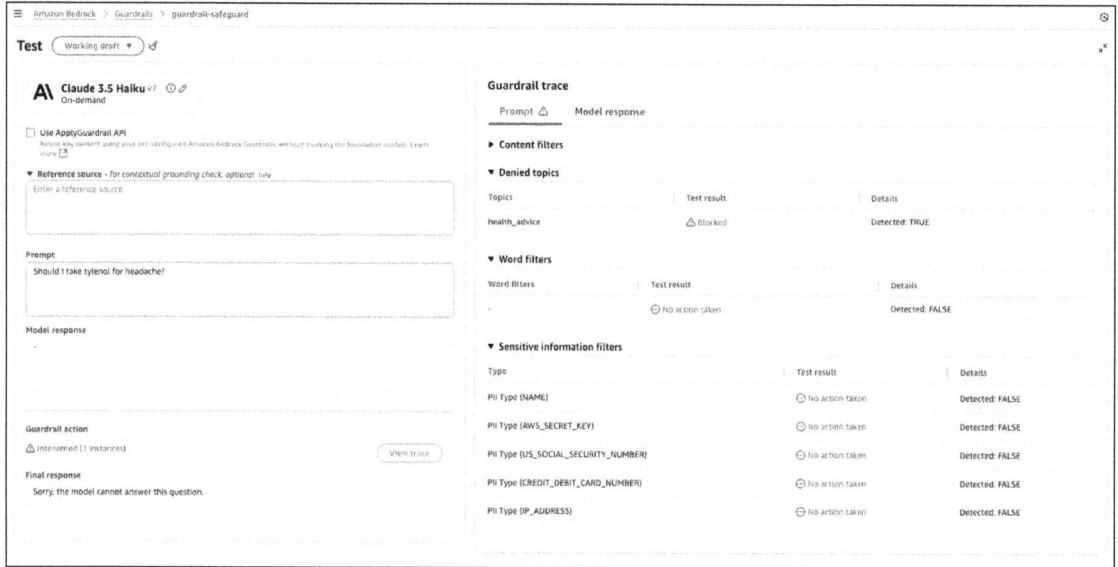

Figure 10.8: Reviewing and tracing guardrail actions

In the **Test** window, you need to select the model and enter a test prompt such as `Should I take tylenol for headache?` Given health advice is a denied topic, we should not see the model response with an answer. You can select **View trace** to validate guardrail behavior along with the category.

You can try out different prompts and optionally supply a reference source to validate guardrail action in various scenarios. Once you are satisfied with the guardrail performance and ready to deploy it in production, you need to create a version of it to invoke in your application. You can utilize Guardrail for Amazon Bedrock with InvokeModel and Converse APIs including with knowledge base and agent as well as independently without invoking the FMs on Amazon Bedrock. ApplyGuardrail API allows you to decouple safeguard implementation from FMs and helps you flexibly integrate anywhere in your application.

Security in Amazon Bedrock

As with any other AWS service, Amazon Bedrock incorporates a comprehensive suite of security capabilities, enabling users to monitor and secure their resources effectively. Amazon Bedrock's security framework encompasses the following key components:

- **Data protection**: Amazon Bedrock does not store or log your prompts and responses. It does not use your prompts and responses to train any AWS models and does not distribute them to third-parties. Additionally, Amazon Bedrock deploys FMs into a deployment account per model provider in each region and model providers do not have access to these accounts.

- **Data encryption**: All internetwork in-transit traffic is encrypted in Amazon Bedrock. Amazon Bedrock supports **virtual private cloud** (**VPC**) interface endpoint with AWS PrivateLink to privately and securely make API calls to all Amazon Bedrock endpoints without needing public IP addresses. Also, Amazon Bedrock supports encryption at rest for all model customization, knowledge base and agent artifacts. By default, it will encrypt these resources with AWS-managed KMS key (using AES-256 encryption algorithm) but you also have an option to utilize customer-managed key.

- **Identity and Access Management**: AWS **Identity and Access Management** (**IAM**) integrates with Amazon Bedrock, allowing administrators to permit or restrict access to Amazon Bedrock resources. Administrators can configure permissions to specific Amazon Bedrock resources such as Amazon Bedrock console, knowledge bases and agents for Amazon Bedrock, Provisioned Throughput. Amazon Bedrock allows granular control to allow or restrict using specific FMs. Amazon Bedrock uses IAM service roles for a number of Amazon Bedrock features to let it carry out tasks on your behalf.

- **Compliance and infrastructure security**: Amazon Bedrock offers comprehensive monitoring and logging capabilities that support governance and audit requirements, enabling you to meet various compliance standards such as *Service and Organization Control (SOC)*, *International Organization for Standardization (ISO)*, *Health Insurance Portability and Accountability Act (HIPAA)*, and the *General Data Protection Regulation (GDPR)*. As a managed service, Amazon Bedrock leverages the robust security measures of the AWS global network infrastructure, as documented in the security pillar of the AWS Well-Architected Framework, and enforces access control through IAM principals or temporary security credentials generated by the AWS **Security Token Service** (**STS**). Importantly, keep in mind, the AWS Shared Responsibility Model applies to data protection in Amazon Bedrock. As per the shared responsibility model, AWS is responsible for protecting the global infrastructure that is used by Amazon Bedrock and other services. You are responsible for maintaining control over your content that is hosted on this infrastructure. You are also responsible for the security configuration and management tasks for the AWS services that you use.

Conclusion

In this chapter, we explored the comprehensive security measures and responsible AI practices implemented by Amazon Bedrock, fostering trust and confidence in the deployment of GenAI solutions. You learned about the powerful guardrails feature, which enables you to configure customized policies and safeguards to maintain control over the content processed and generated by your AI applications, ensuring adherence to organizational policies and responsible AI principles. Additionally, we delved into the robust security capabilities of Amazon Bedrock, spanning data protection, encryption, IAM, and compliance with industry standards. By prioritizing security, privacy, and ethical development, Amazon Bedrock empowers you to harness the power of GenAI while mitigating risks and upholding responsible AI practices. With the knowledge gained from this chapter, you are now equipped to leverage Amazon Bedrock's advanced features and security measures, enabling you to build trustworthy and responsible GenAI applications that align with your organization's values and societal norms.

In the next chapter, we will cover how you can evaluate the performance of FMs and choose the best-suited model for your GenAI applications.

Points to remember

- Responsible AI practices are essential to address potential risks and negative impacts associated with AI technologies, such as biases, privacy violations, and unintended consequences. AWS supports copyright indemnity coverage for outputs of Amazon Titan FMs and GenAI services, promoting transparency and mitigating the spread of misinformation.

- Amazon Bedrock incorporates features like guardrail, watermark detection, and model evaluation to promote responsible AI practices, including content moderation, transparency, and informed model selection.

- The guardrail feature allows users to create customized policies and safeguards, including content filters, denied topics, word filters, sensitive information filters, and contextual grounding checks, to maintain control over the content generated by AI applications.

- Amazon Bedrock implements robust data protection measures, ensuring that user prompts and responses are not stored, logged, or used for training models, and are not distributed to third-parties.

- Amazon Bedrock integrates with AWS IAM for granular control over access to resources, including the ability to restrict access to specific FMs.

Exercises

1. **Configuring guardrails for different scenarios**: Practice creating and configuring guardrails for various scenarios to understand how to implement content moderation and responsible AI practices.

   Imagine you are developing an AI-powered content creation tool for a reputable news and media organization. The tool should prioritize factual accuracy, avoid spreading misinformation, and maintain journalistic integrity. Configure a guardrail with the following settings:

a. Setup a contextual grounding check to ensure that the AI-generated content is factually accurate and relevant to the provided context or source material.

b. Configure content filters to block potentially biased, hateful, or discriminatory language.

c. Add word filters to block profanity, offensive terms, and any language that may be considered defamatory or libelous.

d. Setup sensitive information filters to redact any PII or confidential data that may be inadvertently included in the AI-generated content.

e. Test the Guardrail with various prompts, including some that may violate the configured policies, and observe the behavior.

2. **Testing watermark detection**: Explore Amazon Bedrock's watermark detection feature, which helps identify AI-generated content and promote transparency.

   - Generate a sample text using one of the FMs available in Amazon Bedrock.

   - Use the watermark detection feature to analyze the generated text and determine if it was created by an AI model.

   - Experiment with different types of content, for example, text, images, audio and observe the behavior of the watermark detection feature.

   - Try modifying the generated content and test if the watermark detection feature can still identify it as AI-generated.

   - Discuss the potential applications and limitations of watermark detection in promoting transparency and mitigating the spread of misinformation.

Join our Discord space

Join our Discord workspace for latest updates, offers, tech happenings around the world, new releases, and sessions with the authors:

https://discord.bpbonline.com

CHAPTER 11

RAG and Model Evaluation

Introduction

In the rapidly evolving field of AI, the ability to accurately assess and improve model performance is paramount. As we have explored in previous chapters, technologies like **retrieval augmented generation (RAG)** have significantly enhanced the capabilities of **large language models (LLMs)**. However, with great power comes great responsibility and the need for robust evaluation mechanisms. Model evaluation in the context of **generative AI (GenAI)** presents unique challenges. Unlike traditional **machine learning (ML)** tasks with clear right or wrong answers, assessing the quality of generated text requires nuanced approaches that consider factors such as relevance, coherence, factual accuracy, and even ethical considerations. Amazon Bedrock rises to this challenge by providing a comprehensive suite of evaluation tools designed specifically for LLMs and GenAI applications.

This chapter will guide you through the intricacies of model evaluation using Amazon Bedrock. We will explore both automatic evaluation techniques, which provide quick, scalable assessments, and human-based evaluations, which offer deeper insights into model performance. You will learn how to setup evaluation jobs, interpret results, and use these insights to iteratively improve your models. We will also discuss advanced topics such as using the open source **RAG Assessment (Ragas)** framework for evaluating RAG systems, designing custom evaluation metrics, and integrating evaluation processes into your development workflows.

Structure

The chapter covers the following topics:

- Model evaluation and its significance
- Amazon Bedrock Model Evaluation capabilities
- Fundamentals of model evaluation
- Implementing model evaluation in Amazon Bedrock
- Automatic model evaluation in Amazon Bedrock
- Human evaluation in Amazon Bedrock
- Analyzing and interpreting human evaluation results

Objectives

By the end of this chapter, readers will have gained a comprehensive understanding of model evaluation techniques and their implementation using Amazon Bedrock. You will develop proficiency in setting up and running automatic evaluations, learning to interpret the results to drive model improvements. This chapter will equip you with the skills to design and implement human-based evaluations, providing deeper insights into model performance. You will explore advanced evaluation techniques, including the use of Ragas for assessing RAG systems, and learn to design custom evaluation metrics tailored to specific use cases.

You will gain valuable knowledge about best practices for integrating evaluation processes into AI development workflows. This multifaceted approach to learning will ensure that you can confidently assess the performance, reliability, and ethical considerations of your AI models, ultimately enabling you to develop more robust and trustworthy AI solutions.

By the end of this chapter, you will have the skills to implement comprehensive evaluation strategies that ensure your AI models perform well in controlled environments and meet the rigorous demands of production deployments.

Model evaluation and its significance

Model evaluation is a critical process in the development and deployment of AI systems, particularly for LLMs and GenAI applications. It involves assessing the performance, reliability, and potential biases of AI models to ensure they meet the required standards for their intended use cases.

The significance of model evaluation in AI development cannot be overstated, as it serves several crucial purposes, as follows:

- **Quality assurance**: Evaluation helps ensure that AI models perform as expected and produce high-quality outputs. This is especially important for GenAI, where the quality of generated content can vary widely based on input and context.

- **Performance measurement**: Through evaluation, developers can quantify various aspects of model performance, such as accuracy, relevance, coherence, and response time. These metrics provide objective measures of how well the model is functioning.

- **Bias detection**: Evaluation processes can help identify potential biases in model outputs, ensuring that AI systems are fair and do not discriminate against particular groups or perpetuate harmful stereotypes.

- **Comparative analysis**: By evaluating different models or versions of a model, developers can make informed decisions about which one is best suited for a particular task or application.

- **Continuous improvement**: Regular evaluation provides insights into areas where a model can be improved, guiding further training or fine-tuning efforts.

- **Trust and transparency**: Thorough evaluation and reporting of results build trust with users and stakeholders by demonstrating the capabilities and limitations of AI systems.

- **Regulatory compliance**: As AI regulations evolve, robust evaluation processes help ensure that AI systems meet legal and ethical standards.

- **Resource optimization**: Evaluation helps in understanding the trade-offs between model complexity, performance, and computational resources, allowing for more efficient use of resources.

In the context of GenAI and LLMs, it presents unique challenges. Unlike traditional ML tasks with clear right or wrong answers, assessing the quality of generated text requires more nuanced approaches. Evaluators must consider factors such as contextual relevance, factual accuracy, coherence, creativity, and even the appropriateness of the language used.

Amazon Bedrock Model Evaluation capabilities

Amazon Bedrock provides a comprehensive suite of tools and features designed to address the complex needs of evaluating GenAI models. These capabilities streamline the evaluation process, allowing developers to assess and improve their models efficiently.

Key features include the following:

- **Automatic evaluation**:
  - Bedrock offers a range of pre-defined metrics for automatic evaluation, covering aspects like accuracy, robustness, and toxicity.
  - It offers two options for evaluation:
    - **Programmatic**: Evaluate performances using just the model and metrics you select.

- **Model as a judge**: A pre-trained model evaluates your model's responses using metrics you have selected.

  o Supports various task types including text generation, summarization, **question answering** (**QA**), and classification.

  o Provides built-in datasets for different evaluation scenarios, as well as the option to use custom datasets.

- **Human-based evaluation**:

  o Enables the creation and management of human evaluation workflows.

  o Supports the formation of work teams for conducting evaluations.

  o Offers customizable interfaces for human evaluators to assess model outputs based on specific criteria.

- **Flexible evaluation jobs**:

  o Allows the creation of evaluation jobs that can assess one or more models simultaneously.

  o Supports both single-model assessments and comparative evaluations between models.

- **Comprehensive metrics**:

  o Includes a wide range of evaluation metrics suitable for different aspects of model performance.

  o Allows for the definition of custom metrics to address specific use case requirements.

- **Integration with foundation models**:

  o Seamlessly works with various **foundation models** (**FMs**) available in Amazon Bedrock, ensuring compatibility and ease of use.

- **Scalability and performance**:

  o Leverages AWS infrastructure to handle large-scale evaluations efficiently.

  o Enables parallel processing of evaluation tasks for faster results.

- **Detailed reporting**:

  o Generates comprehensive reports with visualizations to help interpret evaluation results.

  o Provides both overview statistics and detailed breakdowns of performance across different metrics and datasets.

- **API support**:

  o Offers API access for programmatic creation and management of evaluation jobs.

o   Enables integration of evaluation processes into broader AI development workflows and CI/CD pipelines.

- **Security and compliance**:
   o   Adheres to AWS security standards, ensuring data privacy and protection during the evaluation process.
   o   Supports compliance with various regulatory requirements through detailed logging and access controls.

By leveraging these capabilities, developers can implement robust evaluation strategies that cover both quantitative and qualitative aspects of model performance. This comprehensive approach to evaluation ensures that AI models developed and deployed using Amazon Bedrock meet high standards of quality, reliability, and ethical considerations.

In this chapter, we will explore how to effectively use these features to design and implement thorough evaluation processes for your AI models, enabling you to develop more trustworthy and high-performing AI solutions.

Fundamentals of model evaluation

Let us explore the core concepts and methodologies used in evaluating AI models, with a focus on GenAI and LLM. Understanding the core components of model evaluation is crucial for effectively assessing and improving AI models, especially in the context of GenAI and LLMs. Let us explore each component in detail.

Evaluation metrics

Evaluation metrics are quantitative measures used to assess various aspects of model performance. They provide objective ways to compare models and track improvements. Different tasks and model types often require specific metrics.

The following are the common metrics for GenAI (not all are supported by Amazon Bedrock):

- **Perplexity**:
   o   Measures how well a model predicts a sample.
   o   Lower perplexity indicates better performance.
   o   Useful for assessing language models' general predictive power.
   o   **Example**: A perplexity of 10 means the model is as confused as if it had to choose uniformly between 10 options for each word.

- **Bilingual Evaluation Understudy score**:
   o   Primarily used for machine translation tasks.
   o   Measures the similarity between model-generated text and reference translations.

- o Scores range from 0 to 1, with 1 being a perfect match.
- o **Example**: A **Bilingual Evaluation Understudy** (**BLEU**) score of 0.7 indicates high similarity to reference translations.

- **Recall-Oriented Understudy for Gisting Evaluation score**:
  - o **Recall-Oriented Understudy for Gisting Evaluation** (**ROUGE**) used for evaluating text summarization.
  - o Measures overlap between generated and reference summaries.
  - o Various types like ROUGE-N, ROUGE-L, ROUGE-W, focus on different aspects.
  - o **Example**: A ROUGE-1 score of 0.6 indicates 60% unigram overlap with reference summaries.

- **Coherence and fluency metrics**:
  - o Assess the logical flow and readability of generated text.
  - o Often requires combination with human evaluation.
  - o Can use metrics like sentence embedding similarity or language model perplexity as proxies.

- **Task-specific metrics**:
  - o **For QA**: Exact match and F1 scores.
  - o **For classification tasks**: Accuracy, precision, recall, F1 score.

Evaluation datasets

Evaluation datasets are carefully curated sets of data used to test model performance. They play a crucial role in ensuring comprehensive and fair assessment.

The following are the types of evaluation datasets:

- **Built-in datasets**: Provided by platforms like Amazon Bedrock, these standardized datasets offer consistent benchmarks across multiple FMs, enabling fair comparison and performance validation against established metrics.

  Examples:
  - o TriviaQA is a dataset that contains over 650K QA-evidence-triples. This dataset is used in question and answer tasks.
  - o WikiText2 is a Hugging Face dataset that contains prompts used in general text generation.

  Advantage: Standardized, allows comparison across different models and research.

- **Custom datasets**: Created specifically for your use case or domain.

Example: A dataset of customer queries and ideal responses for a customer service chatbot.

Advantage: Highly relevant to specific application, can test domain-specific knowledge.

- **Adversarial datasets**: Designed to challenge models with difficult or edge cases.

    Example: Winograd Schema Challenge for testing common sense reasoning.

    Importance: Helps identify model weaknesses and potential failure modes.

The following are the characteristics of good evaluation datasets:

- **Diversity**: Covers a wide range of inputs and scenarios.
- **Relevance**: Reflects real-world use cases and challenges.
- **Balance**: Represents different categories or types of inputs fairly.
- **Size**: Large enough to provide statistically significant results.

Evaluation tasks

Evaluation tasks are specific scenarios or problems designed to test particular aspects of model performance. They help assess how well a model performs in real-world applications.

The following are the common evaluation tasks for GenAI:

- **Open-ended text generation**: Assesses the model's ability to generate coherent and relevant text given a prompt.

    Example: Generating a story continuation or a product description.

- **Summarization**: Tests the model's capability to condense longer texts while retaining key information.

    Types: Abstractive, that is, generating new sentences and extractive, that is, selecting important sentences.

- **QA**: Evaluates the model's ability to understand context and provide accurate answers.
- **Varieties**: Closed-book, that is, without external knowledge and open-book, that is, with access to reference material.
- **Translation**: Assesses language translation capabilities between different languages. It considers accuracy, fluency, and preservation of meaning.
- **Sentiment analysis**: Tests the model's ability to discern and classify the sentiment in text. It is often used in conjunction with human evaluation for nuanced understanding.
- **Dialogue generation**: Evaluates the model's ability to maintain context and generate appropriate responses in a conversation. It assesses aspects like coherence, engagement, and staying on-topic.

- **Code generation and completion**: For models trained on programming tasks, assesses the ability to generate or complete code snippets. It evaluates correctness, efficiency, and adherence to coding standards.

Implementing model evaluation in Amazon Bedrock

Let us explore how Amazon Bedrock incorporates these key components and provides specific types of evaluation for comprehensive model assessment, as follows:

- **Automatic evaluation**: Bedrock offers automated evaluation for various task types:
  - **General text generation**: Assesses the quality of open-ended text generation.
  - **Text summarization**: Evaluates the model's ability to create concise and accurate summaries.
  - **QA**: Tests the model's capability to provide accurate and relevant answers to questions.
  - **Text classification**: Assesses the model's proficiency in categorizing text into pre-defined classes.
- **Human-based evaluation**:
  - Bedrock supports creating and managing human evaluation workflows for more nuanced assessments.
  - Allows for customizable evaluation criteria and rating methods tailored to specific use cases.
- **Metrics and datasets**:
  - Utilizing built-in metrics such as accuracy, robustness, and toxicity for automatic evaluations.
  - Leveraging Bedrock's pre-built datasets for standard evaluation scenarios.
  - Option to integrate custom datasets for domain-specific evaluations.
- **Evaluation jobs**:
  - Ability to create evaluation jobs that can assess one or more models simultaneously.
  - Support for both single-model assessments and comparative evaluations between models.
- **Custom metrics and evaluation criteria**: Flexibility to define custom metrics and evaluation criteria for both automatic and human-based evaluations.
- **Ragas integration**: Support for advanced evaluation techniques like Ragas for comprehensive assessment of RAG systems.

By leveraging these evaluation types and features in Amazon Bedrock, you can perform the following:

- Design thorough evaluation strategies that cover both quantitative and qualitative aspects of model performance.

- Tailor evaluations to your specific use case and domain requirements.

- Conduct comprehensive assessments that ensure your AI models meet the high standards required for real-world applications.

Challenges in evaluating LLMs

It is crucial to understand the unique challenges posed by evaluating LLMs. These challenges stem from the complexity, versatility, and often unpredictable nature of LLMs.

Let us examine these challenges as follows:

- **Lack of definitive ground truth**: Unlike many traditional ML tasks, generative outputs from LLMs often do not have a single correct answer.

  o **Example**: For a prompt like `Write a story about a robot learning to love`, there are countless valid and creative responses.

  o **Challenge**: Evaluating quality or correctness becomes highly subjective when dealing with diverse, creative outputs that have multiple valid expressions.

  o **Implication**: Traditional metrics like accuracy become less meaningful, necessitating more nuanced evaluation approaches.

- **Contextual dependency**: The quality and appropriateness of LLM outputs can vary significantly based on the context and nuances of the input.

  o **Example**: A model might perform well on general knowledge questions but struggle with domain-specific or culturally nuanced queries.

  o **Challenge**: Creating evaluation datasets that cover a wide range of contexts and scenarios.

  o **Implication**: Need for diverse, representative evaluation sets and context-aware evaluation methods.

- **Subjectivity in quality assessment**: Many aspects of language quality, such as creativity, coherence, and style, are inherently subjective.

  o **Example**: What one evaluator considers a witty response, another might find inappropriate or off-topic.

  o **Challenge**: Achieving consistency and reliability in human evaluations.

  o **Implication**: Necessity for well-defined rubrics, multiple evaluators, and methods to handle subjectivity.

- **Handling ethical considerations and biases**: LLMs can inadvertently produce biased, unfair, or potentially harmful content.

  o **Example**: A model might generate text that perpetuates gender stereotypes or contains subtle racial biases.

  o **Challenge**: Detecting and quantifying biases, especially subtle ones, across vast output possibilities.

  o **Implication**: Need for specialized evaluation techniques focused on fairness, bias detection, and ethical considerations.

- **Evaluating factual accuracy**: LLMs can generate plausible-sounding but factually incorrect information, a phenomenon known as **hallucination**.

  o **Example**: A model confidently stating an incorrect historical date or inventing non-existent scientific facts.

  o **Challenge**: Verifying the factual correctness of generated content, especially for specialized or less common knowledge.

  o **Implication**: Requirement for fact-checking mechanisms and evaluations that assess the model's ability to distinguish between fact and speculation.

- **Assessing consistency across multiple interactions**: LLMs should maintain consistency in their knowledge and persona across a conversation or multiple related queries.

  o **Example**: A model giving contradictory information about a topic in different parts of a conversation.

  o **Challenge**: Designing evaluation methods that assess long-term consistency and coherence.

  o **Implication**: Need for evaluation techniques that go beyond single-turn interactions to assess multi-turn consistency.

- **Evaluating safety and robustness**: LLMs should be resilient to adversarial inputs and maintain safe, appropriate outputs even with challenging prompts.

  o **Example**: Ensuring the model does not produce harmful content when given provocative or malicious inputs.

  o **Challenge**: Creating comprehensive test sets that probe the model's boundaries and failure modes.

  o **Implication**: Necessity for adversarial testing and safety-focused evaluation metrics.

- **Keeping up with rapid model improvements**: The field of LLMs is advancing rapidly, with new models and techniques emerging frequently.

  o **Example**: A new model architecture that renders certain evaluation methods less effective or irrelevant.

  o **Challenge**: Continuously updating evaluation methodologies to keep pace with model advancements.

  o **Implication**: Need for flexible, adaptable evaluation frameworks that can evolve with the technology.

- **Balancing comprehensive evaluation with efficiency**: Thoroughly evaluating an LLM across all possible use cases and scenarios can be extremely time-consuming and computationally expensive.

  o **Example**: Running extensive evaluations on a large model like Nova Pro or Claude 3.5 Sonnet can take significant time and resources.

  o **Challenge**: Finding the right balance between comprehensive evaluation and practical constraints.

  o **Implication**: Need for efficient evaluation strategies that provide meaningful insights without excessive resource consumption.

Addressing evaluation challenges with Amazon Bedrock

Amazon Bedrock offers a comprehensive suite of tools and features designed to address many of the challenges in evaluating LLMs. As we proceed, we will explore the two main types of evaluation provided by Bedrock: automatic evaluation and human evaluation. These complementary approaches allow for a multi-faceted assessment strategy. Automatic evaluation enables efficient, scalable assessments using pre-defined metrics and datasets, while human evaluation facilitates nuanced, qualitative assessments of subjective aspects. By leveraging both of these evaluation types in Amazon Bedrock, you will be equipped to conduct thorough assessments of your LLMs. This comprehensive approach ensures that your models meet the high standards required for real-world applications while addressing the unique challenges posed by these sophisticated AI systems.

Automatic model evaluation in Amazon Bedrock

Automatic model evaluation is a crucial feature of Amazon Bedrock that enables efficient, scalable assessments of LLMs. This section will guide you through the process of setting up and running automatic evaluations, interpreting the results, and using these insights to improve your models.

Available metrics and its interpretations

Amazon Bedrock offers a range of pre-defined metrics for automatic evaluation, each designed to assess specific aspects of model performance. The available metrics vary depending on the task type, as follows:

- **Accuracy**:
    - **Applicable to**: Text classification, QA.
    - **Interpretation**: Percentage of correct predictions. Higher is better.
    - **Example**: An accuracy of 0.85 means the model correctly classified or answered 85% of the test cases.

- **Robustness**:
    - **Applicable to**: All task types.
    - **Interpretation**: Measures model's consistency when input is slightly modified. Ranges from 0 to 1, higher is better.
    - **Example**: A robustness score of 0.9 indicates the model's outputs remain consistent for 90% of slightly modified inputs.

- **Toxicity**:
    - **Applicable to**: All task types.
    - **Interpretation**: Measures the presence of toxic or offensive content in model outputs. Lower is better.
    - **Example**: A toxicity score of 0.1 indicates that 10% of the model's outputs contain potentially toxic content.

Built-in datasets for different task types

Amazon Bedrock provides several built-in datasets for standard evaluation scenarios, as follows:

- **General text generation**:
    - **Real toxicity**: RealToxicityPrompts is a dataset for measuring the degree to which racist, sexist, or otherwise toxic language is present in pre-trained neural language models.
    - **WikiText-2**: The WikiText language modeling dataset is a collection of over 100 million tokens extracted from the set of verified good and featured articles on *Wikipedia*.

- **Text summarization**:
  - o **Gigaword**: A large corpus of news articles with headlines, useful for evaluating summarization capabilities.

- **QA**:
  - o TriviaQA is a dataset that contains over 650K QA-evidence-triples. This dataset is used in question and answer tasks.
  - o **Natural questions**: Real queries from *Google search*, useful for evaluating open-domain QA.

- **Text classification**:
  - o **Women's E-Commerce Clothing Reviews**: The Women's E-Commerce Clothing Reviews dataset revolves around the reviews written by customers. Its nine supportive features offer a great environment to parse out the text through its multiple dimensions. Because this is real commercial data, it has been anonymized, and references to the company in the review text and body have been replaced with retailer.

Creating and using custom evaluation datasets

While built-in datasets are useful for standardized evaluations, custom datasets allow for domain-specific assessments.

To create a custom dataset, following are the steps:

1. Prepare your data in **JSON lines (JSONL)** format. Each line should contain a JSON object with the following fields:
   a. **prompt**: The input text.
   b. **referenceResponse (optional)**: The expected output.
   c. **category (optional)**: For classification tasks.

2. Upload your JSONL file to an S3 bucket.

3. When setting up the evaluation job, specify the S3 URI of your custom dataset.

   ```
   {prompt: Summarize the benefits of regular exercise, referenceResponse:
   Regular exercise improves cardiovascular health, strengthens muscles and
   bones, enhances mental well-being, and helps maintain a healthy weight.}
   ```

The following is the step-by-step guide to running an automatic evaluation:

1. **Open Amazon Bedrock console**: Navigate to the **Model evaluation** section.

2. **Create an evaluation job**:
   a. Click **Create automatic evaluation**.

b. Provide a name for your evaluation job.

The intuitive interface allows teams to efficiently compare model performance, track evaluation metrics, and make data-driven decisions when selecting the optimal FM for your specific application needs. Refer to the following figure:

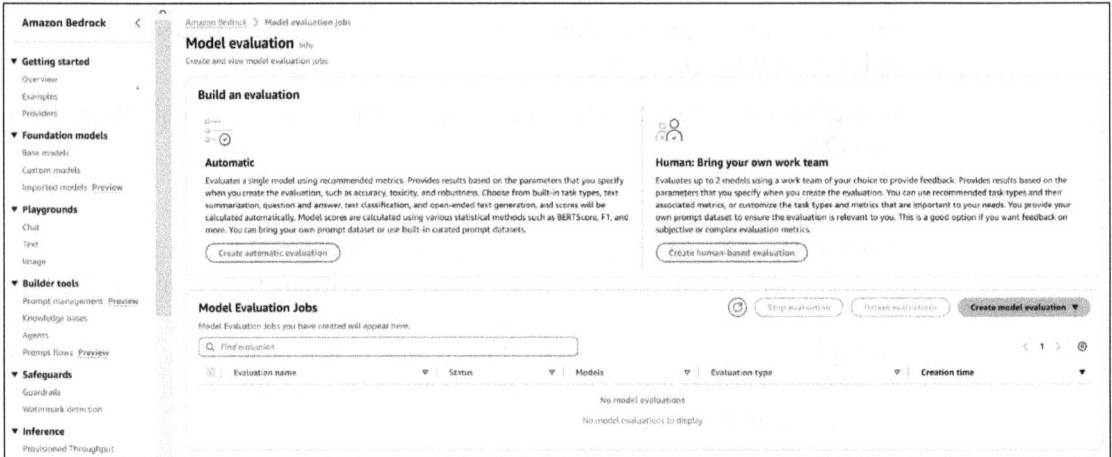

Figure 11.1:Amazon Bedrock Model Evaluation interface

3. **Select model**: Choose the model you want to evaluate from the available options in Bedrock.

The form allows developers to specify evaluation details, description information, and model selection options, enabling data-driven comparisons to identify the optimal FM for specific use cases. Refer to the following figure:

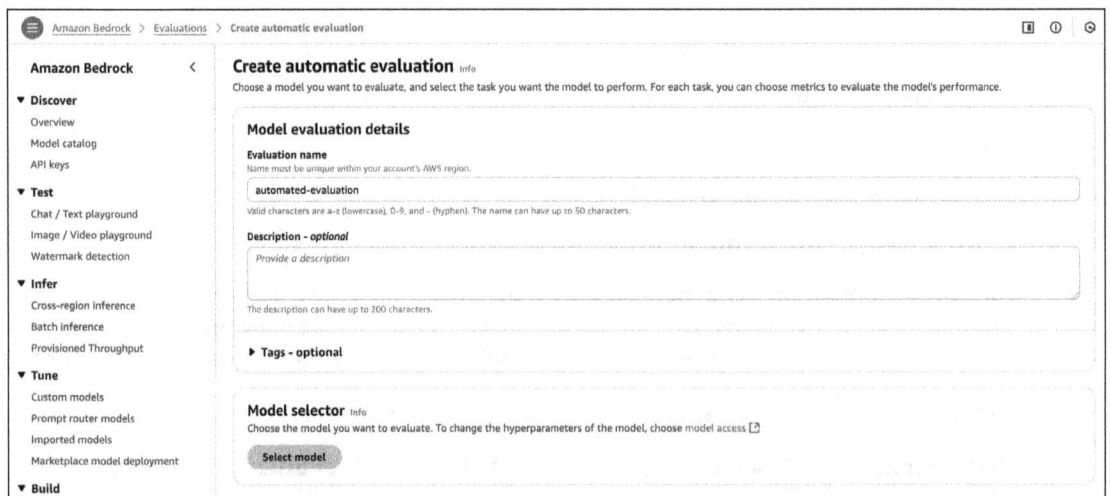

Figure 11.2: Create automatic evaluation in Amazon Bedrock

4. **Choose task type**: Select from **General text generation**, **Text summarization**, **Question and answer**, or **Text classification**.

5. **Select metrics**: Choose the metrics relevant to your task type.

The interface allows developers to define metrics, datasets, and precise evaluation criteria, enabling thorough performance assessment across different model parameters to optimize outcomes for specific use cases. Refer to the following figure:

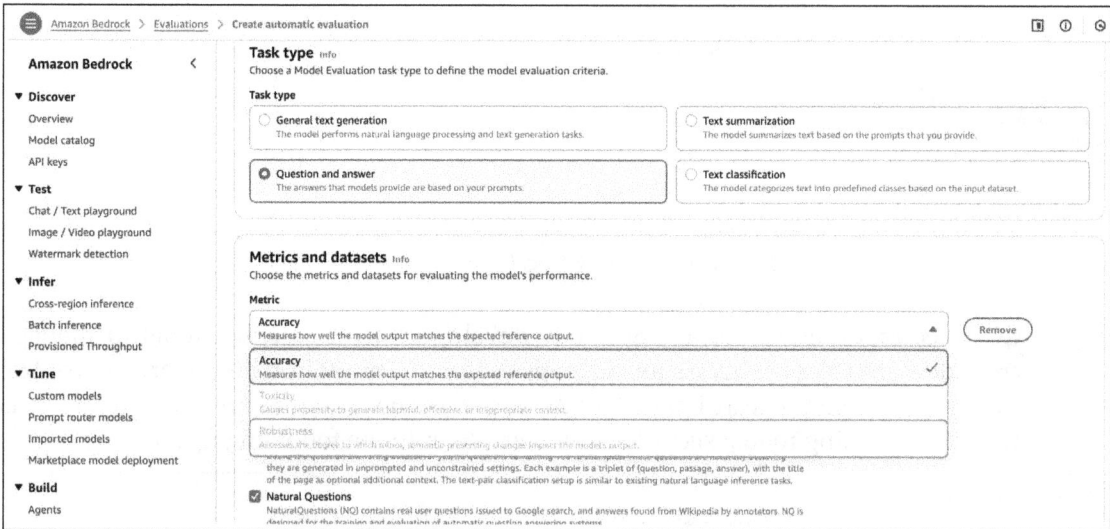

Figure 11.3: Task type configuration in Amazon Bedrock

6. **Choose dataset and create role**:

   a. Select a built-in dataset or specify the S3 URI of your custom dataset.

   b. Setup the **Cross-origin resource sharing (CORS)** configuration for the S3 bucket as shown in the *Figure 11.5*.

   c. Create or use existing Bedrock IAM role.

The comprehensive evaluation setup interface in Amazon Bedrock provides developers with structured sections for defining test parameters and success criteria. This multi-component dashboard enables users to configure evaluation details, API keys, advanced settings, and specific metrics to systematically assess FM performance. Refer to the following figure:

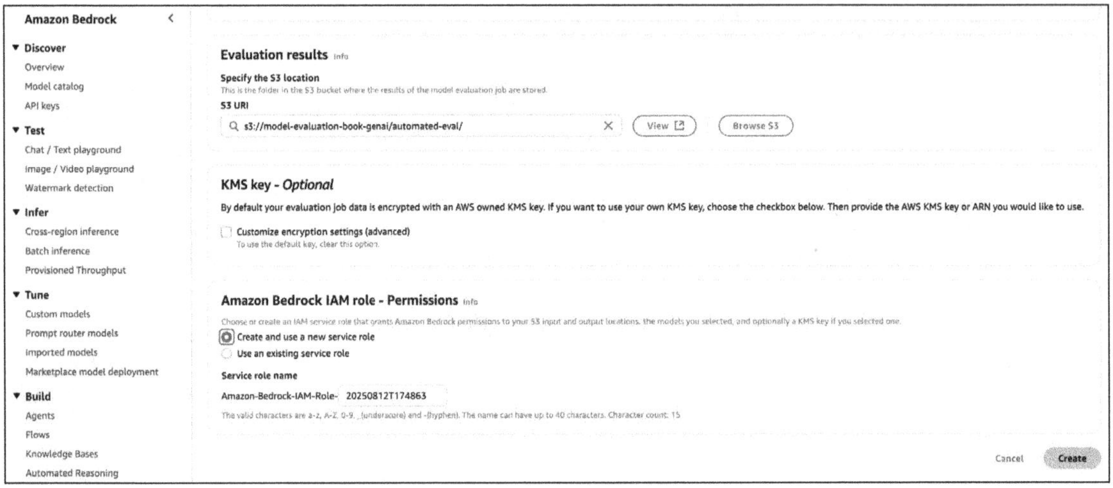

Figure 11.4: *Amazon Bedrock Model Evaluation configuration*

CORS configuration interface provides developers with essential tools to manage cross-domain resource access for web applications. This editor allows precise control over which domains can interact with resources, enabling secure API integrations while maintaining robust security protocols. Refer to the following figure:

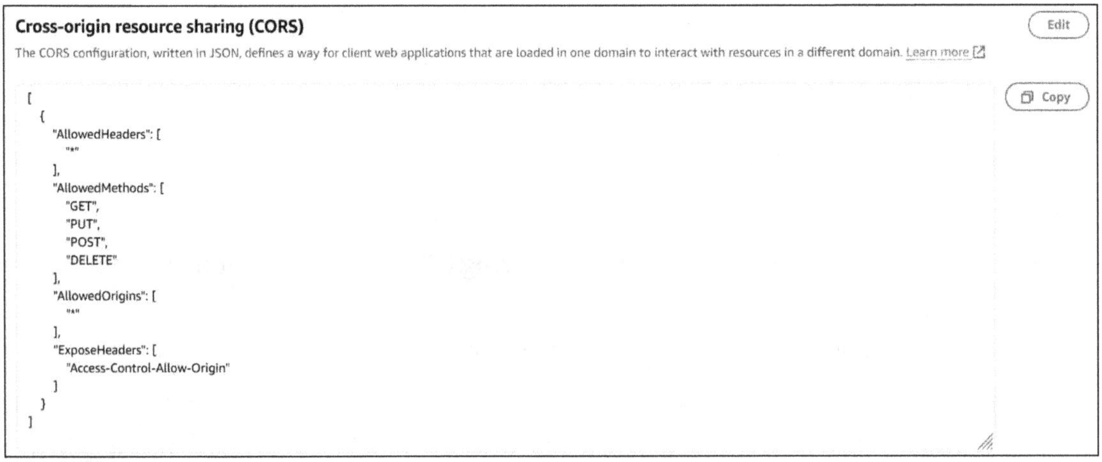

Figure 11.5: *CORS configuration*

7. **Review and create**: Review your settings and create the evaluation job.

The comprehensive Amazon Bedrock interface provides a structured workflow for configuring AI model evaluations through multiple interconnected sections. This organized dashboard enables users to define evaluation details, API keys, advanced settings, and success metrics to assess FM performance across various parameters thoroughly. Refer to the following figure:

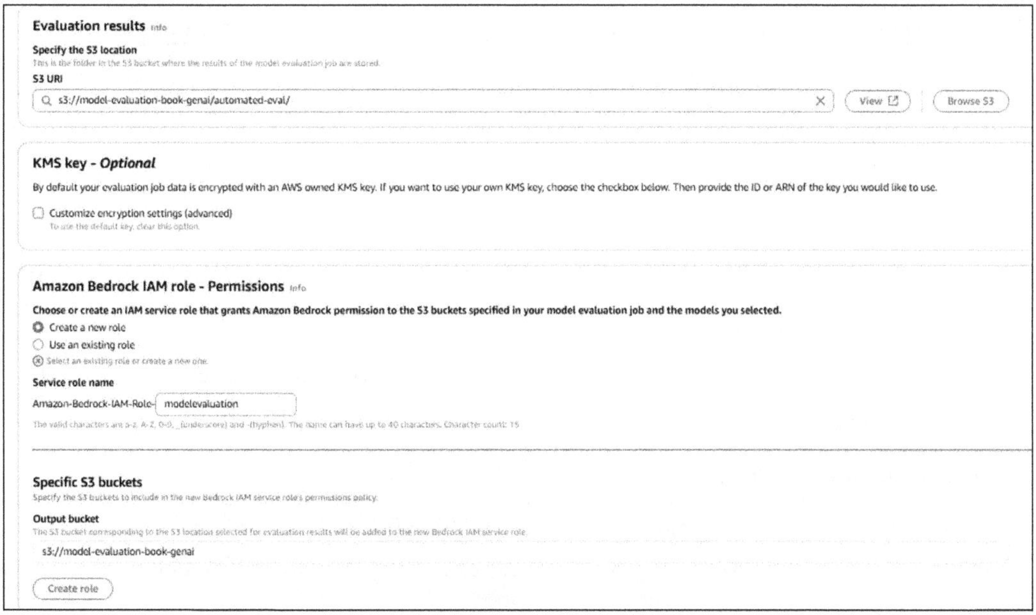

Figure 11.6: Amazon Bedrock Model Evaluation configuration

8. **Monitor progress**: Track the status of your evaluation job in the Bedrock console.

Amazon Bedrock's evaluation interface provides a comprehensive workspace for systematically testing FM performance. The platform combines intuitive configuration panels with detailed metrics tracking, enabling developers to efficiently compare model outputs and identify the optimal AI solution for specific use cases. Refer to the following figure:

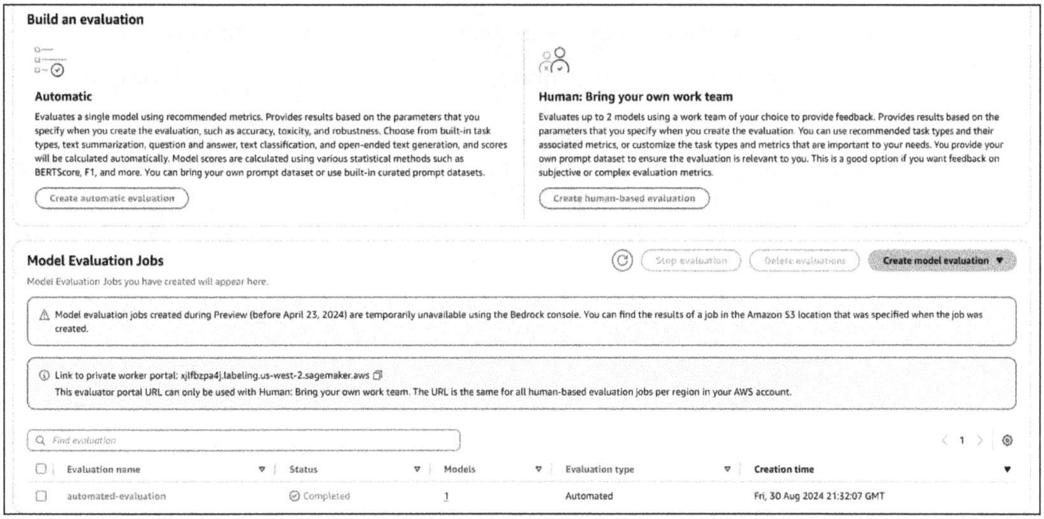

Figure 11.7: Build an evaluation in Amazon Bedrock

Interpreting and analyzing evaluation results

Once the evaluation job is complete, Bedrock provides a comprehensive report.

The following is how to interpret the results:

- **Overall metrics**:
  - Review the aggregate scores for each metric.
  - Compare these to baseline performance or previous versions of your model.

- **Per-sample analysis**:
  - Examine individual samples to understand where the model excels or struggles.
  - Look for patterns in high and low-performing samples.

- **Distribution of scores**:
  - Analyze the distribution of scores for metrics like accuracy or toxicity.
  - Identify any outliers or clusters that might indicate specific strengths or weaknesses.

- **Comparative analysis**: If evaluating multiple models, compare their performance across different metrics and task types.

- **Error analysis**:
  - For tasks like classification or QA, examine misclassified or incorrectly answered samples.
  - Look for common themes in errors to guide further model improvements.

- **Robustness check**:
  - Review how the model's performance changes with slight variations in input.
  - Identify any areas where the model is particularly sensitive to input changes.

Amazon Bedrock's comprehensive results interface displays performance metrics from completed AI model evaluations. The dashboard provides clear visualization of evaluation summaries, analytics with comparative model performance data, and detailed job configuration information, enabling data-driven decisions when selecting the optimal FM. Refer to the following figure:

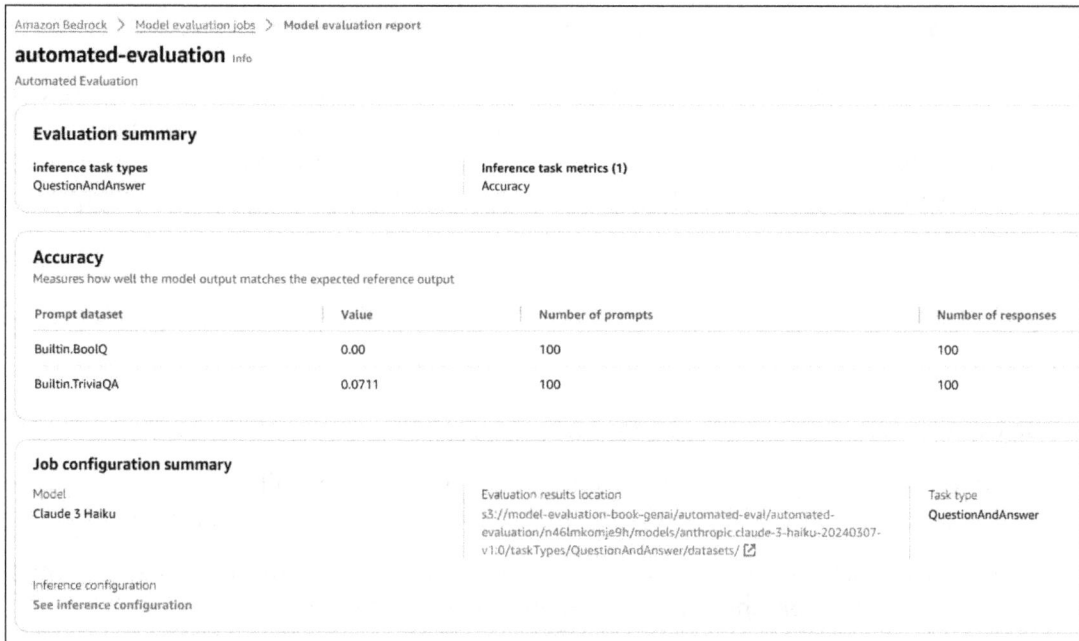

Figure 11.8: *Automated evaluation results dashboard*

The interface provides a centralized hub for tracking and organizing project resources. This powerful dashboard enables users to efficiently filter, sort, and manage various artifacts through an intuitive tabular display, enhancing workflow organization and team collaboration. Refer to the following figure:

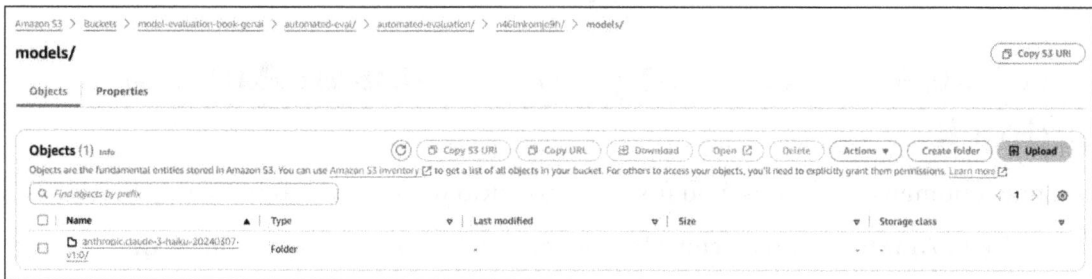

Figure 11.9: *Model artifacts*

By leveraging these automatic evaluation capabilities in Amazon Bedrock, you can gain deep insights into your model's performance, identify areas for improvement, and make data-driven decisions in your AI development process.

Note: While automatic evaluation provides valuable quantitative insights, it should be complemented with human evaluation for a comprehensive assessment, especially for subjective aspects of language quality and appropriateness.

Human evaluation in Amazon Bedrock

While automatic evaluations provide efficient, scalable assessments of model performance, human evaluation is crucial for assessing subjective aspects of language models such as coherence, relevance, and appropriateness. Amazon Bedrock offers robust tools for implementing human-based evaluations, allowing for nuanced assessments that complement automatic metrics.

Importance of human evaluation in assessing AI models

Human evaluation is essential for several reasons, as follows:

- **Subjective quality assessment**: Humans can evaluate aspects like creativity, coherence, and contextual appropriateness that are difficult to quantify automatically.

- **Ethical and safety checks**: Human reviewers can identify subtle biases, potentially harmful content, or ethical issues that automated systems might miss.

- **Contextual understanding**: Humans can assess whether responses are appropriate given cultural, social, or domain-specific contexts.

- **User experience simulation**: Human evaluators can provide insights into how end-users might perceive and interact with the model.

- **Complementary to automatic metrics**: Human evaluation can validate or provide context to automatic evaluation results.

Creating and managing work teams in Amazon Bedrock

To conduct human evaluations, you first need to setup work teams, as follows:

1. **Open Amazon Bedrock console**: Navigate to the **Model evaluation** section.
2. **Create evaluation job**:
   a. Click **Create human-based evaluation**.
   b. Provide a name for your evaluation job.

The Amazon Bedrock interface provides a structured form for defining essential parameters of AI model evaluation jobs. This user-friendly configuration page allows developers to input **Evaluation name**, **Description**, and **Tags**, creating a comprehensive framework for systematic assessment of FM performance. Refer to the following figure:

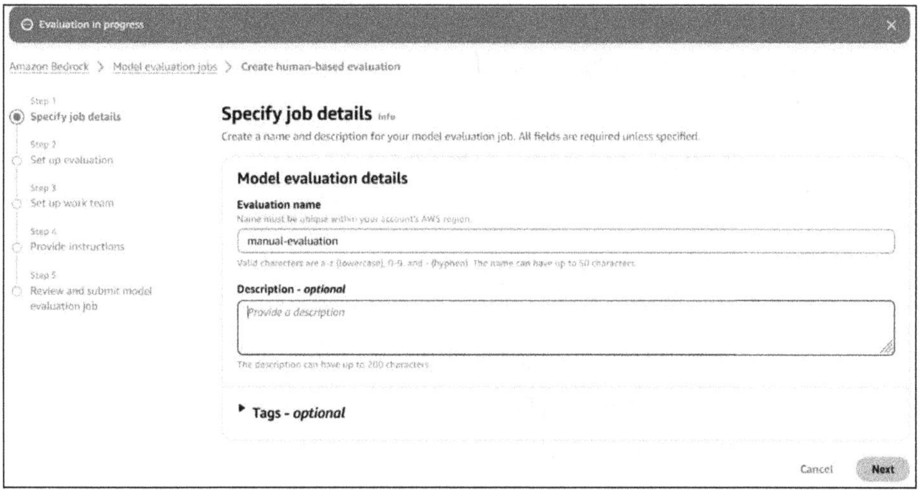

Figure 11.10: *Specify job details for model evaluation*

3. **Select model and choose task type**:

    a. Choose the model you want to evaluate from the available options in Bedrock.

    b. Select from **General text generation**, **Text summarization**, **Question and answer**, **Text classification**, and **Custom**.

The comprehensive interface offers a structured workflow for configuring AI model testing parameters in Amazon Bedrock. Users can select FMs and define specific evaluation tasks, including content generation, text summarization, and QA, providing flexible assessment options to determine optimal model performance for specific applications. Refer to the following figure:

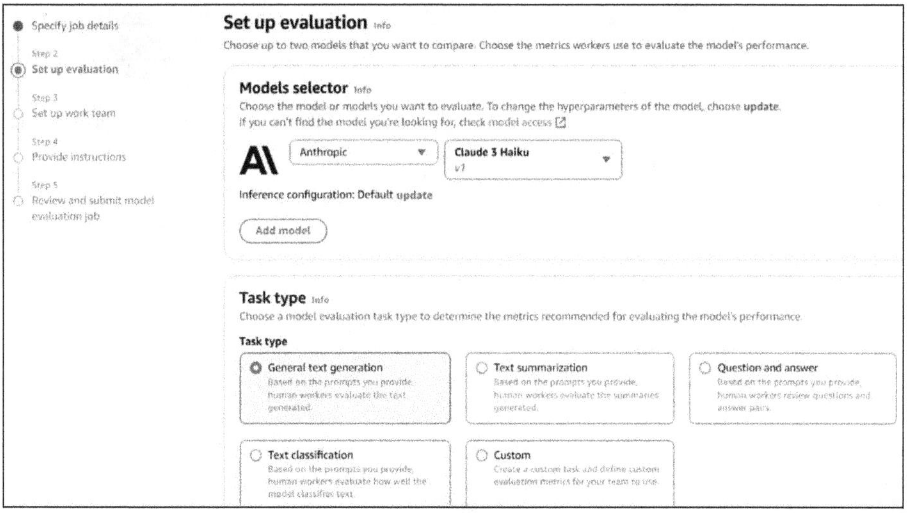

Figure 11.11: *Set up evaluation in Amazon Bedrock*

4. **Select metrics**: Choose the metrics relevant to your task type, as follows:

    a. **Define clear evaluation criteria**:

        i.   What aspects of the model output should be evaluated, for example, **Relevance**, **Coherence**, **Accuracy**.

        ii. Provide clear definitions for each criterion.

    b. **Create comprehensive instructions**:

        i.   Explain the context and purpose of the evaluation.

        ii.   Provide examples of good and bad responses.

        iii. Address potential biases and how to avoid them.

    c. **Design rating scales**:

        i.   Choose appropriate rating methods, for example, Likert scales, binary choices, or free-form feedback.

        ii. Clearly define what each point on the scale represents.

The Amazon Bedrock metrics configuration interface enables precise definition of AI model evaluation criteria and scoring methods. Through customizable **Metric** selections including **Toxicity**, **Accuracy**, **Factuality**, and **Coherence**, developers can establish comprehensive assessment frameworks to objectively measure FM performance across specific use cases. Refer to the following figure:

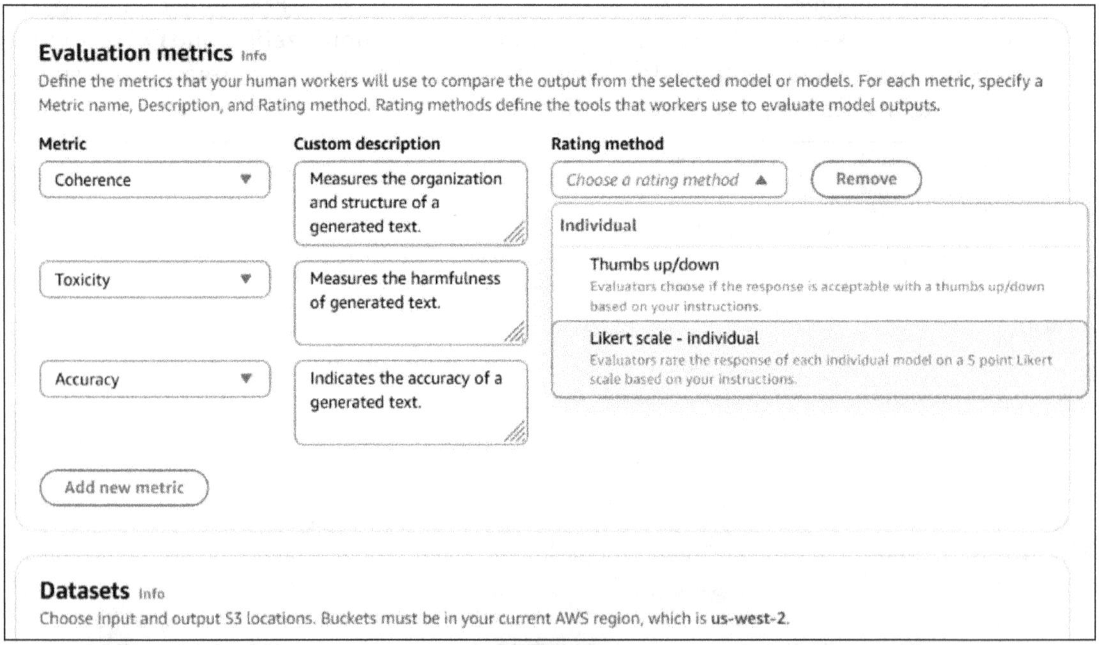

Figure 11.12: Evaluation metrics configuration in Amazon Bedrock

The detailed metrics configuration panel in Amazon Bedrock provides comprehensive options for customizing AI model evaluation criteria. With specialized categories including **Fluency**, **Coherence**, **Relevance**, **Accuracy**, **Toxicity**, and **Comprehensiveness**, developers can establish multidimensional assessment frameworks tailored to their specific model evaluation requirements. Refer to the following figure:

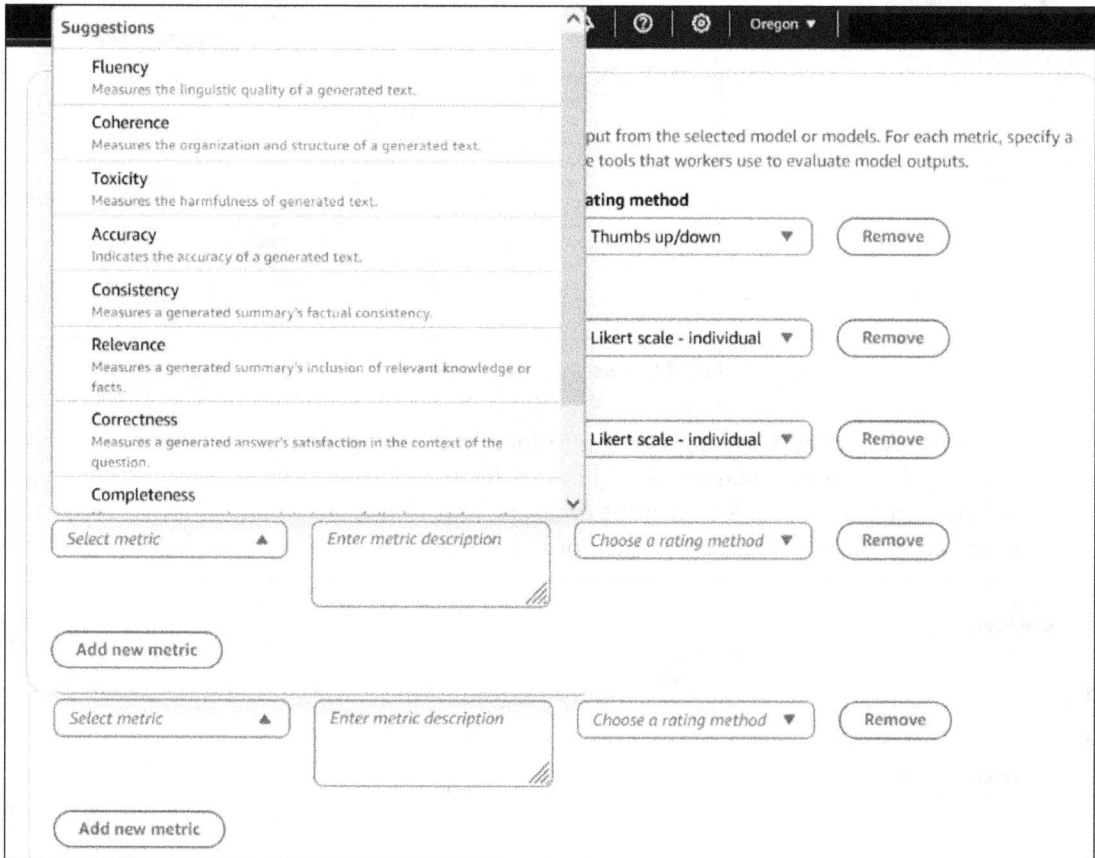

Figure 11.13: Amazon Bedrock Evaluation metrics selection interface

d. **Choose dataset and create role**:

    i.   Select a built-in dataset or specify the S3 URI of your custom dataset.

    ii. Using your own dataset requires you to set your dataset up in the correct format.

    iii. Setup the CORS configuration for the S3 bucket as shown in the image.

    iv. Also create or use existing Bedrock IAM role.

The structured knowledge dataset displays a comprehensive collection of QA pairs formatted in JSON for ML applications. This robust reference repository contains definitions and explanations across diverse domains including fitness, philosophy, science, and technology, providing essential training data for **natural language processing** (**NLP**) models. Refer to the following figure:

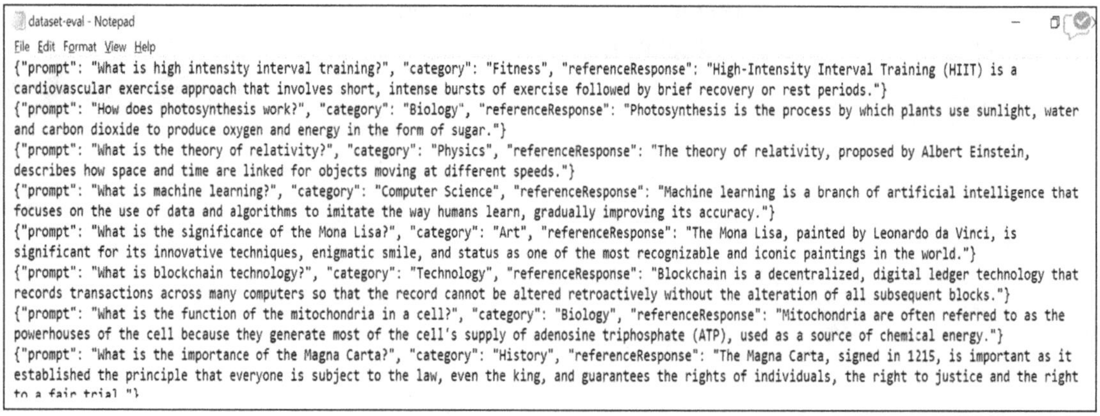

Figure 11.14: *JSON knowledge base dataset for AI training*

The comprehensive dataset management interface in Amazon Bedrock enables developers to configure evaluation data sources for AI model testing. This structured setup allows users to upload custom datasets, select prompt datasets, and define evaluation inputs, providing essential test cases for thorough assessment of FM performance. Refer to the following figure:

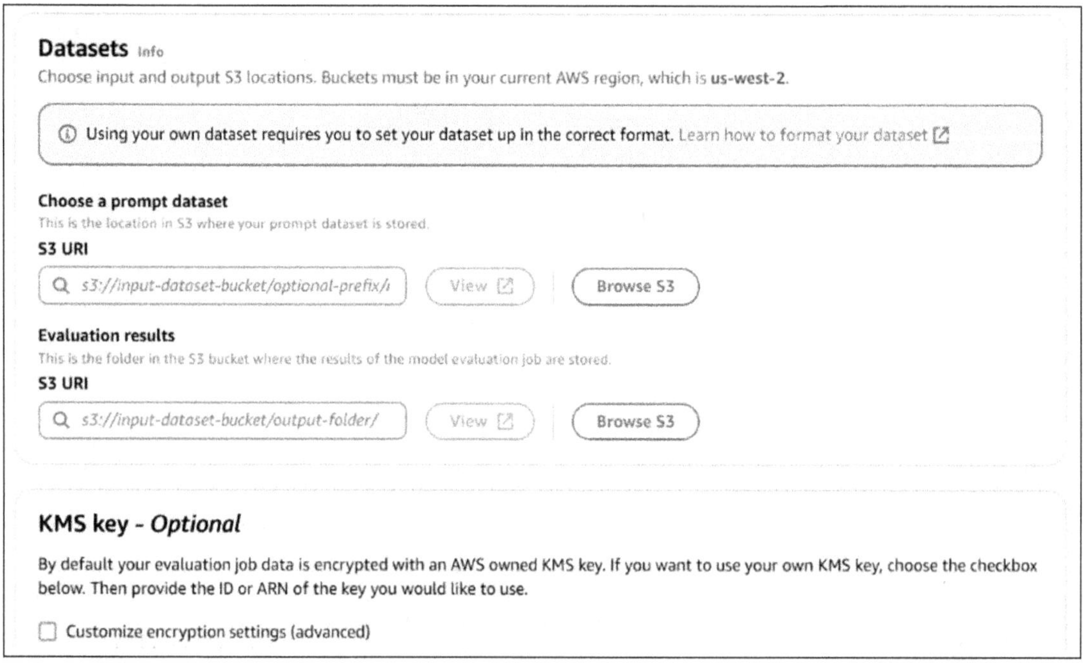

Figure 11.15: *Amazon Bedrock datasets configuration*

The setup interface provides developers with essential tools for integrating FMs into their applications. This structured configuration panel allows users to specify create IAM role, specifying S3 bucket preferences. Refer to the following figure:

Amazon Bedrock IAM role - Permissions Info

Choose or create an IAM role that grants Amazon Bedrock permissions to your S3 input and output locations, the models you selected, and optionally a KMS key if you selected one.

Choose or create an IAM service role that grants Amazon Bedrock permission to the S3 buckets specified in your model evaluation job and the models you selected.

⦿ Create a new role
◯ Use an existing role

Service role name

Amazon-Bedrock-IAM-Role- | 20240830T174220

The valid characters are a-z, A-Z, 0-9, _(underscore) and -(hyphen). The name can have up to 40 characters. Character count: 15

Specific S3 buckets

Specify the S3 buckets to include in the new Bedrock IAM service role's permissions policy.

Input bucket(s)

The S3 bucket corresponding to the input dataset will be added automatically.

s3://input-bucket

Choose additional input buckets

You can add more custom prompt dataset(s) to the Bedrock IAM service role by adding another input bucket.

+ Add another input bucket

Output bucket

The S3 bucket corresponding to the S3 location selected for evaluation results will be added to the new Bedrock IAM service role.

s3://output-bucket

Create role

Cancel | Previous | **Next**

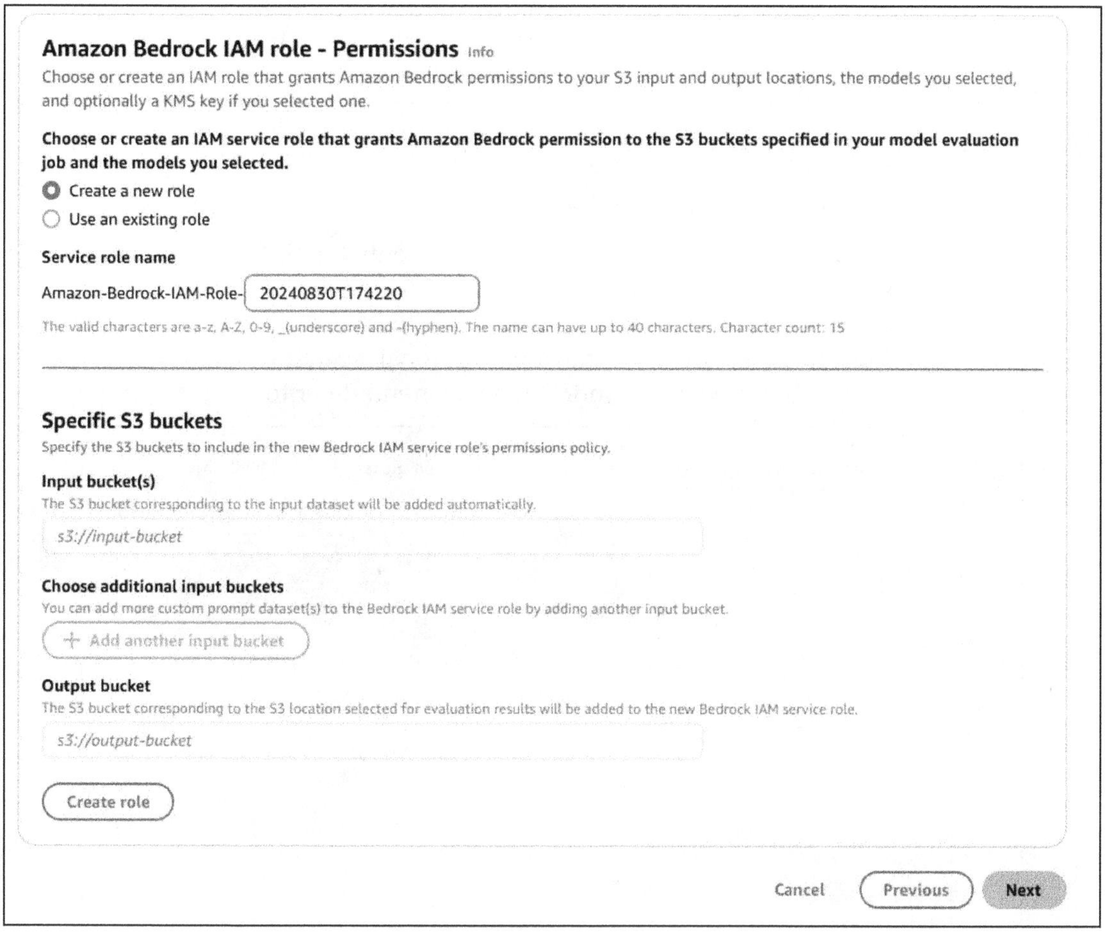

Figure 11.16: Amazon Bedrock LLM configuration

5. **Create a new work team**:

  a. Go to **SageMaker Ground Truth** | select **Labeling workforces** | click on **Private**.

  b. Click **Create private team**.

  c. Provide a team name and description.

  d. Add team members by entering their email addresses.

   This streamlined console allows data scientists to create a private workforce. Refer to the following figure:

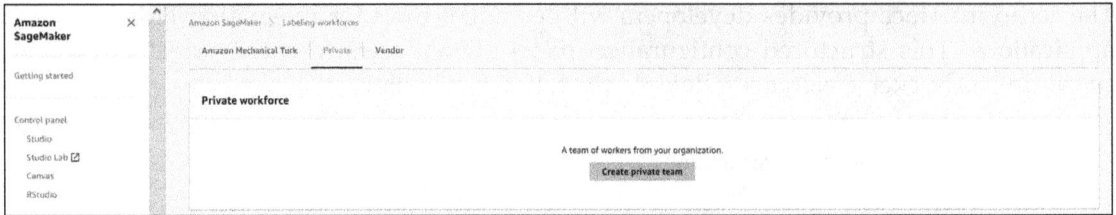

Figure 11.17: Private workforce creation

e. Provide the **Team details** and **Add workers**.

The team management interface provides essential tools for configuring worker access and permissions within a collaborative environment. This streamlined setup form enables administrators to define team details and add workers with specific roles, establishing the organizational structure needed for efficient project collaboration and resource management. Refer to the following figure:

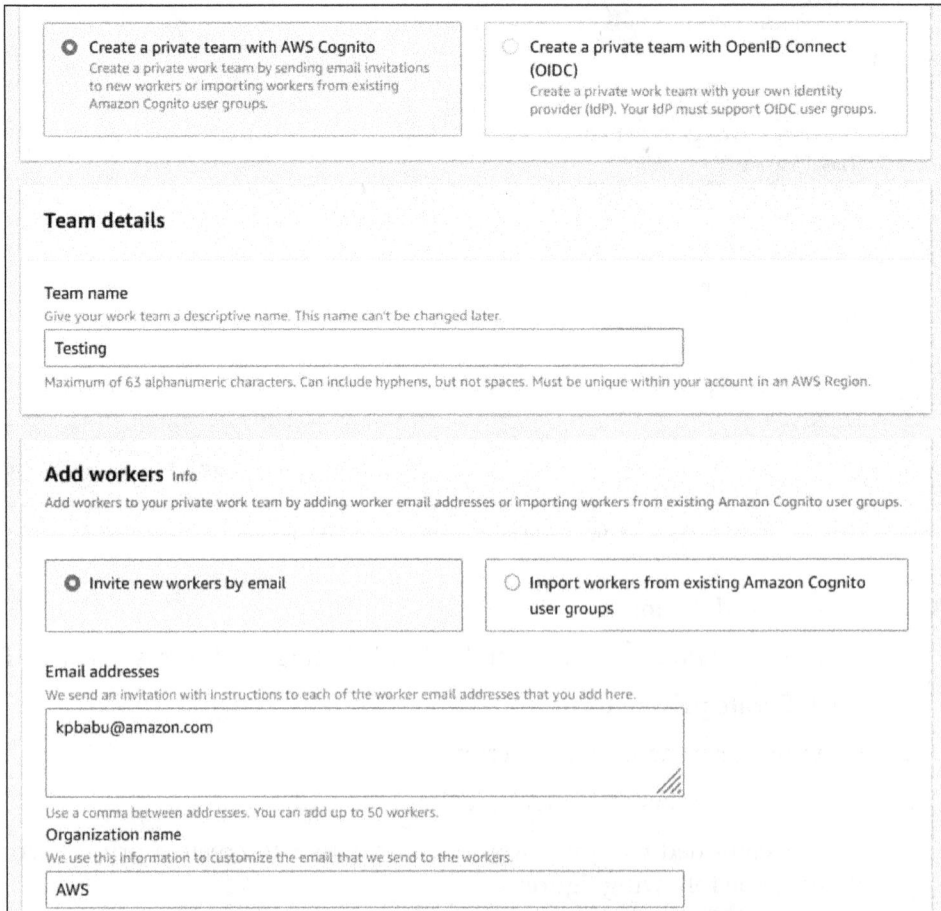

Figure 11.18: Team setup and worker configuration interface

f.   For adding workers, provide the **Email addresses**, **Organization name** and **Contact email**.

g.   Click on **Create a private team with Amazon Cognito**.

The interface provides detailed configuration options for team collaboration and communication preferences. This user-friendly form allows administrators to specify team attributes, control security settings, and establish notification protocols, ensuring effective information sharing among team members. Refer to the following figure:

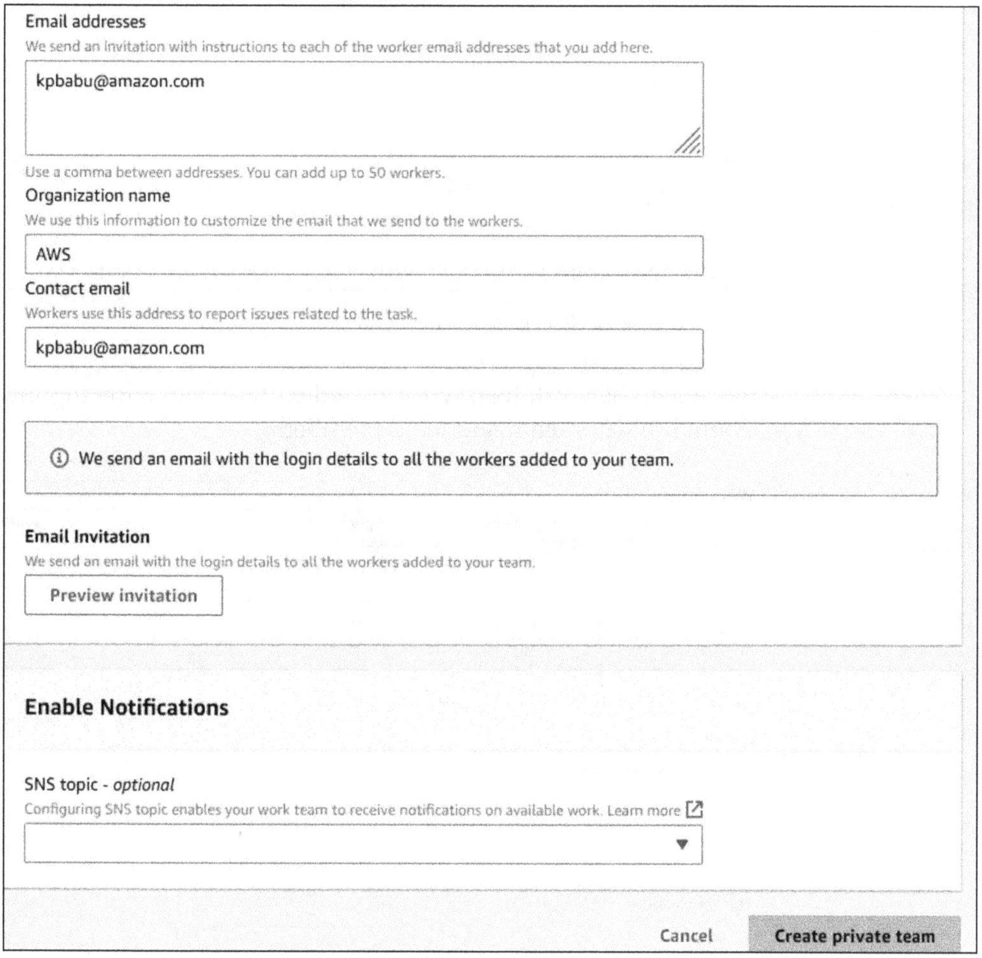

Figure 11.19: *Team configuration and notification settings*

The following interface provides a summary of the private workforce and the team details:

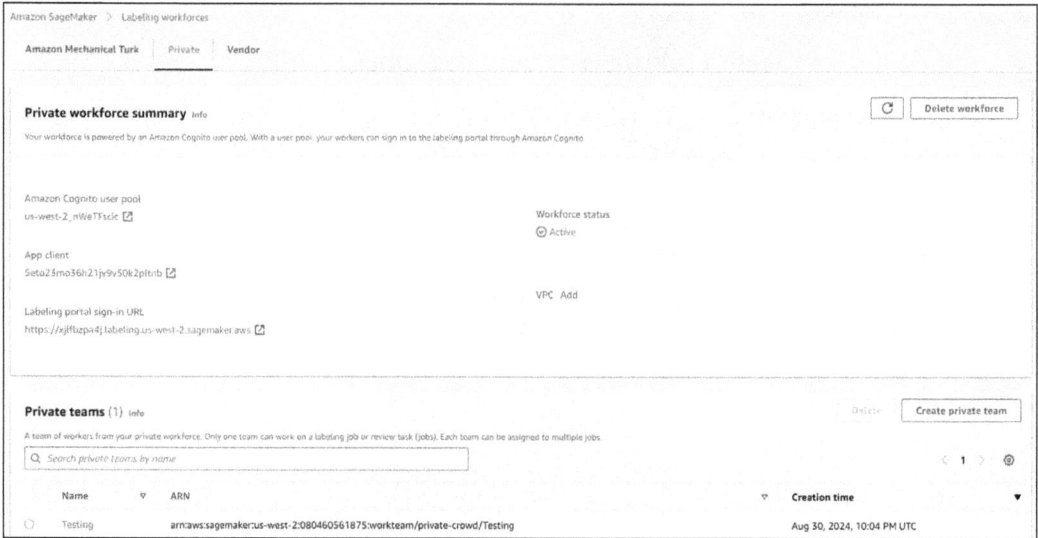

Figure 11.20: Private workforce summary

6.   **Assign work team**: Select the work team you created earlier. The following interface gives the details about the work team and team members:

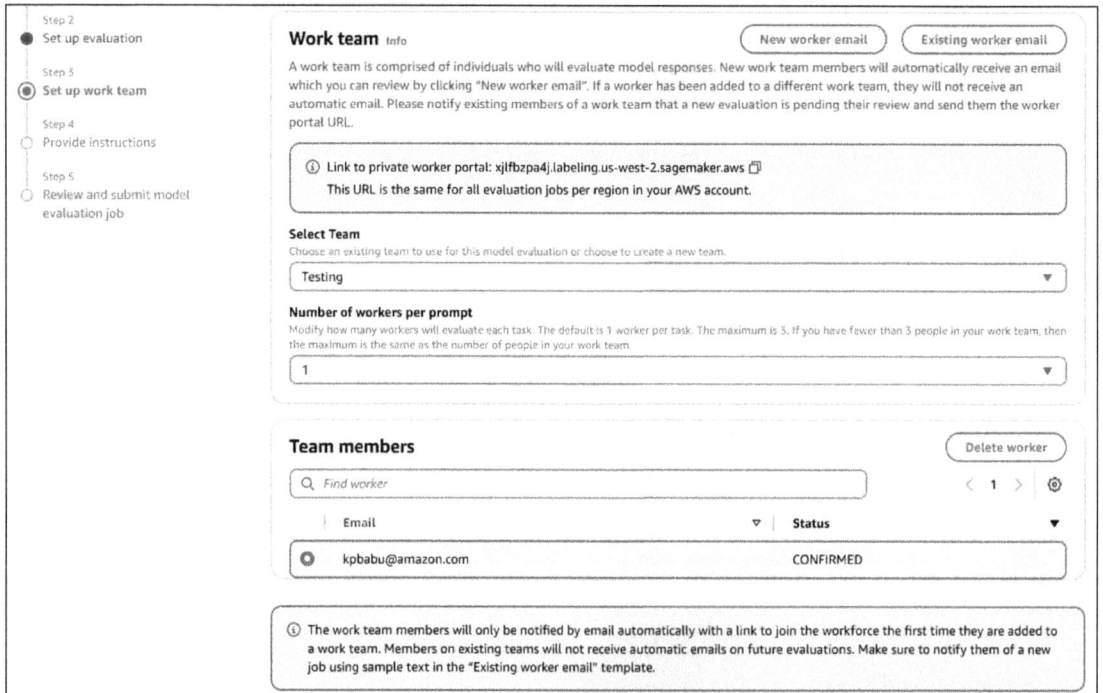

Figure 11.21: Work team and members

7. **Create human workflow role**:

   a. Create or use existing role for **Human workflow IAM role.**

   b. Specify the **S3 bucket** for the output. The following interface enables the user to provide the details for IAM role and S3 bucket details:

Human workflow IAM role - Permissions Info

Choose or create an IAM role that grants the human workflow access to your S3 input and output locations, and optionally a KMS key if you selected one.

◉ Create a new role
○ Use an existing role

Service role name

HumanWorkflow-ModelEvaluation-IAM-Role-[20240830T175997]

The valid characters are a-z, A-Z, 0-9, _(underscore) and -(hyphen). The name can have up to 25 characters. Character count: 15

S3 buckets

Specify the S3 buckets to include in the new Bedrock IAM service role's permissions policy.

○ **Any S3 bucket**
   Grant access to all S3 buckets on your account.

◉ **Specific S3 buckets**
   Specify the S3 buckets to include in the new Bedrock IAM service role's permissions policy.

   Output bucket
   The S3 bucket corresponding to the S3 location selected for evaluation results will be added to the new Bedrock IAM service role.

   [s3://model-evaluation-book-genai]

   Choose additional buckets
   You can add more custom prompt dataset(s) to the Bedrock IAM service role by adding another bucket.

   (+ Add another bucket)

(Create role)

Cancel   (Previous)   **Next**

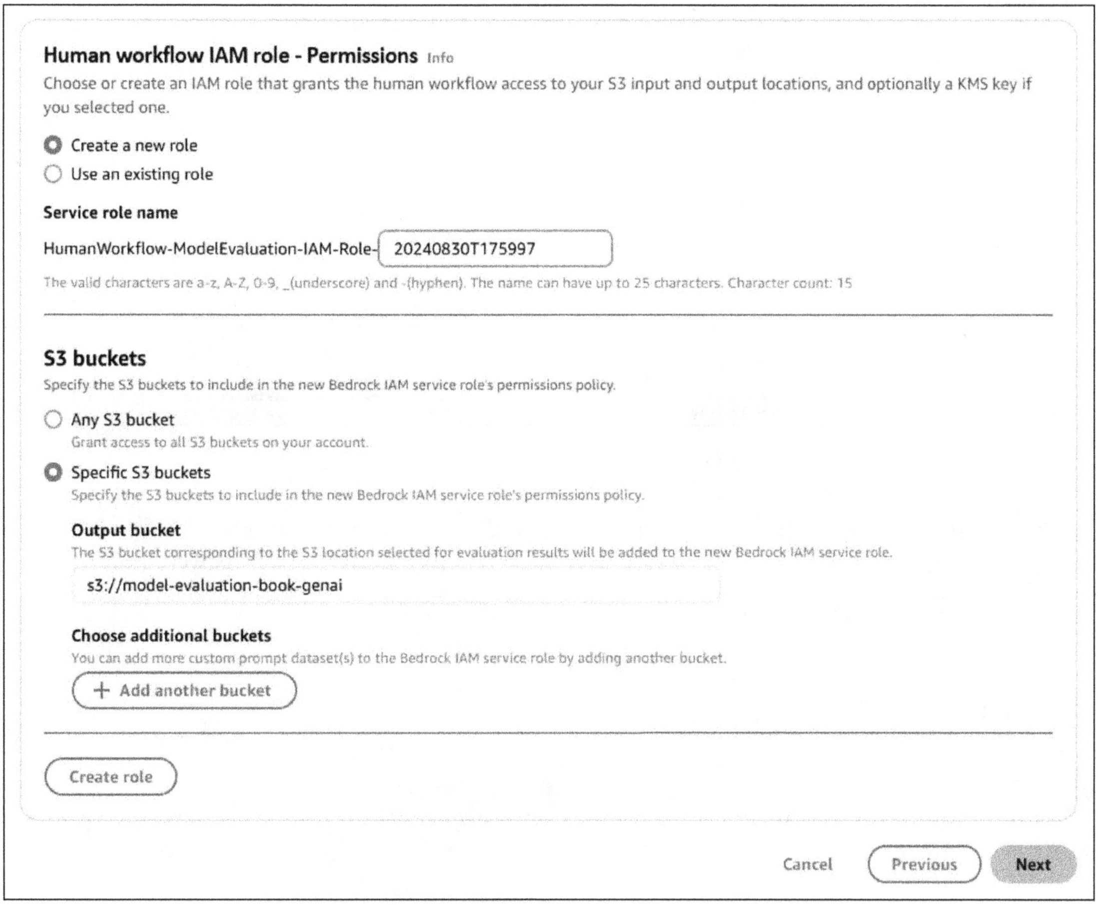

Figure 11.22: Role and S3 bucket details

8. **Create comprehensive instructions**:

   a. Explain the context and purpose of the evaluation.

   b. Provide the instructions for how to use the tools. The following figure is an interface to provide instructions for using the tool for evaluation:

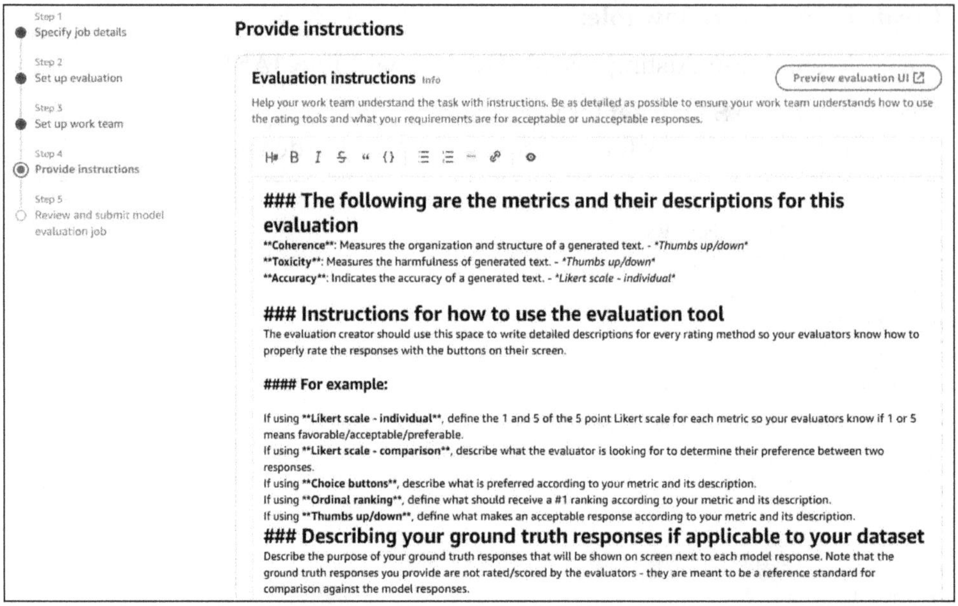

Figure 11.23: Evaluation instruction

9. **Review and launch**: Review all settings and launch the evaluation job. The following interface provides the details to review and submit the evaluation job details:

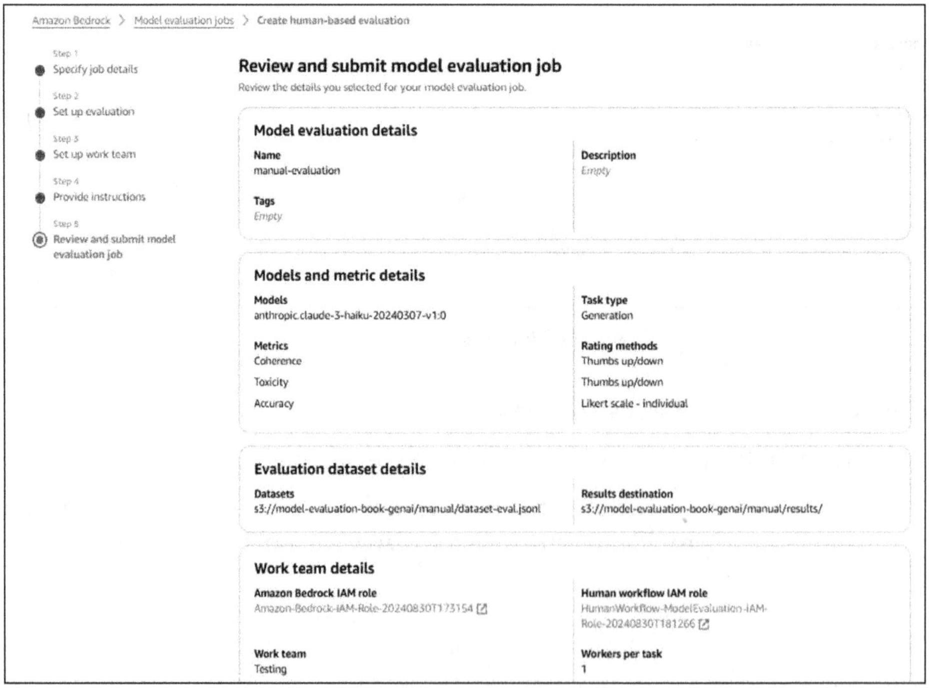

Figure 11.24: Review evaluation job details

The following interface shows the dataset and team details for evaluations:

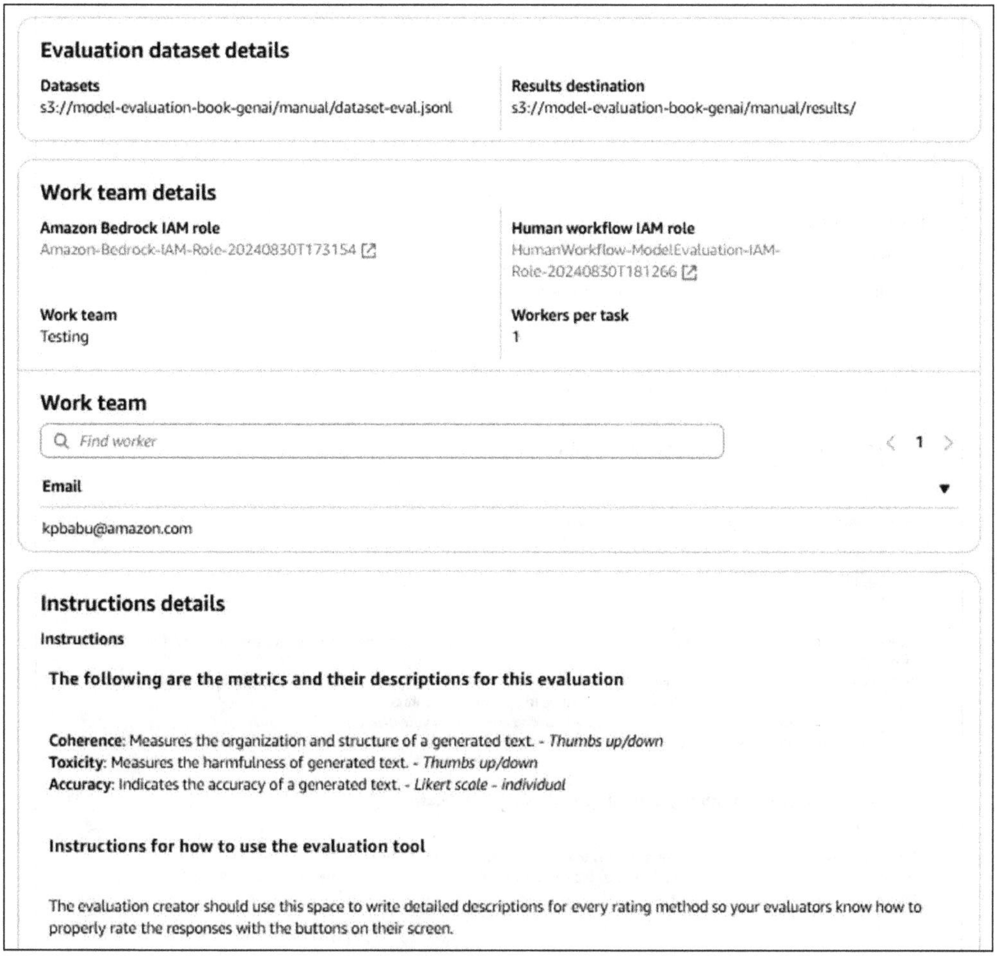

Evaluation dataset details

Datasets
s3://model-evaluation-book-genai/manual/dataset-eval.jsonl

Results destination
s3://model-evaluation-book-genai/manual/results/

Work team details

Amazon Bedrock IAM role
Amazon-Bedrock-IAM-Role-20240830T173154 ☑

Human workflow IAM role
HumanWorkflow-ModelEvaluation-IAM-Role-20240830T181266 ☑

Work team
Testing

Workers per task
1

Work team

Q Find worker

‹ 1 ›

Email ▼

kpbabu@amazon.com

Instructions details

Instructions

The following are the metrics and their descriptions for this evaluation

Coherence: Measures the organization and structure of a generated text. - *Thumbs up/down*
Toxicity: Measures the harmfulness of generated text. - *Thumbs up/down*
Accuracy: Indicates the accuracy of a generated text. - *Likert scale - individual*

Instructions for how to use the evaluation tool

The evaluation creator should use this space to write detailed descriptions for every rating method so your evaluators know how to properly rate the responses with the buttons on their screen.

Figure 11.25: Evaluation dataset and team details

The following interface provides the details for instruction details review:

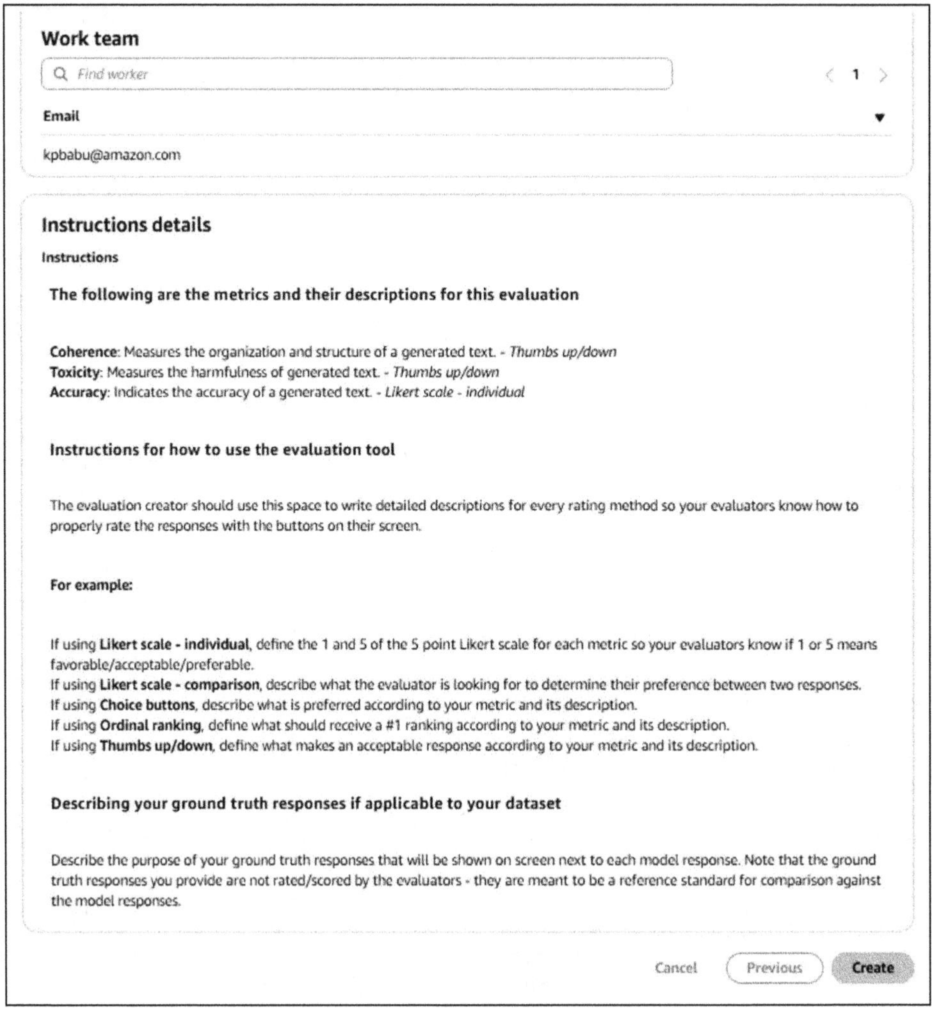

Figure 11.26: Instruction details review

The following interface shows the details of the **Model Evaluation jobs**:

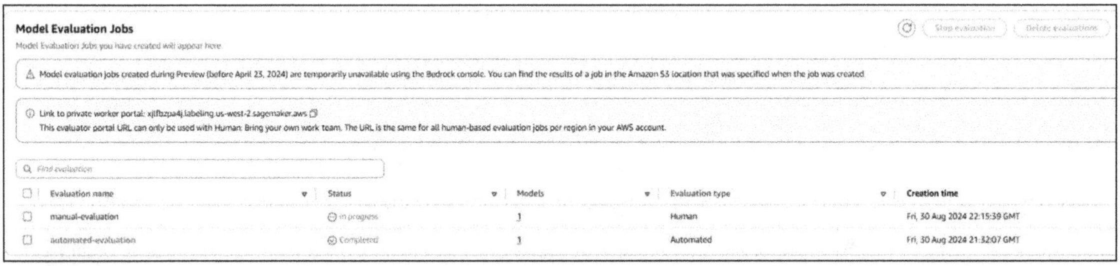

Figure 11.27: Model evaluation job details

Analyzing and interpreting human evaluation results

Once evaluators complete their tasks, Bedrock provides tools to analyze the results, as follows:

- **Overview dashboard**:
  - View aggregate scores across all evaluation criteria
  - See distribution of ratings for each aspect evaluated

- **Inter-rater agreement**:
  - Check consistency among different evaluators
  - Identify any outliers or discrepancies

- **Sample-level analysis**:
  - Examine individual samples and their ratings
  - Identify patterns in high and low-scoring outputs

- **Comparative analysis**:
  - If evaluating multiple models, compare human evaluation results
  - Correlate human evaluation results with automatic metrics

- **Qualitative feedback**:
  - Review any free-form comments provided by evaluators
  - Look for common themes or specific areas for improvement

- **Action items**:
  - Based on the analysis, identify concrete steps for model improvement
  - Consider refining prompts, fine-tuning on specific areas, or addressing detected biases

By effectively utilizing human evaluation in Amazon Bedrock, you can gain deep, nuanced insights into your model's performance that go beyond what automatic metrics can provide. This holistic approach to evaluation ensures that your AI models not only perform well technically but also meet the subjective quality standards necessary for real-world applications.

RAG evaluation

Evaluating RAG systems presents unique challenges due to their hybrid nature, combining both retrieval and generation components. This section focuses on the Ragas framework and its implementation using Amazon Bedrock.

Ragas framework

Ragas provides a comprehensive, reference-free evaluation framework for RAG systems. It addresses the unique challenges of evaluating RAG architectures, offering a more nuanced and accurate assessment of their performance across all components of the RAG pipeline.

Traditional metrics often fall short in evaluating the hybrid nature of RAG systems. Ragas offers several key advantages, as follows:

- **Holistic evaluation**: Assesses both retrieval and generation components
- **Context-aware assessment**: Considers retrieved context when evaluating answer quality
- **Reference-free evaluation**: Does not require human-annotated answers for every query
- **Multi-dimensional analysis**: Covers various aspects like factual accuracy, relevance, and coherence
- **Adaptability**: Applicable across different domains and RAG implementations

Ragas and RAG components

Ragas provides metrics and methodologies to evaluate each component of the RAG pipeline, as follows:

- **Query understanding**:
  - **Metric**: Answer relevancy
  - **Evaluation**: Assesses how well the system understands and addresses the user's query
  - **Importance**: Ensures the RAG system correctly interprets the user's information need

- **Retrieval**:
  - **Metrics**: Context precision, context recall, context entity recall
  - **Evaluation**: Measures the quality and relevance of retrieved information
  - **Importance**: Ensures the system retrieves accurate and pertinent information from the knowledge base

- **Generation**:
  - **Metrics**: Faithfulness, answer correctness, coherence
  - **Evaluation**: Assesses the quality, accuracy, and coherence of the generated response
  - **Importance**: Ensures the final output is factual, relevant, and well-formulated

- **Overall system performance**:
  - o **Metrics**: Combination of all above metrics
  - o **Evaluation**: Provides a comprehensive view of how well the entire RAG pipeline is functioning
  - o **Importance**: Allows for holistic assessment and targeted improvements

Ragas addresses RAG-specific challenges through the following:

- Faithfulness metrics to detect hallucinations in generated content
- Relevance evaluations for both retrieved context and generated answers
- LLM-based techniques to assess quality without pre-defined correct responses
- Balanced assessment of retrieval and generation quality
- Detection of subtle errors like partial hallucinations
- Adaptability to various RAG architectures
- Support for continuous evaluation and improvement

By providing targeted metrics for each component of the RAG system, Ragas enables developers to pinpoint areas for improvement and optimize the entire pipeline, leading to more reliable, accurate, and contextually appropriate RAG applications.

Ragas metrics

Ragas offers several metrics to evaluate different aspects of RAG system performance, as follows:

- **Faithfulness**: Measures the factual consistency of the generated answer against the given context. It is calculated from the answer and retrieved context, with scores ranging from 0 to 1. Higher scores indicate better faithfulness.

- **Answer relevancy**: Assesses how pertinent the generated answer is to the given prompt. It penalizes incomplete answers or those containing redundant information. Scores typically range between 0 and 1, with higher scores indicating better relevancy.

- **Context precision**: Evaluates whether the relevant items in the contexts are ranked higher. Ideally, all relevant chunks should appear at the top ranks. Scores range from 0 to 1, with higher scores indicating better precision.

- **Context recall**: Measures the extent to which the retrieved context aligns with the annotated answer (ground truth). Scores range from 0 to 1, with higher values indicating better performance.

- **Context entity recall**: Assesses the recall of entities in the retrieved context compared to the ground truth. This is particularly useful for fact-based use cases. It measures what fraction of entities are recalled from ground truths.

- **Answer similarity**: Evaluates the semantic resemblance between the generated answer and the ground truth. Scores range from 0 to 1, with higher scores indicating better alignment.

- **Answer correctness**: Gauges the accuracy of the generated answer compared to the ground truth. It combines semantic similarity and factual similarity. Scores range from 0 to 1, with higher scores indicating better correctness.

Implementing Ragas with Amazon Bedrock

Amazon Bedrock provides a robust platform for implementing and evaluating RAG systems.

The following is how to implement Ragas evaluation using Amazon Bedrock and open source Ragas library (**https://docs.ragas.io/**):

1. **Setup and dependencies**:

```
%pip install langchain>0.1 Ragas==0.1.9 --force-reinstall --quiet
import boto3
from botocore.client import Config
from langchain.llms.bedrock import Bedrock
from langchain_community.chat_models.bedrock import BedrockChat
from langchain.embeddings import BedrockEmbeddings
from langchain.retrievers.bedrock import AmazonKnowledgeBasesRetriever
```

2. **Configure Bedrock clients**:

```
bedrock_config = Config(connect_timeout=120, read_timeout=120,
retries={'max_attempts': 0})
bedrock_client = boto3.client('bedrock-runtime')
bedrock_agent_client = boto3.client("bedrock-agent-runtime",
config=bedrock_config)
```

3. **Setup language models and embeddings**:

```
llm_for_text_generation = BedrockChat(model_id="anthropic.claude-3-
haiku-20240307-v1:0", client=bedrock_client)
llm_for_evaluation = BedrockChat(model_id="anthropic.claude-3-sonnet-
20240229-v1:0", client=bedrock_client)
bedrock_embeddings = BedrockEmbeddings(model_id="amazon.titan-embed-
text-v1", client=bedrock_client)
```

4. **Create retriever and QA chain**:

```
retriever = AmazonKnowledgeBasesRetriever(
    knowledge_base_id=kb_id,
    retrieval_config={"vectorSearchConfiguration": {"numberOfResults": 5}}
)
qa_chain = RetrievalQA.from_chain_type(
```

```
    llm=llm_for_text_generation, retriever=retriever, return_source_
documents=True
)
```

5. **Prepare evaluation data**:

```
from datasets import Dataset
questions = [
    "What was the primary reason for the increase in net cash provided
by operating activities for Octank Financial in 2021?",
    # Add more questions...
]
ground_truths = [
    ["The increase in net cash provided by operating activities was
primarily due to an increase in net income and favorable changes in
operating assets and liabilities."],
    # Add more ground truths...
]
answers = []
contexts = []
for query in questions:
    answers.append(qa_chain.invoke(query)["result"])
    contexts.append([docs.page_content for docs in retriever.get_
relevant_documents(query)])
data = {
    "question": questions,
    "answer": answers,
    "contexts": contexts,
    "ground_truths": ground_truths
}
dataset = Dataset.from_dict(data)
```

6. **Run Ragas evaluation**:

```
from Ragas import evaluate
from Ragas.metrics import (
    faithfulness, answer_relevancy, context_recall, context_precision,
    context_entity_recall, answer_similarity, answer_correctness
)
from Ragas.metrics.critique import (
    harmfulness, maliciousness, coherence, correctness, conciseness
)
metrics = [
    faithfulness, answer_relevancy, context_precision, context_recall,
    context_entity_recall, answer_similarity, answer_correctness,
```

```
        harmfulness, maliciousness, coherence, correctness, conciseness
]
result = evaluate(
    dataset=dataset,
    metrics=metrics,
    llm=llm_for_evaluation,
    embeddings=bedrock_embeddings,
)

df = result.to_pandas()
print(df)
```

Interpreting Ragas results

The Ragas evaluation provides scores for each metric, helping you understand different aspects of your RAG system's performance, as follows:

- High faithfulness scores indicate that the generated answers are consistent with the retrieved context.

- High answer relevancy scores suggest that the answers directly address the questions.

- High context precision and recall scores indicate that the retrieval system is effectively finding relevant information.

- Low scores in any metric highlight areas for improvement in your RAG pipeline.

Best practices for RAG evaluation

Following are the best practices for RAG evaluation:

- **Use diverse question sets**: Ensure your evaluation covers various types of questions and topics.

- **Balance automatic and human evaluation**: While Ragas provides automated metrics, incorporate human evaluation for nuanced understanding.

- **Iterative improvement**: Use evaluation results to continually refine your RAG system, adjusting retrieval strategies and fine-tuning generation models.

- **Consider domain-specific metrics**: Depending on your use case, you may need to develop additional custom metrics.

- **Regular re-evaluation**: As your knowledge base grows or changes, regularly re-evaluate your RAG system to ensure consistent performance.

By leveraging the Ragas framework with Amazon Bedrock, you can gain comprehensive insights into your RAG system's performance across multiple dimensions. This approach allows for data-driven optimization and helps ensure that your RAG system meets the high standards required for real-world applications.

Practical applications for model and RAG evaluation

The knowledge gained from this chapter can be applied in various scenarios:

- Developing QA systems with high accuracy and relevance
- Creating summarization tools that maintain faithfulness to source documents
- Building conversational AI systems that provide contextually appropriate responses
- Implementing domain-specific knowledge retrieval systems in fields like healthcare or legal services

Best practices for model and RAG evaluation

To effectively leverage model and RAG evaluation in your GenAI development process, apply these best practices:

- Implement a combination of automatic and human-based evaluations for comprehensive assessment.
- Regularly update your evaluation datasets to reflect changing real-world scenarios.
- Use a diverse set of metrics to capture different aspects of model and RAG system performance.
- Integrate evaluation feedback into your development cycle for continuous improvement.
- Stay informed about the latest advancements in evaluation techniques and metrics.

Future trends

As the field of GenAI continues to evolve, we can anticipate several trends in model and RAG evaluation, as follows:

- **More sophisticated evaluation metrics**: Development of metrics that capture nuanced aspects of language understanding and generation.
- **Automated evaluation pipelines**: Increased integration of evaluation processes into CI/CD pipelines for AI development.
- **Multimodal evaluation**: Extension of evaluation techniques to cover multimodal AI systems incorporating text, images, and audio.

- **Personalization in evaluation**: Tailoring evaluation methods to account for individual user contexts and preferences.

- **Explainable evaluation**: Greater focus on making evaluation results interpretable and actionable for both technical and non-technical stakeholders.

Conclusion

In this chapter, we explored the critical aspects of model evaluation and RAG evaluation using Amazon Bedrock. As AI systems become increasingly sophisticated and integral to various applications, the ability to accurately assess and optimize their performance is paramount. We began by examining model evaluation fundamentals, highlighting the importance of comprehensive evaluation in AI development, various metrics tailored to different tasks (such as accuracy, perplexity, and BLEU score), and the unique challenges presented when evaluating LLMs. We then delved into Amazon Bedrock's evaluation capabilities, including its automatic evaluation features for various task types, human-based evaluation workflows, and seamless integration with FMs. Our discussion extended to RAG-specific evaluation techniques, where we addressed methods for assessing both retrieval and generation components, metrics for measuring faithfulness to retrieved information, and approaches for end-to-end evaluation of RAG systems. We implemented the Ragas framework, demonstrating comprehensive evaluation using metrics like faithfulness, answer relevancy, and context precision, and showcased its integration with Amazon Bedrock Knowledge Bases. Finally, we shared best practices and optimization strategies, including techniques for improving retrieval and generation quality, methods for balancing different evaluation metrics, and approaches for ensuring fairness while reducing bias in model evaluations.

In the next chapter, we will explore how to leverage Amazon Q's capabilities to develop custom assistants that transform how your users interact with information and systems across your enterprise.

Points to remember

- Evaluation is an ongoing process, not a one-time task in AI development.

- Different tasks and use cases may require different evaluation approaches and metrics.

- Balance between various evaluation metrics is key to developing well-rounded AI systems.

- Ethical considerations should be a fundamental part of your evaluation strategy.

- Amazon Bedrock provides a robust ecosystem for implementing, evaluating, and optimizing both traditional AI models and RAG systems.

CHAPTER 12

Building Generative AI Assistant using Amazon Q

Introduction

Businesses are constantly looking for better ways to work with their data and automate routine tasks. Amazon Q, a new **generative AI (GenAI)** assistant from AWS, addresses this need by helping organizations work more efficiently with their information and systems. As an enterprise-ready AI solution, Amazon Q transforms how teams interact with company data, generate content, and streamline workflows. It acts as an intelligent assistant that understands your organization's context while ensuring security and accuracy. This chapter will explore Amazon Q's capabilities and demonstrate how it enables businesses to harness the power of GenAI for improved productivity and decision-making.

Structure

The chapter covers the following topics:

- Amazon Q
- Amazon Q Business
- Amazon Q Apps

Objectives

By the end of this chapter, readers will understand how to leverage Amazon Q to build AI-powered solutions that can enhance productivity and automate tasks within your organization. You will gain practical skills in setting up, customizing, and managing Amazon Q Business applications, preparing you to implement these solutions in real-world scenarios.

Amazon Q

Amazon Q is a fully managed, GenAI-powered assistant built on Amazon Bedrock. Designed to streamline enterprise tasks and accelerate software development. It provides accurate and comprehensive responses to user queries based on an organization's data.

This service assists developers with coding, testing, and debugging, while also supporting business users by answering questions, generating content, and completing workflows. Amazon Q can be used to create AI-powered chatbots for various applications, from customer service to internal knowledge management, and serves as a powerful tool for both technical and non-technical teams across an organization.

The following are the key features of Amazon Q:

- **Fully managed and serverless**: Amazon Q is a fully managed, serverless solution. There is no infrastructure to manage and no LLM models to deploy. This means you can focus on using the tool rather than worrying about maintenance or updates.

- **Intelligent information retrieval**: Amazon Q sifts through vast amounts of your enterprise data to provide accurate answers. It is like having a highly efficient research assistant who always cites their sources.

- **Comprehensive developer assistant**: Amazon Q accelerates software development by generating code, debugging, testing, and optimizing applications. It can perform complex tasks like Java version upgrades, security scanning, and implementing new features based on natural language requests.

- **Configurable and customizable**: Amazon Q provides flexibility in selecting and configuring enterprise data sources and controlling response generation. A marketing team, for instance, can configure Amazon Q to pull data only from the marketing department's documents, ensuring that responses are always relevant and up-to-date with the latest campaign details.

- **Data and application security**: Amazon Q support access control and ensures responses are permissions-aware, protecting sensitive data. The finance department, for example, can easily restrict access to sensitive financial documents, ensuring that only authorized personnel can access specific data through Amazon Q.

- **Broad connectivity**: Amazon Q offers out-of-the-box connectors to over 40 data sources and can integrate with third-party applications via plugins. For instance, Amazon Q can be integrated with *Salesforce*, allowing sales representatives to quickly retrieve client information and past interactions, streamlining the sales process.

Amazon Q products

Amazon Q is available in several products, each tailored to specific use cases and customer needs. In the following sections, we will explore these products in detail.

Refer to the following figure for details:

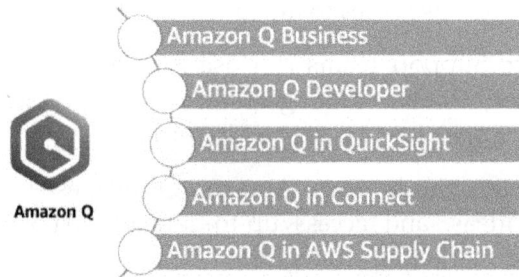

Figure 12.1: Amazon Q products

Let us begin by examining Amazon Q Business, designed for enterprise-wide deployment.

Amazon Q Business

Amazon Q Business is designed to help organizations securely access and leverage their vast amounts of data spread across multiple documents, systems, and applications. It enables employees to efficiently retrieve information, generate insights, and automate tasks based on enterprise data.

Amazon Q Business comes in two versions: Amazon Q Business Pro, which provides the full suite of capabilities including advanced integration options and access to Amazon Q Apps for task automation, and Amazon Q Business Lite, which offers essential GenAI capabilities at a lower cost, focusing on accurate, permissions-aware responses and basic task automation.

Amazon Q Developer

Amazon Q Developer is designed for developers who want to integrate Amazon Q functionalities within custom applications and workflows. It assists with coding and non-coding tasks such as debugging, testing, and managing infrastructure, allowing developers to focus on creating unique experiences without leaving their **integrated development environment (IDE)** such as **Visual Studio Code (VS Code)** or JetBrains.

In the next section, we will explore Amazon Q Business in detail, including how to setup and configure it, integrate data sources, and leverage its features to enhance your organization's productivity and decision-making processes. While Amazon Q includes other products, this chapter will focus exclusively on Amazon Q Business.

Amazon Q Business

Having introduced Amazon Q Business earlier, let us explore its use cases, key features and capabilities in more detail. Amazon Q Business is designed to revolutionize how enterprises handle information and automate tasks across various departments.

Let us explore some real-world use cases to illustrate its versatility:

- **Customer support**: Support teams can use Amazon Q Business to quickly access product information, troubleshooting guides, and customer history, enabling faster and more accurate responses to customer inquiries.

- **Marketing**: Marketers can leverage Amazon Q Business to analyze campaign data, generate content ideas, and access up-to-date market research, streamlining the creation of targeted marketing strategies.

- **Legal**: Legal departments can utilize Amazon Q Business to search through vast repositories of legal documents, contracts, and case law, speeding up research and document preparation processes.

- **HR**: **Human resource (HR)** professionals can use Amazon Q Business to automate onboarding processes, answer employee queries about policies, and assist in performance review preparations.

- **Finance**: Finance teams can employ Amazon Q Business to analyze financial data, generate reports, and access regulatory information, enhancing decision-making and compliance efforts.

- **IT support**: **Information technology** (IT) teams can leverage Amazon Q Business to automate responses to common technical issues, provide step-by-step troubleshooting guides, and quickly access system documentation, significantly reducing resolution times and improving overall IT efficiency.

These use cases demonstrate how Amazon Q Business can be applied across an organization to improve efficiency, decision-making, and employee productivity.

The Amazon Q Business interface reflects its role as your enterprise AI assistant, establishing its ability to work with your company's information. With its clean chat interface, users can type their business questions or requests, and Q responds using authorized company data.

Refer to the following figure:

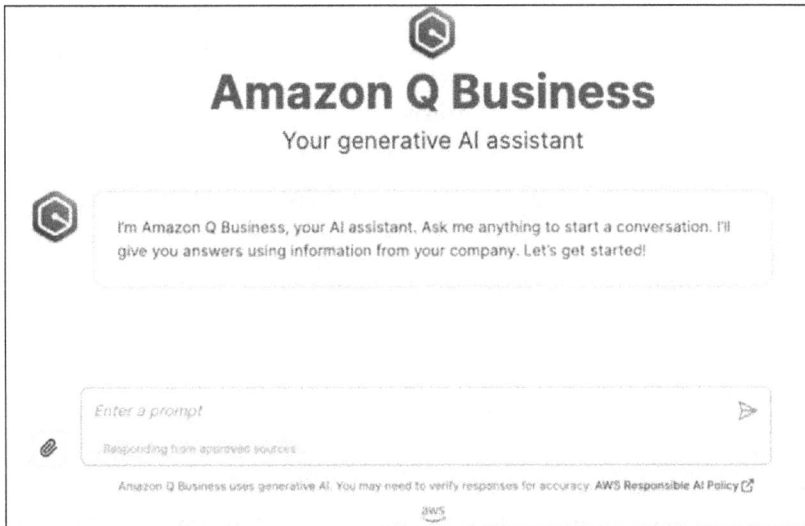

Figure 12.2: Amazon Q Business and GenAI assistant

The following are the key features that enable these capabilities:

- Comprehensive data access and analysis is a cornerstone of Amazon Q Business. It connects to over 40 commonly used enterprise systems and business tools, such as wikis, intranets, Atlassian, Gmail, Microsoft Exchange, Salesforce, ServiceNow, Slack, and Amazon S3. This wide-ranging connectivity allows enterprises to access and analyze information from multiple sources seamlessly.

- Permissions-aware question and answer are a crucial feature that ensures data security and compliance. Amazon Q Business provides responses based on the user's access level, guaranteeing that only authorized information is shared. An employee can query Amazon Q about a specific internal policy, and the AI assistant will retrieve and provide information only from documents they have permission to access. This feature is particularly valuable in maintaining data confidentiality and adhering to organizational security protocols.

- Amazon Q Business can also personalize responses using employee profiles from your organization's **identity provider (IdP)**. Leveraging data such as department, role, or location, Q Business customizes its responses to be more relevant and contextually accurate for each employee. For instance, if an HR team member queries about a policy, the AI assistant can automatically provide relevant information tailored specifically to HR roles, ensuring highly targeted and useful responses.

- Task automation with Amazon Q Apps is a powerful capability, especially in the pro version. Users can describe the type of app they want in natural language, and Amazon Q will generate an app to accomplish the desired task. These apps excel at handling repetitive tasks and sharing information efficiently within organizations. For example, a Q App could automatically summarize lengthy reports, extracting key points and action items, or assist in project status reporting by organizing team members' conversational updates into a structured format. By streamlining routine tasks, Q Apps enhance productivity and improve information flow across departments.

- Amazon Q Business also supports multimedia data including images, audio, and video. This capability enables teams to extract insights and automate tasks involving various types of media. For instance, marketing teams can analyze product images to quickly generate relevant promotional content, while HR departments can upload recorded audio or video meetings and instantly receive summarized notes with identified key points and actionable items. This significantly reduces manual work and enhances productivity across departments.

- Hallucination mitigation is a built-in feature of Amazon Q Business that helps ensure the accuracy and trustworthiness of generated responses. By grounding its answers in your organization's indexed enterprise content and enforcing strict access controls, Q Business reduces the risk of generating speculative or incorrect information. For example, when a user asks for HR policy details, the response will reference specific documents the user is authorized to access minimizing confusion and supporting informed decision-making across compliance-sensitive domains like finance, legal, or healthcare.

- Security and privacy are built into the core of Amazon Q Business. It integrates with existing identities, roles, and access permissions, ensuring that sensitive data is only accessible to authorized personnel. For instance, the finance department can use Amazon Q to ensure that sensitive financial data is only accessible to authorized personnel, protecting confidential information while still providing useful insights. This robust security framework allows organizations to leverage the power of AI while maintaining strict control over their data.

These features work in concert to provide a comprehensive, secure, and efficient AI-powered assistant for enterprises.

In the next section, we will explore how Amazon Q Business works behind the scenes to deliver these capabilities.

Working mechanics of Amazon Q Business

To understand how Amazon Q Business operates, let us start with a high-level view of how Amazon Q Business creates a secure and intelligent workspace environment.

Figure 12.3 illustrates the three core pillars of the system: secure authentication, enterprise data integration, and interactive AI assistance. Through secure IdP authentication, Amazon Q Business ensures authorized access while seamlessly connecting to over 40 enterprise data sources, including popular platforms like *Salesforce*, *SharePoint*, and *Microsoft Teams*. As we examine the detailed architecture in subsequent sections, this high-level framework illustrates how Q orchestrates secure data access and AI-powered interactions across your enterprise ecosystem.

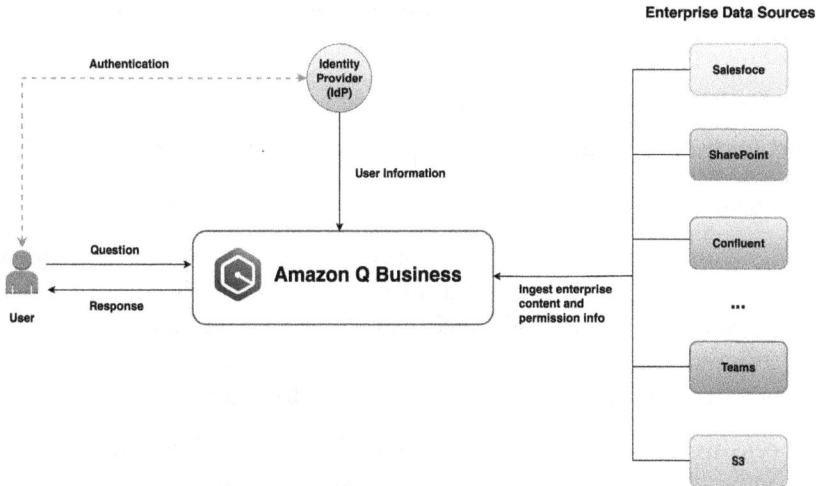

Figure 12.3: *Amazon Q with enterprise data source connectors*

The following figure provides a simplified view of how Amazon Q Business connects with various data sources, processes information, and interacts with users while maintaining security and permissions:

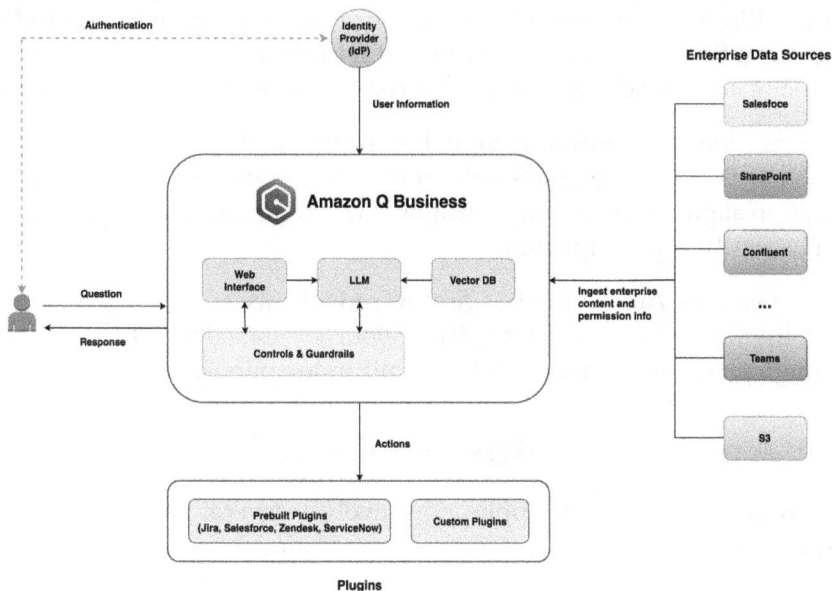

Figure 12.4: *Detailed Amazon Q Business architecture with data source connectors and plugins*

Figure 12.4 illustrates the various components of Amazon Q Business, including:

- Data ingestion from enterprise content and permission information using built-in connectors.

- The use of LLMs and a vector database to provide responses to user queries.
- The web interface for user interaction.
- Enforcement of controls and guardrails based on ingested permissions.
- Support for built-in and custom plugins for integrating with third-party applications.

Now, let us break down the key components of Amazon Q Business:

- **Data ingestion and indexing**: Amazon Q Business supports over 40 pre-built data source connectors to ingest data from your enterprise applications, document repositories, collaboration tools, websites, databases, and more. This ingested content is then indexed, making it easily searchable. Custom connectors can also be created to integrate with proprietary data sources specific to your organization.

- **AI processing and retrieval**: Amazon Q Business utilizes multiple foundation or LLMs powered by Amazon Bedrock. These LLMs enable the RAG approach. RAG retrieves relevant information from your indexed enterprise repositories and uses it to augment and enrich responses to user queries or prompts. This grounding in your organization's knowledge base helps minimize hallucinations, ensuring that the AI assistant's responses are accurate and based on your proprietary data.

- **Security and permissions**: Along with indexing your enterprise knowledge and content, Amazon Q Business also ingests the associated permissions and **access control lists (ACLs)**. This ensures that users can only access and retrieve information they are authorized to view, maintaining strict data security and compliance within your organization.

- **Authentication and authorization**: For secure authentication and authorization, Amazon Q Business integrates with your existing IdPs, such as *Okta* or *PING*. This integration aligns with your organization's identity management practices, enhancing overall security and compliance.

This architecture enables Amazon Q Business to provide accurate, context-aware responses while maintaining the security and integrity of your organization's data, all while offering flexibility through plugin integrations and customization options.

Creating Amazon Q Business application

Setting up an Amazon Q Business application involves several key steps. While the exact interface may change over time, the general process remains consistent.

The following are the steps:

1. **Create application**: Navigate to the **Amazon Q Business** in the AWS Management Console and click on **Create application**. Follow the wizard to define application settings, including name and service role.

   The following figure shows how to create and manage Amazon Q Business applications:

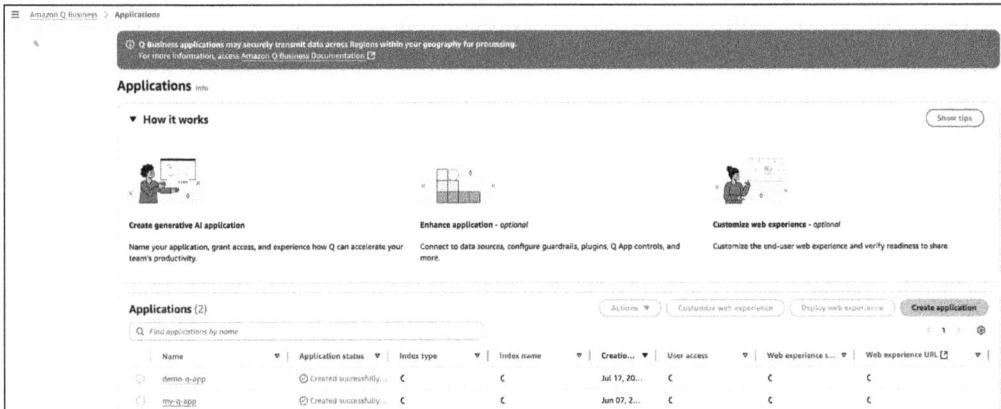

Figure 12.5: Creating an application with Amazon Q Business

Ensure that **IAM Identity Center** is enabled in your AWS account to manage user access. This step is crucial for controlling who can access your Amazon Q Business instance.

Let us begin by creating an application in Amazon Q Business, as shown in *Figure 12.6*:

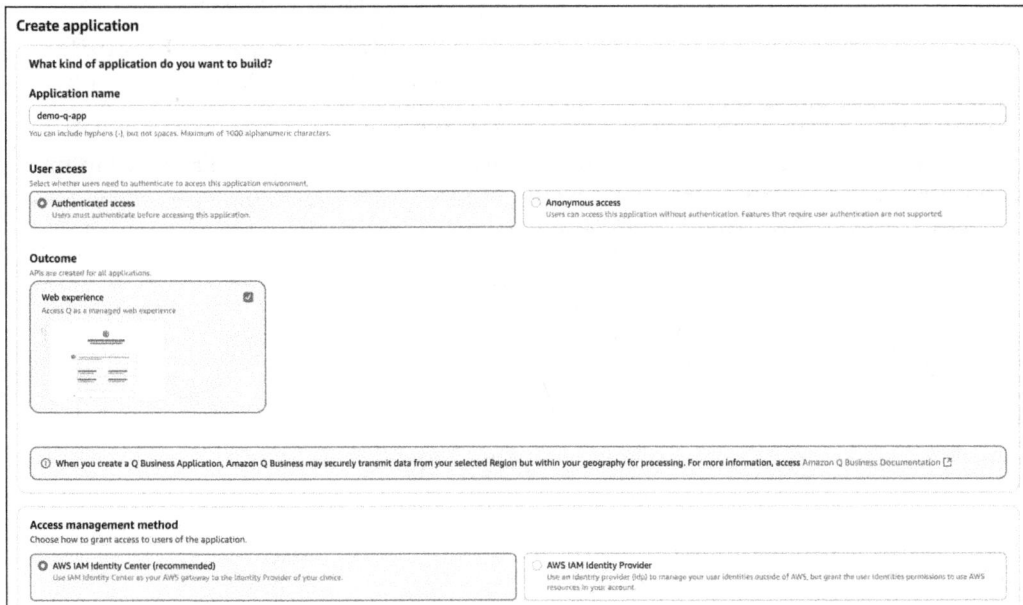

Figure 12.6: Creating an application with Amazon Q Business

> **Note: For detailed instructions on IAM Identity Center setup, refer to the AWS IAM Identity Center documentation**.

2. Select **Retrievers** choose the **Use native retriever** option. For **Index provisioning**, select either **Enterprise**, recommended for production workloads or **Starter**, suitable for non-production environments and **proof-of-concept** (PoCs).

Next, select and configure your retriever setting, as shown in the following figure:

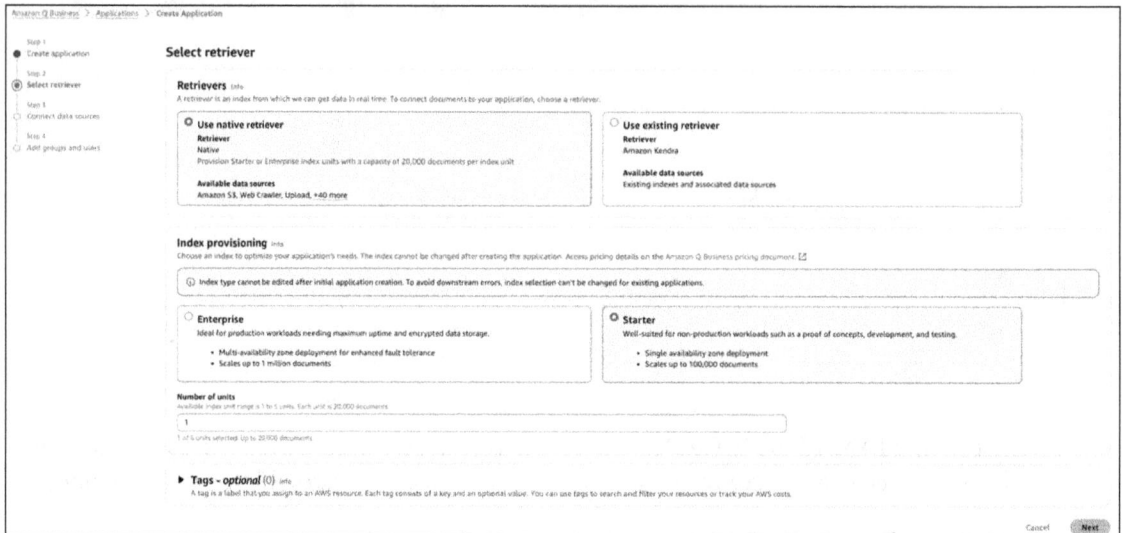

Figure 12.7: Choosing a retriever and index with Amazon Q Business

This selection is crucial as it determines your application's capacity. **Enterprise** option allows scaling up to one million documents across multiple Availability Zones, while **Starter** is limited but suitable for PoC and testing.

3. **Connect data sources**: This step enables Amazon Q to access and retrieve information from your organization's data repositories. You can connect up to five data sources for a single application (15 for enterprise edition).

Next, configure your data source connections for Amazon Q Business using available connectors, as shown in *Figure 12.8*:

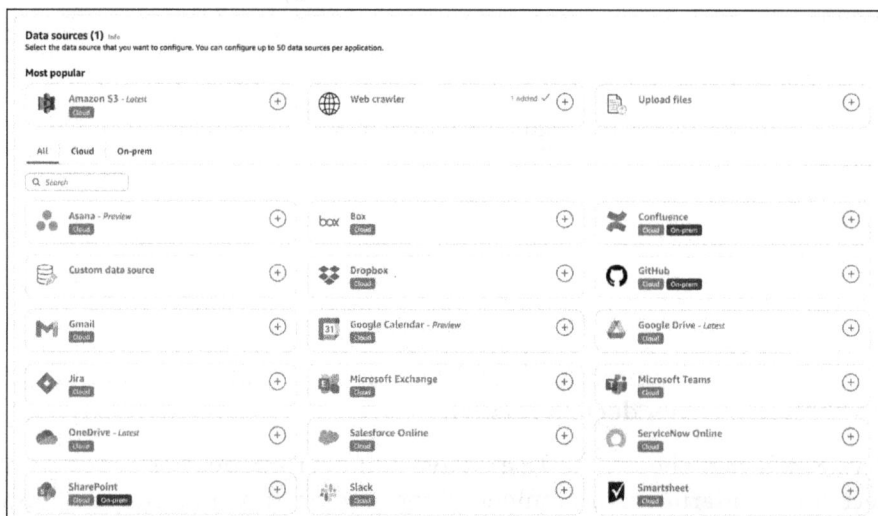

Figure 12.8: Data sources connectors with Amazon Q Business

For example, let us add two data sources, as follows:

a. **Upload a PDF file**: This could be your company's latest product catalog or annual report.

b. **Web crawler**: You might use this to index your company's internal wiki or knowledge base.

Let us look at the web crawler setup, as follows:

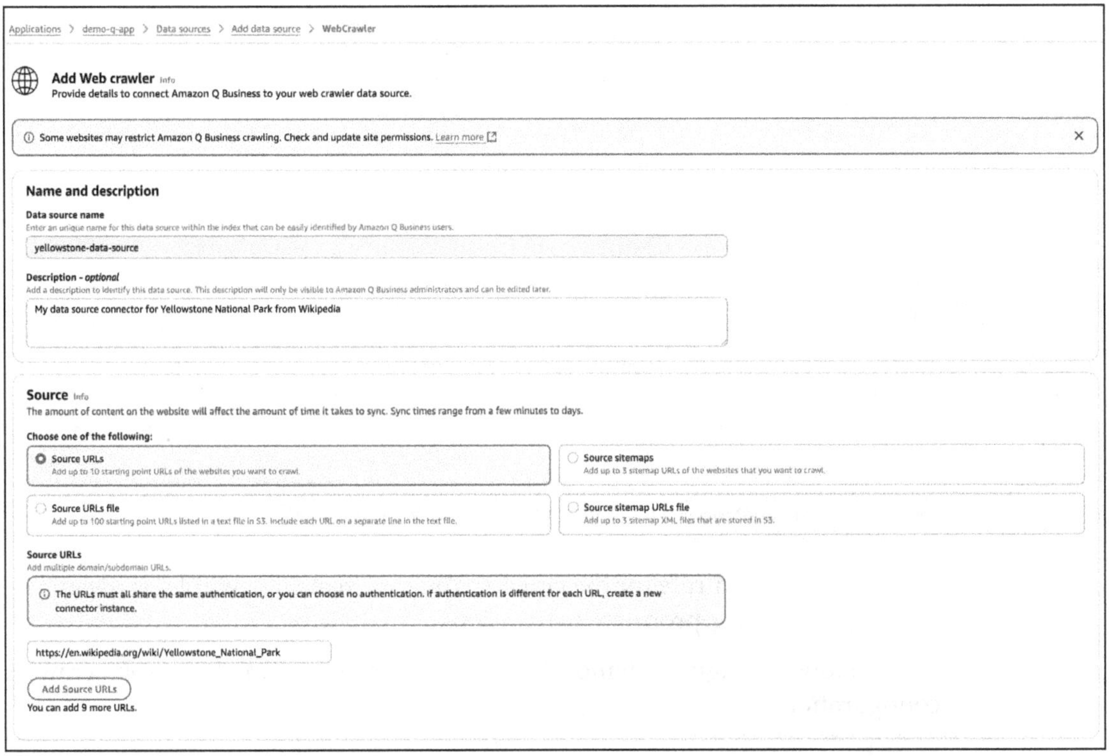

Figure 12.9: Web crawler data source connector with Amazon Q

c. Enter the URL of the website you want to crawl. For internal sites, ensure you have the necessary permissions.

d. Configure the crawler's behavior:

  i. Set the crawl scope, for example, limit to specific subdomains or paths.

  ii. Define the crawl depth to control how many links deep the crawler should go.

  iii. Setup exclusion patterns for pages you do not want to index.

e. Setup authentication if the site requires it. This is crucial for internal company sites.

Figure 12.10 demonstrates how to configure web crawler data sources and their security settings:

Authentication info

Select an authentication method to allow Amazon Q Business to access your data source instance.

Select the type of authentication to apply to all of the source URLs or to the source URLs file that you added above.

○ **No authentication**
This is to crawl a public website.

○ **Basic authentication**
Enter the username and password to access the website you want to crawl.

○ **NTLM/Kerberos authentication**
Enter NTLM/Kerberos username and password.

○ **Form authentication**
Enter the user name and password, and XPaths (XML Path Language) for the user name and password fields. You can find the XPaths of elements using your browser's developer tools.

○ **SAML authentication**
Enter the user name and password, and XPaths (XML Path Language) for the user name and password fields, user name and password buttons, and login page URL.

Web proxy - *optional* info

You can use a web proxy to connect to internal websites you want to crawl.

Host name
Enter the host name of the proxy server. For example, the host name of https://a.example.com/page1.html is "a.example.com".

```
a.example.com
```

Port number
Enter the port number of the proxy server. For example, the standard port for HTTPS is 443.

```
443
```

Authentication credentials

You use an AWS Secret Manager secret if the websites you want to crawl using a web proxy require authentication to access the websites. If you have a secret containing your credentials, you can use it. Otherwise, create one.

AWS Secrets Manager secret
Choose an existing secret that starts with 'QBusiness-' or create a new one.

```
Choose a secret                                                    ▼
```

▼ **Configure VPC and security group - *optional*** info

Virtual Private Cloud (VPC)
Select a VPC that defines the virtual networking environment for this repository instance. Manage VPCs ⬏

```
No VPC                                                             ▼
```

Figure 12.10: Web crawler data source connector and security configuration with Amazon Q Business

f. Configure the **IAM role** for the crawler. You can create a new role or use an existing one with appropriate permissions.

The following figure demonstrates **IAM role** setup for web crawler configurations:

IAM role info

ⓘ **IAM role guidance**
IAM roles used for applications can't be used for data sources. If you are unsure if an existing role is used for an application, choose "Create a new role" to avoid an error.

IAM role
Amazon Q Business requires an IAM role to access repository credentials and application content.

```
Create a new service role (Recommended)                            ▼
```

Role name
The role name uses the prefix 'QBusiness-DataSource-'. The created role will only work for this data source and its specific configuration.

```
QBusiness-DataSource-qnyt5
```

Figure 12.11: Web crawler data source connector, IAM role configuration with Amazon Q

g. Set the sync schedule. You can choose to run the crawler on-demand, hourly, daily, or weekly. For frequently updated sites, consider a more frequent sync.

Configure the sync settings for your web crawler, as shown in *Figure 12.12*:

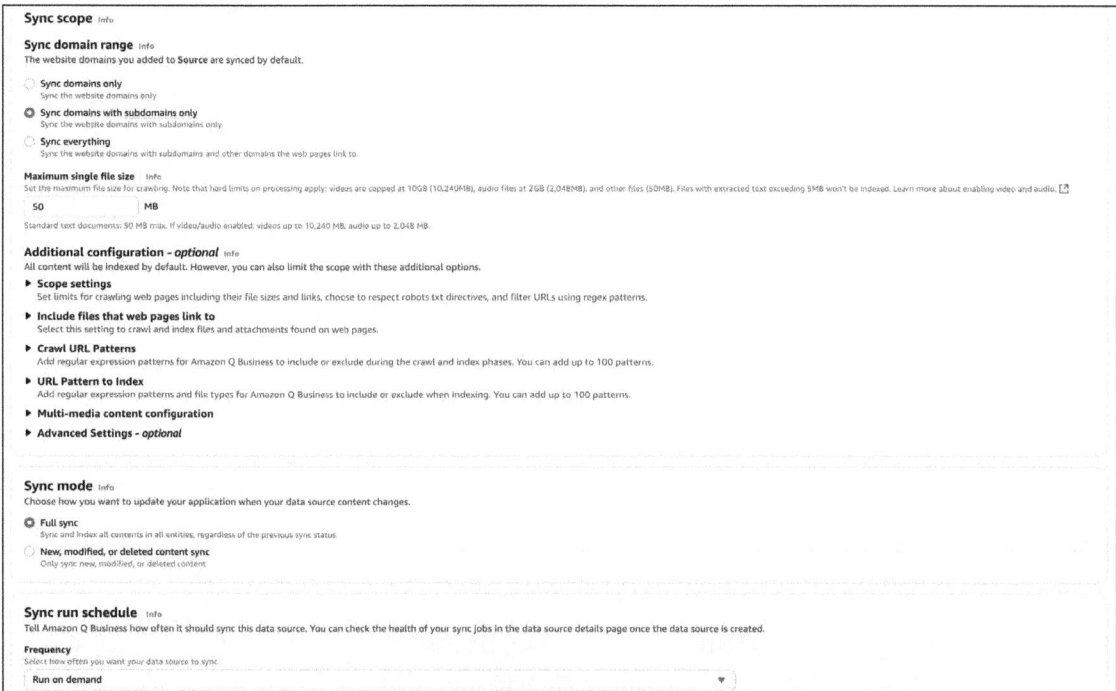

Sync scope Info

Sync domain range Info
The website domains you added to **Source** are synced by default.

○ **Sync domains only**
  Sync the website domains only

◉ **Sync domains with subdomains only**
  Sync the website domains with subdomains only.

○ **Sync everything**
  Sync the website domains with subdomains and other domains the web pages link to.

Maximum single file size Info
Set the maximum file size for crawling. Note that hard limits on processing apply: videos are capped at 10GB (10,240MB), audio files at 2GB (2,048MB), and other files (50MB). Files with extracted text exceeding 5MB won't be indexed. Learn more about enabling video and audio. ↗

50	MB

Standard text documents: 50 MB max. If video/audio enabled: videos up to 10,240 MB, audio up to 2,048 MB.

Additional configuration - *optional* Info
All content will be indexed by default. However, you can also limit the scope with these additional options.

▶ **Scope settings**
  Set limits for crawling web pages including their file sizes and links, choose to respect robots.txt directives, and filter URLs using regex patterns.

▶ **Include files that web pages link to**
  Select this setting to crawl and index files and attachments found on web pages.

▶ **Crawl URL Patterns**
  Add regular expression patterns for Amazon Q Business to include or exclude during the crawl and index phases. You can add up to 100 patterns.

▶ **URL Pattern to Index**
  Add regular expression patterns and file types for Amazon Q Business to include or exclude when indexing. You can add up to 100 patterns.

▶ **Multi-media content configuration**

▶ **Advanced Settings - *optional***

Sync mode Info
Choose how you want to update your application when your data source content changes.

◉ **Full sync**
  Sync and index all contents in all entities, regardless of the previous sync status.

○ **New, modified, or deleted content sync**
  Only sync new, modified, or deleted content

Sync run schedule Info
Tell Amazon Q Business how often it should sync this data source. You can check the health of your sync jobs in the data source details page once the data source is created.

Frequency
Select how often you want your data source to sync.

Run on demand	▼

Figure 12.12: *Web crawler data source connector and sync configuration with Amazon Q*

h. After setup, initiate the first sync by clicking **Sync now**. The initial crawl may take some time depending on the size of the website.

Refer to the following figure:

yellowstone-data-source Info   [Sync now] [Stop sync] [Actions ▼]

Data source details

Name	**Status**	**Last sync status**
yellowstone-data-source	⊘ Active	-
Description	**Type**	**Last sync time**
-	WEBCRAWLER	-
Data source ID	**IAM role ARN**	**Current sync state**
6f2be9c9-d577-4ad0-ab05-0cccd5fe1644	arn:aws:iam::771197545841:role/service-role/QBusiness-DataSource-puntk	Idle

Sync history   Troubleshooting tools - *new*   Settings   Tags

Sync history (0)

‹ 1 › ⚙

Status / Summary	Start time	End time	Total items scanned	Failed ↗	Logs ↗	Actions ↗

This data source has not been synced
[Sync now]

Figure 12.13: *Web crawler data source connector and sync frequency in Amazon Q Business*

Note: Start with a smaller subset of your website to test the crawler's behavior before expanding to your entire site.

    i.   Setup web experience by creating a dedicated web URL for Amazon Q Business access. Assign users or groups who should have access, controlling their subscription level (Q Business Lite or Q Business Pro).

Configure user and group access through the interface, as shown in *Figure 12.14*:

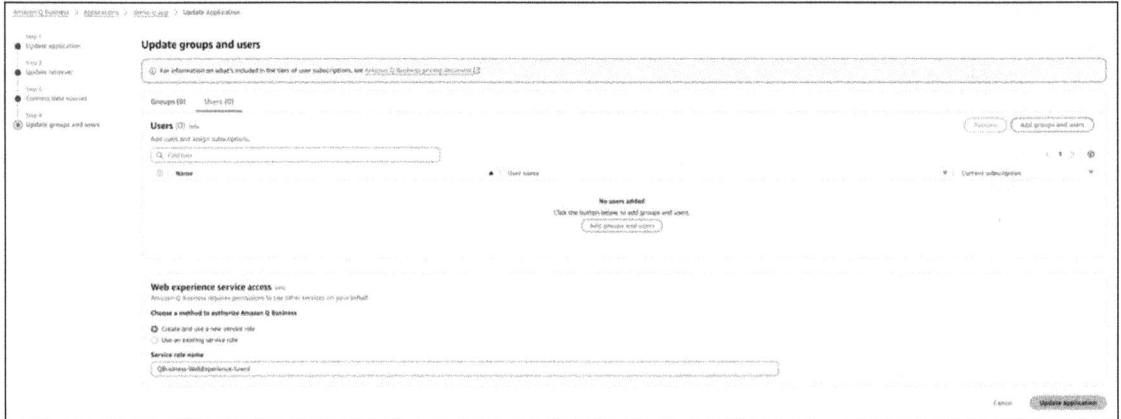

Figure 12.14: Update users and groups in Amazon Q Business

Once you complete this step, you will be assigned a dedicated web URL similar to **https://example.chat.qbusiness.us-west-2.on.aws/**

The following figure shows URL after going to application details:

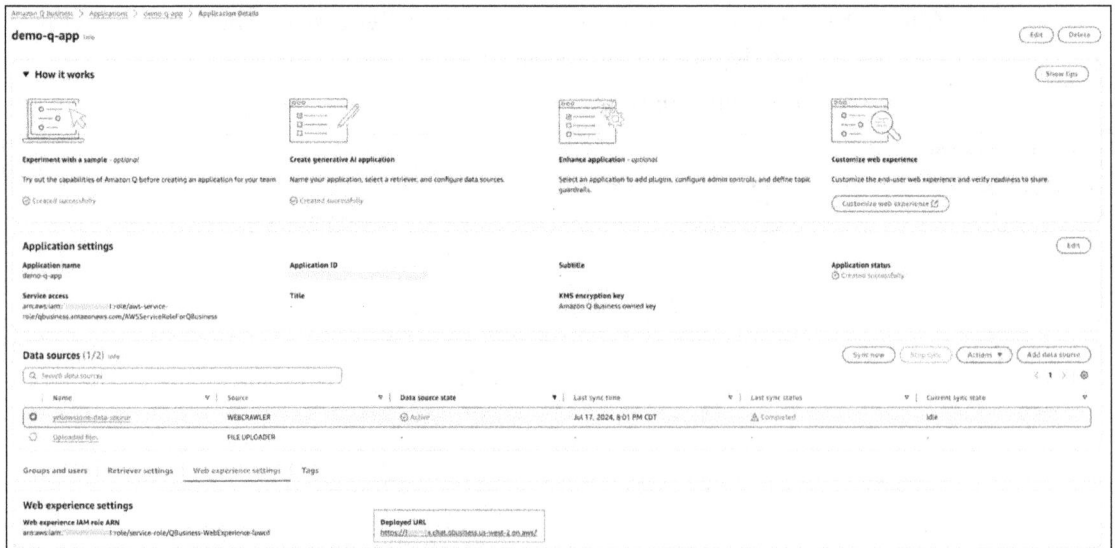

Figure 12.15: Web experience in Amazon Q Business

You can further customize the experience by clicking the **Customize web experience** button.

j. Test and share the Amazon Q Business as web experience access the provided URL, log in, and start a conversation to test the setup. Verify that Amazon Q Business responds accurately based on the data sources you have provided.

Figure 12.16 demonstrates how to test your web crawler data source connections:

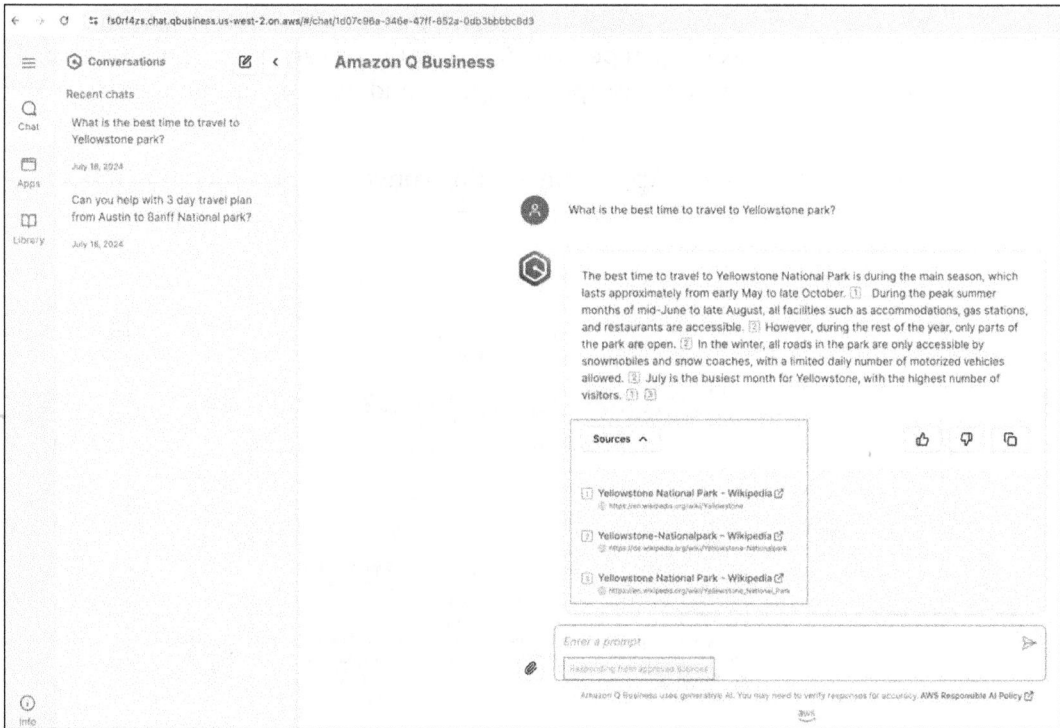

Figure 12.16: Testing web crawler data source connector in Amazon Q Business

By following these steps, you will have a functional Amazon Q Business application tailored to your organization's needs. Remember, the power of Amazon Q Business lies in its ability to integrate with your specific data sources and provide insights based on your organization's unique knowledge base.

For the most up-to-date and detailed instructions on each step, always refer to the official AWS Documentation for Amazon Q Business.

In the next section, we will explore how you can easily convert any of your conversation to a Q App if you have Q Business Pro subscription.

Amazon Q Apps

Amazon Q Apps allow users to create lightweight applications directly within the Amazon Q web experience. These apps can fulfill specific tasks and can be securely shared with colleagues or published to your organization's catalog.

Q Apps are designed to automate repetitive tasks and streamline workflows. They leverage the power of Amazon Q's language understanding to create custom tools based on natural language descriptions.

Creating Q App

Users can easily convert an existing repetitive Amazon Q conversation into a Q App. This process involves defining the app's purpose, inputs, and desired outputs using natural language instructions.

Figure 12.17 shows how to create Q Apps from existing conversations:

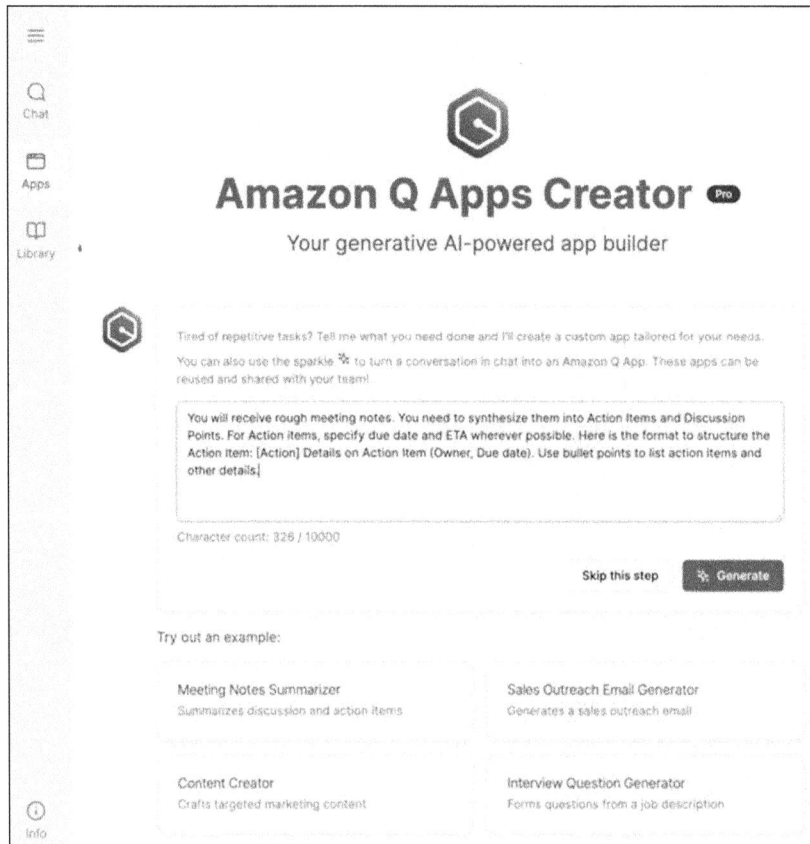

Figure 12.17: *Amazon Q Apps creator with Amazon Q Business*

Let us explore a practical example of a Q App, that is, **Meeting Notes Synthesizer**. This app can do the following:

- Analyze raw meeting minutes
- Automatically identify key discussion points

- Extract decisions made
- List action items with assigned owners
- Highlight important information

Let us see the **Meeting Notes Synthesizer** Q App at work, as shown in *Figure 12.18*:

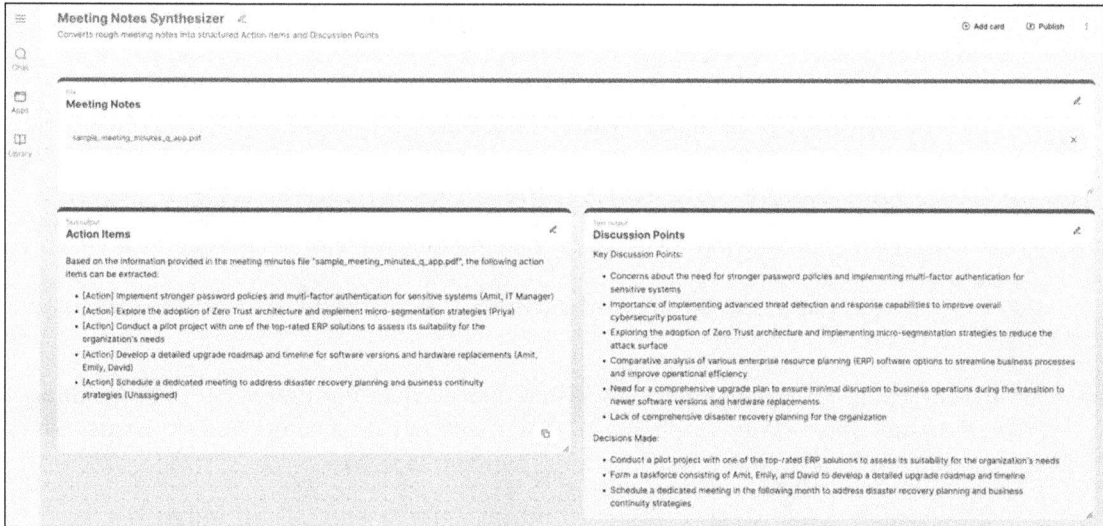

Figure 12.18: *Amazon Q App and Meeting Notes Synthesizer with Amazon Q Business*

The app synthesizes unstructured text into a structured format with dedicated sections for highlights, decisions, assigned tasks, and summaries. This streamlines post-meeting workflows and ensures consistent formatting.

Using Q App

Once created, using a Q App is straightforward, following are the steps:

1. Select the app from your catalog.
2. Provide the required input, for example, upload raw meeting notes.
3. Run the app.
4. Review and utilize the generated output.

Here are the key features of Q App that enhance your productivity:

- **Customization and sharing**: After creating a Q App, you can further customize it using the **Add card** option. This allows you to refine the app's functionality or add additional steps. Once satisfied, you can publish the app to share it with others in your organization. By leveraging Q Apps, enterprises can significantly enhance productivity by automating routine tasks and ensuring consistency in various business processes.

- **Plugins**: Amazon Q Business includes a powerful plugins feature that seamlessly integrates with third-party services, enhancing its capabilities and streamlining workflows.

- **Built-in plugins**: Amazon Q Business comes with built-in plugins for popular applications like Jira, Salesforce, ServiceNow, and Zendesk. These plugins allow users to perform tasks directly within the Amazon Q interface without leaving the chat.

  Following is an example:

  o An IT representative can create a new incident in ServiceNow using natural language commands.

  o A sales manager can quickly update customer information in Salesforce without switching platforms.

  o A project manager can create and assign tasks in Jira directly from a conversation about project updates.

- **Custom plugins**: Organizations can also develop custom plugins to integrate Amazon Q with any third-party application that meets their specific requirements. These tailored solutions unlock a world of possibilities, as follows:

  o Custom plugins can connect to proprietary or specialized enterprise systems like ADP for HR processes or Dynamics 365 for finance operations.

  o They leverage the OpenAPI specification to ensure seamless integration with your systems.

  For example, a sales representative could query real-time customer data, update records, and generate reports directly from the Amazon Q interface, all through a custom plugin that integrates with your organization's unique **customer relationship management** (**CRM**) system.

By leveraging both built-in and custom plugins, organizations can create a truly tailored AI assistant that handles specific tasks relevant to their unique workflows, enhancing productivity and efficiency across the board.

Accessing Amazon Q Business through extensions

Amazon Q Business extends its reach beyond the core interface through a broad set of integrations with browsers, collaboration platforms, and productivity tools. These extensions allow users to access Q's capabilities in the flow of their daily work, enhancing adoption and minimizing context switching.

Browser extensions are available for *Chrome, Firefox,* and *Edge,* letting users ask questions, summarize web content, or retrieve enterprise knowledge directly while browsing.

Slack and Microsoft Teams integrations enable team members to interact with Amazon Q in chats and channels. For example, during a discussion in Teams, an employee can ask Q for the latest project update or retrieve a policy document and instantly share it with colleagues.

Microsoft Word and Outlook (Microsoft 365) integrations empower users to generate summaries, draft responses, or insert structured insights while working with documents or emails.

These integrations are centrally configured by administrators in the Amazon Q Business console and deployed through organizational app directories like Microsoft 365 Admin Center or Slack's App Directory. By embedding Q into familiar platforms, organizations encourage broader use, speed up workflows, and increase the value of their internal data.

These integrations streamline everyday workflows and encourage broader adoption by bringing Amazon Q Business into the tools employees already use.

Security, controls and guardrails

Amazon Q Business prioritizes robust security and compliance to protect your organization's sensitive data. Key security features include the following:

- **Identity and access management**: Amazon Q Business integrates with existing IdPs like Azure AD, Okta, or Ping for seamless authentication and authorization. This ensures that only authorized personnel can access the system, maintaining data confidentiality.

- **Data protection**: As a regional service, all your data is stored within the region where your Q Business endpoint and app are created. This feature aids in compliance with local data protection regulations and simplifies data governance. Additionally, Amazon Q Business uses tailored LLMs specifically designed for enterprise use cases, ensuring your data is never used for training or improving any GenAI or ML models.

- **Network security**: For enhanced security, you can access Amazon Q Business using a **virtual private cloud** (**VPC**) endpoint, keeping your traffic within the Amazon network and reducing the risk of unauthorized access.

- **Customizable guardrails**: One of the powerful features of Amazon Q Business is the ability to configure application guardrails, allowing you to align the AI's responses with your organization's policies and guidelines.

  Figure 12.19 shows how Amazon Q Business implements security through global and topic-specific controls. Administrators can configure these guardrails to manage AI interactions while ensuring appropriate use of company information.

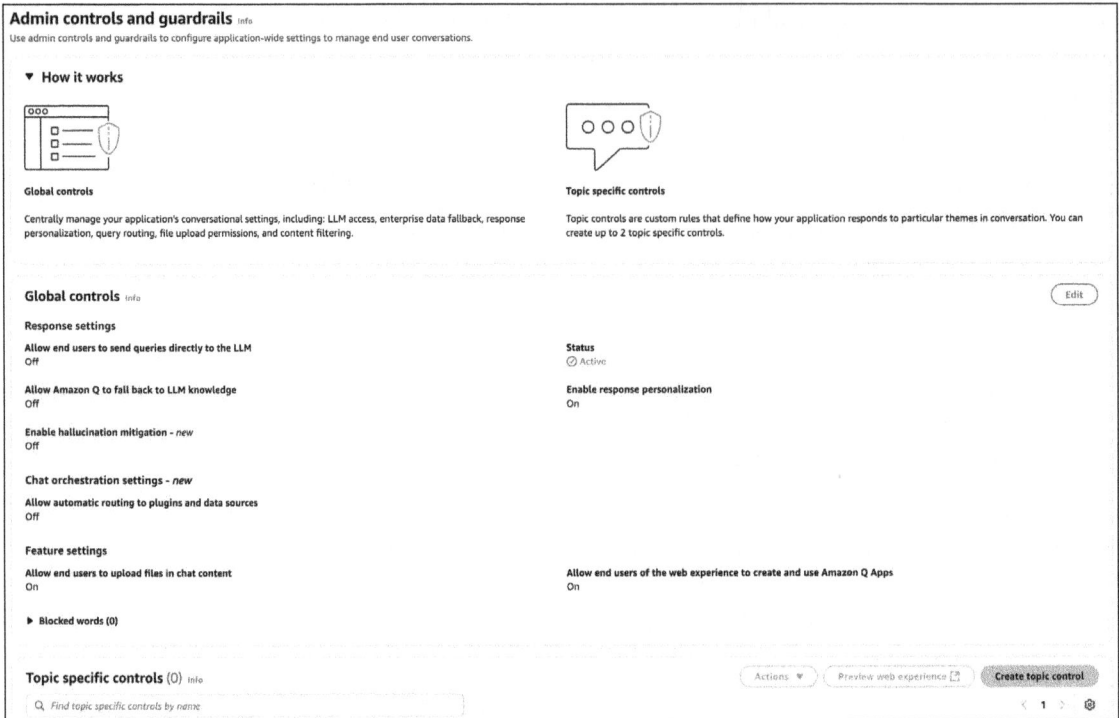

Figure 12.19: *Admin controls and guardrails with Amazon Q Business*

You can configure Amazon Q Business for the following:

- Generate responses using only enterprise data sources
- Restrict certain topics or block specific words
- Implement custom policies for data handling and response generation

For example, an organization could set guardrails to ensure that Amazon Q Business only accesses and provides information from approved internal documents, automatically excludes sensitive employee data or financial figures from responses, and restricts queries related to any sensitive topics. This approach allows employees to use Amazon Q Business effectively for their daily work while protecting sensitive internal information and maintaining appropriate access controls.

Monitoring and auditing

Amazon Q Business integrates with AWS CloudTrail and Amazon CloudWatch for comprehensive monitoring and auditing. CloudTrail captures API calls and related events for Amazon Q Business, storing detailed log files in an Amazon S3 bucket. This enables tracking of user activities, system changes, and API calls, supporting security analysis and compliance audits.

CloudWatch collects and processes raw data from Amazon Q Business into readable, near real-time metrics, stored for 15 months. To use CloudWatch, specify the metric namespace as **AWS/QBusiness** and use dimensions like **ApplicationId** to identify specific metrics. Key metrics include **DocumentsIndexed** for tracking successfully indexed documents, and **ThumbsUpCount** and **ThumbsDownCount** for monitoring end-user experience.

Through the AWS Management Console, CLI, or API, you can view metrics, setup alarms for specific thresholds, and create custom dashboards. Regular review of these logs and metrics helps maintain optimal system performance, address potential issues proactively, ensure compliance, and gain insights into user engagement and system utilization.

For detailed setup instructions, refer to the *AWS CloudTrail User Guide, Amazon CloudWatch User Guide*, and *Amazon Q Business* documentation.

The following are the best practices:

- **Structure complex queries**: For multi-step or complex queries, start new conversations for distinct topics. Provide clear context and specific questions. When necessary, specify examples or expected output formats to ensure accurate and structured responses.

- **Monitor and optimize**: Use AWS CloudTrail and Amazon CloudWatch to track performance, analyze usage patterns, and identify areas for improvement.

- **Customize for efficiency**: Utilize Amazon Q Apps for repetitive tasks and develop custom plugins and data source connectors for specific organizational needs.

- **Encourage effective user interactions**: Train users to provide clear context in queries and start new conversations for distinct topics, improving response accuracy and relevance.

- **Continuously refine**: Regularly assess the effectiveness of your Amazon Q Business implementation. Review user feedback and usage patterns to refine configurations, Q Apps, and plugins.

These practices will help organizations maximize the benefits of Amazon Q Business, ensuring accurate responses, enhancing functionality, optimizing performance, and improving overall productivity.

Conclusion

In this chapter, we explored Amazon Q, with a focus on Amazon Q Business, a fully managed GenAI assistant designed to transform enterprise productivity. We examined its capabilities, including secure access to internal data, automation of routine tasks, integration with familiar tools, and intelligent conversation-to-app conversions via Q Apps.

Key capabilities such as hallucination mitigation, multimedia data support, and personalized responses based on employee profiles strengthen Amazon Q Business's reliability and usability.

By embedding Q Business into everyday platforms like Teams, Slack, Word, and Chrome, organizations can drive adoption and increase the impact of their internal knowledge.

With thoughtful setup, guardrails, and monitoring, Amazon Q Business empowers teams to work smarter, faster, and more securely unlocking GenAI for real business outcomes.

In the next chapter, we will explore ML hub for foundational models, built-in algorithms and prebuilt ML solutions that you can deploy with just a few clicks.

Points to remember

- Amazon Q Business enables secure, enterprise-wide deployment of GenAI, with role-based access control and integration into organizational identity systems.

- The setup process involves selecting retriever types, configuring index capacity, and connecting data sources such as S3, SharePoint, web crawlers, and proprietary systems.

- Multimedia support allows Amazon Q Business to process and extract insights from images, audio, and video, extending its utility beyond text-based data.

- Hallucination mitigation ensures that responses are grounded in enterprise data and permissions-aware, with document-level citations to increase trust and transparency.

- Personalized responses leverage employee profile data (e.g., department or role), delivering more relevant and context-aware interactions.

- Users can build, run, and share lightweight Q Apps to automate repetitive workflows like meeting summaries, policy generation, or report synthesis.

- Amazon Q Business integrates directly into everyday tools including Slack, Microsoft Teams, Microsoft Word and Outlook, and major browsers like Chrome, Edge, and Firefox—enabling users to interact with Q in the flow of work.

- Built-in and custom plugins extend Q Business functionality by connecting it to tools such as Jira, Salesforce, ServiceNow, or any OpenAPI-compliant system.

- Monitoring and auditing are supported through AWS CloudTrail and Amazon CloudWatch, helping administrators track performance, usage, and compliance.

By keeping these points in mind, you can effectively implement and utilize Amazon Q Business to drive significant improvements in employee productivity within your organization.

Exercises

1. **Integrate Amazon Q Business with Amazon S3**: Learn how to connect Amazon Q Business with Amazon S3 and understand its integration capabilities.

   - Setup an Amazon S3 bucket and upload sample data such as FAQ or support documentation.

- Use S3 data source connector to integrate with Amazon Q Business.
- Query the data using Amazon Q Business and generate insights.
- Compare your experience with the integration of web crawler and File Upload connectors.

Document the steps, challenges, and outcomes. Reflect on the ease of use and potential applications.

2. **Specific data source connectors**: Connect Amazon Q Business to popular enterprise applications like Confluent, SharePoint, or Salesforce etc.

   a. Choose one of the supported data sources, for example Confluent, SharePoint, Salesforce.

   b. Review and follow the official AWS Documentation to configure the connector.

   c. Use Amazon Q Business to query and analyze the data from the chosen source.

Create a step-by-step guide based on your experience, noting any difficulties and how you overcame them. Evaluate the integration's usefulness in a real-world scenario.

3. **Configure a custom data source connector:** Learn to create a custom data source connector in Amazon Q Business for unsupported data sources.

   a. Identify a data source not natively supported by Amazon Q Business.

   b. Use the custom data source connector' capability to setup the connection.

   c. Follow the instructions on AWS Documentation for guidance.

   d. Test the custom connector by querying the data and generating insights.

Reflect on the configuration process, including any challenges and solutions. Discuss potential use cases for custom connectors in your organization.

Join our Discord space

Join our Discord workspace for latest updates, offers, tech happenings around the world, new releases, and sessions with the authors:

https://discord.bpbonline.com

CHAPTER 13
Getting Started with Generative AI on Amazon SageMaker JumpStart

Introduction

This chapter explores Amazon SageMaker JumpStart, a powerful toolkit for rapidly developing and deploying GenAI applications. We will dive into the various ways to access and use foundation models with SageMaker JumpStart, focusing on pre-trained GenAI models. Through step-by-step guides, you will learn to navigate the JumpStart interface, select and deploy text generation models, and fine-tune them on custom datasets. We will also cover best practices and optimization techniques for your AI applications.

Amazon SageMaker JumpStart addresses key challenges in AI development by providing easy access to several hundred built-in algorithms and pre-trained foundation models. This comprehensive eliminates the complexity typically associated with model selection, infrastructure setup, machine learning hub and deployment pipelines, allowing users to focus on solving business problems rather than managing technical overhead. Whether through the intuitive visual interface or programmatic approaches using the SageMaker Python SDK, JumpStart enables both novice and experienced practitioners to leverage advanced AI capabilities without specialized expertise.

Structure

The chapter covers the following topics:

- Introduction to Amazon SageMaker JumpStart
- Exploring pre-trained GenAI models
- Deploying text generation model in practice
- Fine-tune and deploy models with SageMaker Jumpstart
- Best practices

Objectives

In this chapter, you will possess a comprehensive understanding of Amazon SageMaker JumpStart and its capabilities for GenAI development. You will learn various methods to access and utilize foundation models through SageMaker JumpStart. You will gain expertise in exploring and selecting pre-trained GenAI models suitable for your projects. Through hands-on experience, you will master the process of deploying a text generation model and fine-tuning pre-trained models on custom datasets. Additionally, you will acquire knowledge of best practices and optimization techniques for SageMaker JumpStart, ensuring efficient resource utilization and improved model performance. By the end of the chapter, you will be equipped with the skills to effectively leverage SageMaker JumpStart for rapid prototyping, experimentation, and deployment of sophisticated GenAI solutions on the AWS platform.

Introduction to Amazon SageMaker JumpStart

Amazon SageMaker JumpStart is the machine learning hub of Amazon SageMaker that helps customers to easily discover built-in contents including algorithms, pre-trained models and solution templates and deploy them easily with just few clicks. While **large language models (LLMs)** and other AI models offer incredible capabilities, they also present several challenges when used directly, as follows:

- **Complexity**: Setting up the infrastructure and importing the publicly available algorithms and models into SageMaker.
- **Model selection**: Choosing the right pre-trained model for a specific task can be overwhelming.
- **Customization**: Adapting pre-trained models to specific use cases often requires significant expertise.
- **Deployment**: Setting up the infrastructure to run AI models at scale can be complex.
- **Cost and time**: Training models from scratch is expensive and time-consuming.

Amazon SageMaker JumpStart benefits

Amazon SageMaker JumpStart addresses the challenges by providing the following:

- **Easy access**: A curated collection of pre-built solutions, pre-trained models, and examples, all accessible through a user-friendly interface.

- **Simplified integration**: One-click deployment of models, reducing the complexity of integrating AI into applications.

- **Customization options**: Tools for fine-tuning pre-trained models on custom datasets without deep ML expertise.

- **Scalable deployment**: Built-in capabilities for deploying models at scale using Amazon's cloud infrastructure.

- **Time and cost efficiency**: By offering pre-trained models and solutions, it significantly reduces development time and costs.

In simpler terms, SageMaker JumpStart acts as a launchpad for ML model development, providing the building blocks and tools needed to quickly create and deploy ML models for Generative AI applications. It allows developers and data scientists to focus on solving business problems rather than dealing with the complexities of model development and infrastructure management.

By leveraging SageMaker JumpStart, users can rapidly prototype ideas, experiment with state-of-the-art models through UI without writing any code. Whether you're working on text generation, image creation, or other AI tasks, JumpStart provides 400+ built-in algorithms with pre-trained foundation models and example notebook making advanced AI capabilities accessible to a broader range of developers and organizations.

Accessing foundation models with Amazon SageMaker JumpStart

Amazon SageMaker JumpStart offers several methods to access and use foundation models, catering to different user needs and expertise levels, as follows:

- **SageMaker Studio UI**: User can access SageMaker JumpStart from SageMaker Studio UI. On the SageMaker JumpStart landing page in Studio, you can explore various model hubs, including both public and private models. Use the search bar to find specific hubs or models. Within each hub, you can sort models by popularity, downloads, or recent updates, and filter them by task. Click on a model to see its details. From the model card, you can choose to fine-tune, deploy, or evaluate the model (if these options are available) by clicking the corresponding buttons in the upper right corner. Remember, not all models offer all these options.

Key aspects of SageMaker Studio UI options are as follows:

- o   Access through the visual interface in SageMaker Studio.
- o   Ideal for users who prefer a graphical environment.
- o   Allows for easy browsing, selection, and deployment of models.
- o   Provides options for fine-tuning and customization.

To access SageMaker JumpStart in Amazon SageMaker Studio, the following are the steps:

1.   Create a domain in SageMaker AI and open **SageMaker Studio**:

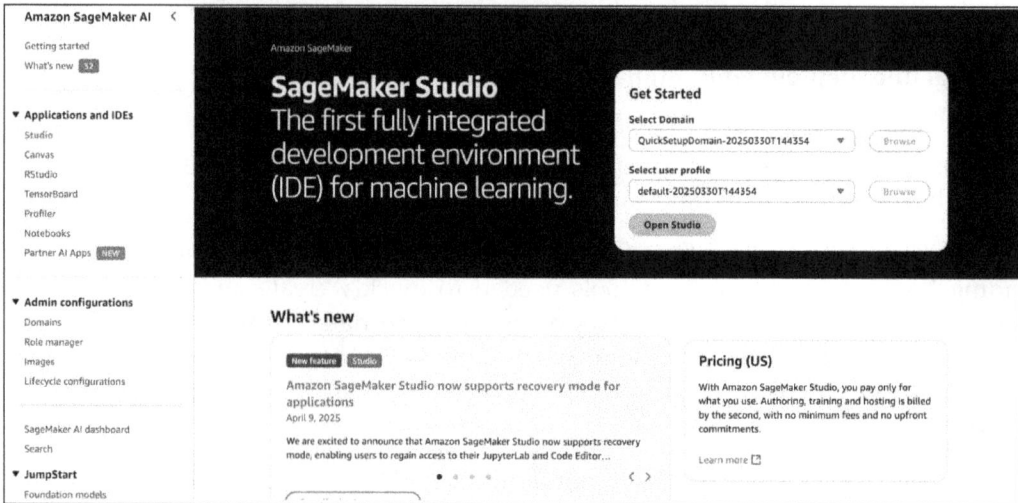

Figure 13.1: Amazon SageMaker AI Console

2.   Locate and select JumpStart inside **SageMaker Studio**. The following figure shows the home screen of SageMaker Studio:

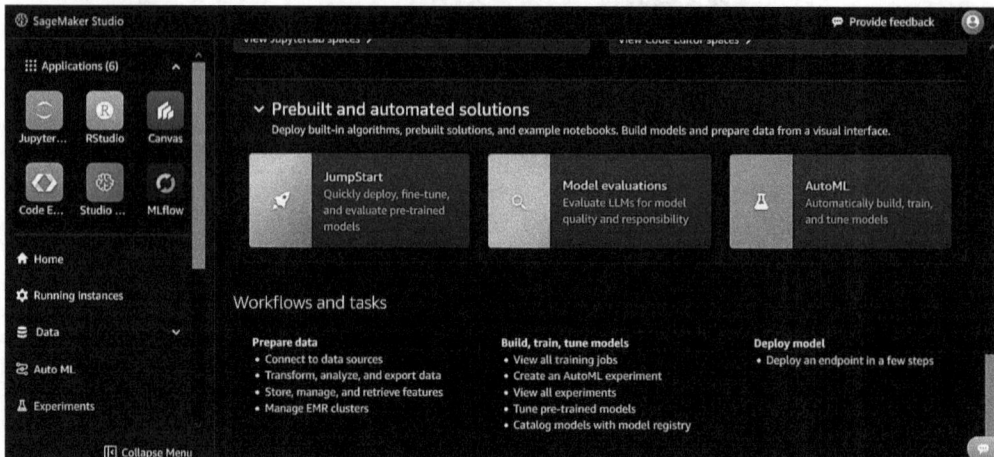

Figure 13.2: SageMaker Studio

The following figure shows the home screen of JumpStart in SageMaker Studio:

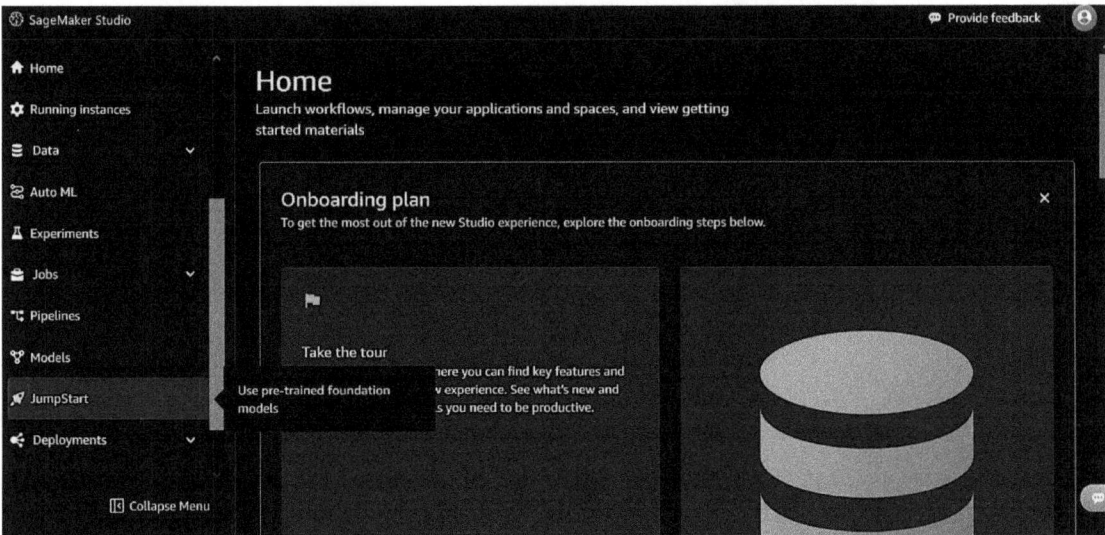

Figure 13.3: *SageMaker Studio Home menu*

3. Once you are on the SageMaker JumpStart landing page, you can browse different models or use the search feature to find specific models. The following figure shows the different public models available:

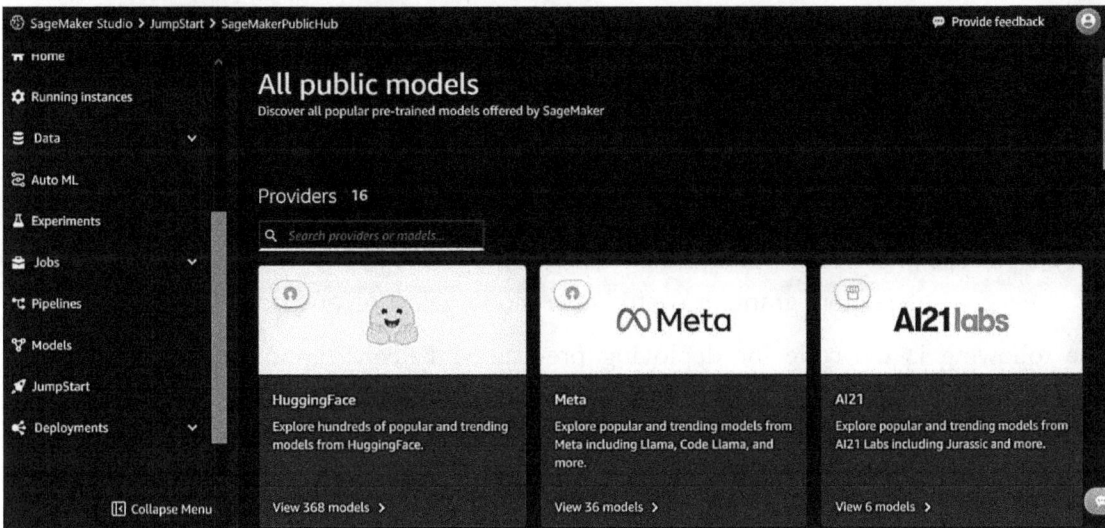

Figure 13.4: *SageMaker Studio JumpStart Models*

The following figure shows the results of the search with **Llama 3**:

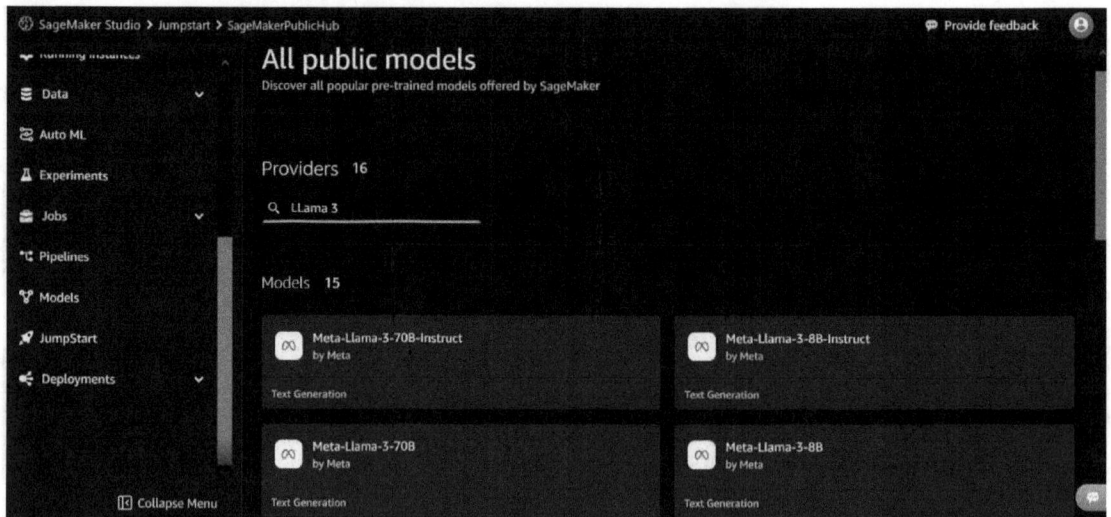

Figure 13.5: SageMaker Studio JumpStart Model Providers

- **SageMaker Python SDK**: You can deploy all JumpStart foundation models using the SageMaker Python SDK. For public text generation models, you just need the model ID from the provided table. For private models, you first need to subscribe to the model in AWS Marketplace. After subscribing to the model of your choice in AWS Marketplace, you can deploy the foundation model using the SageMaker Python SDK and the SDK associated with the model provider.

  Key aspects of SageMaker JumpStart API are as follows:

  o Programmatic access using the SageMaker Python SDK

  o Suitable for developers and data scientists who prefer code-based workflows

  o Enables automation and integration into existing pipelines

  o Offers more granular control over model selection and deployment

The following is the code for deploying pre-trained Falcon-7B model using SageMaker JumpStart:

```
from sagemaker.serve.builder.model_builder import ModelBuilder
model_builder = ModelBuilder(
model="huggingface-llm-falcon-7b-bf16",
schema_builder=SchemaBuilder(sample_input, sample_output),
role_arn=role)
sagemaker_model = model_builder.build()
predictor = sagemaker_model.deploy()
prediction = predictor.predict(sample_input)
```

The following is the code for fine tuning of the Falcon-7B model using :

```
from sagemaker.JumpStart.estimator import JumpStartEstimator
domain_adaptation_estimator = JumpStartEstimator(
model_id="huggingface-llm-falcon-7b-bf16",
hyperparameters=my_hyperparameters,
instance_type="ml.p4dn.24xlarge")
domain_adaptation_estimator.fit(
{"train": training_dataset_s3_path,
"validation": validation_dataset_s3_path},
logs=True)
```

- **SageMaker Console:** You can explore JumpStart foundation models directly through the Amazon SageMaker Console.

  The following are the steps:

  1. Open the Amazon SageMaker AI console at **https://console.aws.amazon.com/ sagemaker/**

     Find JumpStart on the left navigation panel and choose Foundation models. Refer to the following figure:

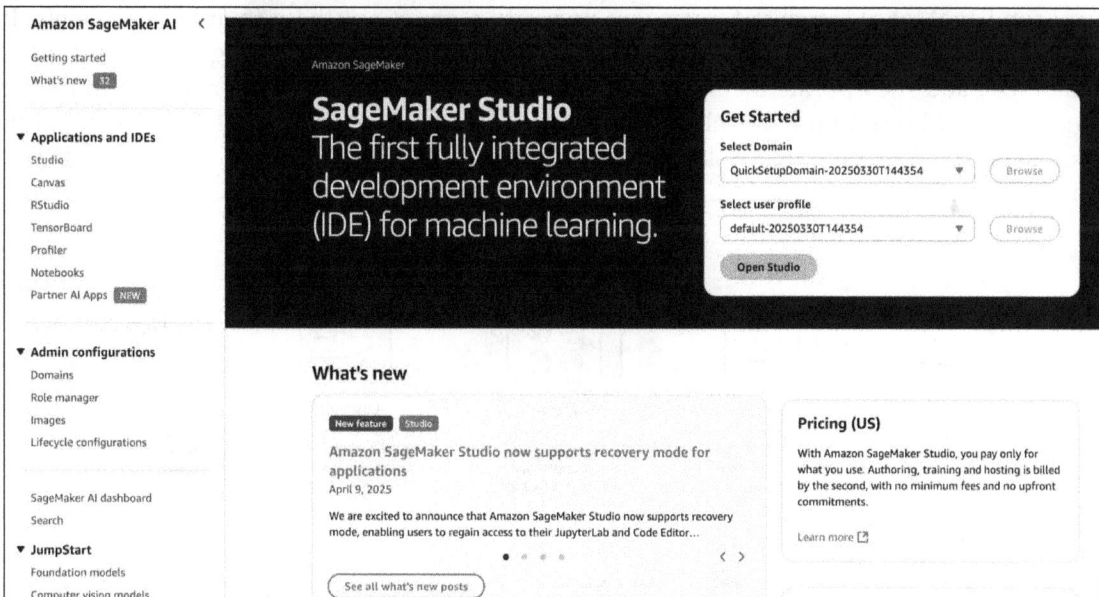

Figure 13.6: SageMaker Studio JumpStart Model Providers

  2. Browse models or search for a specific model. If you need guidance for model selection, see Explore the latest foundation models. Choose View model to view the model detail page for the foundation model of your choice.

Each method of access provides different levels of control and ease of use, allowing users to choose the most appropriate approach based on their technical expertise and project requirements. The chapter would delve into the specifics of each method, providing examples and use cases to illustrate when and how to use each approach effectively.

Exploring pre-trained GenAI models

Amazon SageMaker JumpStart provides cutting-edge foundation models for a wide range of applications. These include creating content, generating code, answering questions, writing copy, summarizing text, classifying information, and retrieving data, among others. With these foundation models, you can develop your own GenAI solutions. Additionally, you can combine these custom solutions with other features offered by SageMaker to enhance their capabilities.

Foundation models are large, versatile AI models trained on vast amounts of data. They can be adapted for various specific tasks and often serve as a starting point for more specialized models. Examples include Meta Llama 2 7B Chat, Flan-T5 XL, Falcon 7B Instruct BF16, and Mixtral-8x22B-Instruct-v0.1. These models are pre-trained on enormous text datasets and can be fine-tuned for specific language tasks. Amazon SageMaker JumpStart is built with the broadest selection of foundation models.

Amazon SageMaker JumpStart gives you access to a variety of these foundation models. It takes care of setting up and maintaining publicly available models, allowing you to easily use, customize, and incorporate them into your machine learning projects. In addition to public models, SageMaker JumpStart also offers proprietary foundation models from third-party providers. The following figure shows how it works:

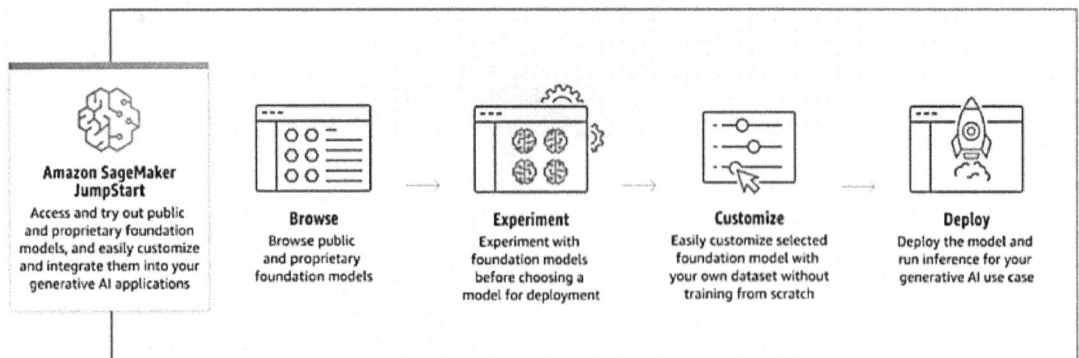

*Your training and inference data is not shared by nor used by AWS or foundation model providers

Figure 13.7: Working of SageMaker Studio JumpStart

The figure illustrates the workflow for using Amazon SageMaker JumpStart to develop GenAI applications. The process begins with accessing and exploring both public and proprietary foundation models. Users can then browse through these models, experimenting with different options to find the best fit for their needs. Once a suitable model is selected, SageMaker JumpStart allows for easy customization using the user's own dataset, without the need to train a model from scratch. Finally, the customized model can be deployed for inference in GenAI use cases. The image emphasizes that throughout this process, user data for training and inference remains private and is not shared with or used by AWS or foundation model providers, ensuring data security and privacy.

Deploying text generation model in practice

This section demonstrates the practical application of Amazon SageMaker JumpStart for deploying and utilizing a powerful text generation model.

The exercise focuses on two key aspects, as follows:

- **Deploying the Llama 2 7B model using the SageMaker JumpStart Console**: There is a step-by-step process of selecting and deploying the Llama 2 7B model directly from the SageMaker JumpStart console. This showcases the user-friendly, no-code approach to deploying sophisticated AI models. You will learn how to navigate the console, select the appropriate model, and configure deployment settings with just a few clicks.

- **Invoking the text generation endpoint using a notebook**: Once the model is deployed, we will demonstrate how to interact with it programmatically. Using a Jupyter Notebook, you will learn to craft API calls to the deployed endpoint, send prompts, and receive generated text responses. This part illustrates the seamless integration between SageMaker's visual tools and programmatic interfaces.

Through this exercise, you will gain a hands-on experience in leveraging SageMaker JumpStart to quickly deploy a state-of-the-art language model and incorporate it into your development workflow. This practical approach highlights how SageMaker JumpStart simplifies access to advanced AI capabilities, enabling developers to focus on building innovative applications rather than managing infrastructure. Whether you are creating a chatbot, a content generation tool, or any text-based AI application, this hands-on section equips you with the essential skills to get started with powerful text generation models on AWS.

The following steps show the details of how to fine-tune and deploy Llama 2 7B model using SageMaker JumpStart:

1. Launch SageMaker Studio and access the JumpStart section within the SageMaker Public Hub. To deploy Meta's Llama 2 7B model, use the search bar to locate **Meta** providers. From the results, select the Llama 2 7B model from the available Meta models. The following figure shows the results of the search term `meta`:

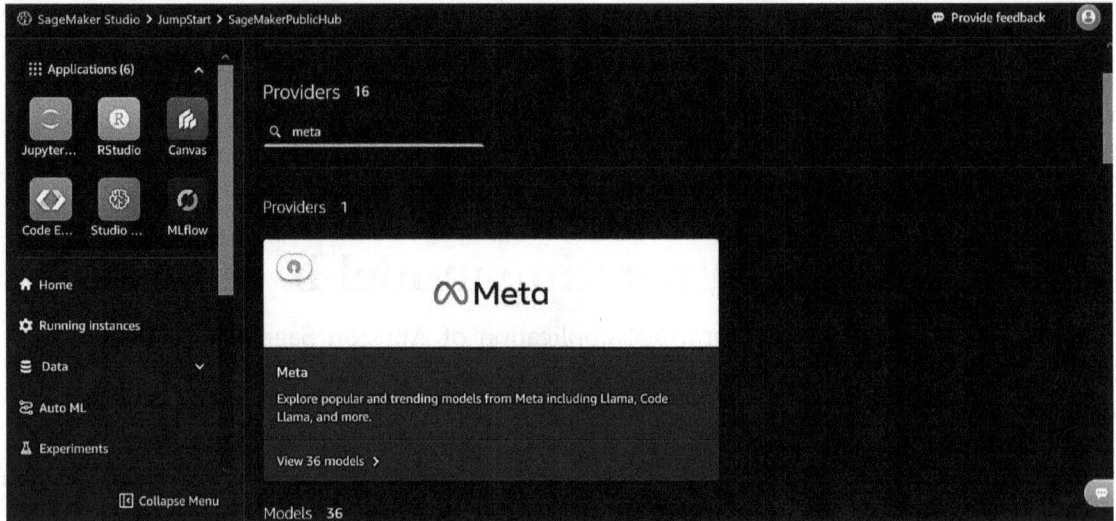

Figure 13.8: *SageMaker Studio JumpStart, Meta model*

2. Upon selecting the Llama 2 7B model in SageMaker JumpStart, you will see a detailed model card. At the top right of this card are four action buttons: Train, Deploy, Optimize, and Evaluate. For the Llama 2 7B model, all four options are available, giving you full flexibility to train, deploy, optimize, or evaluate the model directly from the SageMaker Studio interface. These options allow you to customize and utilize the model according to your specific needs without leaving the SageMaker environment. The following figure shows the model details of the Llama 2 7B:

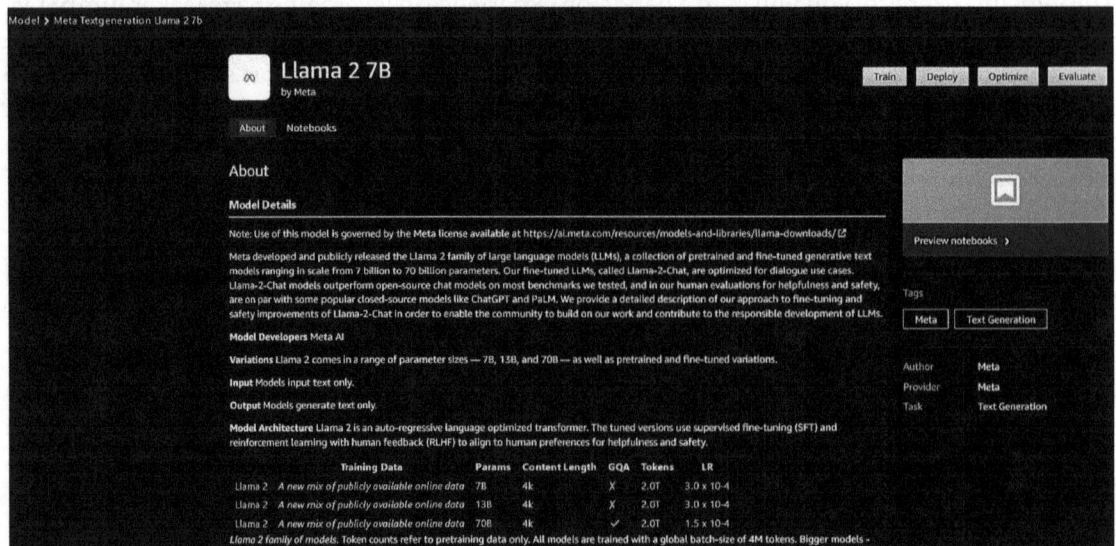

Figure 13.9: *SageMaker Studio JumpStart, Llama 2 7B*

3. The model card includes a preview of a sample notebook for deploying the Llama 2 7B model. This preview shows Python code snippets that demonstrate how to use the SageMaker Python SDK to deploy the model and invoke its endpoint. At the top of the preview, there's an option to **Open in JupyterLab**, allowing you to directly access and execute this deployment code in a full Jupyter Notebook environment. This feature provides a seamless transition from exploring the model to deploying it, with ready-to-use code examples. Refer to the following figure:

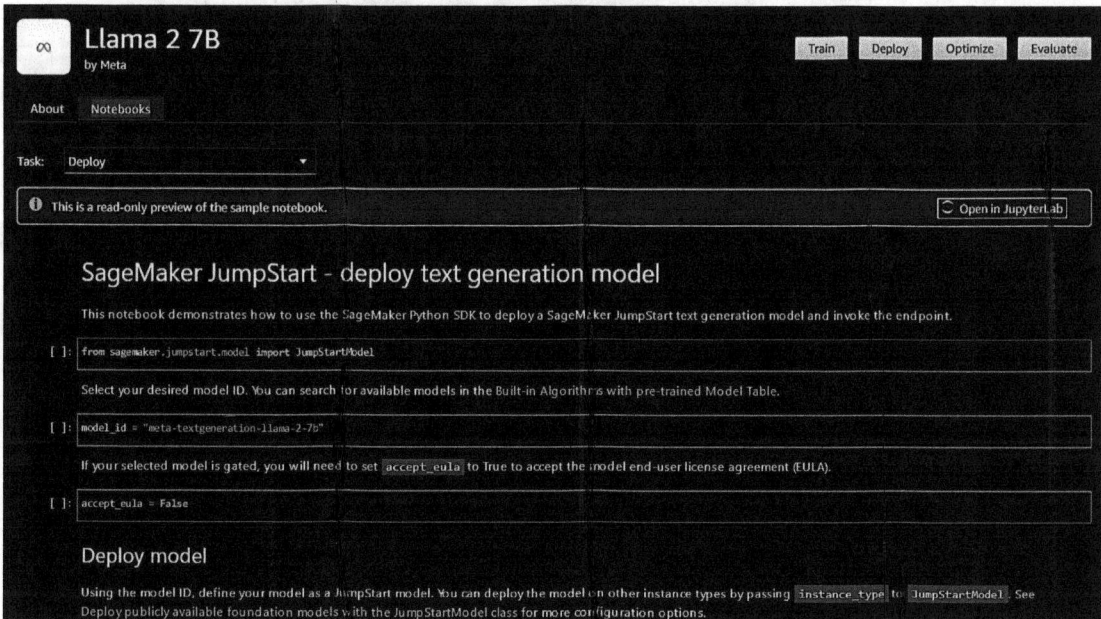

Figure 13.10: *SageMaker Studio JumpStart, Deploy model*

4. To deploy the Llama 2 7B model endpoint, follow these steps in the SageMaker Studio interface:

    a. First, review and accept the **End User License Agreement** (**EULA**) for the Llama 2 model.

    b. In the **Endpoint settings** section:

       o Confirm or modify the auto-generated **Endpoint name**, for example, **JumpStart-dft-meta-textgeneration-1-20240710-155335**

       o Select the **Instance type** (default is ml.g5.2xlarge)

       o Set the **Initial instance count** (default is 1)

    c. The **Inference type** is set to **Real-time** for sustained traffic and low latency.

    d. Leave other options as default if not specified.

    e. Click the **Deploy** button to start the deployment process.

The deployment will take a few minutes to complete, during which SageMaker will setup the specified resources and make the model available at the endpoint.

The following figure shows the details of the **End User License Agreement (EULA)** and option to accept:

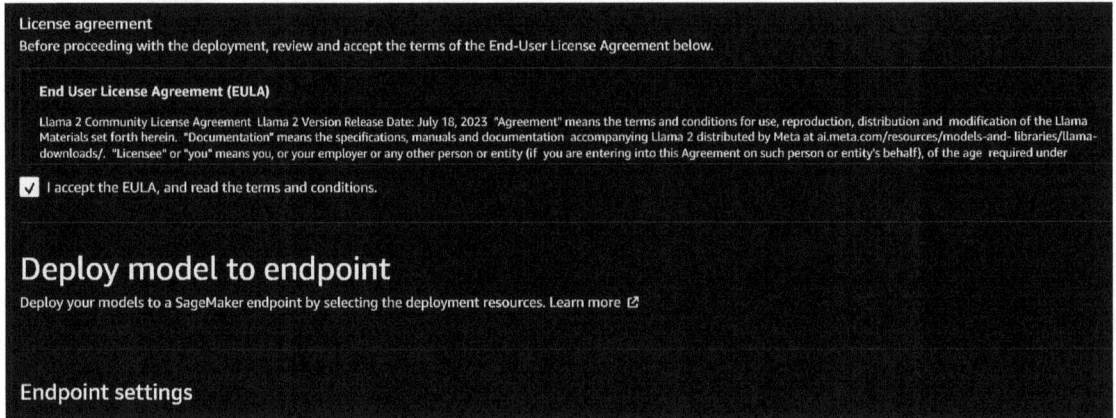

Figure 13.11: SageMaker Studio JumpStart, Deploy model endpoint EULA

The following figure shows the details of the different settings required for the endpoint:

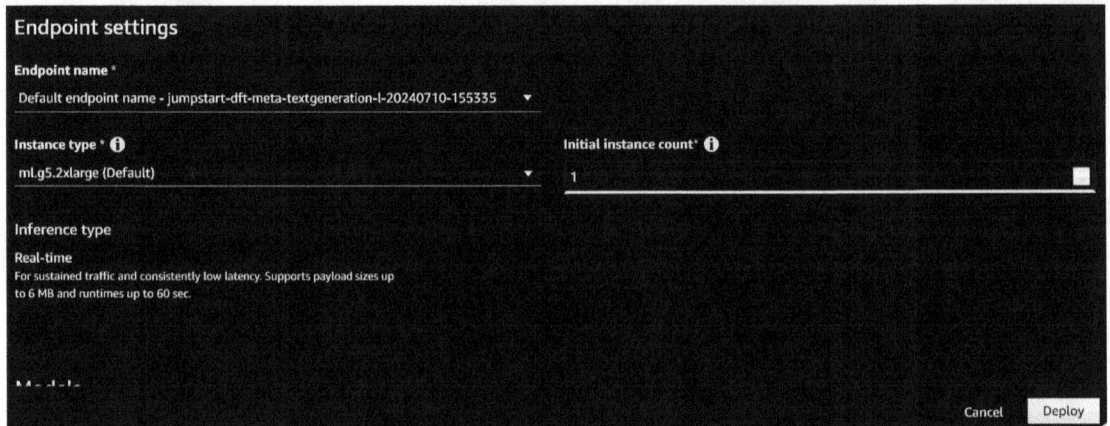

Figure 13.12: SageMaker Studio JumpStart, Deploy model endpoint setting

The following figure shows the endpoint summary details:

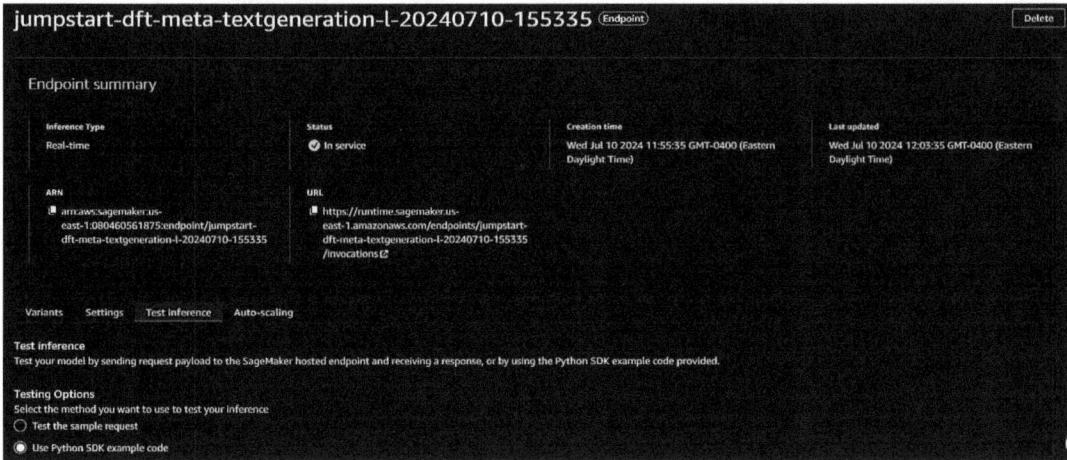

Figure 13.13: SageMaker Studio JumpStart, Deploy model endpoint generation

5. Using test inference tab option, you can click on Open in JupyterHub option and open the deployed Llama 2 7B model in a notebook and execute the code to generate the text. Accessing and Utilizing the Deployed Llama 2 7B Model can be done, as follows:

    a. Navigate to the **Test inference** tab.

    b. Locate and select the **Open in JupyterLab** option.

    c. This action will launch a notebook environment containing the deployed Llama 2 7B model.

    d. Within the notebook, you can execute the provided code to generate text using the model.

This approach allows you to interactively work with the Llama 2 7B model, enabling you to experiment with text generation in a flexible Jupyter environment.

The following figure provides the details to open Jupyter Notebook in SageMaker studio:

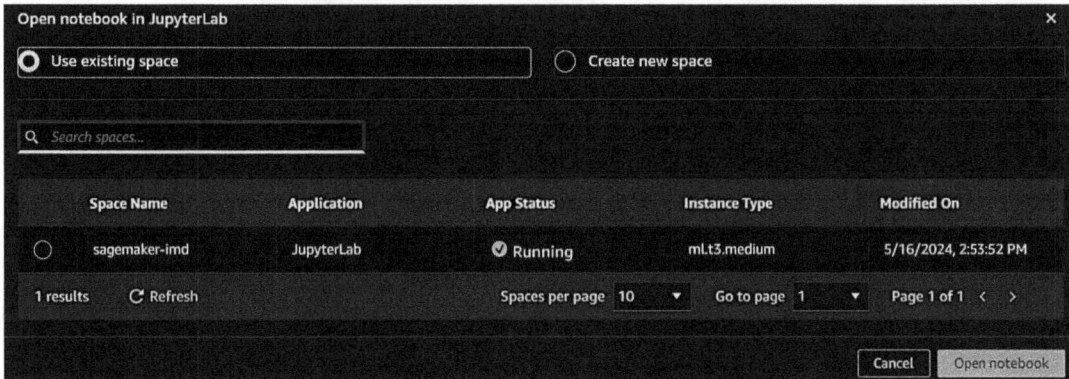

Figure 13.14: SageMaker Studio JumpStart, Deploy model endpoint open notebook

Fine-tune and deploy models with SageMaker JumpStart

SageMaker JumpStart provides a streamlined process for fine-tuning and deploying large language models on AWS.

The following are the key approaches:

- **Domain adaptation**:
  - o Adapts pre-trained models to specific domains or industries
  - o Uses unlabelled data from the target domain
  - o Helps models understand domain-specific language and context

- **Supervised fine-tuning**:
  - o Uses labelled datasets to improve model performance on specific tasks
  - o Involves training on input-output pairs
  - o Enhances accuracy for targeted applications

- **Instruction fine-tuning**:
  - o Trains models to follow specific instructions or prompts
  - o Improves model's ability to understand and execute diverse tasks
  - o Enhances model versatility and task-specific performance

- **LORA/ Parameter-efficient fine-tuning (PEFT)**:
  - o **LORA**: Low-Rank Adaptation technique
  - o **PEFT**: Umbrella term for efficient fine-tuning methods
  - o Reduces computational resources needed for fine-tuning
  - o Allows fine-tuning of large models with limited hardware
  - o Maintains model quality while updating only a subset of parameters

In this hands-on project, we will perform the following:

- Fine-tune a Llama 3 8B model using the Dolly-15K dataset
- Deploy the fine-tuned model using SageMaker python SDK
- Compare outputs from the original Llama 3 model and the fine-tuned, deployed version
- Analyse improvements in task-specific performance and instruction-following capabilities

This practical example will demonstrate the effectiveness of fine-tuning techniques and showcase the deployment capabilities of SageMaker JumpStart. By comparing the original and fine-tuned models, we'll illustrate the benefits of adapting large language models to specific datasets and tasks.

SageMaker JumpStart simplifies the implementation of these techniques, allowing users to fine-tune and deploy models efficiently on AWS infrastructure, as we will see in our Llama 3 example.

Let us get into the details of the code for the fine-tuning of Llama 3 8B model using Amazon SageMaker JumpStart:

1. This code sets up and deploys the Llama 3 8B model using Amazon SageMaker JumpStart. It starts by specifying the model ID (**meta-textgeneration-llama-3-8b**) and version (**2.***). Then, it uses the JumpStartModel class from SageMaker to create a **pretrained_mode** object. Finally, it deploys this model with the **deploy()** method, accepting the EULA. This deployment creates a predictor that can be used for making inferences.

   Refer to the following code:

   ```
   model_id, model_version = "meta-textgeneration-llama-3-8b", "2.*"

   from sagemaker.JumpStart.model import JumpStartModel

   pretrained_model = JumpStartModel(model_id=model_id, model_version=model_version)
   pretrained_predictor = pretrained_model.deploy(accept_eula=True)
   ```

2. After deploying the Llama 3 8B model, the next step is to interact with it for text generation. We define a helper function **print_response()** to display inputs and outputs clearly. Then, we create a payload dictionary containing our prompt *I believe the meaning of life is* along with generation parameters like **max_new_tokens, top_p,** and **temperature**.

   Using the **pretrained_predictor** we obtained from the deployment, we call its **predict()** method with our payload. This sends the prompt to the model and retrieves the generated text. The **custom_attributes** parameter ensures we comply with licensing requirements.

   Finally, we print the input and the model's response, or any errors that occur. This process demonstrates how to use our newly deployed Llama 3 model for practical text generation tasks, showing the seamless transition from model setup to actual use in generating AI-driven responses.

   Refer to the following code:

   ```
   def print_response(payload, response):
       print(payload["inputs"])
       print(f"> {response.get('generated_text')}")
       print("\n==================================\n")
   ```

```
payload = {
    "inputs": "I believe the meaning of life is",
    "parameters": {
        "max_new_tokens": 64,
        "top_p": 0.9,
        "temperature": 0.6,
        "return_full_text": False,
    },
}
try:
    response = pretrained_predictor.predict(
        payload, custom_attributes="accept_eula=false"
    )
    print_response(payload, response)
except Exception as e:
    print(e)
```

3. We will now discuss the data preparation phase for fine-tuning our Llama 3 model. We use the datasets library to load the Databricks Dolly-15k dataset, a diverse collection of instruction-following data.

   We then filter this dataset to focus on summarization tasks, though it is noted that we could easily adapt this for other tasks like QA or information extraction. The category column is removed as it is no longer needed. To evaluate our fine-tuned model's performance, we split the dataset, reserving 10% for testing.

   Finally, we save the training portion as a JSONL file, preparing it for use in the fine-tuning process. This data preparation step is crucial as it tailors the general-purpose Llama 3 model to our specific summarization task, setting the stage for improved performance in this domain.

   Refer to the following code:

```
from datasets import load_dataset
dolly_dataset = load_dataset("databricks/databricks-dolly-15k",
split="train")

# To train for question answering/information extraction, you can
replace the assertion in next line to example["category"] == "closed_
qa"/"information_extraction".
summarization_dataset = dolly_dataset.filter(
    lambda example: example["category"] == "summarization"
)
summarization_dataset = summarization_dataset.remove_columns("category")

# We split the dataset into two where test data is used to evaluate at
the end.
```

```
train_and_test_dataset = summarization_dataset.train_test_split(test_
size=0.1)

# Dumping the training data to a local file to be used for training.
train_and_test_dataset["train"].to_json("train.jsonl")
```

4. We define a JSON template that formats our training examples in a way the Llama 3 model can understand. This template includes a prompt section with placeholders for an instruction and context, followed by a completion section for the model's response.

The prompt guides the model to treat the input as a task with specific instructions and context. We then save this template as a JSON file. This step is crucial because it standardizes how we present data to the model during fine-tuning, ensuring consistency in the input format.

By using a well-structured template, we help the model learn to distinguish between the instruction, context, and the expected response, which is essential for effective instruction-following and task completion after fine-tuning.

Refer to the following code:

```
import json

template = {
    "prompt": "Below is an instruction that describes a task, paired
with an input that provides further context. "
    "Write a response that appropriately completes the request.\n\n"
    "### Instruction:\n{instruction}\n\n### Input:\n{context}\n\n",
    "completion": " {response}",
}
with open("template.json", "w") as f:
    json.dump(template, f)
```

5. We use SageMaker's S3Uploader to transfer our prepared data to Amazon S3. First, we determine the default S3 bucket for our SageMaker session. We then specify the local paths of our training data (**train.jsonl**) and the template file (**template.json**) we created earlier.

We construct an S3 location within our bucket specifically for the Dolly dataset. Using S3Uploader, we upload both the training data and the template to this S3 location. This step is crucial because SageMaker Python SDK's requires training data to be in S3 for easy access during the training process.

By moving our data to S3, we are ensuring that our fine-tuning job can efficiently access the necessary files.

Refer to the following code:

```
from sagemaker.s3 import S3Uploader
import sagemaker
```

```
import random

output_bucket = sagemaker.Session().default_bucket()
local_data_file = "train.jsonl"
train_data_location = f"s3://{output_bucket}/dolly_dataset"
S3Uploader.upload(local_data_file, train_data_location)
S3Uploader.upload("template.json", train_data_location)
print(f"Training data: {train_data_location}")
```

6.　We use SageMaker's **JumpStartEstimator** to configure our fine-tuning job for the Llama 3 model. We specify the model ID and version, accept the EULA, and disable output compression for better visibility. We choose a powerful GPU instance (**ml. g5.24xlarge**) to handle the computational demands of fine-tuning. The code notes that for larger models like Llama-3-70b, an even more robust instance might be necessary.

We then set hyperparameters for the fine-tuning process. By setting **instruction_ tuned** to **True**, we are telling the model to expect our instruction-following dataset format. We set the number of training epochs to 3 and the maximum input length to 1024 tokens. Finally, we call the **fit()** method, pointing to our S3-stored training data.

This initiates the fine-tuning process, where SageMaker will train the Llama 3 model on our Dolly dataset, adapting it to our specific task of summarization (or whichever task we chose earlier).

In this step, our general-purpose Llama 3 model is being tailored to our specific needs, learning from our curated dataset to improve its performance on our chosen task.

Refer to the following code:

```
from sagemaker.JumpStart.estimator import JumpStartEstimator

estimator = JumpStartEstimator(
    model_id=model_id,
    model_version=model_version,
    environment={"accept_eula": "true"},  # Please change {"accept_
eula": "true"}
    disable_output_compression=True,
    instance_type="ml.g5.24xlarge",  # For Llama-3-70b, add instance_
type = "ml.g5.48xlarge"
)
# By default, instruction tuning is set to false. Thus, to use
instruction tuning dataset you use
estimator.set_hyperparameters(
    instruction_tuned="True", epoch="3", max_input_length="1024"
)
estimator.fit({"training": train_data_location})
```

The code above represents the final stage of our fine-tuning process, where we evaluate and compare the performance of our original and fine-tuned Llama 3 models, as follows:

a. We start by deploying our fine-tuned model using **estimator.deploy()**.

b. We then setup a testing process using a portion of our dataset that we previously set aside.

c. The **predict_and_print** function is defined to handle individual predictions. It formats the input using our template, sends it to both the original and fine-tuned models, and collects their responses.

d. We iterate through a small subset of our test data (5 examples) to generate predictions.

e. The results are organized into a pandas DataFrame, as follows:

    •   The input prompts

    •   The ground truth (correct responses from our dataset)

    •   Responses from the original, non-fine-tuned model

    •   Responses from our newly fine-tuned model

f. Finally, we display this DataFrame as an HTML table, allowing for easy visual comparison of the results.

This step is crucial as it allows us to directly compare the performance of our original Llama 3 model with our fine-tuned version. We can observe how well the fine-tuned model has adapted to our specific task (summarization in this case) and whether it produces more accurate or relevant responses compared to the original model. This comparison helps validate the effectiveness of our fine-tuning process and demonstrates the practical improvements achieved through task-specific adaptation of the large language model.

Refer to the following code:

```
finetuned_predictor = estimator.deploy()

import pandas as pd
from IPython.display import display, HTML

test_dataset = train_and_test_dataset["test"]

(
    inputs,
    ground_truth_responses,
    responses_before_finetuning,
    responses_after_finetuning,
) = (
    [],
    [],
    [],
    [],
```

```
)

def predict_and_print(datapoint):
    # For instruction fine-tuning, we insert a special key between input
and output
    input_output_demarkation_key = "\n\n### Response:\n"

    payload = {
        "inputs": template["prompt"].format(
            instruction=datapoint["instruction"],
context=datapoint["context"]
        )
        + input_output_demarkation_key,
        "parameters": {"max_new_tokens": 100},
    }
    inputs.append(payload["inputs"])
    ground_truth_responses.append(datapoint["response"])
    # Please change the following line to "accept_eula=true"
    pretrained_response = pretrained_predictor.predict(
        payload, custom_attributes="accept_eula=false"
    )
    responses_before_finetuning.append(pretrained_response.
get("generated_text"))
    # Fine Tuned Llama 3 models doesn't required to set "accept_
eula=true"
    finetuned_response = finetuned_predictor.predict(payload)
    responses_after_finetuning.append(finetuned_response.get("generated_
text"))

try:
    for i, datapoint in enumerate(test_dataset.select(range(5))):
        predict_and_print(datapoint)

    df = pd.DataFrame(
        {
            "Inputs": inputs,
            "Ground Truth": ground_truth_responses,
            "Response from non-finetuned model": responses_before_
finetuning,
            "Response from fine-tuned model": responses_after_finetuning,
        }
    )
    display(HTML(df.to_html()))
except Exception as e:
    print(e)
```

The following figure provides the snapshot of the evaluate and compare the performance of our original and fine-tuned Llama 3 models:

	Inputs	Ground Truth	Response from non-finetuned model	Response from fine-tuned model
0	Below is an instruction that describes a task, paired with an input that provides further context. Write a response that appropriately completes the request.\n\n### Instruction:\nPlease summarize the challenges faced by the factory workers in The Matchgirls musical.\n\n### Input:\nThe Matchgirls is a musical by Bill Owen and Tony Russell about the London matchgirls strike of 1888. It premiered at the Globe Theatre, London, on 1 March 1966, directed and choreographed by Gillian Lynne.\n\nThe musical focuses on the lifestyle of the match cutters at the Bryant and May factory in Bow, London, with strong references to the condition Phossy jaw and the political climate of the era.\n\nProduction history\nAfter out-of-town tryouts in Leatherhead, Surrey, the show opened on the West End in March 1966. The show closed about three months later.\n\nA cast recording was made of the 1966 Globe Theatre London production. The musical was published by Samuel French Ltd in 1979.\n\nSynopsis\nThe central character of the musical is Kate, a tenement girl and factory worker, who writes to Annie Besant to ask for help in seeking reform at the Bryant and May factory. The story follows Kate and Annie's attempts to rally the girls, leading Kate to become a reckless strike-leader and a key player in the creation and recognition of the union. With much of the action set in the incongruously named, but fictional, 'Hope Court', the musical portrays Bryant and May as callous and uncaring employers, with factory foreman 'Mr Mynel' representing the threatening and imposing regime in which the girls were forced to work.\n\nThere is also a sub plot in which Kate's involvement in the strike puts strain on her relationship with docker Joe.\n\nDespite the subject matter of the musical, a strong emphasis is placed on the positive mentality and natural ebullience of the so-called 'cockney sparrows', this leading to a number of cheerful and entertaining vocal numbers and dance routines.\n\n\n### Response:\n	The Bryant and May factory was a popular employer in the 1960's and 70's in the fictional town of Hope Court. This factory hired many semi-skilled workers to produce their goods. The story focuses on Kate who felt that the working conditions needed reform and put together a union to demand better working conditions for her and her peers. The musical follows the highs and lows of Kate and peers as they fight for better working conditions.	The Matchgirls musical is a musical about the London matchgirls strike of 1888. The musical focuses on the lifestyle of the match cutters at the Bryant and May factory in Bow, London, with strong references to the condition Phossy jaw and the political climate of the era. The musical is set in the 1880s and is about the matchgirls strike of 1888. The musical is about the matchgirls strike of 1888 and the conditions they worked in. The	The Matchgirls is a musical by Bill Owen and Tony Russell about the London matchgirls strike of 1888. It premiered at the Globe Theatre, London, on 1 March 1966, directed and choreographed by Gillian Lynne. The musical focuses on the lifestyle of the match cutters at the Bryant and May factory in Bow, London, with strong references to the condition Phossy jaw and the political climate of the era.

Figure 13.15: Evaluate and compare the performance of our original and fine-tuned Llama 3 models

Best practices

When working with Amazon SageMaker JumpStart for your GenAI projects, following these best practices can help you maximize efficiency, performance, and cost-effectiveness:

- **Model selection**:
    - Carefully evaluate the available models based on your specific use case and requirements.
    - Consider factors such as model size, performance, and licensing when choosing a foundation model.
    - Experiment with different models to find the best balance between accuracy and computational resources.

- **Efficient fine-tuning**:
    - Start with a pre-trained model that closely aligns with your target task to reduce fine-tuning time and resources.
    - Use a representative but manageable dataset for fine-tuning to avoid overfitting and excessive computational costs.
    - Leverage SageMaker's distributed training capabilities for larger models to speed up the fine-tuning process.

- **Optimize deployment**:
    - Choose the appropriate instance type based on your model's size and performance requirements.

- o   Consider using SageMaker's multi-model endpoints for deploying multiple models on a single endpoint to reduce costs.
- o   Implement auto-scaling to handle varying workloads efficiently.

- **Monitor and iterate**:
  - o   Utilize SageMaker's built-in monitoring tools to track model performance and resource utilization.
  - o   Regularly evaluate your model's outputs and gather user feedback for continuous improvement.
  - o   Be prepared to iterate on your model selection or fine-tuning approach based on real-world performance.

- **Cost management**:
  - o   Take advantage of SageMaker's managed spot training for non-time-sensitive workloads to reduce costs.
  - o   Implement a systematic approach to clean up unused endpoints and resources to avoid unnecessary charges.
  - o   Use SageMaker's cost allocation tags to track and manage expenses across different projects or teams.

- **Security and compliance**:
  - o   Ensure that you comply with the licensing terms of the foundation models you asre using.
  - o   Implement proper IAM roles and permissions to control access to your SageMaker resources.
  - o   Use SageMaker's built-in encryption features to protect your data and model artifacts.

- **Version control and reproducibility**:
  - o   Maintain clear versioning for your datasets, fine-tuned models, and deployment configurations.
  - o   Use SageMaker Experiments to track and compare different runs and model versions.
  - o   Document your workflow, including pre-processing steps and hyperparameters, for reproducibility.

- **Leverage SageMaker's ecosystem**:
  - o   Integrate JumpStart with other SageMaker features like SageMaker Pipelines for end-to-end ML workflows.

- o Use SageMaker Feature Store to manage and share features across different models and teams.

- o Explore SageMaker's built-in algorithms and frameworks to complement your foundation model-based solutions.

By following these best practices, you can effectively leverage SageMaker JumpStart to build, deploy, and manage GenAI solutions while optimizing for performance, cost, and scalability. Remember that the field of GenAI is rapidly evolving, so staying updated with the latest features and capabilities of SageMaker JumpStart is crucial for maintaining a competitive edge in your AI development process.

Conclusion

This chapter provided a comprehensive guide to leveraging Amazon SageMaker JumpStart for developing and deploying sophisticated Generative AI applications. We began by introducing SageMaker JumpStart and its key features, highlighting how it addresses the challenges associated with AI model development and deployment. We then explored the various methods to access and utilize foundation models through SageMaker JumpStart, including the SageMaker Studio UI, SageMaker Python SDK, and SageMaker Console. Each approach caters to different user needs and expertise levels, offering varying degrees of control and ease of use. The chapter delved into the extensive collection of pre-trained GenAI models available through SageMaker JumpStart, covering their capabilities and applications.

We demonstrated hands-on how to deploy a text generation model using SageMaker JumpStart, guiding you through the step-by-step process. Furthermore, we discussed the fine-tuning capabilities of SageMaker JumpStart, which enable customizing pre-trained models with your own data without the need for extensive training from scratch. This feature empowers developers to tailor models to their specific use cases, unlocking greater accuracy and relevance. Throughout the chapter, we emphasized best practices and optimization techniques to ensure efficient resource utilization and improved model performance when working with SageMaker JumpStart. By leveraging the power of SageMaker JumpStart, developers and data scientists can significantly reduce development time and complexity, allowing them to focus on creating innovative AI-powered applications on the AWS platform. With its comprehensive toolset and extensive model library, SageMaker JumpStart streamlines the entire GenAI development lifecycle, from model selection to deployment and optimization.

In the next chapter, we will discuss the details of best practices for developing GenAI applications.

Points to remember

- Amazon SageMaker JumpStart acts as a centralized hub, providing easy access to a vast collection of pre-built solutions, pre-trained models, and examples across various domains, including GenAI.

- JumpStart simplifies the integration of AI models into applications by offering one-click deployment capabilities, reducing the complexity associated with model integration and infrastructure setup.

- JumpStart empowers users to customize and fine-tune pre-trained models using their own datasets, without the need for extensive training from scratch, enabling the development of tailored solutions for specific use cases.

- JumpStart supports scalable deployment of models, leveraging Amazon's cloud infrastructure, allowing users to run AI models at scale with ease.

- By providing pre-trained models and solutions, JumpStart significantly reduces development time and costs, enabling organizations to prototype ideas and experiment with state-of-the-art models efficiently.

- JumpStart offers multiple access methods, including the SageMaker Studio UI, SageMaker Python SDK, and SageMaker Console, catering to different user preferences and expertise levels.

- When deploying GenAI models through JumpStart, it is essential to consider best practices and optimization techniques to ensure efficient resource utilization and optimal model performance.

- JumpStart empowers developers and data scientists to focus on solving business problems and creating innovative AI-powered applications, rather than dealing with the complexities of model development and infrastructure management.

Exercises

1. Build a text generation model that can generate 10-K reports based on the input provided. In this exercise, you will fine-tune the GPT-J 6B model using domain adaptation techniques with SEC data. The goal is to create a specialized model that can generate detailed and accurate 10-K reports tailored to specific company inputs. You will utilize Amazon SageMaker JumpStart to streamline the fine-tuning process and implement the text generation model.

2. Fine-tune a state-of-the-art code generation model to enhance its performance on specific programming tasks. In this exercise, you will fine-tune the Code Llama 7B model using domain adaptation techniques with the Dolphin Coder dataset. The goal is to create a specialized model that can generate more accurate, efficient, and context-aware code snippets across various programming languages and tasks. You will implement the fine-tuning process and compare the performance of the original and fine-tuned models in code generation tasks.

## CHAPTER 14

Best Practices for Developing Generative AI Applications

Introduction

In this chapter, we will focus on best practices for developing high-performance, cost-effective, and low-latency generative AI applications. Adhering to these best practices is crucial for optimizing your applications, ensuring efficient resource utilization, and delivering a seamless user experience. For example, by carefully selecting the appropriate LLM and fine-tuning it for your specific use case, you can significantly improve performance and reduce latency, ultimately enhancing the responsiveness of your application. Furthermore, implementing caching strategies and leveraging serverless architectures can greatly reduce costs while maintaining scalability and availability.

By following the best practices outlined in this chapter, you will gain valuable insights into tuning your generative AI applications for optimal performance, minimizing latency, and managing costs effectively, enabling you to deliver high-quality, efficient, and scalable solutions to your customers.

Structure

The chapter covers the following best practices:

- Best practices for developing generative AI applications on AWS
- Cost considerations and strategies for efficient resource utilization

- Security and privacy considerations for generative AI applications
- Monitoring and continuous improvement strategies

Objectives

By the end of this chapter, you will understand how to choose the right foundation model for your specific use case, significantly improving performance and reducing latency in your generative AI applications. You will learn to implement optimization techniques such as token streaming and caching, while also applying cost-effective strategies including prompt optimization and efficient resource utilization. You will gain practical knowledge of data management best practices and security safeguards using AWS services to protect sensitive information and maintain regulatory compliance in your AI solutions. You will develop skills to establish monitoring processes and continuous improvement strategies, ensuring your applications deliver consistently high-quality outputs while adapting to changing requirements. These best practices will enable you to build scalable, high-performance generative AI applications that provide seamless user experiences while effectively managing resources and costs.

Best practices for developing generative AI applications on AWS

When developing generative AI applications on AWS, adhering to best practices is crucial for maximizing effectiveness, efficiency, and reliability. These practices encompass a wide range of considerations, from selecting the right foundation model to ensuring robust security measures. By following these guidelines, you can create powerful, cost-effective, and secure generative AI solutions that leverage the full potential of AWS services. The following best practices provide a comprehensive framework for building successful generative AI applications: choosing the right foundation model, selecting the appropriate development approach, optimizing performance and latency, managing costs effectively, implementing sound data management strategies, ensuring security and privacy, and establishing robust monitoring and continuous improvement processes. Additionally, integrating with other AWS services creates end-to-end solutions that harness the full power of the AWS ecosystem. By implementing these best practices, you can navigate the complexities of generative AI development and deliver high-quality applications that meet the diverse needs of users and businesses alike.

Choosing right FM for use case

The choice of the FM is crucial as it directly impacts the performance, accuracy, and capabilities of your generative AI application. Different FMs have varying strengths and weaknesses, and selecting the right one can significantly enhance the user experience and overall application quality. When choosing an FM, consider factors such as the model's size, specialized training, for example, code generation, QA, reasoning etc., and the trade-offs between performance and cost. With AWS, you can leverage services like Amazon Bedrock and Amazon SageMaker JumpStart to experiment with different pre-trained FMs and customize them for your specific use case. When selecting a FM for a specific use case, various LLM leaderboards can provide valuable initial insights into model performance across different tasks and metrics. Platforms like LMSYS Chatbot Arena Leaderboard, Hugging Face's Open LLM Leaderboard, and Stanford's HELM benchmark offer comparative data on model capabilities, helping you narrow down your options. However, it is crucial to approach these leaderboards with caution and not rely solely on their rankings. While they offer a useful starting point, the best practice is to thoroughly test potential models with your specific use case and dataset. This hands-on evaluation ensures that the chosen model aligns with your unique requirements and performs optimally with your particular data and tasks.

To choose the right model for your use case, you can leverage model evaluation from Amazon Bedrock as we covered in *Chapter 11, RAG and Model Evaluation*. There are several other evaluation frameworks and tools such as MLFlow, DeepEval, Langfuse, Ragas, axeval, and many more with variety of metrics to evaluate performance of FMs. These frameworks are often selected when more customization, specific metrics, or integration with existing ML pipelines is required, especially when evaluating models and systems are not hosted on Amazon Bedrock.

Design considerations

Selecting the right approach for developing generative AI applications is crucial for success and efficiency. The decision-making process involves evaluating several factors, including the specific task requirements, data sources, and desired output characteristics. When developing generative AI applications, the choice of technique depends on the interplay of external data sources, real-time data needs, and domain-specific output requirements. When external data isn't necessary, **prompt engineering (PE)** alone suffices for basic tasks, while combining PE with agents addresses real-time data needs. For applications requiring external data, the approach becomes more nuanced. If domain-specific output is crucial and real-time data is needed, a comprehensive strategy employing PE, **retrieval augmented generation (RAG)**, agents, and fine-tuning is recommended. Without real-time data requirements, PE combined with RAG and fine-tuning is suitable for domain-specific tasks. In scenarios where domain-specificity is not critical but real-time data is essential, integrating PE with RAG and agents proves effective. Lastly, for tasks utilizing external data without real-time or domain-specific demands, a combination of PE and RAG is adequate. This systematic approach ensures that the chosen technique aligns with the task's specific requirements, optimizing the effectiveness and efficiency of the generative AI solution.

Leveraging multi-model routing for enhanced AI capabilities

Implementing a multi-model approach with LLM routers can significantly optimize both performance and cost in generative AI applications. By intelligently routing queries based on complexity, simpler tasks can be directed to smaller, more cost-effective models, while complex queries are handled by larger, more sophisticated models. This strategy not only ensures efficient resource utilization but also maintains high-quality outputs across various types of user inputs. LLM routers, acting as intelligent traffic directors, can analyze incoming queries in real-time and make informed decisions on which model is best suited to handle each request, balancing factors such as response quality, latency, and operational costs. LLM routing typically works by analyzing incoming queries and directing them to the most appropriate model based on factors like complexity, task type, and required expertise. While routing can introduce a small amount of additional latency due to the decision-making process, the benefits often outweigh this cost. The trade-offs include balancing response quality, processing speed, and operational expenses. LangChain's Router offers flexibility and customization options for routing logic, while Amazon Bedrock Intelligent Prompt Routing provides a managed solution that can automatically route requests between different models within the same family, optimizing for both cost and response quality.

Imagine a customer service application where you are summarizing conversations, you might choose a smaller, faster LLM like the Llama 3.1 8B parameter model from Meta on Amazon Bedrock for real-time interaction, while using a larger and more powerful model like the Llama 3.1 405B parameter model for more complex or open-ended queries that require deeper understanding and reasoning.

Optimizing performance and latency for generative AI applications

Generative AI applications often require real-time or near real-time response times to provide a seamless user experience. Optimizing performance and minimizing latency is crucial, especially for interactive applications like chatbots or conversational AI assistants. To enhance the user experience and provide a more responsive interface, you can leverage token streaming. This technique enables the incremental display of the model's output as it is being generated, rather than waiting for the entire response to be completed before presenting it to the user. By streaming the output in real-time, applications can create a perception of lower latency, leading to a more engaging and interactive experience for end-users. There are a number of LLMs on both Amazon Bedrock and Amazon SageMaker JumpStart that support streaming responses. For example, for a conversational AI assistant integrated with Amazon Connect, you can leverage the LLM Amazon Bedrock that supports token streaming to ensure prompt responses, enhancing the customer experience during live interactions.

Another key technique in optimizing latency and performance is response caching. Response caching is a powerful optimization technique for generative AI applications, offering significant benefits in both latency reduction and cost efficiency. By storing and reusing previously generated responses for identical or similar prompts, caching minimizes the need for repeated model invocations. This approach substantially reduces response times, as cached results can be retrieved almost instantaneously compared to generating new responses. Additionally, caching leads to considerable cost savings by decreasing the number of API calls to the language model. For frequently asked questions or common prompts, caching can dramatically improve the application's performance and user experience while simultaneously lowering operational expenses. However, you must carefully manage cache invalidation and updates to ensure the accuracy and relevance of cached responses over time. Tools such as LangChain provide built-in components for caching FM calls, and it integrates with a variety of data stores such as Redis, OpenSearch, Couchbase, MongoDB etc.

Guardrails for Amazon Bedrock supports two modes of operation, allowing you to optimize safety and latency for your use cases. Synchronous mode buffers and scans the generated output against configured policies before sending it to the user, ensuring adherence to guidelines but introducing some latency. Asynchronous mode immediately streams the output to the user while concurrently scanning in the background, providing low-latency responsiveness but risking the delivery of inappropriate content until the scanning process catches up. If you are leveraging agents for Amazon Bedrock, it offers built-in latency optimization for simpler use cases where agents contain a single knowledge base.

Data management and pre-processing best practices

Generative AI models often require large datasets for training and fine-tuning, and effective data management and pre-processing are crucial for achieving accurate and reliable results. Leveraging AWS analytics and machine learning services can streamline this process significantly. Services like Amazon S3 for storage, AWS Glue for **extract, transform, load (ETL)** operations, and Amazon SageMaker for data processing pipelines enable robust data preparation workflows. These tools facilitate essential tasks such as data cleaning to remove inconsistencies and errors, deduplication to eliminate redundant information, and formatting to ensure data consistency. Amazon Comprehend can assist in text analysis and metadata extraction, while Amazon Athena allows for SQL-based querying of large datasets. Implementing version control ensures traceability of data changes. Additionally, employing AWS Lake Formation helps in implementing data governance policies, managing access controls, and maintaining data lineage. This comprehensive approach to data management not only improves the quality of input for generative AI models but also enhances compliance, security, and scalability of the entire data ecosystem.

Cost considerations and strategies for efficient resource utilization

Generative AI applications can be resource-intensive, and managing costs is a critical consideration, especially for large-scale deployments or applications with high concurrency. Services such as Amazon Bedrock charge based on the number of tokens processed and tokens generated by FMs.

One of the most effective ways to reduce cost is to optimize your prompt. Optimizing prompts is a crucial strategy for enhancing the efficiency and cost-effectiveness of generative AI applications. This involves carefully crafting input prompts to reduce the token count while maintaining clarity and specificity. You can achieve this by eliminating unnecessary preambles, focusing on essential information, and directly requesting specific answers. Additionally, utilizing model parameters such as maximum response length can help control the output size. For instance, instructing the model to *provide a concise answer in no more than 50 words* can significantly reduce token usage. By combining these techniques, such as streamlining input, specifying output requirements, and leveraging model parameters, developers can optimize both the quality and efficiency of their AI-generated content while managing costs effectively.

For example, consider this unoptimized prompt: *Hello, I am working on a project about renewable energy sources. Could you please provide me with a detailed explanation of solar power, including how it works, its advantages and disadvantages, and some information about its current global adoption? I would also appreciate, if you could mention some recent technological advancements in this field. Thanks in advance for your help!*

This prompt can be optimized to: *Summarize solar power: function, pros/cons, global adoption, recent tech advances. Limit to 100 words.*

Based on the pricing information from Amazon Bedrock, we can create a cost comparison table to illustrate the potential savings from different optimization strategies. Here is an example:

Strategy	Cost per 1M tokens	Savings
On-demand (base)	$0.0004	-
Provisioned Throughput	$0.00024 - $0.00016	40-60%
Batch processing	$0.0002	50%
Prompt optimization	Varies	Up to 50-90%

Table 14.1: Cost comparison by optimization strategies

This table demonstrates how different strategies can significantly reduce costs:

1. **Provisioned Throughput**: For consistent workloads, this option can offer 40-60% savings compared to on-demand pricing.

2. **Batch processing**: For non-time-sensitive operations, this can provide up to 50% lower prices compared to on-demand.

3. **Prompt optimization**: While not directly reflected in pricing, optimizing prompts can drastically reduce token usage, potentially leading to 50-90% cost reduction depending on the extent of optimization.

It is important to note that actual savings may vary based on specific models, usage patterns, and implementation details. Additionally, combining these strategies can lead to compounded cost reductions.

Batching requests is another effective strategy for optimizing costs when working with large language models, especially in self-hosted environments or when using services like Amazon SageMaker. By grouping multiple prompts or queries into a single API call, batching significantly reduces the overhead associated with individual requests. This approach maximizes GPU utilization, as the model can process multiple inputs in parallel, leading to improved throughput and reduced idle time. For models hosted on Amazon EC2 or Amazon SageMaker, batching helps amortize the fixed costs of keeping the model loaded in memory across multiple requests. Batching can lead to more efficient use of compute resources, potentially allowing for the use of larger instance types that offer better performance at a lower per-request cost. While implementing batching requires careful consideration of latency requirements and queue management, it can result in substantial cost savings and improved overall system efficiency for high-volume generative AI applications.

Security and privacy considerations for generative AI applications

Generative AI applications often deal with sensitive or personal data, making security and privacy critical concerns. Best practices include implementing access controls, data encryption, secure communication channels, and adhering to relevant compliance standards and regulations. AWS services like AWS **Key Management Service** (**KMS**), AWS Secrets Manager, and AWS **Identity and Access Management** (**IAM**) can help you secure your generative AI applications and protect user data. Amazon Bedrock offers several capabilities to support security and privacy requirements. Notably, Amazon Bedrock Guardrails plays a crucial role in addressing security and privacy concerns by providing fine-grained control over model outputs. It allows you to implement content filtering, setup toxicity detection, and enforce output constraints, thereby mitigating risks associated with generating inappropriate or sensitive content. By integrating these security measures and leveraging AWS's compliance-ready infrastructure, organizations can build generative AI applications that not only innovate but also prioritize data protection and regulatory adherence.

The following is an example:

For a healthcare-related QA application, you can leverage AWS KMS to encrypt sensitive patient data, AWS IAM to control access to your generative AI models and APIs, AWS Secrets Manager to securely store and rotate API keys or other sensitive credentials, and Bedrock Guardrails to filter PII information.

Monitoring and continuous improvement strategies

Generative AI applications often require continuous monitoring and improvement to maintain quality and reliability. Best practices include implementing logging and monitoring strategies, collecting user feedback, and regularly fine-tuning or updating your models. AWS services like Amazon CloudWatch, AWS CloudTrail, and Amazon Bedrock Model Evaluation as well as Amazon SageMaker Model Monitor can help you monitor your applications, track model performance, and detect drift or anomalies. Although in preview at the time of this writing, prompt management in Amazon Bedrock offers valuable features for continuous improvement strategies in generative AI applications. By allowing you to create, save, and version prompts, it facilitates systematic experimentation and refinement of prompt designs. The ability to compare different prompt variants and their outputs enables data-driven decision-making, helping teams iteratively improve their prompts based on real performance data. This approach supports a culture of continuous learning and optimization, ensuring that AI applications can evolve and adapt to changing requirements and use cases over time, ultimately leading to more effective and efficient generative AI solutions.

Refer to the following figure:

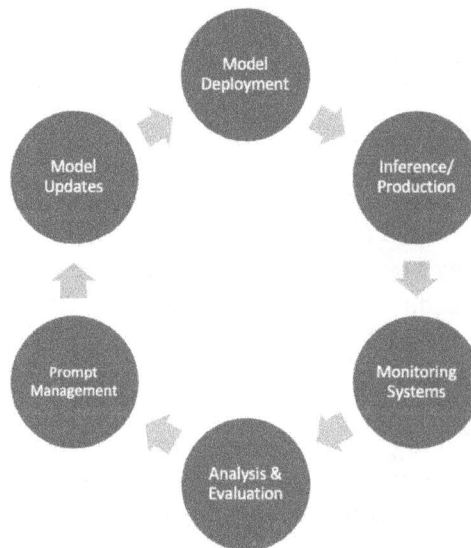

Figure 14.1: Continuous monitoring and improvement cycle

Let us take an example: for a product recommendation application, you can use Amazon SageMaker Model Monitor to track the performance of your generative AI model over time, detect any drift or degradation, and setup alerts to trigger retraining or fine-tuning when necessary, ensuring your recommendations remain relevant and accurate.

Integration with other AWS services for end-to-end solutions

Generative AI applications often require integration with other services and components to create end-to-end solutions. Leverage AWS's wide range of services for tasks such as data ingestion, processing, storage, and delivery to build robust and scalable AI-powered systems. For data ingestion, utilize services like Amazon Kinesis for real-time data streaming. Amazon S3 provides scalable and durable storage for large datasets, while Amazon RDS or DynamoDB can handle structured data storage needs. For data processing and analytics, Amazon EMR enables big data processing, and Amazon Athena allows for SQL queries on S3 data. Use Amazon API Gateway to create, publish, and manage APIs for your generative AI models, ensuring seamless integration with front-end applications. For deployment and scaling, leverage Amazon ECS or EKS for containerized applications, and implement Amazon CloudFront for content delivery and caching. Finally, use AWS Lambda for serverless compute to handle event-driven processing or to create microservices architecture around your generative AI core. By effectively combining these services, you can create comprehensive, scalable, and efficient generative AI solutions that leverage the full power of the AWS ecosystem.

Figure 14.2 describes an LLM-powered QA system that leverages multiple AWS services for secure, scalable, and accurate responses. The system uses Amazon Bedrock for accessing FMs (for example, Nova Pro for multilingual responses and Titan Embedding V2 for embeddings), with data storage distributed across Amazon S3 (documents and logs), DynamoDB (conversation history), and Amazon OpenSearch (vector storage). The authentication is handled by Cognito, while API Gateway and Lambda manage the backend API endpoints. Knowledge base for Amazon Bedrock provides a managed RAG capability that can connect to data source, parse and chunk data, convert into embedding and store it in the defined vector store. Lastly, Amazon Athena can be used for analyzing conversation and service logs.

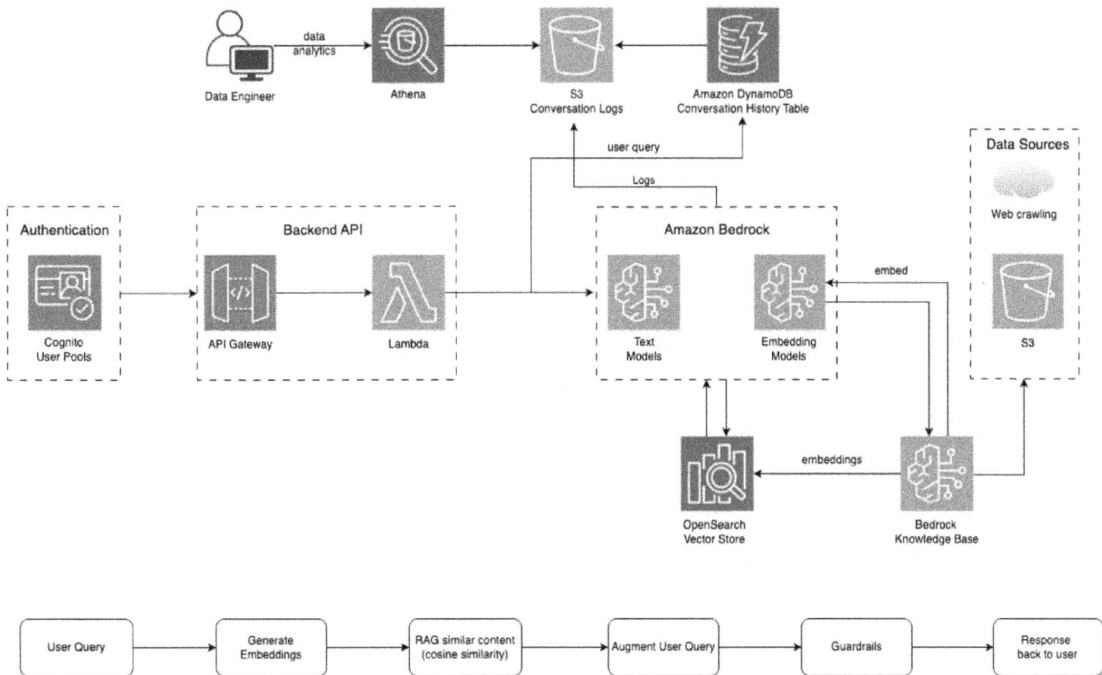

Figure 14.2: AWS architecture for a GenAI-powered RAG chatbot application

Overall pipeline follows these key steps:

- Generate embeddings for the user query using embedding models
- Retrieve similar documents using vector search
- Augment user query with relevant context and send it to text generation model
- Apply guard rails to the response
- Format and deliver the answer

An architecture diagram, as shown in *Figure 14.2* shows the flow from user authentication through Cognito, API Gateway/Lambda for request handling, interaction with various storage services (S3, DynamoDB, OpenSearch), and the core LLM processing pipeline through Bedrock, with Athena handling log analytics.

Conclusion

Developing generative AI applications on AWS requires a holistic approach that balances performance, cost, security, and scalability. By carefully selecting the right foundation model, implementing efficient data management practices, and leveraging AWS's comprehensive suite of services, you can create powerful and responsive AI solutions. The integration of advanced techniques such as token streaming, response caching, and batching requests significantly enhances application performance and user experience. As the field of generative AI continues to evolve, staying abreast of new AWS offerings and continuously refining your approach will be key to maintaining competitive and innovative applications. Remember that successful generative AI development is an iterative process, requiring ongoing monitoring, evaluation, and optimization to ensure your solutions remain effective and aligned with business objectives.

In the next chapter, we will cover common architecture patterns for different real-world generative AI use cases.

Points to remember

- Experiment with different model sizes and customization options to find the optimal balance between performance and cost for your specific use case.
- Implement a systematic approach for selecting technique based on external data needs, real-time requirements, and domain-specificity.
- Utilize token streaming for improved user perception of response times in interactive applications.
- Optimize prompts by focusing on essential information and specifying output requirements to reduce token usage and costs.

- Implement a robust error handling strategy, including graceful degradation and fallback mechanisms, to ensure your generative AI application remains functional even when encountering unexpected inputs or model failures.

- Implement a feedback loop system that collects and analyzes user interactions and responses, using this data to continually refine your models and improve the relevance and quality of generated content over time.

- Consider implementing A/B testing frameworks to systematically compare different prompts, models, or configurations in production environments, allowing for data-driven optimization of your generative AI applications.

- Stay informed about new AWS offerings and updates in the generative AI space to continuously enhance your applications' capabilities and efficiency.

Exercise

Building a cost-effective product description generator: Create a generative AI application that generates product descriptions for an e-commerce platform, optimizing for cost and performance.

Use case: An online retailer needs to generate unique, engaging product descriptions for thousands of items. They want to automate this process using AI while keeping costs low and ensuring quick response times.

Steps:

1. **Set up the basic application**:
   - Use Amazon Bedrock to create a product description generator using an appropriate LLM.
   - Implement a basic prompt that takes product attributes (name, category, key features) and generates a description.

2. **Optimize the prompt**:
   - Refine your initial prompt to reduce token usage while maintaining description quality.
   - Aim to limit descriptions to a specific word count, for example, 50-75 words.
   - Use the Amazon Bedrock console or API to compare token counts and costs between your original and optimized prompts.

3. **Implement batching**:
   - Modify your application to support batch processing of multiple product descriptions in a single API call.

- Compare the cost and throughput of generating descriptions individually vs. in batches.

4. **Add caching**:

   - Implement prompt caching or a caching layer using Amazon ElastiCache for Redis.

   - Store generated descriptions for frequently accessed products.

   - Measure the impact on response time and API calls for repeated requests.

5. **Evaluate and refine**:

   - Use Amazon Bedrock Model Evaluation to assess the quality of generated descriptions.

   - Fine-tune your prompt based on the evaluation results.

   - Compare the performance and cost metrics of your optimized setup against the baseline.

6. **Expected outcome**: By the end of this exercise, you should have a product description generator that:

   - Produces concise, relevant descriptions

   - Utilizes batching for improved efficiency

   - Implements caching to reduce redundant API calls

   - Demonstrates measurable cost savings compared to the initial implementation

Join our Discord space

Join our Discord workspace for latest updates, offers, tech happenings around the world, new releases, and sessions with the authors:

https://discord.bpbonline.com

## CHAPTER 15

Real-world GenAI

Introduction

GenAI has moved beyond theoretical possibilities, such as academic research papers describing potential language models, to become a transformative force across industries and business processes, with practical applications like customer service chatbots that create human-like responses, medical image generation that assists in diagnosis, and automated content creation tools that help marketers produce customized campaigns at scale. This chapter explores real-world implementations of GenAI using AWS services, particularly Amazon Bedrock, showcasing how organizations across different sectors are leveraging this technology to solve practical challenges, improve efficiency, and create innovative solutions.

Through detailed case studies and practical examples, we will examine how businesses are implementing GenAI to achieve tangible results. We will explore the architectural approaches, implementation strategies, and lessons learned from these deployments, providing you with insights and best practices for your own GenAI initiatives.

Structure

The chapter covers the following topics:

- Enterprise use cases
- Implementation considerations

- Common challenges and solutions in enterprise GenAI implementation
- Future trends and opportunities

Objectives

By the end of this chapter, you will have gained a comprehensive understanding of how different industries are practically implementing GenAI solutions across various sectors. You will learn about specific use cases and their technical implementations using AWS services, providing you with concrete examples of successful deployments. This chapter will offer valuable insights into the challenges encountered in real-world GenAI implementations and the corresponding solutions that organizations have developed to overcome them. You will discover best practices for implementing GenAI in various business contexts, ensuring you can avoid common pitfalls while maximizing effectiveness. Additionally, you will explore the tangible impact and return on investment that organizations have achieved through GenAI implementations, with metrics and case studies illustrating their success. Finally, you will learn how to adapt these use cases to your own business needs, enabling you to develop a customized approach to GenAI implementation that aligns with your specific objectives and constraints.

Enterprise use cases

GenAI is rapidly transforming enterprise operations across multiple industries, creating new efficiencies and capabilities that were previously unattainable. As organizations seek competitive advantages in increasingly complex markets, these technologies are moving from experimental projects to mission-critical implementations that deliver measurable business impact. The following use cases demonstrate how leading enterprises are leveraging GenAI to solve real business challenges, highlighting both the technical implementations and the tangible outcomes achieved. Each example represents a proven approach that has delivered significant return on investment while addressing specific industry pain points and operational challenges. By examining these implementations in detail, organizations can gain valuable insights to inform their own GenAI strategies and accelerate their transformation initiatives.

Customer service and support

Customer service and support has emerged as a primary adoption area for GenAI, transforming how organizations handle customer interactions and support operations. This technology enables organizations to provide intelligent, automated responses to customer inquiries while maintaining personalization and context-awareness. Industries actively implementing these solutions include retail, telecommunications, financial services, technology companies, and travel and hospitality sectors. E-commerce giants like Amazon and Shopify, major banks, and telecommunications providers are leading adopters, using AI to handle millions of customer interactions daily while maintaining service quality and reducing operational costs.

The architecture features a logical separation between:

- User-facing components (AWS Amplify, CloudFront, Cognito) that handle the front-end experience and authentication
- Middle-tier services (API Gateway connected to compute resources like Lambda/Fargate/ECS) that process requests
- Core AI capabilities (Amazon Bedrock) that provide the GenAI foundation models
- Data persistence (DynamoDB) for storing conversation history and interactions
- Cross-cutting concerns (IAM, CloudWatch, CloudTrail, AWS Budgets) that address security, monitoring, and cost management

This design enables organizations to rapidly develop sophisticated GenAI applications by leveraging managed AWS services, while ensuring proper security, scalability, and operational visibility throughout the solution lifecycle. The architecture demonstrates how enterprises can implement production-grade GenAI without managing complex infrastructure.

Figure 15.1 illustrates a comprehensive AWS architecture for a GenAI-powered customer service solution. At a high level, it illustrates how various AWS components work together to create a complete, production-ready GenAI application:

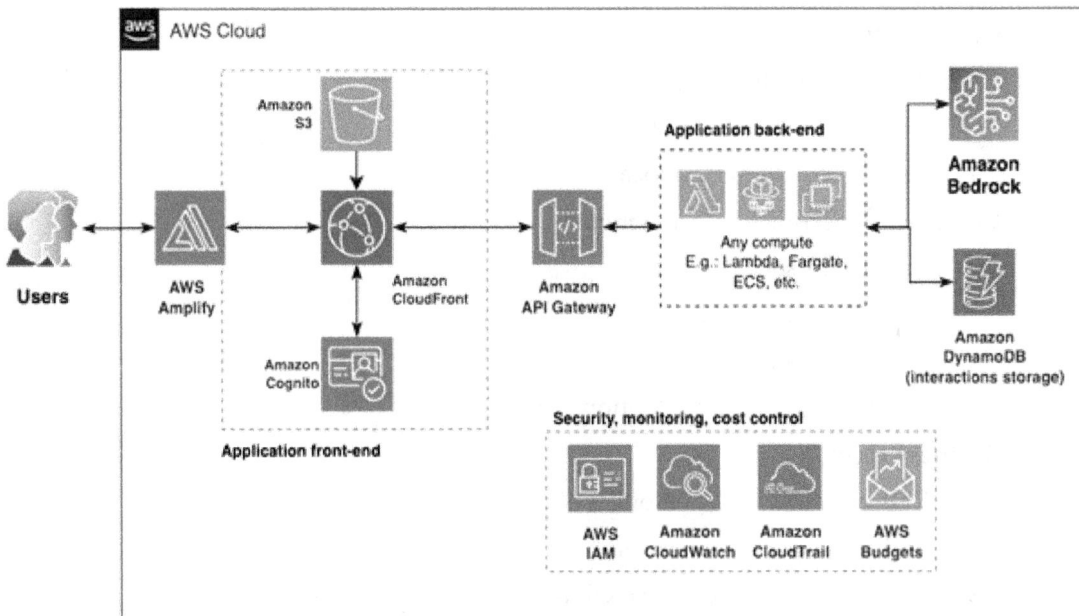

Figure 15.1: *AWS architecture for GenAI-powered customer service solution*

The following are the key features of the above customer service architecture:

- Multi-turn conversations with context retention, enabling natural, continuous interactions

- Real-time product information integration that provides accurate, up-to-date responses

- Automated ticket classification and routing to optimize resource allocation and response times

- Sentiment analysis for escalation that detects customer frustration and ensures timely human intervention

- Comprehensive multilingual support enabling global customer engagement without language barriers

Benefits of GenAI in customer service

The implementation of GenAI in customer service delivers transformative advantages across operations, costs, and customer experience, with organizations reporting dramatic efficiency improvements and substantial financial returns, as follows:

- **Operational improvements**:
  o Reduced response times
  o Lower support ticket volumes
  o 40-60% efficiency gains

- **Cost benefits**:
  o 25-40% reduction in support costs
  o Automated handling of routine queries
  o Optimized resource allocation

- **Customer experience improvements**:
  o Consistent service quality
  o Immediate response times
  o Higher satisfaction scores
  o Improved customer retention rates

- **Business case**:
  o ROI achieved within months of implementation
  o Reduced operational costs
  o Improved customer satisfaction
  o Increased support team productivity

Financial document analysis

Intelligent document processing in financial services leverages GenAI to transform how financial institutions handle complex financial documents, regulatory filings, and customer documentation. This technology automates the processing and analysis of documents like loan applications, financial statements, investment reports, and compliance documentation. Primary adopters include banks, insurance companies, investment firms, and financial regulatory bodies.

Figure 15.2 illustrates AI-powered financial document processing architecture that orchestrates a comprehensive workflow from initial document classification through extraction, NLP processing like entity recognition, and analytics, leveraging multiple AWS services to deliver intelligent insights from complex financial materials. The pipeline combines Amazon Bedrock foundation models with specialized services like Textract and Comprehend to transform unstructured financial documents into structured, actionable intelligence that supports compliance requirements and business decision-making.

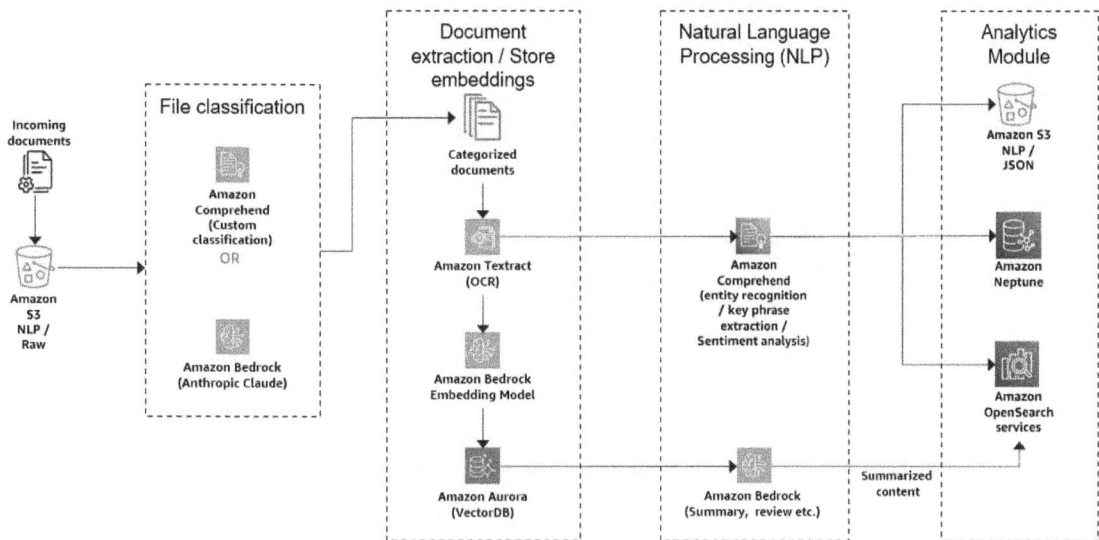

Figure 15.2: *AWS-based intelligent financial document processing pipeline*

The following are the key features of this financial document processing architecture:

- Automated financial document processing that efficiently handles diverse document types with minimal human intervention

- Advanced data extraction and analysis capabilities that transform unstructured financial data into actionable intelligence

- Regulatory compliance engine that identifies, flags, and addresses compliance requirements across multiple jurisdictions

- Real-time analytics and reporting providing immediate insights for time-sensitive financial decisions and audit requirements

Benefits of intelligent document processing

Intelligent document processing transforms financial operations by dramatically accelerating processing speeds while enhancing accuracy, compliance, and security across the document lifecycle.

Refer to the following:

- **Operational efficiency**:
  - o Faster document processing times
  - o Cost reduction in manual processing efforts
  - o Enhanced accuracy in financial data extraction

- **Risk and compliance improvements**:
  - o Improved regulatory compliance
  - o Significant risk reduction through automated fraud detection
  - o Highest standards of security in document handling

- **Business performance**:
  - o Faster decision-making capabilities
  - o Improved customer service with reduced turnaround times
  - o Better resource allocation

- **Strategic advantages**:
  - o Streamlined operations creating competitive edge
  - o Reduced compliance risks and associated costs
  - o Enhanced customer satisfaction through faster service delivery

Healthcare documentation and analysis

Healthcare documentation and analysis using GenAI represents a revolutionary approach to managing medical information and improving patient care. This technology streamlines the creation and analysis of medical documentation while ensuring accuracy and regulatory compliance. The adoption spans across various healthcare sectors, including hospitals, clinical practices, insurance providers, and research institutions. Major healthcare networks, academic medical centres, and health insurance companies are implementing these solutions to improve care quality and operational efficiency while reducing administrative burden on healthcare providers.

Figure 15.3 illustrates a comprehensive AWS architecture integrates GenAI capabilities into healthcare systems, providing a seamless flow from medical image and metadata ingestion through sophisticated processing and user interaction. The solution leverages Amazon

Bedrock for AI capabilities alongside purpose-built vector storage and real-time database components, creating an intelligent healthcare documentation system that improves clinical workflows while maintaining security and compliance standards.

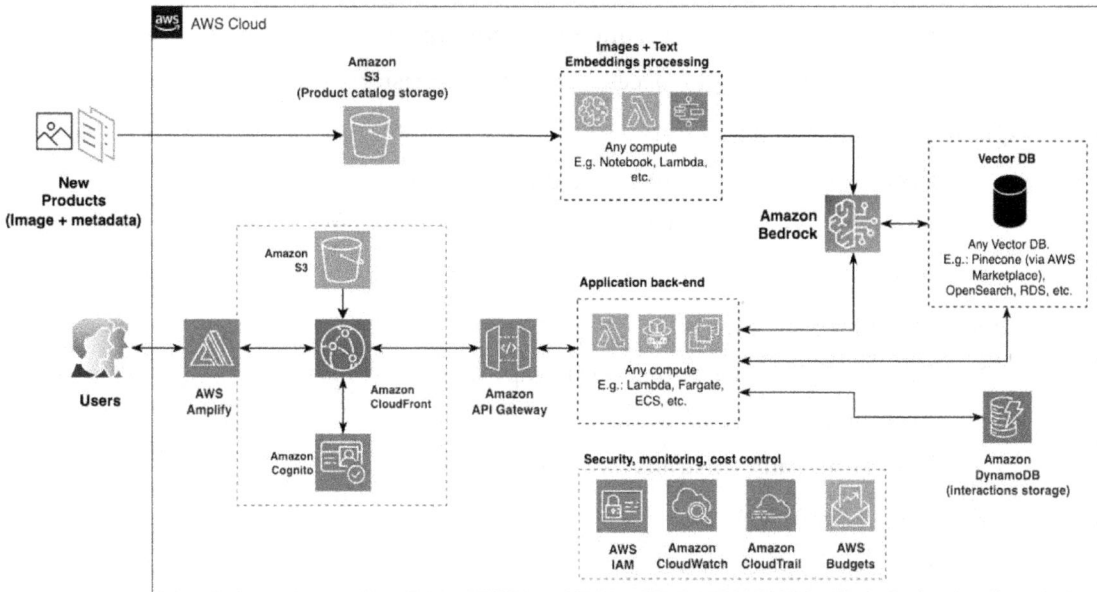

Figure 15.3: Integrated AWS healthcare documentation architecture combining AI-powered processing

The following are the key features of this healthcare documentation architecture:

- Automated medical record analysis that extracts and interprets clinical data from diverse document types
- Patient history summarization that consolidates complex medical histories into actionable clinical overviews
- Risk factor identification leveraging AI to flag potential health concerns based on comprehensive data analysis
- Treatment recommendation support, providing evidence-based guidance to assist clinical decision-making
- Compliance documentation ensuring all processes meet HIPAA, GDPR, and other healthcare regulatory requirements

Benefits of healthcare documentation architecture

The implementation of GenAI in healthcare documentation creates significant value across the entire care continuum, enhancing both provider efficiency and patient outcomes through intelligent automation of critical documentation processes.

Refer to the following details:

- **Clinical efficiency gains**:
  - ○ 40% time savings in administrative documentation tasks
  - ○ Reduced documentation time for providers
  - ○ Improved information access for clinical decision-making

- **Quality enhancements**:
  - ○ More accurate and complete medical records
  - ○ Better compliance with regulatory requirements
  - ○ Enhanced clinical data integrity

- **Operational improvements**:
  - ○ Faster billing cycles and revenue capture
  - ○ Improved resource allocation
  - ○ Streamlined administrative workflows

- **Patient care advantages**:
  - ○ Increased provider-patient interaction time
  - ○ Better-informed clinical decisions
  - ○ Improved patient outcomes and satisfaction levels

Each of these use cases demonstrates how GenAI is driving significant transformation across different industries, with benefits that extend beyond simple automation to create strategic advantages and improved operational outcomes. The key to successful implementation lies in understanding industry-specific requirements, ensuring proper integration with existing systems, and maintaining focus on measurable business outcomes.

Implementation considerations

The successful implementation of GenAI systems requires careful consideration of multiple interconnected factors that significantly impact project outcomes. As organizations embark on their GenAI journey, they must navigate complex technical, operational, and strategic considerations to ensure successful deployment and sustainable operations. These considerations span across various dimensions, from fundamental aspects like data security and system performance to broader concerns such as cost management and quality assurance. Understanding and properly addressing these considerations is crucial as they directly influence the system's effectiveness, reliability, and business value. Organizations must approach these considerations holistically, recognizing that decisions in one area often have ripple effects across others. This section explores key implementation considerations that organizations should carefully evaluate and address throughout their GenAI implementation journey, providing a framework for making informed decisions and establishing robust implementation practices.

Data security and privacy

Implementing GenAI solutions demands a comprehensive security foundation that preserves data integrity while enabling innovation, requiring organizations to adopt sophisticated protection strategies across the entire AI lifecycle.

Data protection strategies

Organizations implementing GenAI must prioritize robust data security measures throughout their implementation process. This begins with comprehensive encryption protocols, implementing both encryption at rest using AWS KMS and encryption in transit using TLS 1.3. Data retention policies must align with regulatory requirements, while data masking techniques should be employed for sensitive information processing. Organizations should establish detailed data handling procedures that cover the entire data lifecycle, from collection to disposal.

Refer to the following details:

- **Access control**: A comprehensive access control framework forms the foundation of secure GenAI implementation. This should incorporate **role-based access control (RBAC)** leveraging AWS IAM for fine-grained permissions management. Organizations must maintain detailed audit logs of all data access and conduct regular reviews of access permissions. The principle of least privilege should be consistently applied, ensuring users and systems have only the minimum necessary access rights to perform their functions.

- **Compliance measures**: Compliance requirements vary by industry and region, requiring careful attention to regulatory frameworks. For organizations handling European user data, GDPR compliance must be built into the system design, incorporating principles such as data minimization and purpose limitation. Healthcare organizations must ensure HIPAA compliance, while service organizations may need to maintain SOC 2 compliance. Regular compliance audits should be conducted to ensure ongoing adherence to these requirements.

By establishing these robust security and compliance frameworks, organizations not only protect sensitive data but also build the trust essential for widespread adoption of GenAI solutions while creating sustainable competitive advantages in an increasingly AI-driven marketplace.

Performance optimization

Achieving exceptional performance in GenAI solutions requires a multifaceted approach to system architecture and resource management, balancing user experience requirements with infrastructure efficiency to deliver consistently responsive interactions.

Performance optimization strategies

The following are the performance optimization strategies:

- **Response time management**: Effective response time management is crucial for maintaining system performance and user satisfaction. Organizations should establish clear response time SLAs and implement comprehensive monitoring systems to track performance against these targets. This includes defining acceptable latency thresholds, monitoring response times across different use cases, and setting up alerting mechanisms for SLA breaches. Prompt design optimization and request queuing mechanisms should be implemented to manage high-load scenarios effectively.

- **Resource management**: Efficient resource management ensures optimal system performance while controlling costs. This involves implementing sophisticated auto-scaling policies based on multiple metrics including CPU utilization, memory usage, and request queue length. Load balancing mechanisms should be implemented to distribute requests effectively across available resources, while resource quotas help prevent overconsumption and ensure fair resource allocation across different system components.

- **Caching strategy**: A well-designed caching strategy is essential for optimizing system performance and reducing response times. This should include implementation of multi-level caching, incorporating application-level caching, response caching, and query result caching. Organizations must develop effective cache invalidation policies and continuously monitor cache hit ratios to ensure optimal cache utilization. The caching strategy should be regularly reviewed and adjusted based on usage patterns and performance metrics.

By implementing these comprehensive performance optimization strategies, organizations can deliver GenAI capabilities that meet or exceed user expectations while maintaining cost efficiency and resource sustainability across fluctuating demand patterns and evolving business requirements.

Cost management

Effective financial governance of GenAI initiatives requires structured approaches to expenditure control and resource utilization, balancing innovation needs with fiscal responsibility to ensure sustainable implementation and continuous value creation.

Strategic cost control approaches

The following are the strategic cost control approaches:

- **Budget control**: Effective cost management begins with comprehensive budget control measures. Organizations should implement detailed cost allocation tags to track expenses across different components and projects. Budget alerts should be established to provide early warning of potential cost overruns, while regular cost optimization reviews help identify opportunities for efficiency improvements. This should be complemented by ongoing monitoring of usage patterns to identify and address any cost anomalies quickly.

- **Usage optimization**: Usage optimization focuses on ensuring efficient utilization of AI resources. This includes implementing token usage monitoring systems, rate limiting mechanisms to prevent abuse, and optimization of prompt lengths to reduce unnecessary token consumption. Organizations should also consider implementing batch processing for bulk operations where real-time processing is not critical, helping to optimize resource utilization and reduce costs.

- **Resource planning**: Effective resource planning ensures optimal allocation of resources while maintaining cost efficiency. This involves detailed capacity planning based on expected usage patterns, accurate cost forecasting using historical data and growth projections, and regular ROI analysis to ensure continued value from AI investments. Organizations should maintain continuous monitoring of resource utilization to identify optimization opportunities and adjust resource allocation accordingly.

- **Model selection strategy**: Implementing a dynamic model selection framework enables organizations to balance performance requirements with cost efficiency. This involves evaluating models based on three key dimensions: latency requirements (response time needs), accuracy thresholds (acceptable quality level for specific use cases), and cost efficiency (price per token or inference). For example, using smaller, less expensive models for initial document classification tasks, while reserving more powerful models for complex financial analysis that requires deeper semantic understanding. Organizations should establish clear performance-cost thresholds that trigger model switching based on business needs and implement continuous evaluation to ensure optimal model utilization across different workflow stages.

By implementing these disciplined cost management practices, organizations can transform GenAI from an experimental cost center into a strategic investment that delivers measurable business value while maintaining financial sustainability throughout deployment cycles and scaling initiatives.

Quality assurance

Building reliable AI systems demands rigorous quality control frameworks that extend beyond traditional software testing approaches, incorporating specialized evaluations for content quality, model performance, and user experience validation across diverse use cases.

Comprehensive quality control mechanisms

Refer to the following for comprehensive quality control mechanisms:

- **Testing framework**: A comprehensive testing framework is essential for maintaining system quality and reliability. This should include automated testing covering unit tests for individual components, integration tests for system interactions, performance tests for system behavior under load, and specialized tests for AI-specific functionality. Human evaluation processes should be incorporated for aspects requiring subjective assessment, while A/B testing methodologies help optimize system performance and user experience.

- **Monitoring and logging**: Robust monitoring and logging systems provide visibility into system performance and behavior. Organizations should implement comprehensive logging strategies capturing all significant system events and interactions. Error tracking and analysis systems should be implemented to identify and address issues quickly, while performance monitoring helps maintain system optimization. User feedback collection mechanisms provide valuable insights for continuous improvement.

- **Content quality**: Maintaining high content quality requires multiple validation layers. Organizations should implement output validation processes to ensure accuracy and appropriateness of AI-generated content. Content moderation systems should be in place to prevent inappropriate or harmful content, while bias detection mechanisms help ensure fairness and objectivity. Regular quality metrics assessment helps maintain high standards and identify areas for improvement.

This comprehensive approach to implementation considerations ensures organizations address key aspects of GenAI deployment effectively, maintaining high standards of security, performance, and quality while managing costs efficiently. Regular review and adjustment of these considerations helps ensure continued effectiveness as systems evolve and requirements change.

Common challenges and solutions in enterprise GenAI implementation

The implementation of GenAI systems represents a significant technological leap for organizations across industries. While the potential benefits are substantial, organizations frequently encounter various challenges during implementation that can impact project success. Understanding these challenges and having proven solutions is crucial for successful GenAI deployment.

Let us get into the details of the key challenges with an example.

Data quality management

Data quality is a fundamental challenge in GenAI implementations. Organizations often struggle with inconsistent, incomplete, or poorly structured data that can significantly impact the quality of AI outputs. The challenge encompasses managing diverse data sources, ensuring data consistency, handling missing information, and maintaining data accuracy over time.

Poor data quality can lead to unreliable AI responses, biased outputs, and reduced system effectiveness.

The following is an example of a financial services company:

A major bank implementing a GenAI system for customer inquiry handling faced challenges with inconsistent customer interaction data across multiple systems.

The following are the challenges faced:

- Customer data spread across legacy CRM, email systems, and chat platforms
- Inconsistent formatting of customer information
- Missing context in historical interactions
- Multilingual customer communications with poor translations

The following solutions can be implemented:

- **Data standardization pipeline**:
    o Created unified data schema for customer interactions
    o Implemented automatic format conversion for legacy data
    o Developed quality scoring system for data entries

- **Data enrichment process**:
    o Added contextual metadata to historical records
    o Integrated customer profile information
    o Created relationship mapping between interactions

- **Quality control measures**:
    o Automated data validation checks
    o Regular data quality audits
    o Feedback loop for data correction

Model performance issues

Model performance issues represent a critical challenge in GenAI implementations. These challenges manifest in various forms, including response accuracy, consistency, processing speed, and the handling of complex queries. Organizations must balance the need for accurate, reliable responses with performance requirements like response time and resource utilization. The challenge is particularly acute when dealing with domain-specific applications where expertise and precision are crucial.

The following is an example of a healthcare provider:

A healthcare network implementing GenAI for medical documentation summarization experienced challenges with accuracy and consistency.

The following are the challenges faced:

- Inconsistent quality in medical terminology processing
- Hallucinations in patient history summaries
- Slow response times for complex medical records
- Missing critical medical information in summaries

The following are the solutions implemented:

- **Enhanced prompt engineering**:
  o Developed specialized medical prompts
  o Created validation checks for critical information
  o Implemented medical terminology verification

- **Context management**:
  o Structured medical record segmentation
  o Prioritized critical medical information
  o Implemented domain-specific knowledge validation

- **Performance optimization**:
  o Parallel processing for large records
  o Cached common medical terms
  o Optimized response generation

Integration complexity

Integration complexity presents a significant challenge when implementing GenAI systems into existing technology ecosystems. Organizations must navigate the intricate process of connecting AI capabilities with legacy systems, ensuring seamless data flow, maintaining security protocols, and managing system dependencies. This challenge is particularly significant in enterprises with complex IT landscapes and strict operational requirements.

The following is an example of a manufacturing company:

A global manufacturer implementing GenAI for maintenance documentation faced challenges integrating with existing systems.

The following are the challenges faced:

- Multiple legacy systems with different protocols
- Real-time data synchronization issues
- Complex workflow requirements
- Security constraints across systems

The following are the solutions implemented:

- **Architecture redesign**:
  - Implemented API gateway for unified access
  - Created middleware for legacy system integration
  - Developed event-driven architecture

- **Data flow optimization**:
  - Established message queuing system
  - Implemented caching layers
  - Created data transformation services

- **Security framework**:
  - End-to-end encryption
  - Role-based access control
  - Audit logging system

Ethical and bias issues

Ethical considerations and bias management are critical challenges in GenAI implementation. Organizations must ensure their AI systems operate fairly, without perpetuating existing biases or creating new ones. This includes addressing concerns about discrimination, ensuring inclusive representation, and maintaining transparency in AI decision-making processes. The challenge extends to maintaining ethical standards while meeting business objectives.

The following is an example of HR technology company:

A company implementing GenAI for resume screening and job matching encountered bias and fairness challenges.

The following are the challenges faced:

- Gender bias in candidate recommendations
- Age-related discrimination in language
- Cultural bias in communication style
- Lack of diversity in recommendations

The following are the solutions implemented:

- **Bias detection framework**:
  - Implemented fairness metrics
  - Created bias detection algorithms
  - Regular bias audit processes

- **Content filtering**:
  - o Neutral language enforcement
  - o Diversity promotion rules
  - o Cultural sensitivity checks

- **Training and validation**:
  - o Diverse training data
  - o Regular fairness assessments
  - o Stakeholder feedback integration

User adoption and training

User adoption and training represent significant hurdles in GenAI implementation. Organizations often face resistance to change, scepticism about AI capabilities, and challenges in effectively training users across different skill levels. The success of AI implementations heavily depends on user acceptance and their ability to effectively utilize the new systems.

The following is an example of legal services firm:

A law firm implementing GenAI for legal document analysis faced challenges with attorney adoption and trust.

The following are the challenges faced:

- Resistance to AI-assisted work
- Lack of trust in AI recommendations
- Training requirements for different user levels
- Integration with existing workflows

The following are the solutions implemented:

- **Change management program:**
  - o Phased implementation approach
  - o Regular training sessions
  - o Success story sharing

- **User experience optimization**
  - o Intuitive interface design
  - o Customizable workflows
  - o Transparent AI decision explanation

- **Support system**:
  - o Dedicated support team

o   User feedback system

o   Regular updates based on feedback

To effectively gauge GenAI implementation success, organizations should focus on these five key performance indicators:

- **Active user rate**: Percentage of eligible users regularly engaging with the AI system, indicating broad organizational adoption

- **Time savings**: Quantifiable reduction in time spent on tasks compared to pre-implementation baselines

- **User satisfaction**: Periodic survey results measuring user confidence, perceived value, and willingness to recommend the system

- **Error reduction**: Measurable decrease in mistakes, corrections, or quality issues when using AI-assisted processes

- **Business impact**: Tangible outcomes tied to organizational goals, such as increased productivity, cost savings, or revenue growth directly attributable to the implementation.

Monitoring and maintenance

Monitoring and maintaining GenAI systems present ongoing challenges for organizations. This includes ensuring consistent performance, tracking system health, managing updates, and maintaining quality standards over time. The dynamic nature of AI systems requires continuous attention to performance metrics, quality control, and system optimization.

The following is an example of media company:

A news organization implementing GenAI for content generation faced challenges in maintaining quality and monitoring performance.

The following are the challenges faced:

- Inconsistent content quality
- Difficulty in tracking performance
- System maintenance issues
- Quality assurance challenges

The following are the solutions implemented:

- **Monitoring framework**:
  - o   Real-time performance tracking
  - o   Quality metrics dashboard
  - o   Automated alerts system

- **Maintenance protocol**:
  - o Regular system health checks
  - o Automated maintenance tasks
  - o Version control system

- **Quality control**:
  - o Content validation pipeline
  - o Performance benchmarking
  - o Regular quality audits

These challenges and their solutions demonstrate the complex nature of GenAI implementation and the importance of comprehensive planning and problem-solving approaches. Organizations should consider these examples when developing their own implementation strategies, while recognizing that solutions may need to be adapted to their specific context and requirements.

Future trends and opportunities

The landscape of GenAI is rapidly evolving, presenting unprecedented opportunities for innovation and transformation across industries. As we look toward the future, several emerging trends are shaping the next generation of AI applications and solutions. These developments are not merely technological advancements but represent fundamental shifts in how organizations and individuals interact with AI systems. Understanding these trends is crucial for organizations to position themselves strategically and capitalize on new opportunities as they emerge. The convergence of improved computational capabilities, advanced algorithms, and growing real-world applications is creating a fertile ground for revolutionary developments in the field of GenAI.

Multimodal AI systems

Multimodal AI represents a significant evolution in GenAI capabilities, moving beyond single-format interactions to integrate multiple forms of input and output. These systems can simultaneously process and generate content across different modalities—text, images, audio, video, and even tactile information. The trend is shifting towards AI systems that can understand and respond to the world more like humans do, through multiple senses and communication channels.

Future applications include the following:

- Virtual assistants that can see, hear, and respond naturally in multiple formats
- Design tools that can generate coordinated brand assets across all media types
- Educational systems that adapt content delivery based on multiple learning modalities

- Healthcare diagnostic tools that integrate visual, verbal, and numerical data
- Customer service solutions that seamlessly blend text, voice, and visual interactions

The impact of multimodal AI will be particularly significant in industries requiring rich, multi-dimensional interaction, such as healthcare, education, and creative industries. Organizations that effectively harness multimodal AI will be able to deliver more intuitive, engaging, and comprehensive solutions to their users.

Autonomous AI agents

Autonomous AI agents represent the next frontier in AI evolution, where systems can independently perform complex tasks, make decisions, and learn from their experiences. These agents will go beyond simple automation to demonstrate genuine autonomy in problem-solving and decision-making, while maintaining appropriate human oversight and control.

The development of autonomous AI agents will revolutionize various sectors, as follows:

- Business process automation with intelligent decision-making capabilities
- Supply chain optimization with real-time adaptation to changes
- Financial trading systems with advanced risk management
- Manufacturing systems with predictive maintenance and quality control
- Customer service with proactive problem resolution

This trend will fundamentally change how organizations approach automation and decision-making, leading to more efficient operations and innovative service delivery models. The key will be balancing autonomy with accountability and maintaining appropriate human oversight.

Personalized AI experiences

The future of AI lies in its ability to deliver highly personalized experiences at scale. Advanced personalization will move beyond simple preference-based customization to deep, context-aware understanding of individual users' needs, behavior, and circumstances. This trend represents a shift from one-size-fits-all AI solutions to truly individualized experiences.

Key developments in this area include the following:

- Dynamic content adaptation based on user context and behavior
- Personalized learning and development pathways
- Customized healthcare interventions and treatment plans
- Individualized financial advice and planning
- Tailored consumer experiences across all touchpoints

This trend will enable organizations to deliver unprecedented levels of personalization while maintaining privacy and security. The challenge will be balancing personalization with data privacy and ethical considerations.

Edge AI and distributed intelligence

The evolution of edge AI represents a fundamental shift in how AI systems are deployed and operated. By moving AI processing closer to where data is generated, organizations can achieve faster response times, improved privacy, and reduced bandwidth requirements. This trend is particularly important as IoT devices become more prevalent and the need for real-time AI processing grows.

This trend encompasses the following:

- Local processing of AI models on devices
- Reduced latency in AI responses
- Enhanced privacy through local data processing
- Improved reliability in areas with limited connectivity
- Reduced cloud computing costs

The impact will be particularly significant in applications requiring real-time processing, such as autonomous vehicles, smart cities, and industrial IoT. Organizations will need to develop strategies for managing distributed AI systems effectively.

Ethical and responsible AI integration

As AI systems become more sophisticated and ubiquitous, the focus on ethical and responsible AI implementation will intensify. This trend reflects growing awareness of the need to ensure AI systems are developed and deployed in ways that benefit society while minimizing potential harm.

Key aspects of this trend include the following:

- Development of robust fairness and bias detection systems
- Implementation of transparent AI decision-making processes
- Creation of accountability frameworks for AI systems
- Integration of privacy-preserving technologies
- Development of sustainable AI practices

Organizations will need to focus on the following:

- Building ethical considerations into AI development from the start
- Creating governance frameworks for AI deployment

- Ensuring transparency and explainability in AI systems
- Developing mechanisms for continuous monitoring and adjustment
- Training teams in ethical AI practices

This trend will shape how organizations approach AI development and deployment, with increased emphasis on responsible innovation and societal impact. Success in this area will become a key differentiator for organizations in the AI space.

Conclusion

The real-world applications of GenAI explored throughout this chapter demonstrate its profound transformative potential across diverse industries. Our exploration of GenAI applications reveals significant business transformation across multiple industries. Organizations leveraging AWS services, particularly Amazon Bedrock, are creating solutions that address complex challenges while following consistent patterns of success regardless of sector.

Successful GenAI implementations begin with understanding specific use case requirements, ensuring technology addresses genuine business needs. These foundations require technical architectures balancing performance, scalability, and cost while integrating with existing systems. Robust security measures and governance frameworks are essential for protecting data and building trust.

The most successful organizations maintain focus on quantifiable business value with clear metrics guiding development. This value-centric approach depends on continuous monitoring and optimization to ensure systems improve over time. The implementation patterns documented provide practical blueprints adaptable to unique organizational contexts.

As GenAI evolves, organizations extracting maximum value will combine technical excellence with strategic alignment, thoughtful governance, and commitment to improvement. Following these practices enables implementation of solutions delivering substantial business impact while maintaining high standards of security, performance, reliability, and ethical operation.

Join our Discord space

Join our Discord workspace for latest updates, offers, tech happenings around the world, new releases, and sessions with the authors:

https://discord.bpbonline.com

Index

www.ingramcontent.com/pod-product-compliance
Lightning Source LLC
Chambersburg PA
CBHW061746210326
41599CB00034B/6799